D1483374

PERSONALITY DISORDERS AND EATING DISORDERS

PERSONALITY DISORDERS AND EATING DISORDERS

Exploring the Frontier

EDITED BY
RANDY A. SANSONE
JOHN L. LEVITT

Routledge
Taylor & Francis Group
New York   London

Routledge is an imprint of the
Taylor & Francis Group, an informa business

Published in 2006 by
Routledge
Taylor & Francis Group
270 Madison Avenue
New York, NY 10016

Published in Great Britain by
Routledge
Taylor & Francis Group
2 Park Square
Milton Park, Abingdon
Oxon OX14 4RN

© 2006 by Taylor & Francis Group, LLC
Routledge is an imprint of Taylor & Francis Group

Printed in the United States of America on acid-free paper
10 9 8 7 6 5 4 3 2

International Standard Book Number-10: 0-415-95324-3 (Hardcover)
International Standard Book Number-13: 978-0-415-95324-5 (Hardcover)
Library of Congress Card Number 2006001827

No part of this book may be reprinted, reproduced, transmitted, or utilized in any form by any electronic, mechanical, or other means, now known or hereafter invented, including photocopying, microfilming, and recording, or in any information storage or retrieval system, without written permission from the publishers.

Trademark Notice: Product or corporate names may be trademarks or registered trademarks, and are used only for identification and explanation without intent to infringe.

Library of Congress Cataloging-in-Publication Data

Personality disorders and eating disorders : exploring the frontier /
    edited by Randy A. Sansone, John L. Levitt.
        p. ; cm.
    Includes bibliographical references.
    ISBN 0-415-95324-3 (hb : alk. paper)
        1. Personality disorders. 2. Eating disorders. I. Sansone, Randy A., 1953- . II. Levitt, John L., 1951-.
    [DNLM: 1. Eating Disorders--epidemiology. 2. Personality Disorders--epidemiology. 3. Eating Disorders--therapy. 4. Personality Disorders--therapy. WM 190 P46672 2006]

RC554.P471 2006
616.85'26--dc22   2006001827

Taylor & Francis Group
is the Academic Division of Informa plc.

Visit the Taylor & Francis Web site at
http://www.taylorandfrancis.com

and the Routledge Web site at
http://www.routledge-ny.com

Contents

About the Editors   ix

Contributors   xi

The Lost Years   xv
By L.M.

Acknowledgments   xxi

Introduction   xxiii
Randy A. Sansone, MD
John L. Levitt, PhD

SECTION I
PERSONALITY CONCEPTUALIZATION   1

1   *Personality Disorder Constructs and
    Conceptualizations*   3
    Henry J. Jackson, PhD, FAPS
    Martina Jovev, MA, PhD

SECTION II
EPIDEMIOLOGY   21

2   *The Prevalence of Personality Disorders in Those
    With Eating Disorders*   23
    Randy A. Sansone, MD
    John L. Levitt, PhD
    Lori A. Sansone, MD

SECTION III
ETIOLOGY   41

3   *Impulsivity Versus Compulsivity in Patients
    With Eating Disorders*   **43**
    Angela Favaro, MD, PhD, MSc
    Paolo Santonastaso, MD

4   *Childhood Trauma, Personality Disorders, and
    Eating Disorders*   **59**
    Randy A. Sansone, MD
    Lori A. Sansone, MD

SECTION IV
ASSESSMENT   77

5   *Clinical Assessment of Personality Disorders*   **79**
    Stephanie D. Stepp, MA
    Rebecca Schwartz, BA
    Marika Solhan, BS
    Timothy J. Trull, PhD

6   *Difficulties in the Assessment of Personality Traits
    and Disorders in Individuals With Eating Disorders*   **91**
    Kelly M. Vitousek, PhD
    Roxanna E. Stumpf

SECTION V
PERSONALITY DISORDERS MOST RELEVANT
TO EATING DISORDERS   119

7   *Obsessive-Compulsive Personality and Eating
    Disorders*   **121**
    Parinda Parikh, MD
    Katharine Halmi, MD

8   *Borderline Personality and Eating Disorders*   **131**
    Randy A. Sansone, MD
    John L. Levitt, PhD

9   *Avoidant Personality Disorder and Eating
    Disorders*   **149**
    John L. Levitt, PhD
    Randy A. Sansone, MD

SECTION VI
TREATMENT APPROACHES   163

10   *Treatment Strategies in the Obsessive-Compulsive*
     Individual With an Eating Disorder   **165**
     Janice Russell, MD, FRACP, FRANZCP, MFCP

11   *A Self-Regulation Treatment Approach for the*
     Patient With an Eating Disorder and Borderline
     Personality Disorder   **183**
     John L. Levitt, PhD

12   *Borderline Personality and Eating Disorders: An*
     Eclectic Approach to Treatment   **197**
     Randy A. Sansone, MD
     Lori A. Sansone, MD

13   *The Treatment of Avoidant Personality Disorder in*
     Patients With Eating Disorders   **213**
     Hendrik Hinrichsen, DClinPsy
     Glenn Waller, DPhil

14   *The Use of Psychotropic Medications in Patients*
     With Eating Disorders and Personality Disorders   **231**
     Randy A. Sansone, MD
     Lori A. Sansone, MD

SECTION VII
OUTCOME   245

15   *Prognostic Implications of Personality Disorders in*
     Eating Disorders   **247**
     Kenneth R. Bruce, PhD
     Howard Steiger, PhD

     Index   **263**

About the Editors

Randy A. Sansone, MD, is a professor in the Department of Psychiatry and the Department of Internal Medicine at Wright State University School of Medicine in Dayton, Ohio, and the director of psychiatry education at Kettering Medical Center in Kettering, Ohio. Dr. Sansone has authored more than 180 published papers, including 25 book chapters; is on the editorial boards of *Eating Disorders: The Journal of Treatment and Prevention, Violence and Victims, Psychiatry 2006,* and *Traumatology;* coauthored the *Self-Harm Inventory,* a measure for self-harm behavior and borderline personality symptomatology; and coedited with John L. Levitt and Leigh Cohn the book *Self-Harm Behavior and Eating Disorders: Dynamics, Assessment, and Treatment.*

John L. Levitt, PhD, is the director of the Eating Disorders and Violence and Abuse Programs of Alexian Brothers Behavioral Health Hospital located in Hoffman Estates, Illinois. He has delivered more than 150 papers and workshop presentations locally and nationally, and has numerous publications with a particular emphasis on the development and application of the self-regulation approach for treating symptomatically complex patients with eating disorders. Dr. Levitt is a coauthor of one book and a coeditor of two other books, including the recently published *Self-Harm Behavior and Eating Disorders: Dynamics, Assessment, and Treatment* with Randy Sansone and Leigh Cohn. He is also on the editorial board of *Eating Disorders: The Journal of Treatment and Prevention.*

Contributors

Kenneth R. Bruce, PhD, is a psychologist at the Eating Disorders Program of the Douglas Hospital and an assistant professor of psychiatry at McGill University in Canada. Dr. Bruce is a clinician, teacher, and researcher, and has published empirical and review articles in the areas of eating disorders and alcohol-use disorders. His recent research focuses on areas of etiological similarity among eating and alcohol-use disorders as well as on biological correlates of eating disorders and personality disorders. He is a member of the Academy for Eating Disorders and serves as a peer reviewer for several journals and extramural funding agencies.

Angela Favaro, MD, PhD, MSc, works in the Department of Neurosciences at the University of Padua, Italy. She is a member of the European Council on Eating Disorders and the Eating Disorders Research Society. Dr. Favaro has a master's of science degree in genetic epidemiology, and her fields of interest are eating disorders, post-traumatic stress disorder, and consultation/liaison psychiatry. She has published more than 200 papers.

Katharine Halmi, MD, is a professor of psychiatry at the Cornell University Medical College and director of the Eating Disorder Program, which she established. She is board certified in both pediatrics and psychiatry. Dr. Halmi began her eating disorder research career while on the psychiatry faculty at the University of Iowa, and in 1979 she moved to the Cornell University Medical College and the New York Hospital–Westchester Division. For the past 20 years, Dr. Halmi has received research support from the National Institute of Mental Health, private foundations, and industry. Her research has focused primarily on eating behavior and the disorders of anorexia and bulimia nervosa. She has investigated these disorders with a broad perspective, with studies in the areas of neuroendocrine functioning, cognitive-behavioral and pharmacological treatment, metabolic and genetic relationships, comor-

bid psychopathology, core eating disorder psychopathology, and longitudinal follow-up studies. Dr. Halmi is well known internationally from
her published research.

Hendrik Hinrichsen, DClinPsy, is a principal clinical psychologist with
the St. George's Eating Disorders Service, London, and a visiting research
fellow at the Eating Disorders Section, Institute of Psychiatry, King's College, London. Dr. Hinrichsen has published peer-reviewed articles on the
subjects of eating disorders and anxiety disorders, and has presented his
research at international conferences. In 2003 he was awarded a South
West London Excellence Award for clinically relevant research.

Henry J. Jackson, PhD, FAPS, is a clinical psychologist, a professor of
psychology, and the head of the School of Behavioral Science at the University of Melbourne in Victoria, Australia. He is also a senior research
fellow at ORYGEN Youth Health. Dr. Jackson has published more than
130 referred articles and book chapters and is on a number of editorial boards. He has coedited two books, one with Peter Cotton titled
Early Intervention and Prevention in Mental Health, published by the
Australian Psychological Society, and the second with Patrick McGorry
titled *The Recognition and Management of Early Psychosis: A Preventive
Approach,* published by Cambridge University Press. Dr. Jackson is the
2005 winner of the Australian Psychological Society's Ian M. Campbell
Prize in clinical psychology.

Martina Jovev, MA, PhD, is a clinical psychologist and research fellow
at ORYGEN Youth Health in Victoria, Australia. Dr. Jovev has published articles in the area of cognitive biases and personality disorders,
and is a researcher on several projects examining psychosocial functioning and processing of psychosocial threat in individuals diagnosed with
personality disorders. She is also an investigator on several projects on
personality disorders in young people.

Parinda Parikh, MD, is an attending psychiatrist in the eating disorder
unit at the Payne Whitney Westchester campus of the New York Presbyterian Hospital in White Plains, New York. She is also an instruc-
tor in psychiatry at the Weill Cornell Medical College in New York.
Dr. Parikh is board certified in adult psychiatry and board eligible in
child and adolescent psychiatry. Her prior publications include survey
research and case reports, and her current research interest is the treatment of eating disorders in children and adolescents.

Janice Russell, MD, FRACP, FRANZCP, MFCP, a psychiatrist, is a
clinical associate professor in the Discipline of Psychological Medicine
at the University of Sydney, and director of the Eating Disorder Programs at the Northside Clinic, Missenden Unit–Royal Prince Alfred

Hospital, and the Rivendell Adolescent Unit–Thomas Walker Hospital. She is a visiting consultant to the Curran Centre Child and Adolescent Service Greater Western Area Health Service in Orange, New South Wales, and the Eating Disorder Program in Canberra. In 2002 Dr. Russell was invited by the Canterbury District Health Board to review services for people with eating disorders in New Zealand, and in 2004 she was invited to review the nongovernmental organization in Wellington, New Zealand. She was an inaugural chair of the Interview Development Subcommittee of the Admissions Committee for the University of Sydney graduate medical program. Her research and publication interests are psychoneuroendocrinology, psychosomatics, adolescent medicine and psychiatry, and eating disorders.

Lori A. Sansone, MD, is a board-certified family medicine physician at Wright-Patterson Air Force Base in Dayton, Ohio. Dr. Sansone was the medical consultant for an eating disorders program for 2 years, has authored more than 80 published papers including 15 book chapters, and coauthored the *Self-Harm Inventory*. She is also coeditor of the local newsletter *Mental Health Issues in Primary Care*.

Paolo Santonastaso, MD, is a professor of psychiatry at the University of Padua, Department of Neurosciences, and is the head of the eating disorders unit of Padua General Hospital in Italy. His main fields of research interest are eating disorders, psychosomatic disorders, posttraumatic stress disorder, and psychotherapy. He has published more than 230 papers.

Rebecca Schwartz, BA, is a graduate student in clinical and developmental psychology at the University of Missouri–Columbia. Her interests include personality disorders, peer relations and socioemotional adjustment, and developmental psychopathology.

Marika Solhan, BS, is a clinical psychology graduate student at the University of Missouri–Columbia. Her research interests include personality disorders, psychometrics, and clinical assessment. She is currently researching affective instability in borderline personality disorder and its relationship to impulsivity, interpersonal stressors, and substance use.

Howard Steiger, PhD, FAED, is the director of the eating disorders program of the Douglas Hospital, professor of psychiatry and associate member in psychology at McGill University, and affiliated with various regional universities. Dr. Steiger directs the only large-scale, specialized program for the treatment of adults suffering from eating disorders in the province of Quebec. Dr. Steiger is active as a clinician, teacher, and researcher, and has published numerous scientific and theoretical articles in the area of eating disorders. His recent research focuses on developmental, neurobiological, and genetic correlates, and commonly associated psychopathology, in sufferers of eating disorders. He is a fellow of the Academy for Eating Disorders and serves on various committees. He is also coeditor of the Academy for Eating Disorders' *Eating Disorders Review* and a member of the editorial board of the *International Journal of Eating Disorders*.

Stephanie D. Stepp, MA, is a doctoral student in clinical psychology at the University of Missouri–Columbia. Her research interests include the validity of current assessment tools in measuring personality pathology, validity and feasibility of dimensional models of personality disorder classification, and relations between Axis I symptoms and personality dysfunction. Ms. Stepp is also interested in providing and disseminating effective treatments for individuals suffering from borderline personality disorder.

Roxanna E. Stumpf is a graduate student in the Clinical Studies Program in the Department of Psychology at the University of Hawaii.

Timothy J. Trull, PhD, is a professor of psychological sciences at the University of Missouri–Columbia. His research interests include personality, personality disorders, self-harm behavior and suicidality, substance-use disorders, psychometrics, and clinical assessment. Dr. Trull currently is an associate editor of the journal *Psychological Assessment*, author of the textbook *Clinical Psychology* (7th edition, 2005), and coauthor of a structured interview for the five-factor model of personality.

Kelly M. Vitousek, PhD, (former name Kelly M. Bemis), is an associate professor of psychology and an adjunct associate professor of psychiatry at the University of Hawaii. She is also codirector of the Center for Cognitive-Behavioral Therapy and director of the eating disorder program in the Department of Psychology. Dr. Vitousek has published more than 50 articles and chapters, and serves on the editorial board of the *International Journal of Eating Disorders*.

Glenn Waller, DPhil, FAED, is head of Outpatients at the Vincent Square Eating Disorders Clinic, Central and North West London Mental Health NHS Trust, and is visiting professor of psychology at the Eating Disorders Section, Institute of Psychiatry, King's College, London. Professor Waller has published more than 170 peer-reviewed articles and a number of book chapters on the subject of eating disorders. He is on the editorial boards of the *International Journal of Eating Disorders*, the *European Eating Disorders Review*, and *Eating and Weight Disorders*.

The Lost Years

BY L.M.

My life began in a seemingly ordinary way. But it didn't remain that way for long. I was born the second out of three girls into a strict European family where the motto was "yours is not to question why, yours is just to do or die." The rules were strict and nonnegotiable. I was never permitted to show any anger or sadness. Ours was a family ruled by fear, with a splash of Catholic guilt to "straighten us out." I learned early that the only way to survive was to follow the rules of authority without question, never express anger, and never ever let them see me cry. A great part of my early childhood went by in a blur. I never questioned them or told them no. They were the adults to be followed without argument. They told me that anything that happens under their roof stays there. It was a perfect breeding ground for a wide variety of emotional issues.

When I was young, my grandfather abused me. He called it playing big girl games. He said it was a way to prove that I loved him and that I was his little angel. Over the next several years his "games" continued.

In high school, when I was 14, my grandfather died. I remember this day even though most of my life was buried. I was supposed to babysit that night and was going to say good-bye to him. He had made comments about my body changing and that he wanted to see it. For the first time I said no. I ran away as the car that was picking me up honked. I felt relief that I could escape for the night. The next morning I got the phone call that my grandfather had been taken to the hospital. He had a massive heart attack and didn't make it. I spent the next several years blaming myself for killing him by saying no to him. Shortly after, I had my first experience with the school psychologist.

It happened purely by accident. By this time I had started to make small scratches on the inside of my left arm. While in driver's education, my teacher asked about the scratches on my arm. From where he was sitting, he had a good view. Panic set in. I thought, "What do I tell him? I can't tell him the truth." I said, "It's nothing. I was playing in the woods and got scratched." Before the day was over, I was called to the nurse's office. I figured I would tell her the same thing that I told the teacher. She gave me some bullshit story that she wanted to see them to make sure that the scratches didn't get infected. Next thing I know she is on the phone with the social worker, saying, "She's here in the office, now—could you come by?" The social worker showed up and asked what had happened. She said that some people do this because they are being abused at home. She asked me if that was happening. I looked her in the eyes and said, "No. I was playing in the woods and got scratched." She called the school psychologist into the room. My panic level was so high I felt like I was going to jump out of my skin. The room became blurry; I felt fuzzy. They said that they had to tell my parents about this. I pleaded with them not to. I choked on my fear and felt like I was going to throw up. I got up and tried to bolt. The social worker had moved in front of the door to block my exit. I yelled at her. "You bitch. Get out of my way." She tried to grab my arm. I recoiled—it felt as though I had been burned. They gave me a choice. They would call my parents or I could tell them, as long as they called the nurse in the morning to prove that I had told them. I got her back later. After school, I stayed late. I tried to figure out how to tell my parents in a way that was all fluff and no substance. I couldn't tell them the truth. They wouldn't do anything, and I would be killed. Several years before my older sister told my parents about what our grandfather had been doing. They went into my grandparents' kitchen and closed the door. I heard screaming coming from behind the door. I heard my grandfather being hit. After several minutes, my parents stormed out of the room right past me. Nothing was ever said about the "incident." My parents continued to let him live in their home and never asked if he was still abusing me. He was, and they didn't even bother to do anything to stop it. They handled this situation in the same way that they handled everything else. They beat the crap out of the guilty party and expected me to be happy about it. Why would I even bother trying to tell them the truth about what my grandfather did?

I was going out to the bus stop to take the late bus home, but there across the street was my mother's van. I started to panic. Should I pretend that I didn't see her? Should I just bite the bullet and tell her the bullshit story that I had concocted? I decided on the latter. She took me to the lake behind the school and asked, "Why would you do that? Haven't your father and I always treated you three the same?" I told her that yes they had. I told her that I didn't know why I had done that. I told her that it made me feel better. When I went back to school the next day, I hunted down the people that had lied to me. I told them exactly how I felt. "You lied to me. You expect me to tell you what is going on with me when you can't even keep your mouth shut for one day? You expect me to trust you when you went back on your word? Think again." A few weeks later, I stayed after school, as I had done so often, to avoid going home. I walked silently into the social worker's office. I had just cut my hand with a piece of glass so that I could bleed on her newly washed floor. She must have heard something because she called out, "Hello . . . anyone there?" I didn't answer. I just let my hand drip blood on her clean floor and walked out.

I wound up spending several hours sitting in the school shrink's office. I looked him straight in the eyes and lied to him, saying, "Nothing is happening at home." What was he going to do—beat an answer out of me? My father and mother already tried that. I didn't even feel the physical pain anymore. I was so numb. There was no one who could hurt me any more than I had already been hurt. In my head, I would repeat, "You do not exist in my world. You can't touch me." I finally graduated from high school without having divulged my secret. I lost a lot of time. My memory was like Swiss cheese. I was accused of having done things or said things that I swore I had never done or said. Truth is, I didn't remember most of my life. There were moments here and there, but nothing made sense. I felt as though a stranger was living my life and I had no control over what this person did or said.

I went away to college in Iowa, relieved that I could leave my family and escape several hundred miles away. I was hoping for a new start. Maybe I could stop cutting to relieve the pressure inside. Maybe I would not be so numb that the sting of a razor's edge was the only thing that I could feel. Maybe I could crawl out of the fog that was always threatening to consume me. Maybe I wouldn't have the dark emptiness inside. Maybe, just maybe, I would find someone that could understand why I felt so crazy inside. This hope didn't last long—only a few weeks. I was back to cutting to feel real. I even went so far as to paint pictures in my own blood and hang them on my side of the dorm room. My dorm mate was not happy. She reported me to the director of the dorm. I couldn't stop the stranger that was living my life from cutting. I just didn't let anyone see the cuts. At around the same time, I had met a guy. He was nice enough at first. I thought that this is what every young woman did. I had never dated before this, so I didn't know what to expect. He started pressuring me to have a sexual relationship. I told him I was a virgin, but he was confused that I knew how to physically please him. He never wanted to touch me because he thought that was "disgusting." This only fed into the core beliefs that I had that my body is disgusting and had only one purpose: to be used. He asked me to dress up in revealing clothes, and pretend that I was sleeping so that he could pretend to sneak into the room and have his way with me. He wanted me to fight back. Sometimes he would tie me up before sex. I went along with it because I didn't know that I could say "no." He would say that I was his f#$* doll. It all seemed familiar—as though I had done this before. I couldn't remember where or how.

During my sophomore year, I took a developmental psychology class. In this class, we were learning about using art to help children express their feelings. We also learned what would be considered to be red flags when children were in trouble or there was a possibility of abuse at home. I felt as though a train had hit me. I thought, "I have a lot of those signs in behavior and in my poetry." I talked to the professor after class to find out ways to make sure that these behaviors were indeed red flags. I knew only that my parents used to beat me at home. I also knew that my grandfather had sometimes touched me inappropriately. I had no idea that this was only the tip of the truth.

My problem with cutting became increasingly worse. The cuts were never deep enough to make me feel like I was alive. I lived day to day in a fog, where nothing felt real. I called it my "unreal reality." I also started to restrict food and purge when I did eat. In an effort to become less attractive to my boyfriend, I had lost 10 pounds in a few weeks. I wanted to be invisible. The cutting became so frequent, as did my desire to end the miserable existence that I had created. My first trip to a psych ward was a result of cutting too deeply. They were able to keep me there on 24-hour observation. They went through their standard questions. I lied to get out of there by telling them that I wasn't trying to kill myself. I told them I didn't know why I cut except that it made me feel more real. They finally let me out AMA (against medical advice). I had to follow up with the psychiatrist. I agreed to see him once a week. At some point, he tried to tell me that I had dissociated myself from my childhood experiences. That's why I could not remember any of it. I told him that the reason I couldn't remember was because there was nothing to remember. I had a small problem with food. I had a difficult time with remembering where I was sometimes. I forgot what I said sometimes or what I had done. I admitted that my parents treated me horribly while I was growing up. I also admitted that my grandfather had sometimes touched me inappropriately.

I spent the next 3 years in and out of the hospital because of cutting, suicide attempts, and my eating disorder. I had a difficult time concentrating, but somehow I managed to graduate from college. The worst part of it was that I lived every day like I was surrounded by a fog that kept trying to consume me. I felt as though I had rocks tied on my feet. They were so heavy that I could hardly move. I noticed that I found strange things appearing in my room. There were baby blankets, pacifiers, and an entire set of art supplies, to name a few. I know that I had not purchased them, so how did they get there? I never spoke of these things to anyone. How would I explain how they got there? I hid them from my boyfriend, and he never found out. I had been with the same person for 6 years. How would I tell him about my memory problems?

I had secretly started seeing an older woman. She seemed kind and nurturing. She never forced me to be sexual or do things that I didn't want to do. I finally moved out of my boyfriend's house and moved in with the older woman. During the 3-year relationship I had with her, I never once was afraid that I would wake up in the middle of the night with someone trying to have sex with me. It was quite the opposite. At first she was very kind. After several months, I felt like she was smothering me. I was constantly taking care of her and her house. I did all of the cleaning and cooking while working full-time. I became more involved with cutting and not eating. It was as though she was sucking all of the energy out of me. My weight dropped lower and lower. I stayed in the second bedroom with the door closed. I couldn't stand to be touched. Every time anyone came near me, I would recoil. I felt as though someone had shocked or burned me. I finally had to quit my job at a day care center. I couldn't lift the kids anymore, and my brain was not working properly. I could not concentrate at work and decided that it was not right to risk the welfare of the children that depended on me to keep them safe.

I quit therapy and decided I had nowhere to go. I could stay with this woman who sucked the life out of me, or I could go back to live with my parents and get treatment for my eating disorder. I knew somewhere inside that I would not survive much longer. The way I saw it, I had three choices: I could stay where I was at and wait to die, I could end it all quickly, or I could ask my parents for help. Some part of me did not want to die and fought to keep me alive. Somehow, I made the decision to ask my parents for help. Somehow, I got into treatment. I don't regret that choice because I am physically and mentally healthier than I ever have been before. I am fortunate to have found the right therapist and the right treatment. I am convinced that I would not be alive had some higher power not intervened. I am choosing healthier relationships. The road is not always easy, and at times I find myself slipping into old habits. But, I am not there as long because I have been offered more effective ways of coping. I just need to make the decision to take the healthier path.

Acknowledgments

This volume represents the culmination of my academic passion to understand and effectively treat individuals suffering from both eating disorders and personality disorders. Consequently, I want to personally acknowledge and sincerely thank the many authors who, in these pages, take risks and share their impressions, clinical experience, and research about these challenging patients. I want to express my deep appreciation to Dr. John Levitt, who has been a wonderful colleague, superb coauthor, and unending source of emotional support, feedback, and novel ideas. I want to acknowledge Nancy Bird Sowards for her deeply valued friendship, ever-present support, and life guidance. I want to thank Dr. Robert Sutton, who provided the initial infrastructural support for me to maintain an active research and writing career at Kettering Medical Center. I must also express my gratitude to the medical administration at Kettering Medical Center for their unrelenting support—specifically, Dr. Stephen McDonald, Dr. Robert Smith, and Dr. Greg Wise. Finally, I want to acknowledge my wife, Lori, who has been a remarkably supportive and truly exceptional companion, while managing to balance her intricate professional roles with me as coresearcher, coauthor, and copresenter—*mi amor para siempre.*

—Randy A. Sansone, MD

Participating with Dr. Randy Sansone in our second major book project together reminds me of how so many individuals touch our lives and have such a profound impact. First, I want to acknowledge the sharing, learning, and growing that this relationship has provided me—thank you, Randy. Second, I want once again to acknowledge the debt that I owe to all those patients I have been fortunate enough to interact with over the years. They continue to teach me daily. I also want to thank my colleagues and friends at Alexian Brothers Behavioral Health Hospital for supporting my efforts to develop innovative treatment programs for these patients. Finally, I want to thank my wife, Janet, and my four children for the constant inspiration, the significant doses of humility, and keeping me young.

—John L. Levitt, PhD

Introduction

RANDY A. SANSONE, MD
JOHN L. LEVITT, PHD

The juncture between personality disorders and eating disorders truly remains one of the challenging frontiers in the eating disorders field. Almost all eating disorder clinicians have pondered this perplexing relationship and grappled with the treatment implications of working with patients with both eating and personality psychopathologies. We first attempted to globally explore this frontier in a special edition of the journal *Eating Disorders: The Journal of Treatment and Prevention*. It is not surprising that this special edition generated even more questions for us, which served as the impetus for this edited book on personality disorders and eating disorders.

In developing a strategy for this volume, we intentionally sought to blend together two disciplines of experts—those anchored in the field of personality pathology and those anchored in the field of eating disorders. In doing so, we anticipated an elite volume consisting of a unique merger of talented and well-qualified experts in their respective fields. We believe that we have achieved this.

In the first chapter of this volume, Martina Jovev and Henry Jackson provide a robust introduction to personality conceptualization and the intricacies of personality disorder diagnosis. These authors dialogue categorical versus dimensional models of personality assessment, the difficulty of assessing *maladaptiveness* in *Diagnostic and Statistical Manual of Mental Disorders* Axis II disorders, and the role of cultural influences on personality. In the second chapter, we review the prevalence of personality disorders among those with eating disorders and provide a literature-review-based summary.

Chapters 3 and 4 explore some of the etiological issues related to personality disorders and eating disorders. Given that many Axis II disorders appear to have various degrees of genetic predisposition, the focus is on other aspects of etiology. Angela Favaro and Paolo Santonastaso discuss the intriguing coexistence of impulsive and compulsive personality traits in patients with eating disorders. We discuss the unfortunate role of childhood trauma as a risk factor for certain types of personality disorders, which in turn appear to function as subsequent risk factors for particular types of eating disorders.

Chapters 5 and 6 of this volume review patient assessment. Stephanie Stepp, Rebecca Schwartz, Marika Solhan, and Timothy Trull provide us with a unique overview of the available assessment tools for use in this comorbid population. Kelly Vitousek and Roxanna Stumpf deftly tackle the challenges of assessing personality functioning in acutely ill patients with eating disorders.

Based on the literature analysis in Chapter 2, the next three chapters provide the reader with an overview of the personality pathologies most commonly encountered in individuals with eating disorders—specifically, obsessive-compulsive, borderline, and avoidant personality disorders. Parinda Parikh and Katharine Halmi review obsessive-compulsive personality disorder, contrasting it with obsessive-compulsive disorder. We review borderline and avoidant personality disorders, emphasizing the potential adaptive roles of eating disorders in patients with these Axis II phenomena.

Justifiably, the largest section of this book is devoted to treatment. We wanted to provide the reader with various approaches to clinical intervention, and we have attempted to do so. However, with the exception of the suggested treatment strategies for borderline personality disorder, few of which are empirically supported, the clinical literature in this area is very sparse. Janice Russell begins this section by reviewing a multicomponent treatment strategy for the many patients with eating disorders that clinicians encounter with comorbid obsessive-compulsive personality traits or disorder. The next two chapters focus on the treatment of comorbid borderline personality disorder. Given that there are a variety of approaches to this Axis II disorder, we selected two approaches, because of space limitations. Specifically, John Levitt discusses the self-regulation approach, a well-rounded model for the treatment of this population. Lori Sansone and Randy Sansone discuss an eclectic approach to the treatment, which readily accommodates the various clinical variations observed in those with borderline personality disorder. As for those patients with comorbid avoidant personality disorder, because of the absolute dearth of information, Hendrik Hinrichsen and Glenn Waller literally introduce to the literature a treatment strategy. Finally, we finish with a discussion of a medication treatment strategy for eating disordered individuals with personality disorders.

The final chapter of this volume focuses on treatment outcome—an aspect of intervention that all clinicians yearn to know about. Specifically, what can clinicians realistically expect in terms of treatment outcome in this population? Kenneth Bruce and Howard Steiger adroitly and explicitly address this issue.

As we completed this project, we became poignantly aware that this is just the beginning. Patients with both eating disorders and personality disorders are truly an uncharted clinical frontier. Each author in this volume has been an explorer, trying to tease out a viable clinical path. We believe that they, the authors, have done a remarkable job in an area with little preexisting data. Although they have, we hope, cut an approximate path through this frontier, we clinicians remain explorers, as well, encountering an ever-changing landscape, trying to do the best that we can for our patients.

NOTE

Please address all correspondence to Randy A. Sansone, MD, Sycamore Primary Care Center, 2115 Leiter Road, Miamisburg, OH, 45342; telephone: 937-384-6850; fax: 937-384-6938; e-mail: Randy.sansone@kmcnetwork.org.

Personality Conceptualization

1

Personality Disorder Constructs and Conceptualizations

HENRY J. JACKSON, PHD, FAPS
MARTINA JOVEV, MA, PHD

The concept of personality disorders (PDs) has existed for some time, although PDs have typically been considered as disorders of exclusion— that is, specifically to the exclusion of psychosis or neurosis (Jackson, 1998). However, the importance of PDs in clinical practice was dramatically emphasized with the inclusion of Axis II in the *Diagnostic and Statistical Manual of Mental Disorders–Third Edition* (*DSM–III*; American Psychiatric Association [APA], 1980). Since the advent of the *DSM–III*, PDs have been separated from the great majority of mental disorders and represented as distinct diagnostic categories on a distinct diagnostic axis (Axis II). This innovation has forced clinicians to think of PDs as (a) coexisting with Axis I disorders such as depression or panic disorder, (b) predisposing individuals toward developing specific Axis I disorders, (c) complicating Axis I presentations, and/or (d) complicating treatment response to Axis I disorders (i.e., interfering with or preventing treatment).

The *Diagnostic and Statistical Manual of Mental Disorders–Fourth Edition* (*DSM–IV*; APA, 1994, p. 629) operationalized the criteria for the various PDs and defined a PD as "an enduring pattern of inner

TABLE 1.1 Comparison of the Classification Systems for Personality Disorders in the *Diagnostic and Statistical Manual of Mental Disorders–Fourth Edition (DSM–IV) and International Classification of Diseases* (10th ed.; ICD–10)

Diagnostic Criteria	
DSM–IV	**ICD–10**
Diagnostic criteria for a personality disorder refer to behaviors or traits that are characteristic of the person's recent and long-term functioning since early childhood. Personality disorder describes a constellation of behaviors or traits that cause either significant impairment in social or occupational functioning or subjective distress.	Diagnostic criteria include a variety of conditions that indicate a person's characteristic and enduring patterns of inner experience (cognition and affect) and behavior(s) that differ markedly from a culturally expected and accepted range.

Classification of Personality Disorder	
DSM–IV	**ICD–10**
Cluster A	
Paranoid	Paranoid
Schizoid	Schizoid
Schizotypal	
Cluster B	
Antisocial	Dissocial
Borderline	Emotionally unstable
Histrionic	Histrionic
Narcissistic	Other (Narcissistic)
Cluster C	
Avoidant	Anxious (Avoidant)
Dependant	Dependant
Obsessive-compulsive	Anankastic

experience and behavior that deviates markedly from the expectations of the individual's culture, is pervasive and inflexible, has an onset in adolescence or adulthood, is stable over time and leads to distress or impairment." This definition explicitly emphasizes notions of convergent validity, inflexibility, temporal stability, pervasiveness, maladaptiveness and impairment, and subjective distress.

There are two major nosological systems that include PDs—the *DSM* and the *International Classification of Diseases* (ICD-10; World Health Organization, 1992). The *DSM–IV* (APA, 1994) identifies 10 distinct

PDs and assigns them to three PD clusters: Cluster A (odd or eccentric: paranoid, schizoid, and schizotypal), Cluster B (dramatic or erratic: antisocial, borderline, histrionic, and narcissistic), and Cluster C (anxious or fearful: avoidant, dependent, and obsessive-compulsive). The *ICD-10* (World Health Organization, 1992) identifies nine specific PDs that approximate the *DSM* system but does not group them into clusters (see Table 1.1). The present chapter focuses on research undertaken using the *DSM* PD rubrics.

Within the *DSM* system (APA, 1980, 1987, 1994) there are four assumptions about the nature of personality and PDs: (a) that there is a point of discontinuity between normal and abnormal personality, (b) that this point can be demarcated by satisfying a number of measurable criteria that are valid for all cases, (c) that there are qualitatively different and mutually exclusive "types" or "categories" of PDs, and (d) that the diagnostic criteria for any specific PD are polythetic, meaning that an individual needs to *meet a specified number of stipulated criteria* to attain a specific PD diagnosis *but not necessarily all of the criteria or a specific combination of the stipulated criteria.*

Practice Point

With the *DSM* classification system, a person with a specific PD, say, borderline personality disorder (BPD), may have a dissimilar presentation from a second person also diagnosed with BPD, because each person may have been accorded a different "constellation" of BPD criteria (i.e., a person needs to meet only any five out of nine BPD criteria to achieve a full diagnosis of BPD).

CHALLENGES TO THE *DSM* PD CONCEPTS

There are a number of challenges or issues pertaining to the *DSM* PD categories, including the reliability of the *DSM* PD categories, the validity of the PD construct, the role of maladaptiveness in the conceptualization and diagnosis of PDs, the distinctness of criteria between different PD categories, and the development of measures to assess PDs.

The Reliability of the DSM *PD Categories and the Validity of the PD Construct*

Since the inception of the *DSM–III* (APA, 1980), the status of PDs as mental disorders has been questioned on two major grounds (e.g., Livesley, Jackson, & Schroeder, 1992; Schroeder & Livesley, 1991). The first issue is the reliability of Axis II diagnostic categories, and the second is a more fundamental concern about the validity of PDs as a distinct construct.

Despite operationalized diagnostic criteria, the categorical nature of the *DSM* PDs (APA, 1980, 1987, 1994) has been criticized for poor reliability among clinicians when used in unstructured interviews and only fair reliability across structured interviews (Perry, 1992). It has been proposed that the low reliability of the PD diagnoses and their associated co-occurrence with other PDs is due to the artificial nature of the PD categories. Although many individuals display evidence of personality dysfunction, only a few actually meet full diagnosable criteria and receive a categorical diagnosis. As such, the categorical judgments of the *DSM* system may result in a loss of information that may be vital to treatment planning (Kass, Skodol, Charles, Spitzer, & Williams, 1985) as well as compromise the reliability and validity of the PD diagnosis (Widiger, 1992).

Validity of PDs

In addition, the *DSM* system of categorizing PDs is challenging because of problems with multiple PD diagnoses and PD overlap. Empirical studies suggest that the average number of PD diagnoses per patient with PD appears to be closer to four rather than one (de Girolamo & Reich, 1993). Furthermore, the degree of similarity observed between the factor structures across personality disordered and non–personality disordered individuals provides evidence that particular dimensions of PDs are organized in a similar way in the two populations (Livesley et al., 1992; Schroeder & Livesley, 1991).

Such research indicates that there may not be a clear demarcation between one PD and the next. Thus, individual categories may fail to adequately capture the concept of a PD, resulting in a substantial overlap between the types of PDs, as well as a substantial number of multiple diagnoses (Skodol, Rosnick, Kellman, Oldham, & Hyler, 1988). Although on their own these studies do not oppose the categorical model, they do suggest that such a model may not adequately capture individual personality dysfunction with only one PD type and that the categorical system may force distinctions that may not otherwise exist (Widiger, 1993).

A second line of criticism has questioned if PD categories represent diagnosable forms of abnormality. Widiger, Sanderson, and Warner (1986) suggested that the categorical diagnoses in the *DSM* do not appear to identify distinct classes of individuals and that these categories do not define discrete disorders. In support of this viewpoint, Livesley et al. (1992) found that the dimensions of PDs are organized in a similar way in "normal" and personality disordered populations (Livesley et al., 1992; Schroeder & Livesley, 1991).

Practice Point

There may not be clear distinctions between normal and abnormal personality. Thus, clinicians may not agree on the presence or absence of a PD. In addition, individuals may meet the criteria for more than one PD, and there may be overlap between the various PDs.

The Role of Maladaptiveness in the DSM

At the core of a *DSM* PD diagnosis is the concept of disordered functioning, which reflects the need for clinicians to assess the impact of personality styles on day-to-day life. The *DSM–IV* states that personality traits are diagnosed as a PD only when they are "inflexible, maladaptive, persisting and cause significant functional impairment or subjective distress" (APA, 1994, p. 630). The delineation of personality traits as being adaptive or maladaptive is essential, as it provides a large part of the justification for defining PDs as mental disorders.

Despite its importance, *maladaptiveness* has an ambiguous role in the *DSM* diagnostic system. First, it is not specifically included in all the criteria sets for individual PD diagnoses. For example, some of the individual criteria sets refer to *social* dysfunction, such as BPD ("a pattern of unstable and intense interpersonal relationships characterized by alternating between extremes of idealization and devaluation"; APA, 1994, p. 654). Yet other criteria sets include features that may not be directly considered as dysfunctional, as in avoidant PD ("unusually reluctant to take personal risks or to engage in any new activities because they may prove embarrassing"; APA, 1994, p. 665). Consequently, the primary diagnostic emphasis is often given to the number of traits satisfied rather than to determining if a set of traits results in significant maladaptiveness.

Second, the maladaptiveness criterion as stated in the *DSM–IV* offers little help in delineating PDs from normal personality traits. The *DSM–IV* even suggests that some personality traits may be adaptive in certain environments—"paranoid traits may be adaptive, particularly in threatening environments" (APA, 1994, p. 637). At the same time, the *DSM* noted, "Only when traits are inflexible, maladaptive, persisting and cause significant functional impairment or subjective distress do they constitute PDs" (APA, 1994, p. 630). However, the *DSM* does not provide *specific* criteria as a basis on which to judge particular descriptors as maladaptive. In reality, personality traits may be considered to be (a) inherently maladaptive, (b) maladaptive only above a certain level, and/or (c) maladaptive only in certain contexts. As such, at least part of the reason for the low reliability of the *DSM* diagnoses may be the inherent lack of an operationalized definition of maladaptiveness.

Practice Point
Despite its importance in the conceptualization of PDs in the *DSM*, maladaptiveness is not specifically included in all of the criteria for individual PD diagnoses, and the *DSM* offers little help in separating PDs from normal personality traits.

The Distinctiveness of Criteria From Different PD Categories

There appear to be high rates of co-occurrence and overlap among the PDs, which could be a consequence of confounding the components of personality style and disordered functioning in the current descriptors of PDs (Parker, 1997; Svanborg, Gustavsson, Mattila-Evenden, & Asberg, 1999). For example, overlap among individual PD categories will be found if they share certain behavioral features of disordered functioning (e.g., avoidance of social situations). In addition, criteria from two or more different PDs might lead to the same behavioral outcomes but may be attributed to different cognitive processes or intentions. For example, a person with BPD and a person with antisocial PD may both be unemployed (a behavioral outcome), but the individual with antisocial PD evinces "repeated failure to sustain consistent work behavior or honor financial obligations" (p. 650), whereas the unemployment for the person with BPD is "due to interpersonal problems, identity or impulsivity" (p. 654). The two criteria have different connotations. In the case of the person with antisocial PD, there is an implicit notion that the unemployment is due to active choice by the person, whereas in the case of the person with BPD, there is clearly the idea that the outcome is a consequence of the person's psychopathology. Consequently, the observed co-occurrence between PD categories is not because they share a common personality style but rather because they share a dysfunctional behavioral component.

Practice Point

There are several problems with the current conceptualization of maladaptiveness in the PD literature:

1. The current diagnostic *criteria* may not adequately capture the impairment and maladaptiveness associated with the PDs.
2. The current *tools* used for diagnosing PDs do not adequately capture the maladaptive criteria needed for a PD diagnosis.
3. The clinician's opinion may or may not reflect the true level of maladaptiveness experienced by those persons who have the traits suggested in the diagnostic criteria.
4. Lack of dysfunction may be associated with the social desirability of certain personality traits, such as being a perfectionist, which may be considered by the respondent, clinician, or society to be more socially desirable than being socially aloof.

DIMENSIONAL MODELS OF PDS

There are several reasons for supporting the categorical conceptualization of PDs. It is a familiar system that has facilitated the conceptualization and communication regarding PDs. In addition, the increased focus on PDs has led to better clinical decisions and selection of more appropriate treatment. Nevertheless, there is limited empirical support for the grouping of PDs into clusters (Bell & Jackson, 1992) or for a clear distinction between one PD and another (Widiger et al., 1986). As a result, a number of researchers have proposed dimensional models of personality and PDs (e.g., Cloninger, 1987; Cloninger, Svrakic, & Przybeck, 1993; Costa & McCrae, 1992). According to this model, normal and abnormal persons share the same basic interpersonal styles, but individuals suffering from PDs can be conceptualized as a small subset of individuals who fall at the extreme end of personality dimensions.

In terms of dimensional models, there is a growing literature that attempts to explain PDs in terms of the Neuroticism Extraversion Openess Personality Inventory (NEO PI) (Costa & McCrae, 1992) five-factor model. In this model, schizoid PD is defined in terms of low extraversion (i.e., introversion), whereas avoidant PD is defined in terms of low extraversion (i.e., introversion) and high neuroticism. Similarly, obsessive-compulsive PD is defined in terms of high conscientiousness. Although this approach may place PDs on a continuum with "normal" personality, the richness of the PD descriptions or diagnostics are not readily captured by the five-factor model. This may be resolved if the 30 facet scales are used instead of the five factors to map onto the 10 PDs of the *DSM–IV.* However, extensive mapping at the facet level is yet to occur.

To date, dimensional models have not been used in the formal diagnosis of personality pathology, and there is limited agreement among the dimensional theorists concerning the number and content of traits necessary to describe personality. This lack of agreement has contributed to the development and publication of many instruments to measure personality dimensions. Unfortunately, there are not many studies analyzing the convergent validity of these inventories.

BLENDED MODELS

One way of overcoming the problems associated with the categorical PD models would be to dimensionalize the *DSM* model. However, there are clear difficulties with this option. First is the difficulty of dimensionalizing the 79 PD criteria found in the *DSM* (i.e., of turning yes–no criteria into dimensional criteria), and second is the question of what it means to have to rate each patient on 79 criteria. What sense would one make of such a complicated profile?

Nonetheless, Oldham and Skodol (2000) created a system dimensionalizing the *DSM* PDs. In this system, both categorical and dimensional representations of the *DSM* PDs have stronger relationships to impairment and functioning in the domains of employment, social relationships with parents and friends, and global social adjustment than do the other dimensional models tested (Skodol et al., 2005). This suggests that the dimensional rating of traditional categorical criteria may be a good compromise in the ongoing debate regarding the use of categories versus dimensions.

Consider the following case illustration. A 26-year-old unmarried woman with BPD presents for long-term therapy, following a recent suicide attempt. The suicide attempt was precipitated by a relationship breakup. She has been referred to the Psychology Service by the hospital's Accident and Emergency Department. She reports a history of self-harming behavior, affective instability, feelings of emptiness and boredom, sexual promiscuity, binge drinking (to modulate her moods), intense anger, and unstable relationships. Currently, she does not meet the criteria for an Axis I disorder, although she has been treated for major depression in the past. She completes the NEO (Costa & McCrae, 1992) for dimensional personality assessment. Results reveal high neuroticism scores, and this is found to be true on the constituent facets of the Neuroticism scale. However, she scores high on several facets of Openness, namely, openness to ideas, feelings, and aesthetics, and two facets of Agreeableness, namely, altruism and tender-mindedness. These can be viewed as assets and indicate strengths that the clinician can engage and use in therapy to explore new ways of dealing with the self-damaging behaviors and cognitions.

Practice Point

The dimensional model represents PDs on a continuum between normal and pathological behavior. It is less arbitrary and more informative, and it avoids multiple diagnoses and heterogeneous categories. Furthermore, it allows assessment and comparison of personality disordered and non–personality disordered individuals. However, there is no consensus among dimensional theorists, and a blended model may be most useful.

OTHER ISSUES IN PDS

Temporal Stability of PDs

The appropriateness of diagnosing PDs in adolescents has often been debated (Bleiberg, 1994; Vito, Ladame, & Orlandini, 1999), both because of the fluid nature of personality in this age group and because of a concern about the impact of being labeled with a PD at such an early age. Both the *DSM–IV* and the ICD–10 diagnostic systems caution against PD diagnosis in adolescents and set arbitrary cutoff ages below which diagnosis is not recommended. Nevertheless, there is emerging evidence that PDs can be reliably diagnosed in adolescents, are valid, and have serious psychosocial consequences (e.g., Bernstein et al., 1993; Grilo et al., 1998).

Reviews of the stability of PDs in adult clinical populations (e.g., Grilo & McGlashan, 1999; Grilo, McGlashan, & Skodol, 2000) and community samples (e.g., Johnson et al., 1997) suggest that when using assessments based on interviews, most PDs have only moderate stability in adults, even when dimensional approaches are employed (Johnson et al., 1997). In contrast, moderate to high levels of stability have been found across the *DSM* clusters. For example, high levels of stability were found for Cluster B disorders in the Children in the Community Study (Bernstein et al., 1993; Johnson et al., 2000). This is consistent with the finding of no sudden increase in normal trait stability in the transition from the second decade to the third decade of life (Roberts & DelVecchio, 2000).

In clinical samples, the Yale Adolescent Follow-Up Study found low stability of categorical PDs over 2 years in adolescent inpatients (Mattanah, Becker, Levy, Edell, & McGlashan, 1995) and low to moderate stability for dimensional PD ratings (Grilo, Becker, Edell, & McGlashan, 2001), but participants' mean age was less than 18 years at follow-up and there was a low rate of participant retention in the follow-up period. In contrast, Chanen et al. (2004) found that the 2-year stability of the global category of PD in an older adolescent sample is high, whereas the stability of dimensionally rated PDs appears to be similar to that found in young adults in a variety of settings, especially for some Cluster A and Cluster B PDs.

On balance, the literature on the stability of normal personality suggests no sudden change between the second and third decades of life. Studies in community and inpatient samples of adolescents do not suggest dramatic differences in patterns of stability to those in adults. It appears that enough stability occurs to justify diagnosis and treatment of PDs in adolescents presenting to clinical services.

Practice Point

The PD construct is just as stable in adolescents as it is in adults, thus justifying intervention in adolescents presenting to clinical services for personality-based problems.

The Role of Culture

Culture may exert manifold influences on personality and PDs. First, culture may play a role in the shaping of personality and PDs, thus increasing their ultimate incidence and prevalence in a community. Paris (1998) labeled this the "cohort effect." The only empirical data in this regard are for antisocial PD, which has doubled in the United States since World War II (Kessler et al., 1994). A number of major authorities in the area (e.g., Millon & Davis, 1996; Paris, 1998) have argued that BPD has also increased in frequency in U.S. society since the 1950s because of rapid technological changes, the breakdown of the family unit, and the unavailability of potentially reparative figures such as extended family members who now need to work. Another factor leading to the increase in PDs may be parental psychopathology (e.g., substance use, depression), which may have increased over time. Add to this mix the role of pernicious role models in the entertainment industry and the disrepute of formerly respected reparative organizations such as the church. The preceding examples illustrate how PD rates may change over time within a single nation because of sociological changes.

Do specific PDs differ among cultures or nations? One reason to suspect cross-cultural differences is that certain personality traits that underpin PDs may be greatly admired and encouraged in certain nations. Paris (1998) argued that traditional societies are more likely to favor dependency traits as this ensures greater cohesion within the social group and binds them together in terms of mutual obligations; in such societies, there is less tolerance of deviancy. On the other hand, Western societies may reward narcissism and individuality, placing less importance on dependency.

There are few data to support cross-cultural differences in the prevalence rates of PDs (Paris, 1998). However, Paris (1998) noted the rates of antisocial PD are lower in Japan and Taiwan compared to South Korea and argued that this is because family cohesion and loyalty is stronger and more strongly encouraged in Japan and Taiwan. Obsessive-compulsive PD demonstrated the highest prevalence of all PDs in a national epidemiological study in Australia (Jackson & Burgess, 2004) and was associated with the lowest levels of disability (Jackson & Burgess, 2004; Skodol et al., 2002). Researchers might speculate that the high conscientiousness underpinning obsessive-compulsive PD might be advantageous in a Western society such as Australia.

In contrast, in war-torn countries (e.g., parts of Africa) where populations have been consistently ravaged and brutalized for many generations, the rates of antisocial PD may be higher than in other safer and secure countries. Individuals with this disorder are more likely to (a) have lost family members such as parents, (b) have experienced loss of nuclear and extended family cohesion, (c) have survived conflict, and (d) assume leadership positions in a lawless society—in some cases, to be in charge of genocidal activities and/or to model and reward others for antisocial behaviors (e.g., disregarding the rights of others, lying, stealing, cheating, lacking empathy, seeking sensation, engaging in brutality and sadism). Of course, there could be a genetic–adaptive component to this, whereby those with antisocial PD characteristics are more likely to survive over others and pass on their genes to offspring.

There may also be differences across cultures in the recognition and detection of PDs, as well as the labeling of them as abnormal. In some cases, it may be that exuberant sexual displays, a focus on the self, and the desire to be the center of attention are not labeled as histrionic but seen as normal (e.g., in Western countries). As Paris (1998) stated, "When personality profiles correspond to social expectations, certain traits may not be considered pathological unless they seriously interfere with functioning" (p. 289). An individual may be deviant on a particular personality dimension but may find an "ecological niche" (Parker, 1997) and not necessarily demonstrate disordered functioning. For instance, a person with histrionic PD may function well at work but not in personal relationships, whereas a person with dependent PD may function well at home but less well at work.

A final point pertains to whether certain subcultures within a single society "promote," "encourage," or "attract" people with certain specific PDs. For example, being narcissistic and histrionic might be career-enhancing attributes within the entertainment industry. Can one persevere and succeed as an actor or actress without having the characteristics of narcissism or histrionicity? The ecological niche argument is that people with such characteristics might be well suited to acting but would not be so well suited to working in another occupation.

Practice Point

Rapid change and social disintegration may lead to higher rates of PDs over time. Particular cultures and subcultures may favor certain personality traits. Individuals may find an ecological niche where their deviant personality traits are supported or even encouraged.

Axis I and Axis II Comorbidity

One of the major threads of research activity stimulated by the *DSM* has been the relationship between Axis I and Axis II disorders. An extensive literature examining Axis I–Axis II comorbidity is now available, and this is soundly reviewed by Bank and Silk (2001). However, continuing to focus on a specific PD at the global level (e.g., obsessive-compulsive PD) may be too gross a level to further our understanding of the relationship of personality to Axis I disorders such as depression or anorexia nervosa. The relationship is more likely to exist at a lower level, that is, at a trait or combinatorial trait level.

There are at least five possible ways of thinking about the relationships between Axis I and Axis II conditions. One model is that a given personality trait, for instance perfectionism, is a risk factor for an Axis I disorder such as depression and takes temporal precedence over it. Using these same examples, a second model is that both perfectionism and depression have independent origins—that is, their own distinct and unique etiologies—and emerge independently and potentially contemporaneously of each another. A third model is that, like the second model, perfectionism and depression have independent, or at least somewhat independent, origins but have a pathoplastic effect on each other—that is, they become mutually intertwined and difficult to disentangle from each other. This model could be relatively silent with regard to the *origins* of both perfectionism and depression but is clearly relevant to *course*, as the argument might be that the combination of depression and perfectionism exacerbates the dysfunctionality of the person and diverts their potential developmental trajectory if the person is young. A fourth model is that both depression and PD have a common underlying predisposition—for example, a latent trait called perfectionism. A fifth model is that a latent trait independently gives rise to both depression and PD, although this latent trait is yet to be identified and labeled.

Practice Point
The relationship between PD and an Axis I disorder(s) may not be straightforward. There may be at least five possible models of the relationship between them.

Comorbidity Between PDs and Eating Disorders

Highly variable rates of comorbidity, ranging from 21% to 97%, have been reported for the presence of any PD in patients with a range of eating disorder diagnoses (Skodol et al., 1993; Vitousek & Manke, 1994). Conversely, high prevalence rates for eating disorders have been reported for patients with PDs (Dolan, Evans, & Norton, 1994). The majority of studies in the area of eating disorders and PDs have been undertaken in bulimia nervosa, where borderline PD has been found to be the most common PD, with a prevalence rate of about 31% (Cassin & von Ranson, 2005), although prevalence rates range from 2% to higher than 50% (Skodol et al., 1993). Although research examining personality traits in patients with bulimia has often found these patients to be extroverted, histrionic, and affectively unstable, traits associated with anorexia nervosa such as perfectionism, shyness, and compliance have also emerged in studies (Cassin & von Ranson, 2005; Vitousek & Manke, 1994). The most frequent PD among individuals with anorexia nervosa is avoidant PD, at about 53%, followed by dependent (37%), obsessive-compulsive (33%), and borderline (29%) PDs (Cassin & von Ranson, 2005).

Interpreting comorbidity between eating disorders and PDs is complex partly because of the extensive comorbidity of anorexic and bulimic subtypes with one another and in part because of the multiple possible meanings and causes of comorbidity (see Lilienfeld, Waldman, & Israel, 1994). Moreover, although certain personality traits are associated with specific eating disordered behavior, many of these traits are the polar opposites (for instance, extroversion and shyness). Interestingly, PD (global category) is more likely to be diagnosed in patients who have a lifetime history of *DSM–IV* anorexia nervosa, binge eating/purging type, or who have concurrent symptoms of both disorders rather than patients with either bulimia or anorexia nervosa, restricting type. In addition, the PD diagnosis is equally likely to be in Cluster B or Cluster C (Herzog, Keller, Lavori, Kenny, & Sacks, 1992). In other words, these individuals are more likely to show severe and widespread pathology and to be more impaired than patients with either anorexia, restricting type, alone, or bulimia, alone.

Westen and Harnden-Fischer (2001) offered several possible reasons for the comorbidity between eating disorders and PDs. First, the comorbidity between eating disorders and PDs could reflect random co-occurrence, such that patients have a random chance of having the two disorders. However, the low probability of such high rates of co-occurrence between these disorders, which have relatively low base rates in the general population, suggests that the possibility of random co-occurrence is unlikely.

Second, the comorbidity between eating disorders and PDs could reflect symptomatic expressions of personality pathology. A third similar explanation for the comorbidity between eating disorders and PDs suggests that there might be a common pathology underlying multiple phenotypically distinct disorders—that is, a common genetic or environmental diathesis might underlie both eating disorders and PDs. Both of these hypotheses have some limited empirical support (Skodol et al., 1993).

One possible explanation for the substantial inconsistency across studies, as well as the comorbidity between eating disorder categories, is that eating disorder categories may be linked to heterogeneous personality factors (Sohlberg & Strober, 1994)—that is, more than one type of personality structure may generate or contribute to the symptoms of each eating disorder.

Some evidence for this possibility comes from the studies separating bulimic individuals into "multi-impulsive" versus "uni-impulsive" subtypes (Lacey & Evans, 1986). Multi-impulsive persons with bulimia display several impulsive behaviors (e.g., stealing, substance abuse) in addition to binge eating, whereas uni-impulsive patients have binge eating as their only symptom or behavior that could be described as impulsive. Studies have shown that multi-impulsive bulimic individuals have significantly greater rates of BPD and mood disorders than uni-impulsive bulimic individuals (Fichter, Quadflieg, & Rief, 1994). Thus, these two groups may represent very different kinds of patients, even though the eating disorder symptoms of patients with multi-impulsive bulimia with comorbid BPD do not typically differ from those of their uni-impulsive counterparts without comorbid BPD.

Westen and Harnden-Fischer (2001) argued that classifying patients with eating disorders by eating symptoms alone groups together patients with anorexic symptoms who are high functioning and self-critical with those who are highly disturbed, constricted, and avoidant. It also groups together patients with bulimic symptoms who are high functioning and self-critical with those who are highly disturbed, impulsive, and emotionally dysregulated. These authors conclude that Axis I symptoms are a useful component, but only one component, in the accurate diagnosis of eating disorders.

To summarize, the general classification of anorexia and bulimia nervosa as Axis I disorders only may not readily differentiate between subtypes that differ in personality, etiology, or function of symptoms. The grouping together of heterogeneous subgroups, such as patients who are highly impulsive with those who are not impulsive or those who are even highly constricted, could not only produce inconsistent findings across studies but also conceal clinically relevant information about etiology, prognosis, or treatment response.

SUMMARY AND CONCLUSION

Our current conceptualization of PDs has been limited by incorporating aspects of both personality and disorder, which hail from two contrasting clinical views. Traditionally, personality has been understood in terms of traits that are quantifiable dimensions, and variations of personality are considered to be a matter of degree rather than type. In contrast, mental disorders are understood to be distinct pathological entities following the standard medical model. Individuals are generally considered to either have or not have a particular disorder. Although degrees of severity and subthreshold forms are acknowledged, a disorder is understood as a categorical entity. Consistent with this view, the *DSM* makes categorical diagnoses by defining a cutoff point on a symptom checklist above which a disorder is judged to be present. In the case of PDs, these two views collide. If a PD is considered to be a mental disorder, it makes sense to use the assumptions embedded in the *DSM–IV* and consider PDs as discrete categories. If a PD is a form of personality, however, a dimensional view seems more appropriate. Nevertheless, the *DSM* does not provide a coherent theory of PDs. Therefore, multiple PD diagnoses and the problematic overlap between the categories are just some of the challenges to the *DSM* model of PDs. There is not a clear distinction between normal and abnormal personality, thus leading to difficulties diagnosing PDs on the basis of arbitrary cutoff scores.

Despite the inclusion of the *general* maladaptiveness criterion into the *DSM* system, the current diagnostic criteria and the tools used for diagnosing PDs do not offer specific criteria for assessing maladaptiveness or adequately capture impairment and distress associated with PDs. The confusion arises with the use of general maladaptiveness or dysfunction in the *DSM* system as a basis for considering PDs as mental disorders, while at the same time failing to offer a specific definition or a set of criteria for assessing dysfunction. As a consequence of having an inadequate definition, the focus in the PD literature has been on maladaptive behaviors, such as acts of impulsivity. The assessment of PDs is thus open to a clinician's interpretation that may be influenced by the social desirability of certain personality traits (e.g., perfectionism).

The current system for diagnosing PDs tends to focus on the behavioral manifestations of the disorder, such as impulsive acts, despite research indicating that behaviors are less stable over time than are personality traits. This has led to mistaken reservations about the validity of the PD construct on the basis of the temporal instability of behavioral expressions of the disorder. This has been particularly relevant when diagnosing PDs in adolescence. However, patterns of stability and psychosocial dysfunction in adolescence are very similar to those in adults, justifying diagnosis and intervention in adolescents presenting to clinical services. One example of an attempt to broaden the current conceptualization of

PDs is Millon and Davis's (1996) proposal for assessment of four levels of data (behavioral, phenomenological, intrapsychic, and biophysical) and across two domains of personality (structural and functional), although such a multilayered measure of personality is not yet available.

The functional impairment associated with PDs has been well documented in the literature (Jackson & Burgess, 2000; Skodol et al., 2002), yet we still tend to use limited measures of functioning, such as the Global Assessment of Functioning scores, instead of examining specific domains of functioning (e.g., intimate relationships, family, work). This leads to the issue of culture in diagnosing PDs. Certain cultures and subcultures may favor certain personality traits. In fact, certain traits may be seen as being socially desirable. In turn, individuals may find an "ecological niche" in which their deviant personality traits may be favored.

Although debate continues regarding the assignment of PDs onto a separate axis from most other psychiatric disorders, there is every indication that PDs and Axis II will continue in the next revision of the *DSM*. Generally high rates of comorbidity or co-occurrence between Axis I and Axis II disorders have contributed to this debate. The effects of state variables such as mood, anxiety, or psychosis can influence trait characteristics and thus PD diagnosis, whereas some symptoms can appear in the criteria set for both Axis I and Axis II disorders. If we take the example of eating disorders, classification on Axis I without consideration of the underlying personality pathology may not readily differentiate between subtypes of the disorder in question and could also conceal clinically relevant information about etiology, prognosis, and treatment response.

NOTE

Please address all correspondence to Martina Jovev, MA, PhD, ORYGEN Youth Health, Parkville Centre, 35 Parkville, 3010, Victoria, Australia; telephone: +61 3 9342 2864; fax: +61 3 9387 3003; e-mail: Martina.Jovev@mh.org.au.

REFERENCES

American Psychiatric Association. (1980). *Diagnostic and statistical manual of mental disorders* (3rd ed.). Washington, DC: Author.

American Psychiatric Association. (1987). *Diagnostic and statistical manual of mental disorders* (Rev. 3rd ed.). Washington, DC: Author.

American Psychiatric Association. (1994). *Diagnostic and statistical manual of mental disorders* (4th ed.). Washington, DC: Author.

Bank, P. A., & Silk, K. R. (2001). Axis I and Axis II interactions. *Current Opinion in Psychiatry, 14*(2), 137–142.

Bell, R. C., & Jackson, H. J. (1992). The structure of personality disorders in *DSM–III*. *Acta Psychiatrica Scandinavica, 85*(4), 279–287.

Bernstein, D. P., Cohen, P., Velez, C. N., Schwab-Stone, M., Siever, L. J., & Shinsato, L. (1993). Prevalence and stability of the *DSM–III–R* personality disorders in a community-based survey of adolescents. *American Journal of Psychiatry, 150*(8), 1237–1243.

Bleiberg, E. (1994). Borderline disorders in children and adolescents: The concept, the diagnosis, and the controversies. *Bulletin of the Menninger Clinic, 58*(2), 169–196.

Cassin, S. E., & von Ranson, K. M. (2005). Personality and eating disorders: A decade in review. *Clinical Psychology Review, 25*(7), 895–916.

Chanen, A. M., Jackson, H. J., McGorry, P. D., Allot, K. A., Clarkson, V., & Yuen, H. P. (2004). Two-year stability of personality disorder in older adolescent outpatients. *Journal of Personality Disorders, 18*(6), 526–541.

Cloninger, C. R. (1987). A systematic method for clinical description and classification of personality variants. *Archives of General Psychiatry, 44*, 573–588.

Cloninger, C. R., Svrakic, D. M., & Przybeck, T. R. (1993). A psychobiological model of temperament and character. *Archives of General Psychiatry, 50*(12), 975–990.

Costa, P. T., & McCrae, R. R. (1992). *Revised NEO Personality Inventory (NEO–PI–R) and NEO Five Factor Inventory (NEO–FFI) [professional manual]*. Odessa, FL: Psychological Assessment Resources.

de Girolamo, G., & Reich, J. H. (1993). *Personality disorders*. Geneva: World Health Organization.

Dolan, B., Evans, C., & Norton, K. (1994). Disordered eating behavior and attitudes in female and male patients with personality disorders. *Journal of Personality Disorders, 8*(1), 17–27.

Fichter, M. M., Quadflieg, N., & Rief, W. (1994). Course of multi-impulsive bulimia. *Psychological Medicine, 24*(3), 591–604.

Grilo, C. M., Becker, D. F., Edell, W. S., & McGlashan, T. H. (2001). Stability and change of *DSM–III–R* personality disorder dimensions in adolescents followed up 2 years after psychiatric hospitalization. *Comprehensive Psychiatry, 42*(5), 364–368.

Grilo, C. M., & McGlashan, T. H. (1999). Stability and course of personality disorders. *Current Opinion in Psychiatry, 12*(2), 157–162.

Grilo, C. M., McGlashan, T. H., Quinlan, D. M., Walker, M. L., Greenfeld, D., & Edell, W. S. (1998). Frequency of personality disorders in two age cohorts of psychiatric inpatients. *American Journal of Psychiatry, 155*(1), 140–142.

Grilo, C. M., McGlashan, T. H., & Skodol, A. E. (2000). Stability and course of personality disorders: The need to consider comorbidities and continuities between Axis I psychiatric disorders and Axis II personality disorders [Special issue: The Twelfth Annual New York State Office of Mental Health Research Conference]. *Psychiatric Quarterly, 71*(4), 291–307.

Herzog, D. B., Keller, M. B., Lavori, P. W., Kenny, G. M., & Sacks, N. R. (1992). The prevalence of personality disorders in 210 women with eating disorders. *Journal of Clinical Psychiatry, 53*(5), 147–152.

Jackson, H. J. (1998). The assessment of personality disorder: Selected issues and directions. In C. Perris & P. D. McGorry (Eds.), *Cognitive psychotherapy of psychotic and personality disorders: Handbook of theory and practice* (pp. 293–314). Chichester, UK: John Wiley and Sons.

Jackson, H. J., & Burgess, P. M. (2000). Personality disorders in the community: A report from the Australian National Survey of Mental Health and Well-being. *Social Psychiatry and Psychiatric Epidemiology, 35*(12), 531–538.

Jackson, H. J., & Burgess, P. M. (2004). Personality disorders in community: Results from the Australian National Survey of Mental Health and Well-Being, Part III; Relationships between specific types of personality disorder, Axis I mental disorders and physical conditions with disability and health consultations. *Social Psychiatry and Psychiatric Epidemiology, 39*(10), 765–776.

Johnson, J. G., Cohen, P., Kasen, S., Skodol, A. E., Hamagami, F., & Brook, J. S. (2000). Age-related change in personality disorder trait levels between early adolescence and adulthood: A community-based longitudinal investigation. *Acta Psychiatrica Scandinavica, 102*(4), 265–275.

Johnson, J. G., Williams, J. B. W., Goetz, R. R., Rabkin, J. G., Lipsitz, J. D., & Remien, R. H. (1997). Stability and change in personality disorder symptomatology: Findings from a longitudinal study of HIV+ and HIV– men. *Journal of Abnormal Psychology, 106*(1), 154–158.

Kass, F., Skodol, A. E., Charles, E., Spitzer, R., & Williams, A. A. (1985). Scaled ratings of DSM–III personality disorders. *American Journal of Psychiatry, 142*(5), 627–630.

Kessler, R. C., McGonagle, K. A., Zhao, S., Nelson, C. B., Hughes, M., Eshleman, S., Wittchen, H. U., & Kendler, K. S. (1994). Lifetime and 12-month prevalence of DSM–III–R psychiatric disorders in the United States: Results from the National Comorbidity Study. *Archives of General Psychiatry, 51*(1), 8–19.

Lacey, J. H., & Evans, C. D. (1986). The impulsivist: A multi-impulsive personality disorder. *British Journal of Addiction, 81*(5), 641–649.

Lilienfeld, S. O., Waldman, I. D., & Israel, A. C. (1994). A critical examination of the use of the term and concept of comorbidity in psychopathology research. *Clinical Psychology: Science and Practice, 1*(1), 71–83.

Livesley, W. J., Jackson, D. N., & Schroeder, M. L. (1992). Factorial structure of traits delineating personality disorders in clinical and general population samples. *Journal of Abnormal Psychology, 101*(3), 432–440.

Mattanah, J. J. F., Becker, D. F., Levy, K. N., Edell, W. S., & McGlashan, T. H. (1995). Diagnostic stability in adolescents followed up 2 years after hospitalization. *American Journal of Psychiatry, 152*(6), 889–894.

Millon, T., & Davis, R. D. (1996). *Disorders of personality:* DSM–IV *and beyond* (2nd ed.). New York: John Wiley and Sons.

Oldham, J. M., & Skodol, A. E. (2000). Charting the future of Axis II. *Journal of Personality Disorders, 14*(1), 17–29.

Paris, J. (1998). Personality disorders in sociocultural perspective. *Journal of Personality Disorders, 12*(4), 289–301.

Parker, G. (1997). Special feature: The etiology of personality disorders; A review and consideration of research models. *Journal of Personality Disorders, 11*(4), 345–369.

Perry, J. C. (1992). Problems and considerations in the valid assessment of personality disorders. *American Journal of Psychiatry, 149*(12), 1645–1653.

Roberts, B. W., & DelVecchio, W. F. (2000). The rank-order consistency of personality traits from childhood to old age: A quantitative review of longitudinal studies. *Psychological Bulletin, 126*(1), 3–25.

Schroeder, M. L., & Livesley, W. J. (1991). An evaluation of *DSM–III–R* personality disorders. *Acta Psychiatrica Scandinavica, 84*(6), 512–519.

Skodol, A. E., Gunderson, J. G., McGlashan, T. H., Dyck, I. R., Stout, R. L., Bender, D. S., et al. (2002). Functional impairment in patients with schizotypal, borderline, avoidant, or obsessive-compulsive personality disorder. *American Journal of Psychiatry, 159*(2), 276–283.

Skodol, A. E., Oldham, J. M., Bender, D. S., Dyck, I. R., Stout, R. L., Morey, L. C., et al. (2005). Dimensional representations of *DSM–IV* personality disorders: Relationships to functional impairment. *American Journal of Psychiatry, 162*(10), 1919–1925.

Skodol, A. E., Oldham, J. M., Hyler, S. E., Kellman, H. D., Doidge, N., & Davies, M. (1993). Comorbidity of *DSM–III–R* eating disorders and personality disorders. *International Journal of Eating Disorders, 14*(4), 403–416.

Skodol, A. E., Rosnick, L., Kellman, D., Oldham, J. M., & Hyler, S. (1988). Validating structured *DSM–III–R* personality disorder assessments with longitudinal data. *American Journal of Psychiatry, 145*(10), 1297–1299.

Sohlberg, S., & Strober, M. (1994). Personality in anorexia nervosa: An update and a theoretical integration. *Acta Psychiatrica Scandinavica, 89*(Suppl. 378), 16.

Svanborg, P., Gustavsson, P. J., Mattila-Evenden, M., & Asberg, M. (1999). Assessment of maladaptiveness: A core issue in the diagnosing of personality disorders. *Journal of Personality Disorders, 13*(3), 241–256.

Vito, E. D., Ladame, F., & Orlandini, A. (1999). Adolescence and personality disorders: Current perspectives on a controversial problem. In J. Derksen, C. Maffei, & H. Groen (Eds.), *Treatment of personality disorders* (pp. 77–95). New York: Kluwer Academic/Plenum.

Vitousek, K., & Manke, F. (1994). Personality variables and disorders in anorexia nervosa and bulimia nervosa [Special issue: Personality and Psychopathology]. *Journal of Abnormal Psychology, 103*(1), 137–147.

Westen, D., & Harnden-Fischer, J. (2001). Personality profiles in eating disorders: Rethinking the distinction between Axis I and Axis II. *American Journal of Psychiatry, 158*(4), 547–562.

Widiger, T. A. (1992). Categorical versus dimensional classification: Implications from and for research. *Journal of Personality Disorders, 6*(4), 287–300.

Widiger, T. A. (1993). The *DSM–III–R* categorical personality disorder diagnoses: A critique and an alternative. *Psychological Inquiry, 4*(2), 75–90.

Widiger, T. A., Sanderson, C., & Warner, L. (1986). The MMPI, prototypal typology, and borderline personality disorder. *Journal of Personality Assessment, 50*(4), 540–553.

World Health Organization. (1992). *International classification of diseases* (10th ed.). Geneva: Author.

Epidemiology

2

The Prevalence of Personality Disorders in Those With Eating Disorders

RANDY A. SANSONE, MD
JOHN L. LEVITT, PHD
LORI A. SANSONE, MD

Every experienced clinician in the field of eating disorders has encountered a multisymptomatic and challenging patient who manifests long-standing symptoms related to personality pathology. However, the genuine prevalence of Axis II disorders among those with eating disorders remains somewhat elusive. This is due, in part, to small sample sizes in empirical studies, the intensifying effects of Axis I pathology (i.e., the eating disorder) on Axis II symptoms, the difficulties inherent in personality disorder diagnosis, and the effects of biased sampling (e.g., using tertiary-care samples with correspondingly higher levels of comorbid individuals).

Although the precise prevalence of Axis II disorders among patients with eating disorders remains unknown, personality disorders and eating disorders seem to exhibit recurrent patterns of association (Dennis & Sansone, 1997). For example, restricting anorexia nervosa is often associated with obsessive-compulsive personality features and/or disorder, whereas eating disorders characterized by impulsivity (e.g., anorexia nervosa, binge eating/purging type; purging type bulimia nervosa) are often associated with impulsive personality features and/or disorders such as borderline personality.

Given these potential associations, why is Axis II assessment important in the evaluation of patients with eating disorders? The presence of a comorbid personality disorder appears to have mediating effects on the overall eating disorder treatment process and prognosis. For example, the presence of a personality disorder often requires extensive and adjunctive treatment(s), which will be described in the ensuing chapters. In addition, some studies indicate that the prognosis of individuals with eating disorders with comorbid Axis II diagnoses is less favorable (Masjuan, Aranda, & Raich, 2003; Steinhausen, 2002). However, these less favorable outcomes may relate more to general psychiatric symptoms (Steiger & Stotland, 1996) rather than eating disorder symptomatology, per se (Grilo et al., 2003).

In this chapter, we summarize the available studies on the prevalence of personality pathology among those with eating disorders. We caution clinicians that this summary still remains but an approximation (i.e., estimate) of prevalence.

THE DEFINITION AND CLASSIFICATION OF PERSONALITY DISORDERS

According to the *Diagnostic and Statistical Manual of Mental Disorders–Fourth Edition* (*DSM–IV*; American Psychiatric Association, 1994), the general definition of a personality disorder is "an enduring pattern of inner experience and behavior that deviates markedly from the expectations of the individual's culture" (p. 633). Personality disorder symptoms typically manifest in the domains of cognition, affectivity, interpersonal functioning, and impulse control. In keeping with other *DSM* disorders, the individual must experience significant personal distress or impairment in social, occupational, or other areas of functioning.

In addition, the *DSM–IV* broadly classifies personality disorders into three primary subtypes or clusters. Cluster A refers to those personality disorders that are characterized by odd or eccentric features (e.g., schizotypal personality disorder). Cluster B refers to personality disorders that are characterized by dramatic or erratic features (e.g., borderline personality disorder). Cluster C refers to personality disorders that are characterized by anxious or inhibited features (e.g., avoidant and obsessive-compulsive personality disorders).

SUMMARY OF THE EMPIRICAL LITERATURE

In a previous paper, we summarized the empirical data on the prevalence of personality disorders among those with eating disorders (Sansone & Levitt, 2005). In our efforts to obtain studies, we searched both the PubMed and the PsycINFO databases, entering a variety of search terms, including the individual personality disorders noted in *DSM–IV* as well as the various eating disorders under study (i.e., anorexia nervosa, bulimia nervosa, binge eating disorder, and their subtypes).

In presenting these data, we must caution the reader about some of the potential limitations of our findings. First, at the outset, we may have missed data or articles that were presented at professional meetings or not elicited by our selected search terms. Second, we excluded those articles that (a) consisted of only male participants (we believed that these data would not be representative of the general eating disorder population) with the exception of males suffering from binge eating disorder; (b) did not explicitly identify *DSM–IV* personality disorders (i.e., ones that analyzed personality pathology as a single conglomerate variable or in terms of personality clusters, or as personality dimensions, traits, or factors); (c) did not clearly distinguish between the diagnostic types (i.e., anorexia versus bulimia) or subtypes (i.e., restricting type versus binge eating/purging type of anorexia nervosa) of eating disorders; (d) reported results only as scores on personality disorder scales, rather than as Axis II diagnoses; and (e) were available only in a foreign language (e.g., Japanese). We also elected to exclude articles that were too expensive to obtain, which included two dissertation theses.

Third, we included studies that reported on recovered individuals because personality is supposedly a relatively stable phenomenon. Fourth, we did not exclude any articles because of the method of participant recruitment (e.g., recruitment through advertisements) or type of study population (e.g., treatment-seeking versus not, clinical versus nonclinical). Fifth, in the rare event that the reported subsample tallies did not match with corresponding percentages, we relied on the numbers (one article). Sixth, at the outset, we decided to track Cluster A personality disorders (odd or eccentric cluster) as a single entity because of their anticipated infrequency among those with anorexia and bulimia nervosa (Dennis & Sansone, 1997). Seventh, for small *descriptive case studies*, we did not include participants when the investigators simultaneously assigned several personality disorders to a given individual. Eighth, in some studies, investigators using a consistent assessment measure may have given a single individual the diagnosis of several personality disorders; we included these data if tallies were identified for each individual personality disorder. Finally, to capture the largest sample of individuals, we included those studies that examined clinical samples of individuals with other forms of psychiatric comorbidity (e.g., bulimic individuals with substance abuse versus those without substance abuse) and combined all participants into one single sample.

Before we present our findings, we wish to emphasize that these data and the corresponding conclusions offer only general impressions or trends with regard to the association of specific personality disorders with various subtypes of eating disorders. Because of the varying methodologies, assessment tools, and study populations, it is not possible to firmly conclude that these summaries are genuinely reflective of eating disorder populations, in general. However, given the absence of large-scale studies or infallible personality disorder assessments, these data represent our current state of empirical knowledge.

Personality Disorders in Anorexia Nervosa

Anorexia nervosa, restricting type. In keeping with our general clinical experience, the findings presented in Table 2.1 and Figure 2.1 indicate that the most frequent personality disorder among individuals with the restricting type of anorexia nervosa is obsessive-compulsive personality disorder (about 22%), closely followed by avoidant personality disorder (about 19%). Around 11% of those with restricting type anorexia nervosa suffer from borderline or dependent personality disorders, and approximately 5% evidence Cluster A personality disorders. Overall, Cluster C personality disorders appear predominant among these individuals.

Practice Point
In restricting type anorexia nervosa, obsessive-compulsive personality disorder appears to be the most common Axis II disorder, closely followed by avoidant personality disorder.

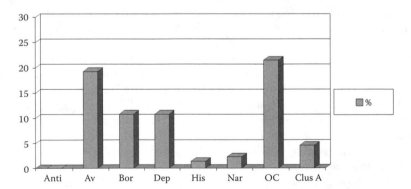

Figure 2.1 The prevalence of personality disorders in anorexia nervosa, restricting type.

Note: Anti = antisocial, Av = avoidant, Bor = borderline, Dep = dependent, His = histrionic, Nar = narcissistic, OC = obsessive-compulsive, Clus A = Cluster A.

TABLE 2.1 Studies of the Prevalence of Personality Disorders in Anorexia Nervosa, Restricting Type

First Author	Year	Measure	N	Anti n (%)	Av n (%)	Bor n (%)	Dep n (%)	His n (%)	Nar n (%)	OC n (%)	Clus A n (%)
Piran	1988	DIB, Int	30	0 (0)	10 (33)	11 (37)	3 (10)	0 (0)	0 (0)	1 (3)	0 (0)
Gartner	1989	PDE	6	0 (0)	2 (33)	2 (33)	1 (17)	0 (0)	1 (17)	1 (17)	2 (33)
Wonderlich	1990	SCID-II	10	NA	2 (20)	2 (20)	4 (40)	2 (20)	NA	6 (60)	NA
McClelland	1991	Int	28	0 (0)	1 (4)	0 (0)	2 (7)	0 (0)	0 (0)	4 (18)	0 (0)
Herzog	1992	SCID-II	31	0 (0)	3 (10)	0 (0)	1 (3)	0 (0)	0 (0)	3 (10)	1 (3)
Thornton	1997	PDE	17	NA	NA	NA	NA	NA	NA	6 (35)	NA
Lilenfeld	1998	SCID-II	26	NA	NA	NA	NA	NA	NA	12 (46)	NA
Matsunaga	1998	SCID-II	36	0 (0)	9 (25)	2 (6)	6 (17)	0 (0)	2 (6)	7 (19)	3 (8)
Diaz-Marsa	2000	SCID-II	25	NA	5 (20)	2 (8)	1 (4)	NA	NA	4 (16)	NA
Matsunaga	2000	SCID-II	10	NA	2 (20)	0 (0)	NA	NA	NA	3 (30)	NA
Total			219	0/131 (0.0)	34/176 (19.3)	19/176 (10.8)	18/166 (10.8)	2/141 (1.4)	3/131 (2.3)	47/219 (21.5)	6/131 (4.6)

Note: Anti = antisocial, Av = avoidant, Bor = borderline, Clus A = Cluster A, Dep = dependent, DIB = Diagnostic Interview for Borderlines, His = histrionic, Int = clinical interview, NA = not available, Nar = narcissistic, OC = obsessive-compulsive, PDE = Personality Disorder Examination, SCID-II = Structured Clinical Interview for *DSM* Personality Disorders; column subtotals may differ as some studies did not either examine or report on all personality disorders.

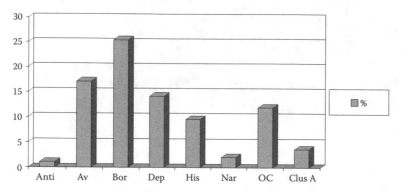

Figure 2.2 The prevalence of personality disorders in anorexia nervosa, binge eating/purging type.

Note: Anti = antisocial, Av = avoidant, Bor = borderline, Dep = dependent, His = histrionic, Nar = narcissistic, OC = obsessive-compulsive, Clus A = Cluster A.

Anorexia nervosa, binge eating/purging type. In those patients suffering from the binge eating/purging type of anorexia nervosa, the most frequent Axis II disorder is borderline personality disorder, with a prevalence rate of around 25% (see Table 2.2, Figure 2.2). Roughly 15% suffer from avoidant or dependent personality disorders, and 10% suffer from histrionic personality disorder. Note that among anorexic individuals with binge eating/purging symptoms, both Cluster B and Cluster C personality disorders are predominant.

Practice Point
In the binge eating/purging type of anorexia nervosa, borderline personality disorder appears to be the most common Axis II disorder.

Personality Disorders in Bulimia Nervosa

The majority of studies in the area of eating and personality disorders have been undertaken in those with bulimia nervosa (i.e., these studies comprise the largest number of participants). This observation probably reflects the traditional predominance of individuals with bulimia nervosa in most treatment settings. In addition, the majority of participants in these studies suffered from the purging type of the disorder.

The prevalence of personality disorders in bulimia nervosa is illustrated in Table 2.3 and Figure 2.3. Among those with this eating disorder, borderline personality disorder is the most frequent Axis II disorder, with a prevalence rate of more than 28%. This is followed by dependent, histrionic, and avoidant personality disorders, with prevalence rates around 20%. Based on these findings for Axis II disorders, the cluster profile for participants in reported studies is predominantly Cluster B, followed to a lesser degree by Cluster C.

TABLE 2.2 Studies of the Prevalence of Personality Disorders in Anorexia Nervosa, Binge Eating/Purging Type

First Author	Year	Measure	N	Anti n (%)	Av n (%)	Bor n (%)	Dep n (%)	His n (%)	Nar n (%)	OC n (%)	Clus A n (%)
Piran	1988	DIB, Int	38	0 (0)	3 (8)	16 (42)	3 (8)	5 (13)	0 (0)	1 (3)	0 (0)
Gartner	1989	PDE	21	0 (0)	7 (33)	7 (33)	4 (19)	1 (5)	2 (10)	8 (38)	1 (5)
Yager	1989	PDQ	15	0 (0)	6 (40)	5 (33)	8 (53)	4 (27)	0 (0)	2 (15)	NA
Wonderlich	1990	SCID-II	10	NA	6 (60)	2 (20)	4 (40)	0 (0)	NA	0 (0)	NA
McClelland	1991	Int	12	0 (0)	0 (0)	2 (4)	0 (0)	0 (0)	0 (0)	1 (2)	0 (0)
Herzog	1992	SCID-II	88	2 (2)	6 (7)	11 (12)	5 (6)	6 (7)	0 (0)	4 (4)	4 (4)
Matsunaga	1998	SCID-II	30	0 (0)	8 (27)	11 (37)	6 (20)	2 (7)	2 (7)	5 (17)	2 (7)
Diaz-Marsa	2000	SCID-II	17	NA	NA	5 (29)	NA	4 (24)	NA	3 (18)	NA
Matsunaga	2000	SCID-II	16	NA	3 (19)	4 (25)	NA	NA	NA	6 (38)	NA
Total			247	2/204 (1.0)	39/230 (17.0)	63/247 (25.5)	30/214 (14.0)	22/231 (9.5)	4/204 (2.0)	30/247 (12.1)	7/189 (3.7)

Note: Anti = antisocial, Av = avoidant, Bor = borderline, Clus A = Cluster A, Dep = dependent, DIB = Diagnostic Interview for Borderlines, His = histrionic, Int = clinical interview, NA = not available, Nar = narcissistic, OC = obsessive-compulsive, PDE = Personality Disorder Examination, PDQ = Personality Diagnostic Questionnaire, SCID-II = Structured Clinical Interview for DSM Personality Disorders; column subtotals may differ as some studies did not either examine or report on all personality disorders.

TABLE 2.3   Studies of the Prevalence of Personality Disorders in Bulimia Nervosa

First Author	Year	Measure	N	Anti	Av	Bor	Dep	His	Nar	OC	Clus A
Gwirtsman	1983	Int	18	0 (0)	1 (5)	8 (44)	0 (0)	0 (0)	0 (0)	0 (0)	0 (0)
Levin	1986	PDQ, Int	24	0 (0)	0 (0)	6 (25)	0 (0)	9 (38)	0 (0)	0 (0)	0 (0)
Pope	1987	DIB	52	—	—	1 (2)	—	—	—	—	—
Frankel	1988	PDE	35	NA	NA	7 (20)	NA	NA	NA	NA	NA
Powers	1988	SCID-II	30	6 (20)	3 (10)	7 (23)	0 (0)	16 (53)	3 (10)	10 (33)	10 (33)
Gartner	1989	PDE	8	0 (0)	2 (25)	3 (38)	3 (38)	1 (13)	1 (13)	0 (0)	0 (0)
Yager	1989	PDQ	300	12 (4)	107 (36)	142 (47)	139 (46)	116 (39)	2 (1)	37 (12)	—
Yates	1989	PDQ	30	1 (3)	1 (3)	4 (13)	10 (33)	10 (33)	1 (3)	11 (37)	12 (40)
Pyle	1990	PDQ-R	46	—	—	18 (39)	—	—	—	—	—
Schmidt	1990	PDE	23	0 (0)	0 (0)	8 (35)	0 (0)	0 (0)	0 (0)	0 (0)	1 (4)
Wonderlich	1990	SCID-II	16	NA	3 (19)	3 (19)	3 (19)	5 (31)	NA	2 (13)	NA
Zanarini	1990	DIPD	34	1 (3)	6 (18)	12 (35)	3 (9)	4 (12)	1 (3)	3 (9)	6 (18)
McCann	1991	PDE	19	0 (0)	3 (16)	3 (16)	3 (16)	3 (16)	3 (16)	4 (21)	0 (0)
Ames-Frankel	1992	PDE	83	NA	9 (11)	19 (23)	10 (12)	8 (10)	NA	NA	NA
Herzog	1992	SCID-II	91	0 (0)	2 (2)	7 (8)	1 (1)	6 (7)	1 (1)	3 (3)	4 (4)
Bossert-Zaudig	1993	Int	24	0 (0)	2 (4)	3 (8)	0 (0)	7 (29)	—	0 (0)	—
Rossiter	1993	PDE	71	8 (11)	10 (14)	15 (21)	10 (14)	5 (7)	7 (10)	7 (10)	3 (4)

Study	Year	Instrument	N								
Sunday	1993	SCID–II	91	NA	NA	44 (48)	NA	NA	NA	NA	NA
Carroll	1996	PDE	30	0 (0)	3 (10)	3 (10)	2 (7)	0 (0)	1 (3)	2 (7)	3 (10)
Steiger	1996	SCID–II	61	NA	NA	14 (23)	NA	NA	NA	NA	NA
Lilenfeld	1998	PDE	47	NA	NA	NA	NA	NA	NA	2 (4)	NA
Matsunaga	1998	SCID–II	42	5 (12)	8 (19)	8 (19)	7 (17)	4 (10)	4 (10)	5 (12)	4 (10)
Rossotto	1998	SCID–II	80	4 (5)	11 (14)	20 (25)	13 (16)	12 (15)	14 (18)	16 (20)	10 (13)
Diaz-Marsa	2000	SCID–II	17	NA	4 (13)	7 (23)	5 (17)	NA	NA	NA	3 (10)
Inceoglu	2000	PDQ–R	34	1 (3)	9 (27)	12 (35)	10 (29)	9 (27)	6 (18)	6 (18)	15 (44.1)
Matsunaga	2000	SCID–II	42	8 (19)	5 (12)	8 (19)	7 (17)	4 (10)	4 (10)	5 (12)	4 (10)
Godt	2002	Int	81	0 (0)	15 (18)	5 (6)	11 (14)	6 (7)	1 (1)	3 (4)	4 (5)
Van Hanswijck de Jonge	2003	IPDE	35	3 (9)	10 (29)	15 (43)	1 (3)	1 (3)	0 (0)	5 (14)	4 (11)
Total			1464	49/1016 (4.8)	214/1132 (18.9)	402/1417 (28.4)	238/1132 (21.0)	226/1115 (20.3)	49/992 (4.9)	121/1079 (11.2)	83/709 (11.7)

Note: Anti = antisocial, Av = avoidant, Bor = borderline, Clus A = Cluster A, Dep = dependent, DIB = Diagnostic Interview for Borderlines, DIPD = Diagnostic Interview for Personality Disorders, His = histrionic, Int = clinical interview, IPDE = International Personality Disorders Examination, NA = not available, Nar = narcissistic, OC = obsessive-compulsive, PDE = Personality Disorder Examination, PDQ = Personality Diagnostic Questionnaire, PDQ–R = Personality Diagnostic Questionnaire–Revised, SCID–II = Structured Clinical Interview for DSM Personality Disorders, — = not studied; column subtotals may differ as some studies did not either examine or report on all personality disorders.

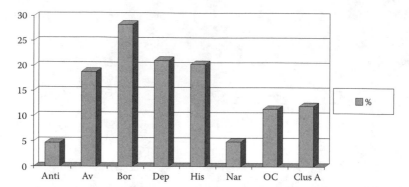

Figure 2.3 The prevalence of personality disorders in bulimia nervosa.
Note: Anti = antisocial, Av = avoidant, Bor = borderline, Dep = dependent, His = histrionic, Nar = narcissistic, OC = obsessive-compulsive, Clus A = Cluster A.

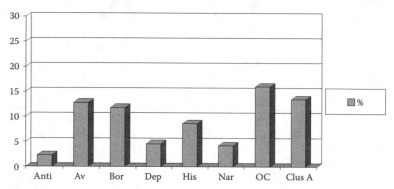

Figure 2.4 The prevalence of personality disorders in binge eating disorder.
Note: Anti = antisocial, Av = avoidant, Bor = borderline, Dep = dependent, His = histrionic, Nar = narcissistic, OC = obsessive-compulsive, Clus A = Cluster A.

Practice Point
In bulimia nervosa purging type, borderline personality disorder appears to be the most common Axis II disorder.

Personality Disorders in Binge Eating Disorder

Among individuals suffering from binge eating disorder (see Table 2.4, Figure 2.4), the available empirical data indicate that obsessive-compulsive personality disorder is most common, closely followed by Cluster A disorders (both groupings with prevalence rates of around 15%). The next most common personality disorders are avoidant and borderline personalities, with prevalence rates around 12%. These data indicate that a broad array of Cluster A, Cluster B, and Cluster C

TABLE 2.4 Studies of the Prevalence of Personality Disorders in Binge Eating Disorder

First Author	Year	Measure	N	Anti n (%)	Av n (%)	Bor n (%)	Dep n (%)	His n (%)	Nar n (%)	OC n (%)	Clus A n (%)
Yanovski	1993	SCID–II	43	0 (0)	4 (9)	6 (14)	0 (0)	0 (0)	0 (0)	3 (7)	0 (0)
Specker	1994	PDQ–R	43	2 (5)	11 (26)	13 (30)	9 (21)	20 (47)	6 (14)	11 (26)	21 (49)
Raymond	1995	PDQ–R	35	2 (6)	9 (26)	10 (29)	6 (18)	15 (43)	4 (11)	11 (31)	16 (46)
Telch	1998	SCID–II	61	0 (0)	4 (7)	4 (7)	2 (3)	0 (0)	0 (0)	3 (5)	3 (5)
Grilo	2000	DIPD–IV	70	4 (6)	15 (21)	6 (9)	2 (3)	1 (1)	4 (6)	18 (26)	11 (16)
Wilfley	2000	SCID–II	162	2 (1)	9 (6)	15 (9)	1 (1)	0 (0)	4 (3)	23 (14)	10 (6)
Picot	2003	SCID–II	50	NA	6 (12)	1 (2)	NA	NA	NA	5 (50)	NA
Van Hanswijck de Jonge	2003	IPDE	15	0 (0)	3 (20)	1 (7)	0 (0)	0 (0)	0 (0)	2 (13)	2 (13)
Total			479	10/429 (2.3)	61/479 (12.7)	56/479 (11.7)	20/429 (4.7)	36/429 (8.4)	18/429 (4.2)	76/479 (15.9)	63/479 (13.2)

Note: Anti = antisocial, Av = avoidant, Bor = borderline, Clus A = Cluster A, Dep = dependent, DIPD–IV = Diagnostic Interview for Personality Disorder–IV, His = histrionic, Int = clinical interview, IPDE = International Personality Disorders Examination, NA = not available, Nar = narcissistic, OC = obsessive–compulsive, PDQ–R = Personality Diagnostic Questionnaire–Revised, SCID–II = Structured Clinical Interview for DSM Personality Disorders; column subtotals may differ as some studies did not either examine or report on all personality disorders.

personality disorders are encountered in those with binge eating disorder, illustrating the heterogeneity in Axis II disorders among this subgroup. It is unknown if the observed Axis II heterogeneity reflects etiological heterogeneity, as well.

Practice Point
Among individuals with binge eating disorder, there does not appear to be any distinct Axis II pattern.

CLINICAL IMPLICATIONS

The preceding findings appear to support general clinical experience. The predominant Axis II disorder in restricting anorexia nervosa is obsessive-compulsive personality disorder, which is a common clinical observation. This particular eating disorder–personality disorder association appears intuitively logical, given the high levels of continual restraint and self-monitoring required to maintain this type of eating pathology. An obsessive overdrive seems necessary for one to sustain the psychological stamina required to gradually and consistently starve oneself.

Likewise, in both the binge eating/purging type anorexia nervosa and purging type bulimia nervosa, borderline personality appears to be the most common personality disorder. For these eating disorders, there are obviously higher levels of impulsivity as exemplified in the behaviors of binge eating and purging. However, we caution clinicians that impulsive eating pathology alone is not a definite indication of borderline personality pathology. Borderline personality disorder typically encompasses a host of adjunctive self-regulation difficulties (e.g., substance and alcohol abuse or addiction, the abuse of prescription medications, promiscuity, difficulty regulating finances) as well as long-standing self-harm behavior (e.g., cutting, burning, hitting oneself; suicide attempts; abusive relationships; high-risk behaviors).

In comparing the four eating disorder diagnoses using a prevalence cutoff of 20% for personality disorders, we find that none emerge in binge eating disorder. This observation may indicate that higher levels of personality pathology are found in anorexia and bulimia nervosa, compared with binge eating disorder. If so, it may be that the use of pathological counterregulatory behaviors is associated with a heightened likelihood of comorbid Axis II psychopathology.

Another way to view these data is to sum the percentages of the individual personality disorders for each eating disorder diagnosis. Because more than one personality disorder might be assigned to a given individual, these summed percentages could exceed 100%. Despite the limitations with this approach, it provides a global sense of the extent of personality psychopathology within an eating disorder diagnostic category. For restricting anorexia nervosa, the sum of Axis II percentages is 70.7; for the binge eating/purging type of anorexia nervosa, 84.8; for bulimia nervosa, 121.2; and for binge eating disorder, 73.1. This analysis suggests that personality pathology is most commonly diagnosed in bulimia nervosa. This finding warrants further research, as it may be tempered by the mean age of the diagnostic groups, rather than reflecting genuine rates of personality pathology.

The broad cluster splay for binge eating disorder is particularly interesting, especially the presence of Cluster A personality disorders. This may relate to the association of binge eating disorder with a variety of Axis I disorders. Perhaps, in some cases, these peculiar findings relate to the substantially different clinical characteristics of this subgroup of eating disorders (e.g., presentation at 30 or 40 years of age, up to 40% males). For example, from a purely speculative point of view, the male loading might account for a large portion of this Cluster A loading. Given the higher expectations for males to function independently in this culture, it could be that those who suffer from Cluster A disorders use food to treat their internal distress secondary to social and occupational demands. Regardless, future personality studies in binge eating disorder may need to be sensitive to gender patterns.

We wish to emphasize that the preceding relationships between eating and personality pathology are reflective of general trends, only. The genuine prevalence of personality disorder pathology among those with eating disorders remains unknown. Accurate determination of prevalence rates is compromised by the fact that there are specific factors that may affect personality assessment in eating disorder populations. For example, actively ill patients are more likely to evidence higher scores on personality disorder measures. In addition, age may confound certain personality disorder assessments (e.g., patients with restricting anorexia nervosa tend to be younger and are less likely to endorse borderline personality items that assess promiscuity, suicide attempts, and interpersonal chaos). Finally, few of these studies are controlled, so we do not know how patient personality disorder rates compare with community prevalence rates when using a specific methodology for personality assessment.

CONCLUSIONS

For the majority of eating disorder diagnoses, there appear to be specific personality disorder trends. Given the preceding findings, those with restricting type anorexia nervosa need to be clinically screened for obsessive-compulsive personality as well as avoidant personality features/disorder, whereas those with binge eating/purging behavior (in either anorexia or bulimia nervosa) need to be clinically screened for borderline personality disorder. Following confirmation, the presence of these comorbid personality disorders needs to be factored into the treatment context as well as the prognosis.

NOTE

Please address all correspondence to Randy A. Sansone, MD, Sycamore Primary Care Center, 2115 Leiter Road, Miamisburg, OH, 45342; telephone: 937-384-6850; fax: 937-384-6938; e-mail: Randy.sansone@kmcnetwork.org.

REFERENCES

American Psychiatric Association. (1994). *Diagnostic and statistical manual of mental disorders* (4th ed.). Washington, DC: Author.

Ames-Frankel, J., Devlin, M. J., Walsh, T., Strasser, T. J., Sadik, C., Oldham, J. M., et al. (1992). Personality disorder diagnoses in patients with bulimia nervosa: Clinical correlates and changes with treatment. *Journal of Clinical Psychiatry, 53,* 90–96.

Bossert-Zaudig, S., Saudig, M., Junker, M., Wiegand, M., & Krieg, J.-C. (1993). Psychiatric comorbidity of bulimia nervosa inpatients: Relationship to clinical variables and treatment outcome. *European Psychiatry, 8,* 15–23.

Carroll, J. M., Touyz, S. W., & Beumont, P. J. V. (1996). Specific comorbidity between bulimia nervosa and personality disorders. *International Journal of Eating Disorders, 19,* 159–170.

Dennis, A. B., & Sansone, R. A. (1997). Treatment of patients with personality disorders. In D. M. Garner & P. E. Garfinkel (Eds.), *Handbook of treatment of eating disorders* (2nd ed., pp. 437–449). New York: Guilford.

Diaz-Marsa, M., Carrasco, J. L., & Saiz, J. (2000). A study of temperament and personality in anorexia and bulimia nervosa. *Journal of Personality Disorders, 14,* 352–359.

Frankel, J. S., Sadik, C., Dantzic, S., Charles, E., Roose, S. P., & Walsh, B. T. (1988, May). *The systematic study of personality disorders in bulimic patients.* Paper presented at the American Psychiatric Association annual meeting, Montreal, Canada.

Gartner, A. F., Marcus, R. N., Halmi, K., & Loranger, A. W. (1989). *DSM–III–R* personality disorders in patients with eating disorders. *American Journal of Psychiatry, 146,* 1585–1591.

Godt, K. (2002). Personality disorders and eating disorders: The prevalence of personality disorders in 176 female outpatients with eating disorders. *European Eating Disorders Review, 10,* 102–109.

Grilo, C. M., & McGlashan, T. H. (2000). Convergent and discriminant validity of *DSM–IV* Axis II personality disorder criteria in adult outpatients with binge eating disorder. *Comprehensive Psychiatry, 41,* 163–166.

Grilo, C. M., Sanislow, C. A., Shea, M. T., Skodol, A. E., Stout, R. L., Pagano, M. E., et al. (2003). The natural course of bulimia nervosa and eating disorder not otherwise specified is not influenced by personality disorders. *International Journal of Eating Disorders, 34,* 319–330.

Gwirtsman, H. E., Roy-Byrne, P., Yager, J., & Gerner, R. H. (1983). Neuroendocrine abnormalities in bulimia. *American Journal of Psychiatry, 140,* 559–563.

Herzog, D. B., Keller, M. B., Lavori, P. W., Kenny, G. M., & Sacks, N. R. (1992). The prevalence of personality disorders in 210 women with eating disorders. *Journal of Clinical Psychiatry, 53,* 147–152.

Inceoglu, I., Franzen, U., Backmund, H., & Gerlinghoff, M. (2000). Personality disorders in patients in a day-treatment programme for eating disorders. *European Eating Disorders Review, 8,* 67–72.

Levin, A. P., & Hyler, S. E. (1986). *DSM–III* personality diagnosis in bulimia. *Comprehensive Psychiatry, 27,* 47–53.

Lilenfeld, L. R., Kaye, W. H., Greeno, C. G., Merikangas, K. R., Plotnicov, K., Pollice, C., et al. (1998). A controlled family study of anorexia and bulimia nervosa. *Archives of General Psychiatry, 55,* 603–610.

Masjuan, M. G., Aranda, F. F., & Raich, R. M. (2003). Bulimia nervosa and personality disorders: A review of the literature. *International Journal of Clinical and Health Psychology, 3,* 335–349.

Matsunaga, H., Kaye, W. H., McConahan, C., Plotnicov, K., Pollice, C., & Rao, R. (2000). Personality disorders among subjects recovered from eating disorders. *International Journal of Eating Disorders, 27,* 353–357.

Matsunaga, H., Kiriike, N., Nagata, T., & Yamagami, S. (1998). Personality disorders in patients with eating disorders in Japan. *International Journal of Eating Disorders, 23,* 399–408.

McCann, U. D., Rossiter, E. M., King, R. J., & Agras, W. S. (1991). Nonpurging bulimia: A distinct subtype of bulimia nervosa. *International Journal of Eating Disorders, 10,* 679–687.

McClelland, L., Mynors-Wallis, L., Fahy, T., & Treasure, J. (1991). Sexual abuse, disordered personality, and eating disorders. *British Journal of Psychiatry, 158,* 63–68.

Picot, A. K., & Lilenfeld, L. R. R. (2003). The relationship among binge eating severity, personality psychopathology, and body mass index. *International Journal of Eating Disorders, 34,* 98–107.

Piran, N., Lerner, P., Garfinkel, P. E., Kennedy, S. H., & Brouillette, C. (1988). Personality disorders in anorexic patients. *International Journal of Eating Disorders, 7,* 589–599.

Pope, H. G., Frankenburg, F. R., Hudson, J. I., Jonas, J. M., & Yurgelun-Todd, D. (1987). Is bulimia associated with borderline personality disorder? A controlled study. *Journal of Clinical Psychiatry, 48,* 181–184.

Powers, P. S., Coovert, D. L., Brightwell, D. R., & Stevens, B. A. (1988). Other psychiatric disorders among bulimic patients. *Comprehensive Psychiatry, 29,* 503–508.

Pyle, R. L., Mitchell, J. E., & Callies, A. (1990, May). *Bulimia nervosa treatment and borderline personality symptoms.* Presented at the 143rd annual meeting of the American Psychiatric Association, New York, NY.

Raymond, N. C., Mussell, M. P., Mitchell, J. E., de Zwaan, M., & Crosby, R. D. (1995). An aged-matched comparison of subjects with binge eating disorder and bulimia nervosa. *International Journal of Eating Disorders, 18*, 135–143.

Rossiter, E. M., Agras, W. S., Telch, C. F., & Schneider, J. A. (1993). Cluster B personality disorder characteristics predict outcome in the treatment of bulimia nervosa. *International Journal of Eating Disorders, 13*, 349–357.

Rossotto, E. (1998). Bulimia nervosa with and without substance use disorders: A comparative study. *Dissertation Abstracts International, 58*, 4469B.

Sansone, R. A., & Levitt, J. L. (2005). The prevalence of personality disorders among those with eating disorders. *Eating Disorders: The Journal of Treatment and Prevention, 13*, 7–21.

Schmidt, N. B., & Telch, M. J. (1990). Prevalence of personality disorders among bulimics, nonbulimic binge eaters, and normal controls. *Journal of Psychopathology and Behavioral Assessment, 12*, 169–185.

Specker, S., de Zwaan, M., Raymond, N., & Mitchell, J. (1994). Psychopathology in subgroups of obese women with and without binge eating disorder. *Comprehensive Psychiatry, 35*, 185–190.

Steiger, H., Jabalpurwala, S., & Champagne, J. (1996). Axis II comorbidity and developmental adversity in bulimia nervosa. *Journal of Nervous and Mental Disease, 184*, 555–560.

Steiger, H., & Stotland, S. (1996). Prospective study of outcome in bulimics as a function of Axis-II comorbidity: Long-term responses on eating and psychiatric symptoms. *International Journal of Eating Disorders, 20*, 149–161.

Steinhausen, H.-C. (2002). The outcome of anorexia nervosa in the 20th century. *American Journal of Psychiatry, 159*, 1284–1293.

Sunday, S. R., Levey, C. M., & Halmi, K. A. (1993). Effects of depression and borderline personality traits on psychological state and eating disorder symptomatology. *Comprehensive Psychiatry, 34*, 70–74.

Telch, C. F., & Stice, E. (1998). Psychiatric comorbidity in women with binge eating disorder: Prevalence rates from a non-treatment-seeking sample. *Journal of Consulting and Clinical Psychology, 66*, 768–776.

Thornton, C., & Russell, J. (1997). Obsessive compulsive comorbidity in the dieting disorders. *International Journal of Eating Disorders, 21*, 83–87.

Van Hanswijck de Jonge, P., Van Furth, E. F., Lacey, J., & Waller, G. (2003). The prevalence of *DSM–IV* personality pathology among individuals with bulimia nervosa, binge eating disorder and obesity. *Psychological Medicine, 33*, 1311–1317.

Wilfley, D. E., Friedman, M. A., Dounchis, J. Z., Stein, R. I., Welch, R. R., & Ball, S. A. (2000). Comorbid psychopathology in binge eating disorder: Relation to eating disorder severity at baseline and following treatment. *Journal of Consulting and Clinical Psychology, 68*, 641–649.

Wonderlich, S. A., Swift, W. J., Slotnick, H. B., & Goodman, S. (1990). *DSM–III–R* personality disorders in eating-disorder subtypes. *International Journal of Eating Disorders, 9*, 607–616.

Yager, J., Landsverk, J., Edelstein, C. K., & Hyler, S. E. (1989). Screening for Axis II disorders in women with bulimic eating disorders. *Psychosomatics, 30*, 255–262.

Yanovski, S. Z., Nelson, J. E., Dubbert, B. K., & Spitzer, R. L. (1993). Association of binge eating disorder and psychiatric comorbidity in obese subjects. *American Journal of Psychiatry, 150,* 1472–1479.

Yates, W. R., Sieleni, B., Reich, J., & Brass, C. (1989). Comorbidity of bulimia nervosa and personality disorder. *Journal of Clinical Psychiatry, 50,* 57–59.

Zanarini, M. C., Frankenburg, F. R., Pope, H. G., Hudson, J. I., Yurgelun-Todd, D., & Cicchetti, C. J. (1990). Axis II comorbidity of normal-weight bulimia. *Comprehensive Psychiatry, 30,* 20–24.

Etiology

CHAPTER
3

Impulsivity Versus Compulsivity in Patients With Eating Disorders

ANGELA FAVARO, MD, PHD, MSC
PAOLO SANTONASTASO, MD

Despite the predominance of a categorical approach when dealing with Axis II issues in eating disorders (EDs), a dimensional approach to the study of personality disorders is particularly interesting and fruitful. A categorical approach is often recommended for a variety of reasons. In particular, it facilitates scientific communication and is more in tune with the medical tradition. However, the variation within diagnostic categories, the presence of symptoms that are characteristic of more than one category, and the influence of Axis I disorders on the clinical manifestations of personality disorders (Rø et al., 2005; Sansone, Levitt, & Sansone, 2006) are good reasons to consider the use of a dimensional approach in the study and clinical assessment of Axis II features in these patients.

A spectrum approach appears to be a more suitable alternative for quantitative models that reflect the etiology of multifactorial diseases such as psychiatric disturbances. Quantitative models more easily explain the effects of multiple genes and multiple risk factors. However, spectrum models have important implications in the clinical field. They provide accurate diagnostic information to successfully individualize the treatment, as many patients with EDs do not respond satisfactorily to standard treatments. To clarify, although the presence of specific traits does not necessarily indicate the presence of a full-syndrome personality disorder, it often provides important information to the therapist to improve the patient's outcome and identify the possible targets of the treatment.

Impulsivity and compulsivity are two dimensions that appear to have specific and important clinical and prognostic implications in EDs. Although the diagnostic criteria for EDs include no mention of the terms *impulsivity* and *compulsivity*, both terms appear in the *Diagnostic and Statistical Manual of Mental Disorders–Fourth Edition* (*DSM–IV*) (American Psychiatric Association, 1994) under the diagnostic criteria for several Axis I and II disorders. Both characteristics, however, are "core" features that appear to have roles as risk factors for the development of EDs and to influence their clinical course. The aim of the present chapter is to briefly describe the relevance of impulsivity and compulsivity in the development, clinical course, and treatment of EDs.

IMPULSIVITY AND COMPULSIVITY: DEFINITIONS

The concept of impulsivity is important in clinical psychiatry and psychology as well as in everyday life. Usually, impulsivity is defined as the tendency to respond quickly and without reflection, and/or to engage in rapid, error-prone information processing without planning before the action (Plutchik & Van Praag, 1995). However, from a psychiatric point of view, impulsivity is often defined as the presence of impulsive behavior (e.g., kleptomania, pyromania, addictions, perversions, binge eating) or emotions that lead to impulsive reactions such as fear or anger, which are difficult to resist and may be harmful to oneself or others (Bech & Mak, 1995). The impulsive behavior is usually ego-syntonic and has the goal of obtaining some immediate gratification or pleasure in the absence of an adequate regard for the consequences of actions, either for oneself or for others (Moeller, Barratt, Dougherty, Schmitz, & Swann, 2001). In the literature, psychiatrists and psychologists tend to consider impulsivity as a trait rather than a state feature.

Practice Point
Impulsive behavior is usually ego-syntonic and has the goal of obtaining some immediate gratification or pleasure in the absence of an adequate regard for the consequences of actions.

Buss (1988) interpreted impulsivity in an evolutionary framework, which is an interesting perspective. He pointed out that traits such as impulsivity do not usually occur in isolation but occur with other traits that can inhibit or amplify one another. For example, the combination of impulsivity and sociability creates extraversion, whereas impulsivity and aggressiveness may lead to antisocial behavior (Plutchik & Van Praag, 1995). Following this hypothesis, impulsive self-injurious behavior (SIB) such as skin cutting or burning might be explained by a combination of impulsivity, the need for self-punishment, and/or a conflictual relationship with one's own body. The presence of an ED is associated with an overwhelming disturbance of one's relationship with the body and usually increases a sense of ineffectiveness and low self-esteem. As a matter of fact, the combination of an ED with impulsive traits could explain why there is a significant association between impulsive SIB and EDs (Favaro, Ferrara, & Santonastaso, 2004).

Compulsivity can also be conceptualized both as a personality trait and as the presence of compulsive behaviors. Compulsions are usually classified into ideational and motor compulsions. This latter category includes aggressive (e.g., coprolalia, compulsive self-mutilation), physiological (e.g., eating or smoking in a compulsive way), and bodily movement compulsions (e.g., touching, tics, compulsive exercising). The compulsive behavior is usually ego-dystonic and has the goal of preventing or reducing anxiety or distress—not to provide pleasure or gratification (American Psychiatric Association, 1994). The compulsion may be performed to reduce the distress associated with an obsession and, in some cases, may consist of stereotypic acts performed without a specific goal. In any case, attempts to resist the compulsion are followed by a sense of mounting anxiety and tension that is usually relieved by performing the compulsion (American Psychiatric Association, 1994).

Practice Point
Compulsive behavior is usually ego-dystonic and has the goal of preventing or reducing anxiety or distress—not to provide pleasure or gratification.

THE RELATIONSHIP BETWEEN IMPULSIVITY AND COMPULSIVITY

Although impulsive and compulsive behaviors may, at first, seem to be extreme opposites on a continuum of control (impulsivity = inadequate or poor control; compulsivity = excessive overcontrol and inhibition), it seems unlikely that both types of behaviors belong to a simple, unidimensional spectrum (Skodol & Oldham, 1996). As in EDs, in many psychiatric disorders, impulsive traits do not exclude the presence of compulsive symptoms and vice versa. Many compulsive features, such as indecisiveness, extreme perfectionism, and overconscientiousness, are present in more than 40% of patients with borderline personality disorders (Zanarini & Weinberg, 1996), whereas patients with obsessive-compulsive (OC) disorders with comorbid psychiatric disorders have shown a significantly increased rate of suicide attempts (Hollander & Wong, 1995). Most likely, the interactions between several biological and psychological systems, including gender, affect regulation, cognitive functioning, stage of illness, and adaptive efforts, explain the variety of presentations of these psychopathological traits (Skodol & Oldham, 1996).

IMPULSIVITY AND COMPULSIVITY
IN THE RISK OF DEVELOPING EDS

From a theoretical point of view, impulsivity could be considered a risk factor for developing an ED, especially bulimia nervosa. As reported in a review by Stice (2002), impulsivity clinically seems to play a small but significant role in increasing the risk of developing bulimic symptoms. However, the measurement of impulsivity remains a problematic question. Typically, impulsivity is measured by the use of self-report questionnaires or the assessment of the presence of behaviors that are supposedly impulsive in nature (Fahy & Eisler, 1993). A more thorough assessment of impulsivity, however, should include an evaluation of the extent to which such behaviors are committed without forethought or conscious judgment, whether behaviors are characterized by acting on the spur of the moment, the inability to focus on a specific task, and the lack of adequate planning (Moeller et al., 2001).

Some authors include temperamental traits, such as sensation seeking and risk taking, in the definition of impulsivity (Eysenck & Eysenck, 1977). However, the typical temperamental characteristics of patients with bulimia nervosa and anorexia nervosa binge eating/purging type (i.e., high novelty seeking and *high* harm avoidance) do not completely coincide with the definition of temperamental impulsivity that is described by Cloninger (1996) (i.e., high novelty seeking, *low* harm avoidance, and low persistence). Yet high novelty seeking is hypothesized to be a risk factor for bulimic symptoms, but no longitudinal studies to date have explored this point.

Few studies have investigated if certain specific impulsive behaviors are risk factors for EDs. There is some evidence for substance use in predicting an increased risk for developing bulimic symptoms (Killen et al., 1996; Stice, 2002). In addition, some studies have found elevated rates of substance or alcohol abuse among the first-degree relatives of patients with bulimia nervosa (Kaye et al., 1996; Lilenfeld et al., 1998).

Compulsivity is also considered a risk factor for EDs, in terms of both personality traits (perfectionism) and OC spectrum symptoms and disorders. For example, Bellodi et al. (2001) found a significant coaggregation of ED and OC spectrum disorders in a family study. A study by Lilenfeld et al. (1998) found that EDs and OC disorders were independently transmitted in families. In addition, the rate of OC disorders was elevated among relatives of ED probands who had OC disorder. On the contrary, rates of OC personality disorders were elevated in relatives of anorexia nervosa probands, irrespective of the presence of OC personality disorder in the probands. This finding suggests that OC personality disorder and anorexia nervosa could represent a continuum of phenotypic expressions of a similar genotype. In support of these findings, perfectionism and obsessions related to symmetry and exactness are traits that are present in many patients with EDs and seem to persist after recovery (Kaye et al., 1998; Srinivasagam et al., 1995). For this reason, the role of perfectionism and other OC personality traits as a part of the ED phenotype has been examined in the recent literature (Anderluh, Tchanturia, Rabe-Hesketh, & Treasure, 2003; Bulik et al., 2003).

From a theoretical point of view, perfectionism seems to be an obvious risk factor for EDs. Perfectionism may promote the relentless pursuit of the thin ideal (Bruch, 1973) and may foster the rigid dieting that can induce and maintain the binge–purge cycle (Stice, 2002) and the anorectic starvation process. However, longitudinal studies that include an assessment of perfectionism do not find a significant effect of this variable on the risk of developing EDs (Jacobi, Hayward, de Zwann, Kraemer, & Agras, 2004; Stice, 2002). Other studies have found that perfectionism is a *retrospective* risk factor (Fairburn, Welch, Doll, Davies, & O'Connor, 1997) and a putative maintenance factor (Santonastaso, Friederici, & Favaro, 1999).

Practice Point
Impulsivity and compulsivity may be risk factors for the development of EDs.

IMPULSIVITY AND COMPULSIVITY AS TRANSDIAGNOSTIC CHARACTERISTICS OF EDS

Impulsive behaviors appear to be a transdiagnostic characteristic in patients with EDs. Although clinically associated with the presence of binge eating, impulsive behavior is not uncommon among various ED subtypes, including restricting anorexia nervosa (Favaro & Santonastaso, 2000; Vandereycken & Van Houdenhove, 1996). Several studies have examined the relationships between EDs and specific impulsive behaviors such as impulsive SIB (Favaro & Santonastaso, 1998, 2000; Favazza, De Rosear, & Conterio, 1989; Paul, Schroeter, Dahme, & Nutzinger, 2002), attempted suicide (Bulik, Sullivan, & Joyce, 1999; Favaro & Santonastaso, 1997), substance and alcohol abuse (Welch & Fairburn, 1996), stealing (Krahn, Nairn, Gosnell, & Drewnowski, 1991; Vandereycken & Van Houdenhove, 1996), and compulsive buying (Lejoyeux, Ades, Tassain, & Solomon, 1996). Others have studied individuals who exhibit a variety of impulsive behaviors and hypothesized the existence of a subgroup of patients with EDs with a multi-impulsive syndrome (Lacey, 1993; Lacey & Evans, 1986; Nagata, Kawarada, Kiriike, & Iketani, 2000). The latter group of patients is characterized by a failure to control impulsive eating behavior (e.g., a purging form of bulimia nervosa) as well as the co-occurrence of various non-ED impulsive behaviors such as alcohol abuse, illicit drug use, deliberate SIB, suicide attempts, sexual disinhibition, and shoplifting.

It is a common clinical experience to observe that pathological impulsive behaviors tend to develop more often *after* the onset of the ED. The presence of an ED, especially those characterized by bulimic symptoms, seems to have a disinhibiting effect on other types of behavior, such as stealing, skin cutting, or hetero-aggressive acts. It appears that the ED has the power to activate a latent tendency toward impulsive behaviors in some vulnerable patients, as hypothesized by Buss (1988).

Practice Point
The ED may have the functional ability to activate a latent tendency toward impulsive behaviors in some vulnerable patients.

Thus, for example, for a correct diagnosis of borderline personality disorder, it is essential to distinguish between the intensifying effects of the ED (Rø et al., 2005; Sansone et al., 2006) and the stable traits of a personality disorder. The diagnostic question becomes even more problematic because many patients have not yet reached the recommended age for the diagnosis of a personality disorder. In addition, the typical onset of an ED during adolescence could suggest that these disturbances could have a role in the development of personality disorders (Halmi, 2003) or, more simply, that they are an expression of difficulties in personality and identity formation. Our clinical observations indicate that the presence of impulsive or multi-impulsive features in patients with EDs is not necessarily an indication of the presence of a personality disorder, because some impulsive behaviors improve or disappear with the remission of the ED. This suggests that the early treatment of an ED could be an important way to prevent the consolidation of personality difficulties (Favaro et al., 2004).

Practice Point
Early treatment of an ED could be an important way to prevent the consolidation of personality dysfunction.

In addition to impulsive features, EDs are characterized by both compulsive traits and behaviors. For example, many of the behaviors used to control body weight are compulsive in nature. In a dimensional study on the different types of SIB in bulimia nervosa, self-induced vomiting loaded on the compulsive dimension (Favaro & Santonastaso, 1998). Additional examples of typical compulsive behaviors in patients with EDs are eating in a compulsive way, exercising excessively to control weight, checking the body, and counting calories. Although some compulsive traits, such as perfectionism and the need for order and symmetry, tend to remain after remission from the ED (and are probably also present before the onset of the ED), many obsessive thoughts and compulsive behaviors tend to develop at the same time as the ED and to improve with its remission. This was observed in the study in Minnesota by Keys and colleagues (1950), in which starvation in an experimental setting induced the onset of obsessive and compulsive symptoms among participants, who were all male.

In a continuum from compulsivity to impulsivity, anorexia nervosa is usually near the compulsive end and bulimia nervosa near the impulsive end. Reviewing studies on the frequency of personality disorder in EDs, Sansone et al. (2006) found that borderline personality disorder is the most frequent diagnosis in bulimia nervosa and that OC personality disorder is the most frequent diagnosis in anorexia nervosa. However, it is noteworthy that borderline personality disorder is not rare in restricting anorexia nervosa (more than 10%) and that OC personality disorder is not rare in bulimia nervosa (more than 10%). It is more clinically appropriate to consider both dimensions as transdiagnostic issues in EDs. The following two clinical vignettes are examples of the importance of impulsivity and compulsivity in both anorexia nervosa and bulimia nervosa.

Anorexia Nervosa and Impulsivity: A Clinical Vignette

Ann was a 23-year-old student at the college of medicine. Ann's family persuaded her to seek consultation for her ED. However, it was very difficult for Ann to accept the fact that she needed help.

Her problems started one year earlier, at the age of 21. During a time of intense stress due to her studies, Ann began to lose weight. She initially weighed 58 kg (BMI = 21.6) and started a brief period of dieting to get down to about 52 kg (BMI = 19.3). She reported that, with no intention to lose weight, she was unable to cope with her studies and started to lose both her appetite and weight. In 1 year, her weight fell to 32 kg (BMI = 11.9). Ann's relatives became very alarmed about her health, and she finally realized that her illness was very severe. Ann accepted the help of her family (and of a doctor, a family friend) and tried to eat more. In our initial meeting, her weight had partially improved (BMI = 14.5), but she was very depressed and would frequently burst into tears.

Ann reported that after the onset of her illness, she started to have various types of impulsive behaviors, such as stealing (e.g., cosmetics, hair accessories), skin cutting, burning, punching, and scratching. She also reported some subjective loss of control over food during the night. She started cognitive-behavioral treatment and experienced a rapid improvement in her psychopathological status and her impulsive behaviors. Although the therapeutic relationship with the therapist was good, Ann was not able to remain in consistent treatment and abandoned the cognitive-behavioral therapy. She continued to periodically come to psychiatric visits. After some attempts to persuade Ann to be more consistent with treatment visits, the therapist agreed to continue with sporadic visits. Ann continued to improve until reaching a full remission of ED and impulsive behaviors.

Comment: The impulsive temperament of this patient is evident not only in the various impulsive behaviors that she described prior to the onset of anorexia nervosa but also in her inability to continue the treatment on a consistent basis. She considered her illness (and, as a consequence, the proposed treatment) to be a loss of control over her behavior and food intake. Thus, in her mind, discontinuing the treatment meant recovering control over her body and her life. Despite this, the patient gained some beneficial effects from the treatment and from the therapeutic relationship.

Bulimia Nervosa and Compulsivity: A Clinical Vignette

Mary was a 22-year-old woman with severe bulimia nervosa. After her mother's death when she was a child, a member of her family sexually abused Mary for years. At the first assessment, her BMI was 18.8. The frequency of binge eating and self-induced vomiting was more than once a day. The typical description of her eating symptoms was as follows: eating something that she considered excessive to maintain her weight (but never more than what other people usually eat), then deliberately eating a large amount of other food (because this was a necessary condition for self-inducing vomiting), and finally vomiting. She described her ED as an irresistible need for vomiting that occurred every time the thought of gaining weight crossed her mind. Despite the importance she gave to the aesthetic aspects of her body (she regularly went to the gym and to the beautician), after vomiting, she always engaged in behaviors such as skin picking and scratching her face.

Comment: Despite the history of sexual abuse, which is usually associated with impulsive behaviors, the main psychopathological characteristic of this patient was the need for control. Vomiting and skin picking were probably methods to improve the absence or deficiency of body sensations and, again, to try to improve the sense of self and the sense of ownership of a violated body. The ED and the skin picking improved significantly with cognitive-behavioral therapy and treatment with sertraline. However, the patient discontinued the drug because of sexual side effects, and because she transferred to another city for work, she was not able to continue cognitive-behavioral treatment. Mary relapsed after a period of complete remission of about 6 months.

SIB AND EDS

Another example of the importance of considering impulsivity and compulsivity in a transdiagnostic way in EDs can be drawn from our studies on SIB. SIBs or moderate or superficial self-mutilation include behaviors such as skin cutting, scratching, picking, or burning; hair pulling;

severe nail biting; and other forms of superficial self-injury. According to Favazza and Simeon (1995), SIBs can be divided into impulsive and compulsive categories according to their clinical characteristics. Compulsive SIBs are usually habitual, repetitive, and "automatic." They are not associated with conscious intent or an affective experience (Favazza, 1998) and have the typical characteristics of compulsions (i.e., a mounting tension when the individual attempts to resist them and a relief of anxiety when the behavior is performed). They usually have ego-dystonic overtones and the goal is not to provide gratification but only to prevent or reduce anxiety and distress. Hair pulling, skin picking, and severe nail biting are examples of this type of SIB.

Impulsive SIBs, on the contrary, are usually episodic, involve little resistance, and provide some form of gratification that is beyond the relief of tension or anxiety. Individuals who perform these types of SIBs report that the behavior helps in the control of negative emotions, such as depression, loneliness, or depersonalization, and also satisfies other needs, such as self-punishment and the manipulation of others (Favazza, 1998). The most common SIBs of the impulsive type are skin cutting, scratching, and burning.

Practice Point
Impulsivity and compulsivity have quite different features and functions in regard to SIB.

To better understand the specific relationship between the phenomenon of SIB and EDs, we investigated from a dimensional point of view the relationship between self-destructive behavior and both anorexia nervosa and bulimia nervosa (Favaro & Santonastaso, 1998, 2000). In the first study of 125 consecutive patients with bulimia nervosa, 90 (72%) reported at least one form of SIB (Favaro & Santonastaso, 1998). The principal component analysis allowed us to examine the grouping of different kinds of behavior into one or more dimensions and to study the position of every patient on the dimensions that emerged. The analysis showed a two-factor solution: hair pulling, severe nail biting, and self-induced vomiting loaded on a factor that we called "compulsive SIB," whereas skin cutting or burning, suicide attempts, substance or alcohol abuse, and laxative or diuretic abuse loaded on another factor that we called "impulsive SIB." These findings have two important implications. First, they support the classification of SIB proposed by Favazza and Simeon (1995). Second, they show that purging behavior belongs to the same dimensions as all the other types of SIB; however, the dimensions were not correlated (Favaro & Santonastaso, 1998).

In a later study, performed on a larger sample of 250 patients with bulimia nervosa, we performed a confirmative factors analysis, which substantially confirmed the presence of the two factors: impulsive and compulsive (Favaro & Santonastaso, 2002). We then performed a second study, sampling a consecutive group of 236 patients with anorexia nervosa (155 restricting type and 81 binge eating/purging type) (Favaro

& Santonastaso, 2000). In this subsequent study, we found that the frequency of SIB in anorexia nervosa is similar to that in bulimia nervosa (Favaro & Santonastaso, 2000). Except for suicide attempts and substance or alcohol abuse, which were more prevalent among bulimics, there were not significant between-group differences with the other types of SIB. The study of the dimensionality of SIB in anorexia nervosa showed similarities and differences in comparison to our study in bulimia nervosa (Favaro & Santonastaso, 1998). The principal components analysis identified three factors: impulsive SIB (suicide attempts, skin cutting and burning), compulsive SIB (severe nail biting, hair pulling), and purging behavior (self-induced vomiting, laxative or diuretic abuse). The distinction between impulsive and compulsive SIB proposed by Favazza and Simeon (1995) appears to be confirmed in anorexia nervosa, as well. But the most important difference is that in anorexia nervosa, purging behavior forms a third different dimension. Weight control in anorexia nervosa can be considered the core feature of the pathology and, probably for this reason, all behaviors with this aim have a different significance and dimensionality. In bulimia nervosa, purging behavior is a compensation for loss of control over food intake and might often be a form of self-punishment. On the other hand, purging behavior in anorexia nervosa is not always associated with binging (e.g., in 44% of cases with recurrent purging in our sample) and may be considered a means of maintaining and increasing control over food and body, even when the patient is not really losing control.

From these studies, we conclude that predictors of the impulsive and compulsive dimensions of SIB are similar in anorexia and bulimia nervosa. The presence of compulsive SIB is predicted by a shorter duration of illness and a more accentuated lack of interoceptive awareness in bulimia nervosa; in anorexia nervosa, it is predicted by a younger age and higher obsessionality. Childhood sexual abuse predicts impulsive SIB in both syndromes (Favaro & Santonastaso, 1998, 2000), supporting the findings reported in the literature (Dohm et al., 2002; Fullerton, Wonderlich, & Gosnell, 1995; van der Kolk, Perry, & Herman, 1991). Furthermore, higher depression in bulimia nervosa and higher anxiety scores in anorexia nervosa predict impulsive SIB.

Practice Point
Predictors of the impulsive and compulsive dimensions of SIB are similar in anorexia and bulimia nervosa.

Finally, in a representative female community sample (Favaro et al., 2004), we again confirmed the dimensional distinction between impulsive and compulsive SIBs and the significant association between some SIBs and EDs. In conclusion, our studies in this field appear to show that impulsive and compulsive dimensions are essential features of EDs and have a serious impact on their clinical presentation as well as important implications in the definition of the therapeutic approach.

IMPULSIVITY AND COMPULSIVITY
IN THE TREATMENT OF EDS

The impulsive and compulsive characteristics of a patient with an ED are important features to be considered for the individualization of the treatment approach, even when a full-criteria diagnosis is not present. Patients with impulsive features are, for example, more likely to drop out of treatment, and therefore strategies to minimize this risk should be used. Impulsive patients with low self-efficacy and high ineffectiveness are at most risk for dropping out, because they often consider the treatment a source of frustration and another manifestation of their failure. An extensive explanation of what we realistically expect from our patients and the communication of a feeling of empathy about the way they feel with themselves are essential before starting any treatment program. It is also useful to verbalize the possibility that they could impulsively abandon the treatment or skip some treatment sessions. In this way, the patient is more prepared to face this possibility and, in the case of dropping out, finds it is easier to come back to treatment, knowing that the therapist will not make the patient feel guilty.

Impulsive acts (such as dropping out from treatment), and impulsive SIB in particular, are hard for the therapist of a patient with an ED to deal with. Feelings of anger, frustration, and denial are common, and it is difficult to be empathic without being sympathetic. The main foci of treatment should be to increase the patient's ability to verbalize and express emotions and to address the difficulty in maintaining a stable sense of self (Suyemoto, 1998). It is important to talk about the impulsive act but also to avoid this type of behavior becoming the only focus of one or more treatment sessions.

The therapist may perceive impulsive SIB or other impulsive behaviors as deliberately hostile or manipulative. For this reason, it is important to avoid either a complete denial or neglect of the acting out or reactions of anger, shock, excessive attention, or monopolization. Several strategies can improve the expression of emotions. These strategies are as follows: (a) increasing the patient's ability to cope with and accept feelings of anger or sexual-related feelings, (b) increasing verbal and other symbolic expressions of the patient's feelings, and (c) developing insight into the meaning and function of the acting out (Suyemoto, 1998). The patient usually considers the impulsive self-injurious act as a method of coping, and it is used despite the fact that it often produces feelings of shame, guilt, and isolation. For this reason, it is important not to discourage self-injury or to emphasize the negative individual and social consequences of the behavior, because they are well-known to the impulsive patient. On the contrary, it is important to help the patient find other useful ways of coping by creating an atmosphere of support and a sense of stability. To improve the stability of the sense of self, the therapist must create a positive relational experience within the therapeutic relationship. The discussion of psychoeducational issues with the patients and their relatives can also be helpful.

The patient with high levels of compulsivity is also a difficult patient. Rigidity and inflexibility make any attempt to induce a modification of behaviors and cognitions more difficult. In patients with EDs, especially in the first stages of the illness, many compulsive symptoms or behaviors are ego-syntonic (e.g., body checks, calorie counting, weight control, excessive exercise). The patient does not regard the reduction of ego-syntonic behaviors as a goal of treatment, whereas the therapist and patient's relatives usually do. The first phases of treatment should address the improvement of the patient's contemplative abilities and focus on some (sometimes few) shared objectives to improve the self-efficacy and self-esteem of the patient. Patients with higher levels of self-esteem are more flexible and can be encouraged to face new aspects of their illness. The ego-dystonic nature of compulsive behavior is the essential premise for dealing with the behavior in the treatment setting. In the absence of that, the therapist should try to help the patient increase his or her awareness of the illness and motivation to change and to assist the family in the containment of the behavior without being controlling or repressing, which would produce an increase in the anxiety in the patient. The presence of ego-dystonic symptoms, such as some types of compulsive SIB and obsessive preoccupations, can represent a protective factor against dropping out (Favaro & Santonastaso, 1998; Halmi et al., 2005) and probably have an important impact in determining treatment-seeking behavior (Favaro et al., 2004). Compulsive behavior and compulsive SIB in EDs are usually addressed using behavioral or cognitive-behavioral techniques. Finally, the therapist should consider the use of antiobsessive pharmacological treatments.

Pharmacotherapy of impulsive and compulsive behaviors and SIBs in EDs may be necessary in patients with severe symptoms or as a measure to facilitate the effects of psychotherapy (Simeon & Hollander, 2001). Unfortunately, no medication for the treatment of SIB has yet been approved in Europe or the United States. In addition, no double-blind controlled study of medications for the treatment of these problems is available in the literature. Some direction can be derived from the clinical experience of expert therapists and from a few uncontrolled studies. These studies seem to indicate that Selective Serotonin Reuptake Inhibitors (SSRIs) are effective in decreasing impulsive behaviors and, probably, impulsive SIB (Simeon & Hollander, 2001). Mood stabilizers may also be helpful in impulsive patients. In patients with high levels of compulsivity and in those with compulsive SIB, SSRIs and clomipramine (Anafranil) are the first-line choices of pharmacological treatment. However, any indication is tentative because no study to date has evaluated the long-term effectiveness of these drugs and their effectiveness in impulsive and compulsive symptoms of patients with EDs.

Practice Point

The consideration of impulsivity and compulsivity dimensions are very important in developing a treatment plan for the patient with an ED and may substantially enhance treatment efficacy.

CONCLUSION

Impulsivity and compulsivity are two important psychopathological dimensions that seem to affect the risk of developing an ED, the clinical characteristics of patients with EDs, and the treatment approach to this type of patient. An extensive assessment of impulsive and compulsive symptoms is necessary in patients with EDs, with a particular attention to SIB. Further research is needed to better understand how to individualize the treatment approach in patients with EDs with impulsive and/or compulsive symptoms.

NOTE

Please address all correspondence to Angela Favaro, MD, PhD, MSc, Psychiatric Clinic, Department of Neuroscience, via Giustiniani 3, 35128 Padova, Italia; telephone: +39 049 8213826 (3831); fax: +39 049 8755574; e-mail: angela.favaro@unipd.it.

REFERENCES

American Psychiatric Association. (1994). *Diagnostic and statistical manual of mental disorders* (4th ed.). Washington, DC: Author.

Anderluh, M. B., Tchanturia, K., Rabe-Hesketh, S., & Treasure, J. (2003). Childhood obsessive-compulsive personality traits in adult women with eating disorders: Defining a broader eating disorder phenotype. *American Journal of Psychiatry, 160*, 242–247.

Bech, P., & Mak, M. (1995). Measurements of impulsivity and aggression. In E. Hollander & D. J. Stein (Eds.), *Impulsivity and aggression* (pp. 25–41). Chichester, UK: Wiley and Sons.

Bellodi, L., Cavallini, M. C., Bertelli, S., Chiapparino, D., Riboldi, C., & Smeraldi, E. (2001). Morbidity risk for obsessive-compulsive spectrum disorders in first-degree relatives of patients with eating disorders. *American Journal of Psychiatry, 158*, 563–569.

Bruch, H. (1973). *Eating disorders, obesity, anorexia nervosa, and the person within.* New York: Basic Books.

Bulik, C. M., Sullivan, P. F., & Joyce, P. R. (1999). Temperament, character and suicide attempts in anorexia nervosa, bulimia nervosa and major depression. *Acta Psychiatrica Scandinavica, 100*, 27–32.

Bulik, C. M., Tozzi, F., Anderson, C., Mazzeo, S. E., Aggen, S., & Sullivan, P. F. (2003). The relation between eating disorders and components of perfectionism. *American Journal of Psychiatry, 160,* 366–368.

Buss, A. H. (1988). *Personality: Evolutionary heritage and human distinctiveness.* Hillsdale, NJ: Lawrence Erlbaum.

Cloninger, C. R. (1996). Assessment of the impulsive-compulsive spectrum of behavior by the seven-factor model of temperament and character. In J. M. Oldham, E. Hollander, & A. E. Skodol (Eds.), *Impulsivity and compulsivity* (pp. 59–95). Washington, DC: American Psychiatric Press.

Dohm, F.-A., Striegel-Moore, R. H., Wilfley, D. E., Pike, K. M., Hook, J., & Fairburn, C. G. (2002). Self-harm and substance use in a community sample of Black and White women with binge eating disorder or bulimia nervosa. *International Journal of Eating Disorders, 32,* 389–400.

Eysenck, S. B., & Eysenck, H. J. (1977). The place of impulsiveness in a dimensional system of personality description. *British Journal of Social and Clinical Psychology, 16,* 57–68.

Fahy, T., & Eisler, I. (1993). Impulsivity and eating disorders. *British Journal of Psychiatry, 162,* 193–197.

Fairburn, C. G., Welch, S. L., Doll, H. A., Davies, B. A., & O'Connor, M. E. (1997). Risk factors for bulimia nervosa: A community-based case-control study. *Archives of General Psychiatry, 54,* 509–517.

Favaro, A., Ferrara, S., & Santonastaso, P. (2004). Impulsive and compulsive self-injurious behavior and eating disorders: An epidemiological study. In J. L. Levitt, R. A. Sansone, & L. Cohn (Eds.), *Self-harm behavior and eating disorders: Dynamics, assessment, and treatment* (pp. 31–43). New York: Brunner-Routledge.

Favaro, A., & Santonastaso, P. (1997). Suicidality in eating disorders: Clinical and psychological correlates. *Acta Psychiatrica Scandinavica, 95,* 508–514.

Favaro, A., & Santonastaso, P. (1998). Impulsive and compulsive self-injurious behavior in bulimia nervosa: Prevalence and psychological correlates. *Journal of Nervous and Mental Disease, 186,* 157–165.

Favaro, A., & Santonastaso, P. (2000). Self-injurious behavior in anorexia nervosa. *Journal of Nervous and Mental Disease, 188,* 537–542.

Favaro, A., & Santonastaso, P. (2002). The spectrum of self-injurious behavior in eating disorders. *Eating Disorders, 10,* 215–225.

Favazza, A. R. (1998). The coming of age of self-mutilation. *Journal of Nervous and Mental Disease, 186,* 259–268.

Favazza, A. R., De Rosear, L., & Conterio, K. (1989). Self-mutilation and eating disorders. *Suicide and Life Threatening Behavior, 19,* 352–361.

Favazza, A. R., & Simeon, D. (1995). Self-mutilation. In E. Hollander & D. Stein (Eds.), *Impulsivity and aggression* (pp. 185–200). Sussex, England: John Wiley and Sons.

Fullerton, D. T., Wonderlich, S. A., & Gosnell, B. A. (1995). Clinical characteristics of eating disorder patients who report sexual or physical abuse. *International Journal of Eating Disorders, 17,* 243–249.

Halmi, K. A. (2003). Classification, diagnosis and comorbidities of eating disorders: A review. In M. Maj, K. Halmi, J. J. Lopez-Ibor, & N. Sartorius (Eds.), *Eating disorders* (pp. 1–33) (WPA series Evidence and Experience in Psychiatry). New York: Wiley and Sons.

Halmi, K. A., Agras, W. S., Crow, S., Mitchell, J., Wilson, G. T., Bryson, S. W., et al. (2005). Predictors of treatment acceptance and completion in anorexia nervosa: Implications for future study designs. *Archives of General Psychiatry, 62,* 776–781.

Hollander, E., & Wong, C. M. (1995). Obsessive-compulsive spectrum disorders. *Journal of Clinical Psychiatry, 56*(Suppl. 4), 3–6.

Jacobi, C., Hayward, C., de Zwaan, M., Kraemer, H. C., & Agras, W. S. (2004). Coming to terms with risk factors for eating disorders: Application of risk terminology and suggestions for a general taxonomy. *Psychological Bulletin, 130,* 19–65.

Kaye, W. H., Greeno, C. G., Moss, H., Fernstrom, J., Fernstrom, M., Lilenfeld, L. R., et al. (1998). Alterations in serotonin activity and psychiatric symptoms after recovery from bulimia nervosa. *Archives of General Psychiatry, 55,* 927–935.

Kaye, W. H., Lilenfeld, L. R., Plotnicov, K., Merikangas, K. R., Nagy, L., Strober, M., et al. (1996). Bulimia nervosa and substance dependence: Association and family transmission. *Alcoholism, Clinical and Experimental Research, 20,* 878–881.

Keys, A., Brozec, J., Henschel, A., Mickelsen, O., & Taylor, H. L. (1950). *The biology of human starvation.* Minneapolis: University of Minnesota Press.

Killen, J. D., Taylor, C. B., Hayward, C., Haydel, K. F., Wilson, D. M., Hammer, L., et al. (1996). Weight concerns influence the development of eating disorders: A 4-year prospective study. *Journal of Consulting and Clinical Psychology, 64,* 936–940.

Krahn, D. D., Nairn, K., Gosnell, B. A., & Drewnowski, A. (1991). Stealing in eating disordered patients. *Journal of Clinical Psychiatry, 52,* 112–115.

Lacey, J. H. (1993). Self-damaging and addictive behaviour in bulimia nervosa: A catchment area study. *British Journal of Psychiatry, 163,* 190–194.

Lacey, J. H., & Evans, C. D. H. (1986). The impulsivist: A multi-impulsive personality disorder. *British Journal of Addiction, 81,* 641–649.

Lejoyeux, M., Ades, J., Tassain, V., & Solomon, J. (1996). Phenomenology and psychopathology of uncontrolled buying. *American Journal of Psychiatry, 153,* 1524–1529.

Lilenfeld, L. R. R., Kaye, W. H., Greeno, C. G., Merikangas, K. R., Plotnicov, K., Pollice, C., et al. (1998). A controlled family study of anorexia nervosa and bulimia nervosa. *Archives of General Psychiatry, 55,* 603–610.

Moeller, F. G., Barratt, E. S., Dougherty, D. M., Schmitz, J. M., & Swann, A. C. (2001). Psychiatric aspects of impulsivity. *American Journal of Psychiatry, 158,* 1783–1793.

Nagata, T., Kawarada, Y., Kiriike, N., & Iketani, T. (2000). Multi-impulsivity of Japanese patients with eating disorders: Primary and secondary impulsivity. *Psychiatry Research, 94,* 239–250.

Paul, T., Schroeter, K., Dahme, B., & Nutzinger, D. O. (2002). Self-injurious behavior in women with eating disorders. *American Journal of Psychiatry, 159,* 408–411.

Plutchik, R., & Van Praag, H. M. (1995). The nature of impulsivity: Definitions, ontology, genetics, and relations to aggression. In E. Hollander & D. J. Stein (Eds.), *Impulsivity and aggression* (pp. 7–24). Chichester, UK: Wiley and Sons.

Rø, Ø., Martinsen, E. W., Hoffart, A., Sexton, H., & Rosenvinge, J. H. (2005). The interaction of personality disorders and eating disorders: A two-year prospective study of patients with longstanding eating disorders. *International Journal of Eating Disorders, 38,* 106–111.

Sansone, R. A., Levitt, J. L., & Sansone, L. A. (2006). The prevalence of personality disorders among those with eating disorders. In R. A. Sansone & J. L. Levitt (Eds.), *Personality disorders and eating disorders: Exploring the frontier* (pp. 23-39). New York: Routledge.

Santonastaso, P., Friederici, S., & Favaro, A. (1999). Full and partial syndromes in eating disorders: A one-year prospective study of risk factors among female students. *Psychopathology, 32,* 50–56.

Simeon, D., & Hollander, E. (Eds.). (2001). *Self-injurious behaviors: Assessment and treatment.* Washington, DC: American Psychiatric Publishing.

Skodol, A. E., & Oldham, J. M. (1996). Phenomenology, differential diagnosis, and comorbidity of the impulsive-compulsive spectrum of disorders. In J. M. Oldham, E. Hollander, & A. E. Skodol (Eds.), *Impulsivity and compulsivity* (pp. 1–36). Washington, DC: American Psychiatric Press.

Srinivasagam, N. M., Kaye, W. H., Plotnicov, K. H., Greeno, C., Weltzin, T. E., & Rao, R. (1995). Persistent perfectionism, symmetry, and exactness after long-term recovery from anorexia nervosa. *American Journal of Psychiatry, 152,* 1630–1634.

Stice, E. (2002). Risk and maintenance factors for eating pathology: A meta-analytic review. *Psychological Bulletin, 128,* 825–848.

Suyemoto, K. L. (1998). The functions of self-mutilation. *Clinical Psychology Review, 18,* 531–554.

Vandereycken, W., & Van Houdenhove, V. (1996). Stealing behavior in eating disorders: Characteristics and associated psychopathology. *Comprehensive Psychiatry, 37,* 316–321.

van der Kolk, B. A., Perry, J. C., & Herman, J. L. (1991). Childhood origins of self-destructive behavior. *American Journal of Psychiatry, 148,* 1665–1671.

Welch, S. L., & Fairburn, C. G. (1996). Impulsivity or comorbidity in bulimia nervosa: A controlled study of deliberate self-harm and alcohol and drug misuse in a community sample. *British Journal of Psychiatry, 169,* 451–458.

Zanarini, M. C., & Weinberg, E. (1996). Borderline personality disorder: Impulsive and compulsive features. In J. M. Oldham, E. Hollander, & A. E. Skodol (Eds.), *Impulsivity and compulsivity* (pp. 37–58). Washington, DC: American Psychiatric Press.

Childhood Trauma, Personality Disorders, and Eating Disorders

RANDY A. SANSONE, MD
LORI A. SANSONE, MD

In this chapter, we explore the nature of the relationships between childhood trauma, personality disorders, and eating disorders. In the past, these types of provocative discussions have been characterized by a variety of perspectives. In this chapter, we specifically focus on exploring and identifying the possible sequential relationships of these experiences in *some* individuals. In an effort to unravel these associations, we begin by reviewing the empirical literature in this area over the past 10 years.

THE LITERATURE SEARCH

In preparing this chapter, we undertook a literature search using the PsycINFO database. We entered a variety of search terms, including *childhood trauma, sexual abuse, physical abuse, emotional abuse, personality disorders, borderline personality, avoidant personality, obsessive-compulsive personality,* and *antisocial personality.* We elected these particular personality disorders because they were more likely to be associated with eating disorders or have a large database. To have as much consistency in Axis II diagnosis as possible, we included only articles published in 1994 or later (i.e., criteria from the *Diagnostic and Statistical Manual of Mental Disorders–Fourth Edition* [*DSM–IV*]) (American Psychiatric Association, 1994). We excluded studies written in foreign languages as well as dissertations and remote journals involving a fee to obtain, unless the abstract contained sufficient information to include findings. It is surprising that we did not encounter a single empirical study that addressed all three areas of inquiry—childhood trauma, personality disorders, and eating disorders.

LIMITATIONS OF THE SEARCH

Before we present the summary of our results, we must note several caveats. First, we may have missed papers in the literature in which none of the designated search terms appeared in the abstract or subject area as well as papers presented as abstracts or at meetings. Second, studies published around the year 1994 may have used personality disorder criteria from a previous version of the *DSM*. We also emphasize the following factors to consider.

Subject Factors

It is important to recognize that childhood trauma is based on subject recollection, which is prone to a variety of psychological compromises. At the outset, many patients lack meaningful recall of events before the ages of 3 or 4. In response to trauma, there may also be a variety of psychological maneuvers by the victim that impair recall, such as suppression, repression, dissociation, and denial.

In addition, the actual recollection of an event may be distorted or misinterpreted in a variety of ways. For example, a male patient adamantly denied any history of abuse, yet casually informed us that his father would beat him with a belt buckle around the head and shoulders. The patient nonchalantly explained that his father was only trying to help him behave because the patient suffered from attention-deficit/hyperactivity disorder: "I needed that type of discipline from my father." In further support of this interpretive dilemma, Bailey and Shriver (1999) acknowledged the importance of subjectivity in labeling a childhood experience as sexual abuse. On a rare occasion, in our clinical experience, some individuals with borderline personality disorder (BPD) may misconstrue or even offer false historical information to engage others. Finally, the difficulties with interpretation may relate to how a society perceives a phenomenon. For example, in some studies, the upper age range of reported abuse is age 18—Is this voluntary participation or victimization?

Because of the preceding psychological and social factors, it is difficult to assess not only the presence of childhood abuse but also its specific characteristics (e.g., duration, relationship of the perpetrator to the victim, level of external parental support, type of sexual imposition)—all of which may affect the eventual evolution of subsequent psychopathology including personality disorders.

Axis II Assessment Factors

Among patients with eating disorders, we are also faced with the difficulties in assessing and confirming diagnoses of personality disorders (see Vitousek & Stumpf, 2005). For example, personality disorder symptoms tend to be artificially elevated among young patients, in individuals in biological crisis such as starvation, and when severe Axis I disorders are present, such as depression. In addition, individual Axis II measures appear to capture slightly different clinical populations. This may be explained, in part, in several ways: (a) the constructs for these measures vary, (b) self-report measures tend to be overinclusive, and (c) the results of semistructured interviews may be dependent on extensive investigator training and inter-rater reliability.

There is also a contemporary tendency in many studies to assess broad personality traits or factors, rather than bonafide *DSM* disorders. Although some of these dimensional approaches are reported to correlate with specific *DSM* Axis II disorders, for the most part, we do not know what level of accuracy these measures actually demonstrate.

Finally, it is difficult to compare personality disorder studies from different *DSM* eras because of the ever-changing Axis II palette. Specifically, the *DSM* has, over time, designated as many as 15 and as few as 10 personality disorders (excluding personality disorder, not otherwise specified). Therefore, a disorder may have existed in a previous version (e.g., passive-aggressive personality disorder) but may no longer be in current diagnostic vogue, thereby crippling the ability to compare data.

Other Limitations

As with any review of studies, there are various types of samples and control groups, varying measures for personality assessment, and varying gender ratios. Therefore, we present this review as an examination of trends or impressions, rather than as absolute conclusions. Despite this cautious framing, we believe that there are a number of valid general conclusions that may be drawn from the existing data.

CHILDHOOD TRAUMA
AND PERSONALITY DISORDERS

A number of studies have examined correlations between specific types of childhood trauma and various personality disorders in adulthood. These populations include community or nonclinical as well as patient samples. We included nonclinical studies in this review because there may be meaningful clinical differences between community populations versus treatment-seeking populations (Sansone, Wiederman, & Sansone, 2000).

Nonclinical Samples

J. J. Johnson, Smailes, Cohen, Brown, and Bernstein (2000) initially assessed 738 children between the ages of 1 and 10 years and then reassessed them as adolescents and young adults. They found that childhood emotional, physical, and supervisory neglect (i.e., inadequate parental monitoring) as well as verbal abuse were associated with an increased risk for personality disorders in adulthood. J. J. Johnson et al. also analyzed specific types of neglect in terms of the resulting type of personality dysfunction. Supervisory neglect was associated with Cluster B personality disorders (i.e., dramatic, emotional, or erratic cluster) including BPD. Emotional neglect was associated with symptoms in Cluster A (i.e., odd or eccentric cluster) as well as avoidant and paranoid personality disorders. Physical neglect was associated with Cluster A symptoms and schizotypal personality disorder. Verbal abuse was associated with a threefold risk of having borderline, narcissistic, obsessive-compulsive, and paranoid personality disorders (J. G. Johnson et al., 2001).

Outpatient Samples

In a sample of 182 outpatients with various personality disorders, Bierer et al. (2003) found that global trauma severity was predictive of Cluster B diagnoses, particularly borderline and antisocial personality disorders. Emotional abuse in men predicted for BPD; sexual and physical abuse predicted for antisocial personality disorder; and sexual, physical, and emotional abuse predicted for paranoid personality disorder.

In the Collaborative Longitudinal Personality Disorders Study (Battle et al., 2004), investigators found that emotional and verbal abuse and caretaker and noncaretaker sexual abuse were associated with BPD, noncaretaker sexual abuse was associated with obsessive-compulsive personality disorder, and verbal and caretaker sexual abuse was associated with antisocial personality disorder.

Combined Inpatient and Outpatient Samples

Hogue (1999) examined both adult inpatients and outpatients and found that high levels of overall family dysfunction were associated with high levels of personality pathology. Paternal psychological maladjustment and sexual abuse were most strongly associated with BPD, maternal emotional abuse and neglect were associated with avoidant personality disorder, maternal emotional abuse was associated with paranoid personality, paternal emotional abuse was associated with schizotypal personality disorder, and maternal emotional abuse was associated with dependent personality. Sexual abuse was associated with antisocial personality disorder.

Substance Abuse Populations

Alcohol abuse. At least three studies have examined the relationship between childhood trauma and subsequent personality pathology among individuals who abuse alcohol. Windle, Windle, Scheidt, and Miller (1995) found that the combination of physical and sexual abuse was associated with high rates of antisocial personality disorder in both men and women. Among inpatients, Lisek (1996) found that in men, childhood abuse was related to antisocial and narcissistic personality disorders, whereas in women it was related to dependent personality disorder and BPD. Glutting (1996) found that among alcoholic men, childhood abuse correlated with antisocial behavior. These studies suggest, among alcoholic individuals, a relationship between childhood trauma and Cluster B disorders.

Mixed substance abuse. There are three studies in mixed substance abuse populations. In the first, Ellason, Ross, Sainton, and Mayran (1996) examined inpatients and found that, compared to those without histories of physical and/or sexual abuse, those with such histories had higher rates of BPD. Ruggiero (1996) found that among male veterans, sexual abuse was related to schizoid personality disorder; physical and emotional abuse had diffuse relationships with most of the Axis II disorders under study (i.e., paranoid, schizoid, schizotypal, antisocial, and borderline personalities); physical neglect had a diffuse relationship with schizoid personality disorder; and emotional neglect had a diffuse relationship with avoidant personality disorder. Bernstein, Stein, and Handelsman (1998) found that physical neglect and abuse were related to antisocial personality traits, emotional abuse contributed to personality traits in all clusters, and emotional neglect was associated with schizoid personality disorder. It is surprising that in this last study, sexual abuse was unrelated to any personality disorder.

Dissociative Identity Disorder

Among inpatients with dissociative identity disorder, Ellason, Ross, and Fuchs (1996) found that 90%, 92%, and 96% reported physical, sexual, and combination abuse, respectively. Clusters B and C were the most common forms of personality pathology, with borderline and avoidant personality disorders being most frequent.

Juvenile Delinquents and Incarcerated Offenders

In juvenile delinquents, Barylnik (2003) found that high rates of physical abuse and neglect contributed to adult antisocial features. Campbell, Porter, and Santor (2004) found among incarcerated male and female adolescents that histories of childhood physical abuse were associated with antisocial personality traits.

Court-Documented Childhood Abuse

Horwitz, Widom, McLaughlin, and White (2001) examined court records for documented cases of childhood abuse and undertook a follow-up assessment of these individuals some 20 years later. Compared with controls, abused and neglected men and women were more likely to have antisocial personality disorder.

Avoidant Personality Disorder

Rettew et al. (2003) found that neither physical abuse nor emotional abuse were related to avoidant personality disorder.

Eating Disorders

Steiger, Jabalpurwala, and Champagne (1996) found among bulimic individuals a correlation between childhood abuse and personality pathology, with BPD being most evident. Grilo and Masheb (2002) found that among outpatients with binge eating disorder, more than 80% reported some form of childhood maltreatment (i.e., emotional, physical, and/or sexual abuse; emotional and/or physical neglect); emotional abuse was associated with Cluster C personality disorders, specifically avoidant personality disorder, but other forms of abuse did not contribute to personality disorders in this sample.

Practice Point

In the overwhelming majority of studies, childhood abuse is correlated with some type of personality pathology. However, the type of abuse and corresponding personality disturbance appear to be highly variable.

CHILDHOOD TRAUMA
AND BORDERLINE PERSONALITY

In the preceding studies, investigators examined various personality dysfunctions and disorders in individuals with histories of childhood trauma. In reviewing the literature, however, we found that the majority of empirical studies have examined specific correlations between childhood trauma and those who presently evidence BPD. In summarizing the research literature up through the mid-1990s, Pfeifer-Tarkowski (1997) concluded that there appears to be a relationship between childhood sexual abuse and borderline-like symptoms in adulthood.

Nonclinical Studies

Screening more than 5,000 participants 18 years of age, Trull (2001) found a relationship between childhood abuse and BPD psychopathology.

Inpatient Studies

Atlas (1995) examined hospitalized adolescent females and found that those with early histories of physical and/or sexual abuse were significantly more likely to be diagnosed with BPD. Oldham, Skodol, Gallaher, and Kroll (1996) found that among applicants to a long-term, inpatient treatment facility, three quarters of the patients with BPD had histories of some type of abuse, whereas only a third of patients without BPD did. C. S. Johnson (1999) examined inpatients with BPD and found that emotional and sexual abuse were significantly associated with the disorder, but only among females (i.e., gender differences). Renneberg, Weibb, Unger, Fiedler, and Brunner (2003) found that 87% of female inpatients with BPD reported traumatic childhood experiences (i.e., sexual and physical abuse). Finally, in an Israeli study of suicidal adolescents (Horesh, Sever, & Apter, 2003), compared to those suffering from major depression, those with BPD reported more sexual abuse. To summarize the preceding studies, there is a high frequency of reported childhood abuse among patients with BPD.

There may also be tempering characteristics of trauma in relationship to BPD. For example, Zanarini et al. (2002) found that among inpatients with BPD, the *severity* of childhood sexual abuse was related to the overall severity of BPD symptoms. Sansone, Gaither, and Songer (2002) found that with the exception of witnessing violence, the *number of types of abuse* (e.g., suffering sexual, physical, and emotional abuse; witnessing violence) correlated with the number of diagnostic confirmations on several measures of BPD. In other words, severity and more types of abuse may be more likely to lead to the borderline disorder.

Borderline Personality in Comparison
With Other Personality Disorders

Several studies have compared childhood abuse histories between individuals with BPD and those with other personality disorders. These studies follow.

Outpatient studies. Compared with other Axis II disorders, several studies indicate that those with BPD have a greater frequency of childhood sexual abuse (Norden, Klein, Donaldson, Pepper, & Klein, 1995; Paris, Zweig-Frank, & Guzder, 1994) as well as physical abuse (Golier et al., 2003; Paris et al., 1994).

Inpatient studies. In a Canadian study, Laporte and Guttman (1996) examined the discharge diagnoses of 751 females with Axis II disorders and found that the BPD subsample reported more abuses (in this study, verbal, physical, and sexual abuse) as well as combinations of abuses from multiple perpetrators. Zanarini, Williams, et al. (1997) found that among a mixed sample of inpatients with personality disorders, those with BPD reported significantly more emotional and physical abuse by a caretaker, as well as sexual abuse by a noncaretaker. In another mixed Axis II inpatient sample, Zanarini, Dubo, Lewis, and Williams (1997) found that more than 90% of the BPD subsample reported childhood abuse and neglect, 80% reported emotional or verbal abuse, and 60% reported physical and sexual abuse. Significant between-group differences (more frequent in the BPD subsample) were physical, noncaretaker sexual, and any sexual abuse; emotional withdrawal of caretakers; and the lack of a genuine relationship with caretakers.

Special populations. Compared with other Axis II disorders, childhood sexual abuse has been associated with BPD among outpatients with major depression (Zlotnick, Mattia, & Zimmerman, 2001) and male forensic patients (Timmerman & Emmelkamp, 2001). In a sample of outpatients with post-traumatic stress disorder (Heffernan & Cloitre, 2000), BPD was associated with maternal physical and verbal abuse as well as earlier age of onset.

Practice Point

In empirical studies, BPD is associated with various forms of abuse, not just sexual abuse. Gender and type of trauma, earlier age of onset, greater severity, multiple perpetrators, and multiple forms of abuse may heighten the risk for the subsequent development of BPD.

PERSONALITY PATHOLOGY AMONG ADULT VICTIMS OF CHILDHOOD SEXUAL ABUSE

Up to this point, we have reviewed studies on the relationship between childhood trauma and personality pathology in various study populations. Yet there is one other group of studies that relate to this topic—

those that explore the current Axis II status of adults who were victims of childhood sexual abuse. The following studies relate to Axis II pathology in adults who were either seeking or receiving treatment for childhood sexual abuse.

Outpatient Studies

BPD. Several studies indicate that among adults with sexual abuse histories, borderline personality features are more common than other personality features (Pope, 1998; Ross-Gower, Waller, Tyson, & Elliott, 1998; Schmidt, 2002). In contrast, Hammond (2000) found that the frequency of childhood sexual abuse was unrelated to BPD but the *severity* of sexual abuse was a significant predictor of BPD, and the number of perpetrators approached significance as a predictor of BPD.

McLean and Gallop (2003) explored the relationship between BPD and the *timing* of childhood sexual abuse, specifically early onset versus late onset. Those with early-onset abuse had a significantly higher prevalence of BPD diagnoses, and paternal incest was a significant predictor for BPD.

Other personality disorders. Other personality disorders have been identified among sexual abuse victims, as well. Pope (1998) confirmed avoidant personality disorder, and D. M. Johnson, Sheahan, and Chard (2003) found, in comparison with BPD, higher frequencies of avoidant, antisocial, and dependent personalities.

Combined Inpatient and Outpatient Samples

Among female inpatients and outpatients with histories of childhood sexual abuse, Shea, Zlotnick, and Weisberg (1999) found that the most frequent personality disorder was paranoid, followed by borderline, and then schizotypal personality disorders.

Practice Point
Among adults with histories of childhood sexual abuse, several Axis II disorders have been reported, including borderline, avoidant, antisocial, dependent, paranoid, and schizotypal personality disorders. Borderline personality is not the invariable Axis II outcome of childhood sexual abuse.

ABUSE FACTORS THAT MAY INTENSIFY
THE LIKELIHOOD OF AN AXIS II DIAGNOSIS

One clinical issue to consider is the possibility that the type of abuse is less relevant than a particular characteristic related to the abuse. For example, perhaps childhood sexual abuse, alone, is less of a predictor for Axis II psychopathology than the age of onset or some characteristic of this type of abuse, such as a malignant threat (e.g., "If you tell, I'll kill your mother!"). Several studies have explored possible modifying characteristics—nearly all in relationship to BPD.

Empirically confirmed factors that may increase the likelihood of a Cluster B or BPD diagnosis include (a) sexual abuse by a parent (Silk, Lee, Hill, & Lohr, 1995), (b) long duration or high frequency of sexual abuse (Paris et al., 1994; Silk et al., 1995), (c) sexual abuse involving penetration (Silk et al., 1995), (d) greater severity of sexual abuse (Paris et al., 1994; Sheahan, 2001), (e) early age of abuse onset (Heffernan & Cloitre, 2000; Kozel, 2001), (f) long duration of physical abuse (Paris et al., 1994), and (g) parental factors such as high control, deficient care, and personality dysfunction (Carter, Joyce, Mulder, & Luty, 2001; Paris et al., 1994).

Practice Point

Rather than the type of abuse, some characteristics of the abuse—such as age of onset, severity or duration, and/or parental psychopathology— may be augmenting factors that intensify the likelihood of an Axis II outcome.

STUDIES THAT REFUTE A RELATIONSHIP BETWEEN CHILDHOOD SEXUAL ABUSE AND AXIS II PSYCHOPATHOLOGY

Not all studies confirm relationships between childhood sexual abuse and adult personality pathology. Again, most of these studies are in the area of BPD. For example, Service (1995) compared women outpatients with and without histories of childhood sexual abuse and found no between-group differences in the prevalence of BPD. Using a path-analytic model, Warren (1996) could not confirm a statistical association between sexual abuse and BPD. Fossati, Madeddu, and Maffei (1999) undertook a meta-analysis of the published literature (21 studies between the years of 1980 and 1995) and observed a moderate pooled effect size ($r = .279$) for the relationship between childhood sexual abuse and BPD; although findings did not support childhood sexual abuse as a major risk factor for BPD, the authors acknowledged, "Childhood sexual abuse could be related to specific BPD psychopathological features" (p. 276).

Other personality disorders have been examined, as well. In a substance abuse sample, Bernstein and colleagues (1998) were unable to correlate childhood sexual abuse with any personality disorder. Carter et al. (2001) found that childhood sexual abuse was not predictive of any specific personality pathology.

Practice Point

Childhood sexual abuse does not invariably predict for personality pathology.

ALTERNATIVE NONTRAUMATIC PATHWAYS TO BPD

Although there appears to be a connection between childhood trauma and BPD, the most commonly studied Axis II disorder, there occasionally are individuals with BPD without such histories. Although the apparent absence of trauma may relate to the psychological mechanisms of repression, suppression, denial, misinterpretation, and dissociation (i.e., these individuals simply do not recall the traumata), there may be alternative explanations, as well. For example, Graybar and Boutilier (2002) discussed the contributory roles to BPD of core emotionality, preexisting temperament, underlying chronic affective disorders, and neurological factors (e.g., attention-deficit/hyperactivity disorder, learning disabilities, abnormalities on neuropsychological testing). However, these intriguing possibilities have not been confirmed by research.

Practice Point

Not all patients with BPD appear to have childhood trauma histories. Therefore, there may be nontraumatic pathways to this disorder.

CLINICAL IMPLICATIONS

Although there are a handful of studies that do not support the contribution of childhood abuse to adult personality pathology, and an existing meta-analysis that also softens support for the contribution of childhood abuse to adult personality pathology, the overwhelming majority of individual studies in this area suggest some relationship between maltreatment in childhood and adult personality dysfunction. Some even suggest specific associations between the type of abuse and the resulting personality pathology. These specific relationships between childhood abuse and adult personality pathology, however, have yet to be empirically reproduced.

Given that maltreatment in childhood is a fairly common experience, it is unlikely that the presence of abuse alone predicts very keenly for any specific personality pathology. This suggests that there may be distinct augmenting factors that heighten this risk (e.g., duration and severity of abuse, relationship of the perpetrator to the victim). In other words, *early developmental trauma in the presence of particular augmenting factors is likely to contribute nonspecifically to adult personality pathology.* This relationship may be stronger in women than men (MacMillan et al., 2001). Conversely, high levels of certain types of personality dysfunction are frequently, but not invariably, associated with childhood trauma.

Practice Point

Early developmental trauma, in combination with augmenting factors, may contribute to nonspecific adult personality pathology.

If there are augmenting factors (i.e., factors that do not directly relate to the characteristics of abuse) that intensify the initiation of personality dysfunction, what might they be? Perhaps the answer resides within the general *context* of early traumata. For example, Zanarini and Frankenburg (1997) emphasized the role of a vulnerable temperament (i.e., genetic predisposition conferred by parents) as well as specific triggering events that appear to unleash symptoms. As another example, Lewis (1997) underscored the role of multiple negative and victimizing life experiences.

Numerous authors have identified possible augmenting factors that relate to the parenting experience and family environment. Yatsko (1996) described unempathic parenting styles. Warren (1996) described perceived low parental support and family dysfunction, and Paris and Zweig-Frank (1997) described the importance of separation from or loss of parents in early life as well as abnormal parental bonding. Hogue (1999) emphasized the overall levels of family dysfunction, and Zanarini, Williams, et al. (1997) emphasized the role of male caretakers and emotional denial as well as inconsistent treatment by female caretakers. Laporte and Guttman (1996) discussed the role of adoption. Norden et al. (1995) described poor parental relationships. Collectively, these preceding findings suggest one consistent theme in the early lives of individuals with personality disorders—unstable parental and familial environments (i.e., multiple possible deficits).

To summarize, these data suggest that genetic predisposition, coupled with unstable or nonsupportive family environments that are highlighted to some degree by various forms of childhood abuse, may lead to some types of personality dysfunction or disorders. According to research findings, these potential disorders commonly include antisocial, borderline, avoidant, paranoid, and perhaps schizotypal personality disorders. These identified risk factors, however, may not consistently predict for all or even a specific type of personality disorder.

Practice Point

Genetic predisposition and unstable family environments characterized by childhood abuse may lead to some types of personality dysfunction or disorders.

Relationship of Abuse, Personality Disorders, and Eating Disorders

How does all of this relate to eating disorders? As noted by de Groot and Rodin (1999) and Everill and Waller (1995), *childhood sexual abuse is a risk factor for eating disorders*, despite statistical analyses suggesting the lack of such an association (Everill & Waller, 1995). This conclusion is likely to include other forms of childhood abuse, as well. This childhood abuse–eating disorder relationship may be mediated by personality dysfunction. At the outset of life's journey, one's endowment with

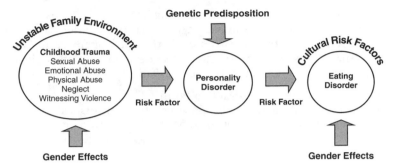

Figure 4.1   Risk-factor model for the relationships between childhood trauma, personality disorders, and eating disorders.

low-adaptive genetics and exposure to an unstable family environment highlighted by abuse appears to establish the risk for personality disorder. *The consolidated personality disorder, in turn, may enhance the risk for an eating disorder* (see Figure 4.1).

How does personality dysfunction heighten the risk for an eating disorder? This relationship can be easily illustrated using the example of purging type bulimia nervosa. If an individual has a heightened level of impulsivity or poor self-regulation, as is the case in BPD, there seems to be an increased risk for poor regulation of food intake. Poor food regulation might lead to weight gain. Weight gain would heighten the risk for the subsequent development of impulsive counterregulatory behaviors (e.g., purging, abusing laxatives) to lose weight. These weight-management behaviors might eventually evolve and function as auxiliary self-harm behaviors (i.e., dual functional roles of weight management and self-harm behavior) in the individual with BPD, resulting in the mutual reinforcement of their existence.

This *childhood trauma–personality dysfunction–eating disorder* sequence may be particularly applicable to those eating disorders that are characterized by impulsivity (i.e., anorexia nervosa, binge eating/purging type; bulimia nervosa/purging type; binge eating disorder). It is not surprising that according to research data, slightly more than one quarter of these individuals suffer from BPD (Sansone, Levitt, & Sansone, 2005), which is much higher than the prevalence observed in restricting type anorexia nervosa.

In contrast, individuals with restricting anorexia nervosa are oftentimes characterized by obsessive-compulsive personality traits (Sansone et al., 2005). In our review of the present literature, there was little consistent evidence to link childhood trauma with obsessive-compulsive personality disorder.

This sequencing model may apply to other eating disorder scenarios, as well. First, it may relate to those individuals who briefly begin their eating disorder experience with restricting anorexia nervosa and promptly shift to a more impulse-ridden eating disorder such as bulimia nervosa. Second, among those restricting individuals whose Axis II pathology is predominantly avoidant personality disorder, there may still be a trauma substrate. In this case, the subsequent eating disorder may function as an adaptation (i.e., the development of a culturally ideal body or shape) to counter the social void.

Practice Point

Childhood trauma is a risk factor for several types of personality disorders. Personality disorders (depending on the type), in turn, may be risk factors for eating disorders.

CONCLUSION

Childhood trauma appears to be a meaningful risk factor for the subsequent development of several types of personality dysfunctions or disorders, particularly in the presence of predisposing genetics and impaired family functioning. Some resulting personality disorders, particularly BPD, may subsequently function as risk factors for eating disorders. In addition, there may also be some relationship between childhood trauma, avoidant personality disorder, and restricting anorexia nervosa. Not all traumatized individuals develop personality disorders, and not all individuals with personality disorders develop eating disorders. Further research is needed to explore the various protective and augmenting factors for this pathway. Through further investigation, we may be able to develop better preventive strategies as well as more effective therapies for this distressed and traumatized subgroup of patients with eating disorders.

NOTE

Please address correspondence to Randy A. Sansone, MD, Sycamore Primary Care Center, 2115 Leiter Road, Miamisburg, OH, 45342; telephone: 937-384-6850; fax: 937-384-6938; e-mail: Randy.sansone@kmcnetwork.org.

REFERENCES

American Psychiatric Association. (1994). *Diagnostic and statistical manual of mental disorders* (4th ed.). Washington, DC: Author.

Atlas, J. A. (1995). Association between history of abuse and borderline personality disorder for hospitalized adolescent girls. *Psychological Reports, 77*, 1346.

Bailey, J. M., & Shriver, A. (1999). Does childhood sexual abuse cause borderline personality disorder? *Journal of Sex and Marital Therapy, 25*, 45–57.

Barylnik, J. (2003). Psychopathology, psychosocial characteristics and family environment in juvenile delinquents. *German Journal of Psychiatry, 6,* 30–32.

Battle, C. L., Shea, M. T., Johnson, D. M., Yen, S., Zlotnick, C., Zanarini, M. C., et al. (2004). Childhood maltreatment associated with personality disorders: Findings from the Collaborative Longitudinal Personality Disorders Study. *Journal of Personality Disorders, 18,* 193–211.

Bernstein, D. P., Stein, J. A., & Handelsman, L. (1998). Predicting personality pathology among adult patients with substance use disorders: Effects of childhood maltreatment. *Addictive Behaviors, 23,* 855–868.

Bierer, L. M., Yehuda, R., Schmeidler, J., Mitropoulou, V., New, A. S., Silverman, J. M., et al. (2003). Abuse and neglect in childhood: Relationship to personality disorder diagnoses. *CNS Spectrums, 8,* 737–740, 749–754.

Campbell, M. A., Porter, S., & Santor, D. (2004). Psychopathic traits in adolescent offenders: An evaluation of criminal history, clinical, and psychosocial correlates. *Behavioral Sciences and the Law, 22,* 23–47.

Carter, J. D., Joyce, P. R., Mulder, R. T., & Luty, S. E. (2001). The contribution of temperament, childhood neglect, and abuse to the development of personality dysfunction: A comparison of three models. *Journal of Personality Disorders, 15,* 123–135.

De Groot, J., & Rodin, G. M. (1999). The relationship between eating disorders and childhood trauma. *Psychiatric Annals, 29,* 225–229.

Ellason, J. W., Ross, C. A., & Fuchs, D. L. (1996). Lifetime Axis I and II comorbidity and childhood trauma history in dissociative identity disorder. *Psychiatry: Interpersonal and Biological Processes, 59,* 255–266.

Ellason, J. W., Ross, C. A., Sainton, K., & Mayran, L. W. (1996). Axis I and II comorbidity and childhood trauma history in chemical dependency. *Bulletin of the Meninger Clinic, 60,* 39–51.

Everill, J. T., & Waller, G. (1995). Reported sexual abuse and eating psychopathology: A review of the evidence for a causal link. *International Journal of Eating Disorders, 18,* 1–11.

Fossati, A., Madeddu, F., & Maffei, C. (1999). Borderline personality disorder and childhood sexual abuse: A meta-analytic study. *Journal of Personality Disorders, 13,* 268–280.

Glutting, J. H. (1996). Childhood abuse, family history, and the development of antisocial personality disorder and alcoholism. *Dissertation Abstracts International, 56,* 7045B.

Golier, J., Yehuda, R., Bierer, L. M., Mitropoulou, V., New, A. S., Schmeidler, J., et al. (2003). The relationship of borderline personality disorder to post-traumatic stress disorder and traumatic events. *American Journal of Psychiatry, 160,* 2018–2024.

Graybar, S. R., & Boutilier, L. R. (2002). Nontraumatic pathways to borderline personality disorder. *Psychotherapy: Theory/Research/Practice/Training, 39,* 152–162.

Grilo, C. M., & Masheb, R. M. (2002). Childhood maltreatment and personality disorders in adult patients with binge eating disorder. *Acta Psychiatrica Scandinavica, 106,* 183–188.

Hammond, B. A. (2000). The relationship of severity of childhood sexual abuse, number of perpetrators, frequency of abuse, and emotional health of the family of origin to borderline personality disorder. *Dissertation Abstracts International, 61,* 1083B.

Heffernan, K., & Cloitre, M. (2000). A comparison of posttraumatic stress disorder with and without borderline personality disorder among women with a history of childhood sexual abuse: Etiological and clinical characteristics. *Journal of Nervous and Mental Disease, 188,* 589–595.

Hogue, S. L. (1999). Relationship between family of origin history and personality pathology. *Dissertation Abstracts International, 59,* 6067B.

Horesh, N., Sever, J., & Apter, A. (2003). A comparison of life events between suicidal adolescents with major depression and borderline personality disorder. *Comprehensive Psychiatry, 44,* 277–283.

Horwitz, A. V., Widom, C. S., McLaughlin, J., & White, H. R. (2001). The impact of childhood abuse and neglect on adult mental health: A prospective study. *Journal of Health and Social Behavior, 42,* 184–201.

Johnson, C. S. (1999). Borderline personality disorder: The influence of childhood trauma and family environment and their associations with different representations of the disorder criteria. *Dissertation Abstracts International, 60,* 2345B.

Johnson, J. G., Cohen, P., Smailes, E. M., Skodol, A. E., Brown, J., & Oldham, J. M. (2001). Childhood verbal abuse and risk for personality disorders during adolescence and early adulthood. *Comprehensive Psychiatry, 42,* 16–23.

Johnson, D. M., Sheahan, T. C., & Chard, K. M. (2003). Personality disorders, coping strategies, and posttraumatic stress disorder in women with histories of childhood sexual abuse. *Journal of Child Sexual Abuse, 12,* 19–39.

Johnson, J. J., Smailes, E. M., Cohen, P., Brown, J., & Bernstein, D. P. (2000). Associations between four types of childhood neglect and personality disorder symptoms during adolescence and early adulthood: Findings of a community-based longitudinal study. *Journal of Personality Disorders, 14,* 171–187.

Kozel, J. J. (2001). Age of abuse onset and its relationship to autonomic arousal in borderline personality disorder. *Dissertation Abstracts International, 61,* 3849B.

Laporte, L., & Guttman, H. (1996). Traumatic childhood experiences as risk factors for borderline and other personality disorders. *Journal of Personality Disorders, 10,* 247–259.

Lewis, R. E. (1997). Childhood experience reports of adult male antisocial inpatients. *Dissertation Abstracts International, 57,* 7264B.

Lisek, V. J. (1996). Family of origin characteristics and personality disorders/tendencies of type 1 male, type 2 male and female alcoholics. *Dissertation Abstracts International, 56,* 3004B.

MacMillan, H. L., Fleming, J. E., Streiner, D. L., Lin, E., Boyle, M. H., Jamieson, E., et al. (2001). Childhood abuse and lifetime psychopathology in a community sample. *American Journal of Psychiatry, 158,* 1878–1883.

McLean, L. M., & Gallop, R. (2003). Implications of childhood sexual abuse for adult borderline personality disorder and complex posttraumatic stress disorder. *American Journal of Psychiatry, 160,* 369–371.

Norden, K. A., Klein, D. N., Donaldson, S. K., Pepper, C. M., & Klein, L. M. (1995). Reports of the early home environment in *DSM-III-R* personality disorders. *Journal of Personality Disorders, 9,* 213–223.

Oldham, J. M., Skodol, A. E., Gallaher, P. E., & Kroll, M. E. (1996). Relationship of borderline symptoms to histories of abuse and neglect: A pilot study. *Psychiatric Quarterly, 67,* 287–295.

Paris, J., & Zweig-Frank, H. (1997). Parameters of childhood sexual abuse in female patients. In M. C. Zanarini (Ed.), *Role of sexual abuse in the etiology of borderline personality disorder* (pp. 15–28). Washington, DC: American Psychiatric Association.

Paris, J., Zweig-Frank, H., & Guzder, J. (1994). Psychological risk factors for borderline personality disorder in female patients. *Comprehensive Psychiatry, 35,* 301–305.

Pfeifer-Tarkowski, V. J. (1997). The role of childhood sexual abuse and the development of borderline personality disorder: A critical review. *Dissertation Abstracts International, 57,* 4720B.

Pope, P. L. (1998). Long-term sequelae of childhood sexual abuse in women. *Dissertation Abstracts International, 58,* 5137B.

Renneberg, B., Weibb, M., Unger, J., Fiedler, P., & Brunner, R. (2003). Etiological factors in borderline personality disorder. *Verhaltenstherapie and Verhaltensmedizin, 24,* 347–364.

Rettew, D. C., Zanarini, M. C., Yen, S., Grilo, C. M., Skodol, A. E., Shea, M., et al. (2003). Childhood antecedents of avoidant personality disorder: A retrospective study. *Journal of the American Academy of Child and Adolescent Psychiatry, 42,* 1122–1130.

Ross-Gower, J., Waller, G., Tyson, M., & Elliott, P. (1998). Reported sexual abuse and subsequent psychopathology among women attending psychology clinics: The mediating role of dissociation. *British Journal of Clinical Psychology, 37,* 313–326.

Ruggiero, J. S. (1996). The personality sequelae of child maltreatment in drug and alcohol dependent male veterans. *Dissertation Abstracts International, 56,* 4592B.

Sansone, R. A., Gaither, G. A., & Songer, D. A. (2002). The relationships among childhood abuse, borderline personality and self-harm behavior in psychiatric inpatients. *Violence and Victims, 17,* 49–56.

Sansone, R. A., Levitt, J. L., & Sansone, L. A. (2005). The prevalence of personality disorders among those with eating disorders. *Eating Disorders: The Journal of Treatment and Prevention, 13,* 7–21.

Sansone, R. A., Wiederman, M. W., & Sansone, L. A. (2000). The prevalence of borderline personality disorder among individuals with obesity: A critical review of the literature. *Eating Behaviors, 1,* 93–104.

Schmidt, S. R. (2002). Personality Assessment Inventory profiles of therapy-seeking women with childhood sexual abuse histories. *Dissertation Abstracts International, 63,* 2074B.

Service, N. M. (1995). Correlates of childhood sexual abuse in adult women outpatients. *Dissertation Abstracts International, 56,* 1710B.

Shea, M. T., Zlotnick, C., & Weisberg, R. B. (1999). Commonality and specificity of personality disorder profiles in subjects with trauma histories. *Journal of Personality Disorders, 13,* 199–210.

Sheahan, T. C. (2001). Predictive variables in the development of Axis II personality traits in childhood sexual abuse survivors. *Dissertation Abstracts International, 61,* 6721B.

Silk, K. R., Lee, S., Hill, E. M., & Lohr, N. E. (1995). Borderline personality disorder symptoms and severity of sexual abuse. *American Journal of Psychiatry, 152,* 1059–1064.

Steiger, H., Jabalpurwala, S., & Champagne, J. (1996). Axis II comorbidity and developmental adversity in bulimia nervosa. *Journal of Nervous and Mental Disease, 184,* 555–560.

Timmerman, I. G. H., & Emmelkamp, P. M. G. (2001). The relationship between traumatic experiences, dissociation, and borderline personality pathology among male forensic patients and prisoners. *Journal of Personality Disorders, 15,* 136–149.

Trull, T. J. (2001). Structural relations between borderline personality disorder features and putative etiological correlates. *Journal of Abnormal Psychology, 110,* 471–481.

Vitousek, K. M., & Stumpf, R. E. (2005). Difficulties in the assessment of personality traits and disorders in eating disordered individuals. *Eating Disorders: The Journal of Treatment and Prevention, 13,* 37–60.

Warren, M. K. (1996). Exploring the causal link between childhood sexual abuse, contextual factors, and borderline personality disorder: A path analytic model. *Dissertation Abstracts International, 56,* 5787B.

Windle, M., Windle, R. C., Scheidt, D. M., & Miller, G. B. (1995). Physical and sexual abuse and associated mental disorders among alcoholic inpatients. *American Journal of Psychiatry, 152,* 1322–1328.

Yatsko, C. K. (1996). Etiological theories of borderline personality disorder: A comparative multivariate study. *Dissertation Abstracts International, 56,* 4628B.

Zanarini, M. C., Dubo, E. D., Lewis, R. E., & Williams, A. A. (1997). Childhood factors associated with the development of borderline personality disorder. In M. C. Zanarini (Ed.), *Role of sexual abuse in the etiology of borderline personality disorder* (pp. 29–44). Washington, DC: American Psychiatric Press.

Zanarini, M. C., & Frankenburg, F. R. (1997). Pathways to the development of borderline personality disorder. *Journal of Personality Disorders, 11,* 93–104.

Zanarini, M. C., Williams, A. A., Lewis, R. E., Reich, R. B., Vera, S. C., Marino, M. F., et al. (1997). Reported pathological childhood experiences associated with the development of borderline personality disorder. *American Journal of Psychiatry, 154,* 1101–1106.

Zanarini, M. C., Yong, L., Frankenburg, F. R., Hennen, J., Reich, D. B., Marino, M. F., et al. (2002). Severity of reported childhood sexual abuse and its relationship to severity of borderline psychopathology and psychosocial impairment among borderline inpatients. *Journal of Nervous and Mental Disease, 190,* 381–387.

Zlotnick, C., Mattia, J., & Zimmerman, M. (2001). Clinical features of survivors of sexual abuse with major depression. *Child Abuse and Neglect, 25,* 357–367.

Assessment

Clinical Assessment of Personality Disorders

STEPHANIE D. STEPP, MA
REBECCA SCHWARTZ, BA
MARIKA SOLHAN, BS
TIMOTHY J. TRULL, PHD

The assessment of personality disorders (PDs) can be a challenging task for clinicians. Not only must the clinician comprehensively evaluate the patient for the presence of the many symptoms of the individual PDs that are presented in the *Diagnostic and Statistical Manual of Mental Disorders–Text Revision* (*DSM–IV–TR*) (American Psychiatric Association [APA], 2000) but the clinician must also determine whether the symptoms are characteristic of the patient's long-term functioning, reflect the patient's functioning across a variety of personal and social contexts, and cause clinically significant impairment or distress. Furthermore, the clinician must determine that the presenting symptoms suggesting personality pathology are not better accounted for by other psychiatric disorders. Clearly, the assessment of PDs can be both daunting and taxing.

   In this chapter, we provide an overview of several measures that are available to the clinician, each of which may provide useful information for the assessment of personality pathology in patients. But, before embarking on this survey, we must make a few general comments. First, it is worth emphasizing that unstructured clinical interviews, although comfortable for the clinician, should not be used to diagnose PDs. Evidence clearly shows that diagnoses based on this traditional method are not reliable (Garb, 2005). So, what methods should the clinician use?

Like others (e.g., Widiger & Samuel, 2005), we advocate a two-step approach to the assessment of PDs. The first step is to administer a self-report inventory that targets maladaptive personality traits. If, based on the results from the inventory, personality pathology is suspected, the clinician should then proceed to administer a semistructured diagnostic interview to confirm PD diagnoses and symptoms. This two-step approach confers several advantages. First, PD evaluations from both self-report inventories and semistructured diagnostic interviews are much more reliable and valid than those from unstructured clinical interviews. Second, administering a self-report inventory, initially, to screen for personality pathology can save valuable time for the clinician. Semistructured interviews can take an hour or more to administer, and it is not efficient to conduct this type of interview assessment with every patient. Because not every patient will exhibit clinically significant personality pathology, the two-step procedure is helpful in identifying those patients who are most likely to receive an Axis II diagnosis. The final advantage of this approach is that the semistructured Axis II interview is recognized as the best way to arrive at the *DSM–IV–TR* PD diagnosis. These diagnostic interviews formally assess the PD criteria, instruct the patient to report only those symptoms that are characteristic of long-term functioning, and solicit examples that will allow the clinician to determine the clinical significance of the symptoms as well as the pervasiveness of these across contexts.

Practice Point

A two-step approach to the assessment of PDs includes first administering a self-report inventory (for screening purposes) and then, if necessary, following up with a semistructured diagnostic interview.

We now turn to a survey of self-report questionnaires that might be used to screen patients for significant personality pathology, the first step in the procedure we previously outlined.

SELF-REPORT INVENTORIES

Self-report inventories are a popular method for assessing PDs and offer many advantages (Widiger & Samuel, 2005). Scores from these inventories are reliable over time and reasonably valid, at least in identifying the general presence of a PD. Furthermore, these inventories are easy to administer and score, and normative data exist to aid in the interpretation of scores. The accuracy of the information obtained from self-report inventories, however, may be compromised at times by negative self-presentation or inadequate insight—two features frequently exhibited by individuals with PDs. Therefore, diagnosing PDs on the basis solely of self-report measures is not advised.

Instead, self-report assessments are most useful when combined with semistructured interviews, to screen for possible PD symptoms prior to the administration of the interview or to augment the information gained from the interview (Widiger & Samuel, 2005). Although many self-report inventories for PDs exist, here we review four of the most commonly used inventories: the Personality Assessment Inventory (PAI) (Morey, 1991), the Morey MMPI Personality Disorder Scales (Colligan, Morey, & Offord, 1994; Morey, Waugh, & Blashfield, 1985), the Millon Clinical Multiaxial Inventory–III (MCMI–III) (Millon, Davis, & Millon, 1997), and the Personality Disorder Questionnaire (PDQ–4) (Hyler, 1994). Scores from each of these inventories have been shown to be reliable and valid.

The Personality Assessment Inventory

The PAI (Morey, 1991) was developed to assess adult personality and a variety of psychopathology symptoms. This self-report measure consists of 344 items and is organized into 11 clinical scales, 4 validity scales, 5 treatment consideration scales, and 2 interpersonal scales. The PAI contains two clinical scales that directly measure maladaptive personality features. The Borderline Features (BOR) clinical scale consists of 4 subscales that assess personality features relevant to a diagnosis of borderline PD, including affective instability, identity problems, negative relationships, and impulsive self-harm behaviors. Elevated BOR scores indicate an individual with clinically significant borderline features, although not necessarily a diagnosis of borderline PD (Morey, 1991). The Antisocial Features (ANT) clinical scale consists of three subscales, assessing antisocial behaviors, egocentricity, and stimulus-seeking. Elevated ANT scores are most common in self-centered, impulsive individuals with little sympathy for others (Morey, 1991). The other PAI clinical scales include Somatic Complaints, Anxiety, Anxiety-Related Disorders, Depression, Mania, Paranoia, Schizophrenia, Alcohol Problems, and Drug Problems.

The four validity scales of the PAI are designed to detect inconsistent or atypical patterns of response and are sensitive to both positive and negative impression management (Morey, 1991). The PAI also contains five scales that assess important issues relevant to clinical treatment, including verbal and physical aggression, suicidal ideation, life stressors, the availability and quality of the examinee's support network, and the examinee's motivation and attitudes toward change in treatment (Morey, 1991). Finally, the PAI contains two scales related to interpersonal functioning, dominance, and warmth.

Morey MMPI Personality Disorder Scales

The Morey MMPI Personality Disorder Scales (Colligan et al., 1994; Morey et al., 1985) assess the *DSM–III* features of 11 PDs in adults. These 11 scales originally consisted of items from the Minnesota Multiphasic Personality Inventory (MMPI) and were revised in 1994 after the release of the MMPI–2 scales. Normative data were also provided at the time of revision (Colligan et al., 1994). Of the 11 scales created, the Borderline, Antisocial, and Dependent scales are the most effective at distinguishing between people with these PDs and nondisordered individuals; the other scales are best used for their negative predictive power as conservative screening tools (Castlebury, Hilsenroth, Handler, & Durham, 1997; Colligan et al., 1994).

Millon Clinical Multiaxial Inventory–III

The MCMI–III (Millon, Davis, & Millon, 1997) is a 175-item, self-report instrument designed for the diagnostic screening and clinical assessment of Axis I and Axis II pathology in a clinical population. The MCMI–III includes 14 scales that assess Axis II PDs from the *DSM–III–R* (APA, 1987) (e.g., masochistic, borderline, histrionic) and *DSM–IV* (APA, 1994), 8 scales that assess structural and functional domains of personality pathology (e.g., expressive acts, object representations, mood and temperament), and 10 scales that assess Axis I clinical syndromes (e.g., dysthymia, post-traumatic stress disorder, delusional disorder). It is important to note that the MCMI–III better assesses personality pathology from Millon's theoretical model than from the *DSM–IV* diagnostic categories, and it typically yields a high false-positive rate (Kaye & Shea, 2000). Therefore, like other inventories we discuss, the MCMI–III is best used as a screening measure for personality and psychopathology.

Personality Disorder Questionnaire–4

The PDQ–4 (Hyler, 1994) assesses PDs with 100 true–false items that directly correspond to the *DSM–IV* diagnostic criteria. Each PD is scored as present or absent, based on the total number of criteria endorsed. Additional advantages of the PDQ–4 include its brevity and low cost of administration. A clinical significance scale section asks patients how long the endorsed traits or behaviors have been present, what situations they occur in, and whether the traits or behaviors cause problems or are distressing. As with many self-report measures of personality pathology, the PDQ–4 is very sensitive and yields a high false-positive rate (Kaye & Shea, 2000). Therefore, despite the attempt to establish chronicity, pervasiveness, and clinical significance, it is best used as a screening method in conjunction with a semistructured interview when determining diagnoses.

SEMISTRUCTURED DIAGNOSTIC INTERVIEWS

We now turn to a second integral component of personality assessment—semistructured diagnostic interviews, which can be used to confirm *DSM–IV–TR* PD diagnoses. Semistructured interviews ask standard questions and then prompt patients to provide examples about each item. Interviewers can also probe further if a patient's responses are unclear and observational data obtained during the interview can inform diagnostic conceptualizations. It is important to keep in mind that interviewees may be reluctant to endorse items if answering in the affirmative leads to more questions. Interviewers should also be aware that the transparency of some interviews might lead to manipulation or distortion (see Rogers, 2001). However, studies have shown that employing a semistructured interview increases the likelihood that a reliable diagnosis will occur (Widiger & Samuel, 2005).

We now review five major semistructured interviews used to assess PDs based on *DSM–IV–TR* criteria (APA, 2000). We want to point out, however, that interviews also exist to assess a specific PD, such as the Revised Diagnostic Interview for Borderlines (Gunderson & Zanarini, 1992) and the Revised Psychopathy Checklist (Hare, 2003), which will be of interest to those wanting more comprehensive information related to a single disorder. Details regarding the reliability and validity of the scores and diagnoses derived from all of these interviews are available elsewhere (e.g., Kaye & Shea, 2000; McDermut & Zimmerman, 2005; Rogers, 2001).

Structured Clinical Interview for DSM–IV *Axis II Disorders*

The Structured Clinical Interview for *DSM–IV* Axis II Disorders (SCID–II) (First, Gibbon, Spitzer, Williams, & Benjamin, 1997) is designed to assess the 10 *DSM–IV* PDs according to their respective criteria. Administration of the SCID–II is a two-part procedure. Respondents first complete a 119-item, self-report questionnaire (SCID–II–Q) (Spitzer, Williams, Gibbon, & First, 1990), whose items correspond to diagnostic criteria for each of the PDs in the *DSM–IV*. Next, individuals whose self-report questionnaires indicate the presence of particular personality features are administered the corresponding portions of the SCID–II. The items of the SCID–II are organized by diagnosis, and each item is scored on a 3-point scale. A major advantage of the SCID–II is that it is easily administered (i.e., criteria grouped by diagnosis and scored in the same direction). Administration time is 30 to 45 minutes.

Structured Interview for DSM–IV *Personality*

The Structured Interview for *DSM–IV* Personality (SIDP–IV) (Pfohl, Blum, & Zimmerman, 1997) is composed of 160 items (rated on a

4-point scale) designed to correspond with specific PD criteria. The SIDP–IV has been used with clinical as well as nonclinical samples and also provides the option for an additional informant (e.g., a family member) to provide collateral data. Items are organized into 10 topical sections (e.g., interests and activities) instead of being organized by disorder. Therefore, this interview has a natural flow and may be less vulnerable to response sets. Also included are items related to the Axis II optional diagnoses, which can be skipped to reduce administration time. Administration time is usually between 60 and 90 minutes. Given that the SIDP–IV relies on the assessment of nonverbal behaviors by interviewer observation, advanced clinical interviewing skills are necessary.

Personality Disorder Interview–IV

The Personality Disorder Interview–IV (PDI–IV) (Widiger, Mangine, Corbitt, Ellis, & Thomas, 1995) consists of 317 items relating to specific diagnostic criteria for the 10 established and 2 proposed PDs in the *DSM–IV*. Each criterion is rated on a 3-point scale. Items are organized in two distinct formats: a thematic format, which groups items according to nine themes (e.g., attitudes toward self), and a disorder format, which groups items according to *DSM–IV* diagnoses. Administration time is approximately 2 hours. Two benefits of the PDI–IV are as follows: (a) the interview values in-depth questioning of the patient, and (b) the manual provides a thorough discussion of the Axis II disorders. However, unlike the SIDP–IV, the PDI–IV places less emphasis on collateral data and gives no guidelines regarding the incorporation of data from multiple informants.

Diagnostic Interview for *DSM* Personality Disorders–IV

The Diagnostic Interview for *DSM* Personality Disorders–IV (DIPD–IV) (Zanarini, Frankenburg, Sickel, & Yong, 1996) consists of 252 items that are scored on a 3-point scale and are organized by disorder. Follow-up questions are also included. The DIPD–IV has received less research (Rogers, 2001) relative to other semistructured interviews.

International Personality Disorder Examination

The International Personality Disorder Examination (IPDE) (Loranger, 1999a) was created to assess Axis II disorders according to both *DSM* and International Classification of Diseases (ICD–10) criteria. The IPDE is composed of two modules: (a) the IPDE *DSM–IV* module and (b) the IPDE ICD–10 module. The *DSM–IV* module closely resembles the original PDE. The ICD–10 module assesses the nine ICD PDs and has been translated into several languages. Administration time is

3 hours for both modules. In addition, two IPDE screening measures are available: the IPDE–Screen and the IPDE–Screening Questionnaire (Loranger, 1999b).

CLASSIFYING PDS DIMENSIONALLY

Before concluding, we feel it is worthwhile to consider several additional measures that may be used to assess personality traits that are believed to underlie the *DSM–IV–TR* PDs, specifically, and personality pathology, in general. Although the preceding measures center on a categorical approach to diagnosis (i.e., a disorder is present or not), dimensional approaches to defining and classifying personality pathology are gaining momentum, and these approaches are likely to be considered in future revisions of the *DSM* (Trull, 2005; Trull & Durrett, 2005).

Measures that assess PDs from a dimensional perspective include the Schedule for Nonadaptive and Adaptive Personality Functioning (SNAP) (Clark, 1993), Dimensional Assessment of Personality Disorder Pathology (DAPP–BQ) (Livesley & Jackson, in press), Revised NEO Personality Inventory (NEO–PI–R) (Costa & McCrae, 1992), and Temperament and Character Inventory (TCI) (Cloninger, Przybeck, Svarkic, & Wetzel, 1994). These measures can be characterized as being developed to assess either normal personality traits or personality pathology. It is surprising that instruments that were developed to measure normal personality functioning have been used to assess personality pathology, and much convergence exists between the measures developed from different traditions (see Clark & Harrison, 2001; Widiger & Coker, 2002). The degree to which the assessor is concerned with adaptive versus maladaptive personality functioning can guide the selection of the appropriate assessment instrument.

Given that the current *DSM* diagnostic manual defines PDs as categorical constructs, why might a clinician be interested in conducting an assessment from a dimensional perspective? First, even in the *DSM–IV–TR* (APA, 2000), PDs are classified as extreme variants of maladaptive traits. Second, given the more limited validity and reliability of the PDs as categorical constructs, some researchers have argued for focusing assessment efforts on fundamental personality traits rather than on diagnostic constructs (e.g., Widiger & Frances, 2002). Third, dimensional models of personality can identify fundamental traits underlying comorbid conditions, informing etiological theories and suggesting possible points of intervention (Trull & Durrett, 2005). Last, clinicians sometimes find that the current classification scheme does not provide accurate coverage of personality pathology (Westen & Arkowitz-Westen, 1998). Dimensional models retain important information about subthreshold traits and symptoms that could warrant clinical attention.

Practice Point
Assessing PDs from a dimensional perspective can provide more comprehensive information about patients' personality functioning, highlighting maladaptive personality traits deserving of clinical attention.

Dimensional Measures of Normal-Range Personality Traits

NEO–PI–R. The NEO–PI–R (Costa & McCrae, 1992) is a self-report measure that assesses the personality traits of the five-factor model of personality. These robust factors have been labeled Neuroticism, Extraversion, Openness to Experience, Agreeableness, and Conscientiousness (McCrae & John, 1992). This measure consists of 240 statements for which participants rate their level of agreement on a 5-point scale. Each of the five broad domains is divided into six facets, and each facet is assessed by eight items. Administration time is approximately 40 to 50 minutes. Much research has been conducted on the validity of the NEO–PI–R in assessing PDs (e.g., Trull, Widiger, Lynam, & Costa, 2003; Widiger & Coker, 2002). However, only limited validity scales are included in this measure, making it more difficult to assess an examinee's level of motivation and willingness to disclose personal information. As a way to address this shortcoming, Trull and Widiger (1997) developed a semistructured interview, the Structured Interview for the Five Factor Model (SIFFM), which allows the assessor the opportunity to ask follow-up questions about each item; the SIFFM assesses both normal and maladaptive variants of five-factor model personality traits.

TCI. The TCI (Cloninger et al., 1994) was developed to assess Cloninger's (1986) biosocial model of personality, which consists of four factors that are posited to be genetically determined: Novelty-Seeking, Harm Avoidance, Reward Dependence, and Persistence. These factors are hypothesized to be stable throughout the life span and have been found to have a significant heritable component (Stallings, Hewitt, Cloninger, Heath, & Eaves, 1996). On the other hand, the three character dimensions, Self-Directedness, Cooperativeness, and Self-Transcendence, are hypothesized to be heavily influenced by environmental factors. This measure contains 226 true–false items. Administration time is approximately 35 to 45 minutes. Low self-directedness and low cooperativeness have been shown to predict the presence of any PD, suggesting that this measure might be an effective screening tool for personality pathology (e.g., Bayon, Hill, Svrakic, Przybeck, & Cloninger, 1996).

Dimensional Measures of Personality Pathology

SNAP. The SNAP (Clark, 1993) is a 375-item, self-report questionnaire that uses a true–false format and evaluates personality characteristics and general temperament. The SNAP contains 3 higher order temperament scales, 12 trait scales, and 6 validity scales. In addition, this questionnaire includes 13 diagnostic scales to assess PDs as outlined with the criteria from the *DSM–III–R* (APA, 1987). This measure was constructed by compiling lists of descriptors of *DSM* and non-*DSM* PDs and related Axis I pathology. These items were then sorted by clinicians into clusters, and these clusters were subjected to factor analysis. This method yielded 22 clusters, and items were generated to assess each of these clusters. Administration times range from 45 to 75 minutes. Scores from this measure have also demonstrated robust relations with interview-based measures of personality pathology. This is, perhaps, not surprising given the manner in which the items were developed for the SNAP.

DAPP–BQ. The DAPP–BQ (Livesley & Jackson, in press) is a 290-item, self-report questionnaire that includes 18 scales of PD symptoms (e.g., Anxiousness, Impulsivity, Compulsivity), which can be organized into four higher order domains: Emotional Dysregulation, Dissocial Behavior, Inhibitedness, and Compulsivity (Livesley, Jang, & Vernon, 1998). The questionnaire takes approximately 60 to 75 minutes to administer. The DAPP–BQ and the SNAP were created in a similar fashion. The authors developed the DAPP–BQ by creating lists of trait descriptors and behavioral acts that typified each of the diagnostic PD categories listed in the *DSM–III* and *DSM–III–R*. Clinicians then rated these descriptors as to the degree of relevance for each of the diagnostic categories. Using these ratings, the authors arrived at the final 18 scales through a series of analyses. The DAPP–BQ scores are internally consistent, are stable over time, and have demonstrated convergent validity with other self-report measures of personality traits and personality pathology (e.g., Bagge & Trull, 2003; Clark, Livesley, Schroeder, & Irish, 1996).

CLOSING COMMENTS

In conclusion, we recommend a two-step strategy to assess PDs. First, the clinician should administer a self-report inventory that assesses personality traits and behaviors that are known to be associated with PDs. Either the PD self-report inventories or the dimensional measures reviewed previously can be readily used for this purpose. If, on the basis of the results of this screening, there is some suspicion that a PD or significant personality pathology is present, the clinician should administer a semistructured diagnostic interview for PDs, for which we have described several examples. This two-step strategy will ultimately save the clinician time and provide a diagnostic formulation that can be effectively used for treatment planning.

NOTE

Please address all correspondence to Timothy J. Trull, PhD, University of Missouri–Columbia, Department of Psychological Sciences, 210 McAlester Hall, Columbia, MO, 65211; telephone: 573-882-0332; fax: 573-882-7710; e-mail: TrullT@missouri.edu.

REFERENCES

American Psychiatric Association. (1987). *Diagnostic and statistical manual of mental disorders* (3rd ed., Revised). Washington, DC: Author.

American Psychiatric Association. (1994). *Diagnostic and statistical manual of mental disorders* (4th ed.). Washington, DC: Author.

American Psychiatric Association. (2000). *Diagnostic and statistical manual of mental disorders* (4th ed., Text Revision). Washington, DC: Author.

Bagge, C., & Trull, T. J. (2003). DAPP–BQ: Factor structure and relations to personality disorder symptoms in a non-clinical sample. *Journal of Personality Disorders, 17,* 19–32.

Bayon, C., Hill, K., Svrakic, D. M., Przybeck, T. R., & Cloninger, C. R. (1996). Dimensional assessment of personality in an outpatient sample: Relations of the systems of Millon and Cloninger. *Journal of Psychiatric Research, 30,* 341–352.

Castlebury, F. D., Hilsenroth, M. J., Handler, L., & Durham, T. W. (1997). Use of the MMPI–2 Personality Disorder Scales in the assessment of *DSM–IV* antisocial, borderline, and narcissistic personality disorders. *Assessment, 4,* 155–168.

Clark, L. A. (1993). *Manual for the Schedule for Nonadaptive and Adaptive Personality.* Minneapolis: University of Minnesota Press.

Clark, L. A., & Harrison, J. A. (2001). Assessment instruments. In W. J. Livesley (Ed.), *Handbook of personality disorders: Theory, research, and treatment* (pp. 277–306). New York: Guilford.

Clark, L. A., Livesley, W. J., Schroeder, M. L., & Irish, S. (1996). The structure of maladaptive personality traits: Convergent validity between two systems. *Psychological Assessment, 8,* 294–303.

Cloninger, C. R. (1986). A unified biosocial theory of personality and its role in the development of anxiety states. *Psychiatric Developments, 3,* 167–226.

Cloninger, C. R., Przybeck, T. R., Svrakic, D. M., & Wetzel, R. D. (1994). *The Temperament and Character Inventory (TCI): A guide to its development and use.* St. Louis, MO: Center for Psychobiology of Personality, Washington University.

Colligan, R. C., Morey, L. C., & Offord, K. P. (1994). The MMPI/MMPI–2 personality disorder scales: Contemporary norms for adults and adolescents. *Journal of Clinical Psychology, 50,* 168–200.

Costa, P. T., & McCrae, R. R. (1992). *Revised NEO Personality Inventory (NEO–PI–R) and NEO Five-Factor Inventory (NEO–FFI), professional manual.* Odessa, FL: Psychological Assessment Resources.

First, M. B., Gibbon, M., Spitzer, R. L., Williams, J. B. W., & Benjamin, L. S. (1997). *User's guide for the structured clinical interview for* DSM–IV *Axis II personality disorders.* Washington, DC: American Psychiatric Press.

Garb, H. N. (2005). Clinical judgment and decision making. *Annual Review of Clinical Psychology, 1,* 67–89.

Gunderson, J. G., & Zanarini, M. C. (1992). *Revised Diagnostic Interview for Borderlines (DIB–R).* Boston: Harvard Medical School.

Hare, R. D. (2003). *Hare Psychopathy Checklist–Revised PCL-R: 2nd edition; Technical manual.* Toronto: Multi-Health Systems.

Hyler, S. E. (1994). *Personality Diagnostic Questionnaire–4.* New York: New York State Psychiatric Institute.

Kaye, A. L., & Shea, M. T. (2000). Personality disorders, personality traits, and defense mechanism measures. In A. J. Rush, H. A. Pincus, M. B. First, D. Blacker, J. Endicott, S. J. Keith, et al. (Eds.), *Handbook of psychiatric measures* (pp. 713–749). Washington, DC: American Psychiatric Association.

Livesley, W. J., & Jackson, D. N. (in press). *Manual for the Dimensional Assessment of Personality Pathology—Basic Questionnaire.* Port Huron, MI: Sigma Press.

Livesley, W. J., Jang, K. L., & Vernon, P. A. (1998). Phenotypic and genotypic structure of traits delineating personality disorder. *Archives of General Psychiatry, 55,* 941–948.

Loranger, A. W. (1999a). *International Personality Disorder Examination (IPDE).* Odessa, FL: Psychological Assessment Resources.

Loranger, A. W. (1999b). *International Personality Disorder Examination (IPDE) Screening Questionnaire.* Odessa, FL: Psychological Assessment Resources.

McCrae, R. R., & John, O. P. (1992). An introduction to the five-factor model and its applications. *Journal of Personality, 60,* 175–215.

McDermut, W., & Zimmerman, M. (2005). Assessment instruments and standardized evaluation. In J. M. Oldham, A. E. Skodol, & D. S. Bender (Eds.), *Textbook of personality disorders* (pp. 89–101). Washington, DC: American Psychiatric Publishing.

Millon, T., Davis, R., & Millon, C. (1997). *Millon Clinical Multiaxial Inventory–III (MCMI–III) manual* (2nd ed.). Minneapolis, MN: National Computer Systems.

Morey, L. C. (1991). *Personality Assessment Inventory: Professional manual.* Odessa, FL: Psychological Assessment Resources.

Morey, L. C., Waugh, M. H., & Blashfield, R. K. (1985). MMPI scales for *DSM–III* personality disorders: Their derivation and correlates. *Journal of Personality Assessment, 49,* 245–251.

Pfohl, B., Blum, N., & Zimmerman, M. (1997). *Structured Interview for DSM–IV Personality.* Washington, DC: American Psychiatric Press.

Rogers, R. (2001). *Handbook of diagnostic and structured interviewing.* New York: Guilford.

Spitzer, R. L., Williams, J. B. W., Gibbon, M., & First, M. B. (1990). *SCID–II questionnaire.* Washington, DC: American Psychiatric Press.

Stallings, M. C., Hewitt, J. K., Cloninger, C. R., Heath, A. C., & Eaves, L. J. (1996). Genetic and environmental structure of the Tridimensional Personality Questionnaire: Three or four temperament dimensions? *Journal of Personality and Social Psychology, 70,* 127–140.

Trull, T. J. (2005). Dimensional models of personality disorder: Coverage and cutoffs. *Journal of Personality Disorders, 19,* 262–283.

Trull, T. J., & Durrett, C. (2005). Categorical and dimensional models of personality disorders. *Annual Review of Clinical Psychology, 1,* 355–380.

Trull, T. J., & Widiger, T. A. (1997). *Structured Interview for the Five-Factor Model of Personality (SIFFM): Professional manual*. Odessa, FL: Psychological Assessment Resources.

Trull, T. J., Widiger, T. A., Lynam, D. R., & Costa, P. T. (2003). Borderline personality disorder from the perspective of general personality functioning. *Journal of Abnormal Psychology, 112*, 193–202.

Westen, D., & Arkowitz-Westen, L. (1998). Limitations of Axis II in diagnosing personality pathology in clinical practice. *American Journal of Psychiatry, 155*, 1767–1771.

Widiger, T. A., & Coker, L. A. (2002). Assessing personality disorders. In J. N. Butcher (Ed.), *Clinical personality assessment: Practical approaches* (2nd ed., pp. 407–434). New York: Oxford University Press.

Widiger, T. A., & Frances, A. J. (2002). Toward a dimensional model for the personality disorders. In P. T. Costa & T. A. Widiger (Eds.), *Personality disorders and the five factor model of personality* (2nd ed., pp. 23–44). Washington, DC: American Psychological Association.

Widiger, T. A., Mangine, S., Corbitt, E. M., Ellis, C. G., & Thomas, G. V. (1995). *Personality Disorder Interview–IV: A semi-structured interview for the assessment of personality disorders; Professional manual*. Odessa, FL: Psychological Assessment Resources.

Widiger, T. A., & Samuel, D. B. (2005). Evidence-based assessment of personality disorders. *Psychological Assessment, 17*, 278–287.

Zanarini, M. C., Frankenburg, F. R., Sickel, A. E., & Yong, L. (1996). *The Diagnostic Interview for DSM–IV Personality Disorders (DIPD–IV)*. Belmont, MA: McLean Hospital.

6

Difficulties in the Assessment of Personality Traits and Disorders in Individuals With Eating Disorders

KELLY M. VITOUSEK, PHD
ROXANNA E. STUMPF

Among the diverse clinical pictures seen in the eating disorder (ED) field, two case summaries make useful referents for a discussion of problems in assessing personality:

Patient A presented as a 15-year-old with a 3-year history of anorexia nervosa, restricting subtype. At interview, her BMI was 17.2 after partial weight restoration during her third inpatient admission. She denied any distress or dysfunction, with the exception of dismay about being "too fat"—a problem she was already working assiduously to correct. With pride, she characterized herself as strong willed and perfectionistic—the sort of person who accomplished every goal she set out to achieve. She outlined patterns of behavior, stretching back to childhood, that matched criteria for obsessive-compulsive personality disorder. Spontaneously, she articulated a close correspondence between her basic nature and her ED—she had *always* liked to do things "just right" and meant to apply those exacting standards to the control of eating and weight.

Patient B began treatment in our program at age 16. Her referral diagnoses from two previous therapists and five hospitalizations included anorexia nervosa, binge-purge subtype, major depressive disorder with psychotic features, borderline personality disorder (BPD), and narcissistic personality disorder. At presentation, she was alternately fasting and binge eating, vomiting several times a day, and abusing laxatives, diet pills, and psychotropic medication. She self-injured by cutting and burning, and she had made one serious suicide attempt. During the intake session, Patient B was emotionally labile and expressive, with bursts of anger and sobbing. She referred to herself as "evil" and "unworthy"; it was not difficult to see, she said bitterly, why her family and therapists had abandoned her as a hopeless case.

These two profiles suggest a number of reasons for attending to personality variables in patients with EDs: (a) the strong impression of continuity between symptoms and stable aspects of the self, (b) the high rate of Axis II comorbidity, (c) the apparent connection between specific personality traits and ED subtypes, and (d) the possibility that personality pathology predicts poor treatment response. Yet the examples also hint at the difficulties we might encounter when we try to make sense of what we see in our patients—particularly with the clarification that Patients A and B are the same individual, evaluated on two occasions 1 year apart. In the period that elapsed between our first and second glimpses of Patient A/B, she appeared to have undergone not only a shift in symptoms but also a startling change in personality.

A third sketch, 6 years later, showed a young woman substantially altered from both of these portraits—a normal eater at a normal weight, out of therapy and off medication, who was successfully balancing graduate school and an active social life. She had not, of course, become a wholly different person in the process of recovery, any more than she had swapped her "anorexic" attributes for a new set of "bulimic" traits when her symptoms shifted during midadolescence. From the perspective gained through working with this patient for 2 years following the second assessment, our best guess is that personality variables did contribute to the development, maintenance, and form of her disorder (and also played a central role in her decision to reject it). At some points along the way, however, stable personality traits were so overwhelmed by the transient effects of her ED symptoms that they were all too easy to misidentify.

Although few patients show such radical changes in apparent personality, the assessment of EDs is routinely complicated by at least some of the factors that converged in this case. These factors include the patient's young age at onset and assessment; the hardwired effects of semistarvation and refeeding; the instability of ED subtypes; the deliberate concealment of symptoms at the initial evaluation and their exaggeration during the second assessment; the acute influences of depression, loss of control, and repeated hospitalization; exposure to clinicians' models and other patients' symptomatic behavior; and subtle intrusions of eating and weight concerns into evidently unrelated domains. In the first section of this review, we outline common difficulties in personality assessment across psychiatric populations, commenting on interactions between these general issues and distinctive features of the EDs. In the second section, we focus more closely on a subset of special challenges in this area.

GENERAL PROBLEMS IN PERSONALITY ASSESSMENT

Problems With the Construct of Personality Disorders

Many experts question the basic assumptions of Axis II diagnosis, noting the false dichotomy implied between healthy and maladaptive personalities, weak support for the presumption of stability over time, and lack of correspondence between clinically and empirically derived symptom clusters (e.g., Clark, Livesley, & Morey, 1997; Widiger & Costa, 1994).

A central focus of discussion is whether the categorical system should be replaced or supplemented by a dimensional approach that provides continuous data about core traits (e.g., Clark et al., 1997; Livesley, Schroeder, Jackson, & Jang, 1994; Oldham & Skodol, 2000; Widiger & Sanderson, 2000; Wonderlich & Mitchell, 2001). Dimensional assessment enhances consistency across raters and over time by eliminating the artificial cutoff point marking the presence or absence of a personality disorder (PD). A corollary is that it better represents the combination of continuity and change associated with the process of recovery, during which many patients slip below PD thresholds while retaining elevated scores on related trait measures. The dimensional model also avoids the awkward practice of assigning multiple Axis II labels to individual patients. In the ED population, it is particularly common for those with mixed anorexic and bulimic features (such as Patient A/B at the second assessment point) to cross cluster boundaries as well as the fuzzy lines between individual PDs, receiving diagnoses from both the "dramatic, emotional, or erratic" and the "anxious or fearful" clusters.

Practice Point

Dimensional assessment provides a clearer and more consistent view of personality variables over time than the presence or absence of Axis II diagnoses.

Although this debate is often framed as if the decision between models were in itself dichotomous, there have been a number of proposals for integrating the two approaches (e.g., Livesley et al., 1994; Oldham & Skodol, 2000; Widiger, 2000). In keeping with this perspective, recent studies in the ED area have begun to report data derived from both categorical and dimensional strategies (Diaz-Marsa, Carrasco, & Saiz, 2000; Karwautz, Troop, Rabe-Hesketh, Collier, & Treasure, 2003; Rø, Martinsen, Hoffart, Sexton, & Rosenvinge, 2005).

Problems With Criteria

Changes in successive editions of the *Diagnostic and Statistical Manual* (*DSM*) make it difficult to compare samples diagnosed under different rule systems. In the ED field, recent shifts in the specifications for subtyping anorexia nervosa and for identifying obsessive-compulsive disorder and obsessive-compulsive personality disorder are particularly relevant (Grilo, 2004; Halmi, Kleifield, Braun, & Sunday, 1999; Speranza et al., 2001; Sunday et al., 2001). Another common problem is that partial overlap in criterion sets can stack the deck for comorbidity between pairs of Axis I and Axis II disorders. One obvious example is binge eating, which is both a sign of impulsivity in BPD and a frequent or required symptom of bulimia nervosa, anorexia nervosa, binge-purge subtype, binge eating disorder, and atypical eating disorders. It is easy to avoid double-dipping in such straightforward cases: patients with a clinical ED must meet criteria for a BPD diagnosis without reference to their erratic eating. More subtle redundancies between Axis I and Axis II criteria also occur, however, and require higher levels of judgment from evaluators; some examples are noted in subsequent sections.

Problems With Measures

Questionnaire measures yield inflated estimates of PD prevalence in both normal and clinical samples (Zimmerman, 1994), an effect consistently observed in the ED area (O'Brien & Vincent, 2003; Rosenvinge, Martinussen, & Ostensen, 2000; Skodol et al., 1993; Vitousek & Manke, 1994). Semistructured interviews produce more plausible figures, although both self-report and clinician-rated scales overestimate pathology in acutely distressed patients. Trained evaluators can achieve excellent agreement when rating the same session. Mismatches are frequent, however, when patients are reassessed by different raters, after brief intervals, or with different interview schedules (Grilo, McGlashan, & Skodol, 2000; Perry, 1992; van Velzen & Emmelkamp, 1996; Zimmerman, 1994). Low stability over the span of months to years may be more attributable to shortcomings in the construct of PDs than to flaws in the methods used to identify them.

A number of problems arise with reference to trait scales as well. Like PD measures, personality inventories are vulnerable to state effects, some to such an extent that they provide little useful information on patients with EDs at intake (Pryor & Wiederman, 1996). Constructs central to many models of the EDs, such as perfectionism and self-control, may not be represented adequately on available instruments (Shafran, Cooper, & Fairburn, 2002; Shafran & Mansell, 2001). In addition, as with changes in the *DSM*, revisions of widely used measures can reduce the comparability of data sets (e.g., Cumella, Wall, & Kerr-Almeida, 2000; Pryor & Wiederman, 1996).

Problems With Samples and Comparison Groups

Sampling bias and selection criteria. The sites from which participants are drawn and the means through which they are recruited influence the degree of personality disturbance found (Fairburn, Welch, Doll, Davies, & O'Connor, 1997; Perkins, Klump, Iacono, & McGue, 2005; Rosenvinge et al., 2000; Skodol et al., 1993). Clinic patients typically show more comorbidity than cases detected in the community, in part as a function of Berkson's bias (i.e., the increased likelihood that individuals with two disorders will turn up in health care systems as a function of seeking treatment for one or the other) (Berkson, 1946; Galbaud du Fort, Newman, & Bland, 1993). Higher rates of personality pathology are also associated with inpatient versus outpatient samples and with specialized versus general services. Recruitment and selection factors can skew the figures obtained in research projects. For example, obese patients hoping to qualify for bariatric surgery may be motivated to conceal psychopathology, whereas those solicited from psychological treatment programs more readily disclose their distress (Sansone, Wiederman, & Sansone, 2000). Rates of BPD may be lower in patients with EDs accepted for treatment trials if parasuicidal behaviors or substance abuse are used as exclusionary criteria (Wonderlich & Mitchell, 1997); however, the widespread belief that only mild, uncomplicated cases survive prescreening is unfounded in this specialty area (Wilson, 1998).

Practice Point
The frequency and severity of personality pathology in ED samples varies widely across recruitment sources and treatment settings.

Comparison groups. No matter how carefully participants are chosen and assessed, the data they provide cannot be interpreted without reference to appropriate comparison groups. Fifteen years ago, we noted, "This principle is so basic to psychopathology research that it should not be necessary to repeat … [however] the omission of essential control data remains one of the most consistent flaws in contemporary eating disorder research" (Vitousek, Daly, & Heiser, 1991, pp. 658–659). Regrettably, that summary still applies. Many recent studies include no comparison group of any kind, reporting tallies of the PD diagnoses or subscale scores obtained by patients with EDs as if the numbers speak for themselves. Others solicit what might be described as *contrast* rather than comparison groups, made up of "healthy normal" participants vetted for any taint of pathology. Of course individuals with no psychiatric history, mood disturbance, weight problems, or dieting behavior will be found to differ from acutely ill patients with anorexia nervosa or bulimia nervosa in dozens of predictable and statistically significant ways; few of these differences clarify the relationships we are attempting to understand.

In all comorbidity research, troubled patients with EDs must be compared to equally troubled patients who do not have EDs, with the most informative choices varying according to the questions posed (Allison, 1993; Vitousek et al., 1991). The inclusion of psychiatric controls erodes the apparent linkage between EDs and PDs and dispels a number of clinical stereotypes about specific risk factors (e.g., Fairburn, Cooper, Doll, & Welch, 1999; Fairburn et al., 1997; Grilo, Sanislow, Skodol, et al., 2003; Zanarini et al., 1990).

Many crucial questions, however, cannot be examined without the addition of another sort of comparison group that is far more difficult to secure—people who match the restrictive eating behavior and low weight status of patients with EDs without sharing their core psychopathology. The recent phenomenon of caloric restriction for longevity is producing a small number of potential candidates (Vitousek, 2004). Inspired by robust evidence that severe dietary restraint extends life span in animals (Weindruch & Walford, 1988), some individuals are beginning to adopt anorexic regimens and reach anorexic weights for apparently nonanorexic reasons. From an ED perspective, the caloric restriction movement is distressing on many levels; however, it does offer an unprecedented opportunity to disentangle vulnerability factors from the secondary effects of chronic food deprivation (Vitousek, 2004; Vitousek, Gray, & Talesfore, in press; see subsequent section on semistarvation and chaotic eating behavior).

Practice Point

Personality disturbances seen in patients with EDs cannot be interpreted without reference to appropriate comparison groups (including both general psychiatric samples and normal individuals exposed to chronic food deprivation).

Although sampling bias, selection criteria, and comparison groups seem like research rather than clinical concerns, sensitivity to the issues they raise is just as important to assessment in therapeutic settings. As clinicians, we cannot seek out matched psychiatric or semistarving individuals to juxtapose with our patients with EDs. We can, however, develop a constant awareness of context that informs our interpretation of symptoms.

Problems With the Timing of Assessment

By definition, when we characterize the variables we are measuring as personality traits or disorders, we sign on to the assumption that they will be stable over time. It is not enough to establish that patients do (or do not) have serious problems; we are asserting that they have particular kinds of problems that turned up early and will persist indefinitely. The obvious difficulty is that we are sometimes forced to judge these temporally defined phenomena from the glimpses we can catch at one point in time—generally while people are thinking, feeling, and acting least like themselves.

We often judge wrong, and we err in a predictable direction. At intake, state variables such as depression leak into the assessment of traits, so that we infer more enduring personality pathology in people who are acutely distressed than we discern in the same individuals once they begin to feel better. Only about half of those assigned PD diagnoses when first evaluated continue to meet criteria at reassessment (Grilo, McGlashan, & Oldham, 1998; Grilo et al., 2000; McDavid & Pilkonis, 1996; Shea et al., 2002; Shea & Yen, 2003; Zanarini, Frankenburg, Hennen, Reich, & Silk, 2004), although constellations of maladaptive traits prove more stable over time (Grilo et al., 2004). The consistent trend toward "recovery" from PDs is more plausibly attributed to initial overdiagnosis than to the healing power of psychotherapy, particularly because such transformations often occur during the first weeks or months of treatment.

Systematic inquiry into characteristic patterns that preceded the current disturbance reduces this effect (Grilo, 2002; Grilo et al., 1998; Loranger et al., 1991) but does not eliminate it. Clearly, it is insufficient simply to ask patients to refer to their "usual selves." Cognitive research confirms that mood has a biasing effect on the retrieval and reporting of information, so that people represent their prior experience differently when depressed or euthymic. On a clinical level, therapists recognize that patients who make statements such as "I have *always* ..." and "I have *never* ..." may be telling us more about their current affect than the consistency of their behavior over time. As discussed in the subsequent section on age effects, problems are compounded when patients develop an Axis I disorder at a young age or have remained ill for so long that their "usual self" has become a stranger.

The contaminating effect of state variables is nowhere more evident than in the ED field. Hospitalized anorexic patients show significant declines on presumed trait measures subsequent to weight restoration (e.g., Kleifield, Sunday, Hurt, & Halmi, 1994; Leon, Lucas, Colligan, Ferdinande, & Kamp, 1985; Pollice, Kaye, Greeno, & Weltzin, 1997; Rø, Martinsen, Hoffart, & Rosenvinge, 2005; Skoog, Andersen, & Laufer, 1984; Stonehill & Crisp, 1977). In bulimia nervosa and mixed ED samples, signs of PD pathology recede over brief periods of treatment (e.g., Ames-Frankel et al., 1992; Garner et al., 1990; Steiger, Leung, Thibaudeau, Houle, & Ghadirian, 1993). In one study, the percentage of patients classified as borderline fell from 80% at intake to 32% by discharge (Kennedy, McVey, & Katz, 1990); in another, only 22% of inpatients with EDs diagnosed with obsessive-compulsive personality disorder remained above diagnostic threshold by 2-year follow-up (Rø, Martinsen, Hoffart, & Rosenvinge, 2005).

Practice Point

Assessment during the early phases of treatment yields inflated estimates of maladaptive traits and PDs in patients with EDs.

There is conflicting evidence about the extent to which depressed mood accounts for the variance in PD symptoms across patients and over time (e.g., Carroll, Touyz, & Beumont, 1996; Kleifield et al., 1994; Pope, Frankenburg, Hudson, Jonas, & Yurgelun-Todd, 1987). Other (interrelated) contributors include the reversal of starvation effects, control over binging and purging, and resolution of the crisis that sometimes triggers treatment entry. In a prospective study of inpatients with mixed EDs assessed on three occasions from hospitalization through 2-year follow-up, improvements in both ED and general psychiatric symptomatology were found to precede reductions in personality pathology (Rø, Martinsen, Hoffart, Sexton, et al., 2005).

Problems With Informant and Clinician Bias

In contrast to the symptoms of most Axis I disorders, many defining characteristics of PDs must be evaluated from an outside perspective to judge the reasonableness of an individual's responses and gauge the reactions he or she elicits from others (Zimmerman, 1994). Most of us make a bad job of objective self-scrutiny, particularly with reference to sensitive domains or when under the influence of strong emotions. For these reasons, the assessment of personality pathology is a collaborative exercise, requiring input from significant others and critical analysis from a rater or therapist as well as data from the individual whose personality is under review. Unfortunately, these differing perspectives do not always converge on the accurate identification of stable traits. Indeed, the biases that observers bring to the process can compound those contributed by the patient.

In theory, family members make optimal informants about the patient's "usual self," offering the views from outside and over time that are crucial to personality assessment (Tyrer, 1995). Some evidence suggests, however, that family members may be even more prone to overgeneralize from the patient's current condition than the patient (Zimmerman, 1994), in part because they are struggling with powerful state variables of their own in reaction to the patient's symptoms. In one study using a mixed psychiatric sample, 50% of cases diagnosed with PD on the basis of informant accounts proved to be false positives (Walters, Moran, Choudhury, Lee, & Mann, 2004). These effects may be exaggerated in the case of EDs, which are notorious for evoking extreme emotional responses (and dispositional attributions) from family members and professionals alike (Beumont & Vandereycken, 1998; Brotman, Stern, & Herzog, 1984; Kaplan & Garfinkel, 1999).

Practice Point

Clinicians should seek information from multiple sources about stable functioning prior to ED onset.

Bias on the part of clinicians can operate at many stages and levels of assessment. It also varies along a continuum of culpability. Differences in the ways that interviewers pose questions, estimate norms, and set cutting points can sum to sharply discrepant conclusions about the same individual. Although raters can be trained to high levels of agreement within sites, assessment cultures and standards vary across settings (Godt, 2002; Widiger & Costa, 1994). Inevitably, clinicians and researchers develop personal models of the likely association between disorders and presumed causal factors, such as personality traits. In the best-case scenario, these are used as working hypotheses; in the worst-case scenario, they become stereotypes impervious to disconfirming data. At all points along the spectrum, raters tend to have different thresholds for detecting relationships they expect to observe relative to those they deem improbable. In the ED literature, the effect of allegiance to favored models is discernible in an apparent correlation between the forms of personality pathology that interest investigators and the pattern of findings they obtain.

At least within the context of research, bias due to preconceived notions about comorbidity can be prevented by ensuring blindness to Axis I status. In the ED field, however, it is both difficult and dangerous to keep raters in the dark. Weight status can be obscured by having one evaluator code transcripts or audiotapes of interviews conducted by another; questions about binge eating can be dropped from the "impulsive behaviors" item of the screen for BPD. Patients can be instructed prior to an interview session that they should avoid mentioning food or weight issues to the clinician who conducts it (e.g., Wentz Nilsson, Gillberg, Gillberg, & Rastam, 1999). The obvious (and insoluble) problem is that blind evaluation requires us to remain ignorant of exactly what we need to know when assessing Axis II conditions, particularly in the case of disorders like the EDs in which Axis I symptoms work their way into every aspect of daily life (see the subsequent section on denial and distortion). The general criteria for diagnosing any PD require the judgment that its features are not better explained by another mental disorder. To honor this directive, it is clearly necessary to know what other mental disorders are in the running. Raters who are uninformed about Axis I status when assigning Axis II diagnoses cannot ask the crucial questions needed to tease them apart.

SPECIAL DIFFICULTIES IN THE ED FIELD

Characteristic features of the ED population compound the problems associated with personality assessment in the general case. We have selected three factors for closer review under the following subheadings: young age at onset and presentation, the effects of semistarvation and chaotic eating behavior, and denial and distortion in self-report.

Other complicating factors include recruitment problems, crossover between ED subtypes, and the persistence of symptoms after patients no longer meet diagnostic criteria. The rarity of anorexia nervosa and bulimia nervosa makes it difficult to secure adequate sample sizes and to examine the linkage between PD risk factors and the emergence of EDs prospectively. The instability of ED subtypes confounds efforts to establish whether personality traits influence the form of symptoms— although the strong hunch that they did provided much of the impetus for research in this area (and has received partial and inconsistent support). The frequent crossover between ED subtypes is one marker of shortcomings in the classification system (Beumont, Garner, & Touyz, 1994; Fairburn, Cooper, & Shafran, 2003); however, recent data suggest that trait variables can help identify meaningful subgroups that partially correspond to current diagnostic categories (Keel et al., 2004) and predict shifts in ED symptoms over time (Tozzi et al., 2005). Finally, the persistence of residual symptoms and the possibility of scarring effects limit the conclusions that can be drawn from follow-up research; the assumption that technically recovered patients return to their "usual selves" may be unwarranted. These and related issues are discussed at greater length in other reviews of the literature on personality and EDs (Grilo, 2002; Halmi et al., 1999; O'Brien & Vincent, 2003; Rosenvinge et al., 2000; Sansone & Levitt, 2005; Skodol et al., 1993; Vitousek & Manke, 1994; Westen & Harnden-Fischer, 2001; Wonderlich, 2002; Wonderlich, Lilenfeld, Riso, Engel, & Mitchell, 2005; Wonderlich & Mitchell, 1997, 2001).

Age at Onset and Assessment

By the typical age of ED onset, young people have undoubtedly developed distinct personalities, but experts disagree about whether they should be diagnosed with distinct Axis II disorders. The *DSM* takes the position that although it is indeed possible to spot personality pathology in children and adolescents, clinicians should be discouraged from affixing it with a PD label. The manual cautions that only in "relatively unusual instances" will young patients satisfy specifications that the maladaptive patterns must be "pervasive, persistent, and unlikely to be limited to a particular developmental stage or an episode of an Axis I disorder" (American Psychiatric Association, 2000, p. 687).

The case of Patient A/B illustrates the problem. She became anorexic at age 12 and had remained severely ill (and been frequently rehospitalized) throughout the 3 to 4 years preceding the first and second assessments. At a minimum, then, any effort to gauge her "usual functioning" when her life was not distorted by the powerful forces of anorexia nervosa would push us back to the age of 11. In fact, a closer look at this patient's personal history indicated that her behavior at ages 10 and 11 had been sharply discontinuous from that characteristic of her early and middle childhood, so that it is not altogether clear to what era we should refer. Moreover, it would be difficult to certify that her maladaptive patterns were independent of a particular developmental period when she had not yet exited the stage during which those patterns had emerged—all in the context of an Axis I disorder with distinctly "developmental" features of its own.

The principle that we should make it especially difficult to qualify for a PD diagnosis during adolescence is affirmed by data showing that it is otherwise all too easy. Within the general population, higher percentages of adolescents than adults meet PD criteria. When figures are based on unfiltered self-report data in questionnaire studies, they sometimes soar into the ludicrous range, with as many as two thirds of college students meeting criteria for at least one PD (Rosen & Tallis, 1995). The numbers obtained through structured interview are somewhat less alarming but still generally double or triple the expected proportion in adults, with a quarter to a third of adolescents crossing one or more Axis II thresholds in some studies (e.g., Bernstein et al., 1993; Gillberg, Rastam, & Gillberg, 1995).

If the discrepancy between adolescent and adult rates fulfills stereotypes about the normative maladjustment of youth, it violates the fundamental assumption of Axis II diagnosis: The disorders we identify should be characteristic of the individual's functioning throughout most of his or her adult life. In general terms, the age-group effect guarantees that stability will be low for PD diagnoses assigned to adolescents, because more than half of these diagnoses vanish during the transition to adulthood. Longitudinal studies that track cohorts over fixed time periods verify this impression (Bernstein et al., 1993; Korenblum, Marton, Golombeck, & Stein, 1990; Lenzenweger, 1999). For example, in one community study, fewer than half of adolescents who had initially received *any* Axis II disorder qualified for *any* Axis II disorder 2 years later; figures for the persistence of *specific* PDs across both assessments fell below 10% for some diagnoses and never exceeded 43% (Bernstein et al., 1993).

It seems reasonable to hypothesize that PD diagnoses might be less ephemeral in clinical populations. Perhaps declining rates in normal samples reflect the fact that many were mild cases who barely made it across the diagnostic threshold in the first place and readily dipped below as they matured, whereas the more severe disturbance that brings adolescents to treatment settings should prove more robust. The data contradict this construction. Across PD categories, only half of adolescents originally diagnosed on an inpatient psychiatric service retained the same PD diagnosis 2 years later (Mattanah, Becker, Levy, Edell, & McGlashan, 1995). For BPD, the correspondence is lower still. Across several studies, just 14% to 33% continued to meet BPD criteria when followed up 2 to 3 years after an index hospitalization (Garnet, Levy, Mattanah, Edell, & McGlashan, 1994; Mattanah et al., 1995; Meijer, Goedhart, & Treffers, 1998). In other words, the *expected* outcome of a BPD diagnosis during adolescence is that it will no longer apply a relatively short time later—which seems a curious state of affairs for a construct defined by the presumption of stability.

None of these figures suggest that Axis II diagnoses during adolescence convey no useful information. If we are not actually measuring the stable patterns we intended to identify, we are picking up something that is meaningfully associated with a number of variables that we would expect a PD to predict (Kasen, Cohen, Skodol, Johnson, & Brook, 1999; Levy et al., 1999; Ludolph et al., 1990; Pinto, Grapentine, Francis, & Picariello, 1996; Westen & Chang, 2000; Westen, Shedler, Durrett, Glass, & Martens, 2003). But although adolescent PD diagnoses are right on the mark in a minority of cases and provide some useful information in many, the cost of false positives may be unacceptably high.

Concern about labeling can be overdone; however, when we predict lifelong personality pathology for adolescents who are still sorting out who they are and who they may become, a certain amount of concern is warranted. On these grounds alone (and there are others), it is distressing that multiple clinicians had given Patient A/B a BPD diagnosis that there was a 67% to 86% chance she would *not* retain 2 years later. It is reprehensible that one had thought it appropriate to pull out a copy of the *DSM* during a therapy session and read the criteria for BPD aloud, emphasizing the closeness of fit to Patient A/B's case. (Presumably, he skipped over the sections specifying that patterns must be characteristic of stable long-term functioning and not better explained by an Axis I disorder, just as he must have neglected those specifications to confer the diagnosis in the first place.) The intended effect was to impress Patient A/B with the gravity of her situation. The actual effect was to increase the number of criteria she fulfilled and bump up their severity. When Patient A/B began treatment in our program some months later, one of our first clinical objectives was to convince her that the diagnosis of BPD had been misapplied. As it turned out, our prediction that BPD symptoms would be transient for this individual proved correct; however, we suspect that if she had remained in treatment with professionals who believed she harbored severe character pathology, their prophecies would have been fulfilled in place of our own.

Practice Point

The assignment of PD diagnoses to adolescents with EDs is usually inappropriate and sometimes harmful.

Semistarvation, Chronic Restraint, and Chaotic Eating Behavior

A challenge unique to this specialty area is the need to disentangle state effects produced by semistarvation from traits that may induce patients to semistarve. The behavior of normal humans and animals is profoundly altered by caloric deprivation (Fessler, 2002; Garner, 1997; Keys, Brozek, Henschel, Mickelsen, & Taylor, 1950; Vitousek, Manke, Gray, & Vitousek, 2004). The consistency of these changes across species, individuals, and conditions suggests that they are hardwired and adaptive, favored in the course of natural selection because they confer survival advantage during periods of famine.

Animals that are underfed or intermittently fed become irritable, asocial, and asexual; some studies also report heightened sensitivity to some kinds of stress, fearfulness in novel situations, and increased rates of stereotypic behavior (Vitousek, Gray, et al., 2004). If there were a veterinary version of the *DSM*, hungry mice and monkeys would presumably receive a range of Axis II diagnoses—at least to the extent that raters missed the distinction between state effects and trait effects in animals as regularly as they do in humans.

Accounts of human semistarvation in the natural environment repeatedly allude to the sense that its victims undergo a startling change in personality. They do not simply behave in different ways; the impression is that they become different *people*, their "usual selves" eroding as chronic hunger "completely alters the character and outlook of the starving man" (Leyton, 1946, p. 78; see also Daws, 1994; Guetzkow & Bowman, 1946; Levi, 1958/1996). The classic Minnesota study provides the most detailed documentation of this effect in volunteers who were semistarving under close scrutiny in atypically benign circumstances (Keys et al., 1950). Marked changes in attitude, mood state, and behavior appeared in 36 previously well-adjusted men during 6 months of underfeeding. On a diet that averaged 1,570 kcals/day and produced a mean 24% weight loss, participants became depressed, irritable, self-centered, socially isolated, and sexually disinterested. Their Minnesota Multiphasic Personality Inventory scores rose as their behavior deteriorated. By the end of the study, the group profile showed a striking resemblance to averaged data from patients with anorexia nervosa, restricting subtype (Vitousek & Manke, 1994). The investigators concluded that participants "suffered from an actual, though temporary, personality disturbance" (Brozek & Erickson, 1948, p. 410), and they coined the term "semi-starvation neurosis" to summarize it. Although the direction of change was consistent, individual differences suggested an interaction between stable traits and the strain of semistarvation. Some of the men developed compulsive patterns; a few displayed uncharacteristic impulsive, self-destructive, and antisocial behaviors; and several showed signs of frank psychopathology. Even a case study chosen to depict a "good" adjustment illustrates the magnitude of effects across participants:

In the control period we had before us a pleasant, cheerful, active young man, full of initiative, cooperative and sociable, highly altruistic, [and] sensitive to the world's social problems. ... Twenty-four weeks later there remains only the shadow of Don's former self. Weak and edematous, lacking physical endurance and mental initiative, he was a childish slave of food, primarily concerned with individual security. (Brozek, 1953, pp. 117–118)

Practice Point

In normal animals and humans, chronic underfeeding has profound effects on cognition, affect, and behavior that resemble changes in "personality."

At least on the surface, all specialists in the ED field acknowledge the significance of semistarvation in the presenting picture of anorexia nervosa. Therapists urge parents not to overinterpret the peculiar behaviors and mysterious moods they witness; their daughter is "not her usual self" because she is starving. Treatment programs are structured around the premise that malnourished patients must be refed before meaningful therapy can occur. Pharmacotherapists emphasize that there are no effective drugs for semistarvation; in the initial stages of treatment, *calories* are the sole specific medication for anorexia nervosa (Walsh, 2002). Articles on personality assessment routinely cite the Minnesota study and caution that chronic restraint and chaotic eating behavior in bulimia nervosa and atypical eating disorders may produce changes similar to those associated with semistarvation, even at normal weight levels.

Yet allusions to starvation effects in the ED literature often have a distinctly pro forma quality, giving a quick nod to the problem before reassuring the reader that it does not, after all, pose any serious impediment to the assessment of personality in this population (e.g., Cumella et al., 2000). Because certain traits measurable at intake (such as obsessionality, perfectionism, and low novelty seeking) appear to precede anorexia nervosa and survive its resolution, we must be capturing something more enduring than the "semi-starvation neurosis" seen in the Minnesota volunteers. After reviewing the data from retrospective, case-control, follow-up, and family genetic studies, many discussions close with the same summary statement: The pathological personality patterns observed during the acute phase of illness are not fully explained as secondary effects of semistarvation.

To our knowledge, no expert in the ED field has ever proposed that they were. Obviously, we must look outside the consequences of starvation to explain why it is self-imposed; traits such as obsessionality and perfectionism have been on the short list of prime suspects for more than 50 years. But this framing of the issue misses the basis for concern in the context of clinical assessment. The question is not whether semistarvation and chaotic eating behavior account for everything we are measuring at the time of intake; the problem is that they make it difficult to sort out which elements are important and enduring and which are exaggerated, distorted, or transient in each of the individuals we assess.

For example, Patient A/B appeared to have obsessional traits at both the first evaluation and the second evaluation. Careful review of her premorbid history and a fast-forward look at her postmorbid future confirmed that this feature was indeed characteristic of her "usual self." At least in her case, obsessionality fit specifications as a trait and was discernible through the noise of state effects. Yet this enduring disposition was greatly exaggerated in the throes of anorexia nervosa, restricting subtype at the initial assessment—the only point at which she met criteria for obsessive-compulsive personality disorder from a categorical perspective—and substantially attenuated subsequent to her recovery. If we had projected the extent to which obsessionality would shape this individual's life from our snapshot view of her "starving self," we would have miscalculated. Dimensional assessment captures the reality that such variables are a matter of degree, but degree *matters* in the interpretation of personality data. Different implications follow from scoring 1 standard deviation above the mean versus 2 or 3. The picture we observed at initial assessment, then, was both accurate and misleading.

In contrast, most of the maladaptive patterns so salient at the second evaluation were atypical of Patient A/B's functioning over time. It would be nice to assume that clinicians could distinguish the state-dependent quality of her "borderline" symptoms from the trait-like properties of her obsessional streak; however, this patient was referred to our treatment program with a pair of technically reliable but invalid PD diagnoses attached. Many experts have made thoughtful observations about the tendency for starvation effects to exaggerate stable features of the "usual self," setting up a vicious cycle in which caloric deprivation intensifies obsessionality and rampant obsessionality leads to increasingly severe restraint (e.g., Bloks, Hoek, Callewaert, & van Furth, 2004; Fairburn, Shafran, & Cooper, 1999; Halmi, 2005; Pollice et al., 1997; Serpell, Livingstone, Neiderman, & Lask, 2002; Thornton & Russell, 1997). It is less often discussed that starvation can have *distorting* effects as well, prompting patterns of thought, feeling, and behavior that are not characteristic of the individual under other conditions. (Of course, one could speculate that the emergence of such phenomena under pressure reveals the "real self" beneath the "usual," but the risk of tautological reasoning should be prohibitive.)

A final point illustrated by the example of Patient A/B is that it is simplistic to equate starvation effects with current BMI. This individual's weight was approximately equivalent at the two assessment points, suggesting that we must look to other variables to explain the patterns observed on one or both occasions. Yet semistarvation effects, more broadly construed, almost certainly help to explain her experience during each of these phases. With additional data collected over time, it became clear that, at least for this individual, steady abstemiousness and gradual weight loss were linked to increasing obsessionality, whereas the pattern of prolonged fasting, bouts of binge eating, and rapid weight fluctuation covaried with emotional instability. The *direction* of relationships between this patient's shifting "traits" and her ED symptoms is obviously difficult to establish; the construct of the vicious cycle may again represent the process most accurately. One generalization does hold across cases: The association between starvation effects and personality pathology is more likely to be a complex function of current eating behavior, current weight, personal weight history, and threshold effects rather than a linear function of BMI.

On the basis of empirical evidence, clinical experience, and common sense, the view that starvation does not impede the assessment of personality is unfounded. In fact, the studies often used to argue against a significant role for starvation make a strong case for the opposite conclusion (e.g., Bloks et al., 2004; Bulik, Sullivan, Fear, & Pickering, 2000; Casper, 1990; Herpertz-Dahlmann et al., 2001; Kleifield et al., 1994; Pollice et al., 1997; Steiger, Stotland, & Houle, 1994; von Ranson, Kaye, Weltzin, Rao, & Matsunaga, 1999; Wentz Nilsson et al., 1999). Some putative traits dissipate rapidly with refeeding and symptom control, whereas others attenuate. Personality variables measured at intake are generally weak predictors of eventual outcome, whereas short-term response to treatment is more informative. At later follow-up points, there is a strong association between persistent personality disturbance and residual eating and weight symptoms, even in patients who no longer qualify for an ED diagnosis.

The commonsense argument for respecting the potency of starvation effects is perhaps equally compelling (and it too draws on a substantial body of data). We are mystified by the assertion that evaluators need not worry about the confounding effects of semistarvation because, after all, patients with EDs had serious problems before restriction began and may well have significant problems after it ends. In view of the fact that caloric deprivation has a profound impact on the apparent "personalities" of normal animals and well-adjusted humans, it seems improbable that it would have *less* effect on the already fragile individuals who are vulnerable to the development of EDs.

Denial and Distortion in Self-Report

Denial of symptoms is a common feature of anorexia nervosa, yet it rarely interferes with its diagnosis. Indeed, a severely underweight patient who insists that she is "fine" and "fit" and cannot fathom all the fuss being made over a matter of "personal preference" does more to clarify her Axis I standing than to obscure it. In the assessment of Axis II variables, however, the same sort of spin complicates the interpretation of self-report.

The operative word is *complicates*, as the effect is seldom quite so simple as across-the-board minimization of symptoms. At the time of initial evaluation, for example, Patient A/B proudly staked her claim to the trait of perfectionism, denied any feelings of self-doubt or inferiority, and misattributed her avoidance of social situations to disdain for the company of others. All of these representations supported her stance in defense of anorexia nervosa; only the first contributed accurate information toward the assessment of PD criteria.

In fact, it is not unusual for patients with EDs to confess to personality pathology they do not possess, manufacturing motives on an ad hoc basis to provide non-ED explanations for ED-inspired behavior. They claim that they never socialize because they prefer to be alone; that they avoid restaurants, movies, and travel because they disapprove of frivolous pursuits and profligate spending; that they opt out of demanding careers because they fear they might fail; and that they shun intimate relationships because they cherish their independence. In some cases, of course, these accounts are valid indicators of Axis II patterns; in others, they are cover stories for Axis I concerns such as reluctance to suspend food rituals or vary exercise routines. At initial assessment, it is difficult to tell which is which, particularly if patients have begun to believe their own material. One of the few things we can count on in this specialty area is that eating and weight issues determine patients' reactions to a wide range of apparently unrelated situations. Understandably, many are reluctant to recognize or concede the degree to which their lives have been distorted by their symptoms. When patients with EDs seem especially eager to attribute eccentric behaviors to their "personal style" rather than their eating and weight concerns, we should be especially wary of the supporting evidence.

Practice Point
A desire to protect ED symptoms can lead patients to minimize or to exaggerate signs of personality disturbance.

A number of other factors can affect the quality of self-report data in this population (Vitousek et al., 1991)—including some of the very traits we are attempting to assess. For example, several theoretical models suggest that individuals with anorexia have limited access to their own internal experience, a deficit that may simultaneously increase the risk of developing this condition and make it more difficult for observers to decode. Characteristics such as conventionalism and compliance could help explain why some young women are particularly susceptible to pressures about weight and shape; however, the same tendencies can also obscure the symptom picture. Paradoxically, Patient A/B's more florid borderline behaviors in part signaled her disposition to do what she believed was expected of her on the basis of models articulated by her therapists, observation of other patients who shared her diagnosis, and knowledge of her own status as a psychiatric inpatient.

For the sake of both accuracy and empathy, the distortion of self-report should not be equated with lying, even when it is both conscious and purposeful (Vitousek, Watson, & Wilson, 1998). Although patients with EDs often take an active role in the maintenance of their disorders, they do not choose the sense of desperation that contributes to their pursuit and defense of symptoms. In addition, they are unable to change the harsh rules set by the biology of appetite and weight regulation. To comply with the terms for practicing self-starvation in the midst of plenty, it is essential to think and act abnormally—and prudent to misrepresent that reality to oneself as well as others. In fact, one of the most interesting aspects of the relationship between personality variables and EDs is that certain "maladaptive patterns of internal experience and behavior" are very nearly job requirements for sustained control over eating and weight (Vitousek, Gray, & Grubbs, 2004). Perfectionism and obsessionality can be construed not only as vulnerability factors but also as *ability* factors for chronic dietary restraint.

CONCLUSION

The evidence affirms the clinical view that personality traits are linked to the EDs, although the nature of the relationship is almost certain to be complex (Lilenfeld et al., 2000; O'Brien & Vincent, 2003; Vitousek & Manke, 1994; Westen & Harnden-Fischer, 2001; Wonderlich et al., 2005; Wonderlich & Mitchell, 1997). The evidence does not affirm the clinical utility of diagnosing Axis II pathology in the individual case, at least during the acute phase of illness. For all the reasons highlighted in this review, the presence of ED symptoms makes it difficult to predict whether pervasive patterns present at intake will prove persistent over time.

In spite of these difficulties, early assessment of Axis II pathology is often recommended on the grounds that the information is needed for treatment planning (Reich & Green, 1991; Zimmerman, 1994; Zimmerman & Mattia, 1999). Unfortunately, the data suggest that if we tailor interventions to match initial PD diagnoses, we may be planning treatment incorrectly for 50% to 85% of the cases we identify. Decision-tree models that specify different lengths or modes of therapy for patients with PDs will direct many toward unnecessary or inappropriate treatment. Because BPD in particular carries substantial stigma even (or perhaps especially) among mental health professionals (Linehan, 1993), a premature diagnosis carries the potential added risks of serving as a self-fulfilling prophecy, creating emotional distance in therapists, and/ or leading to exclusion from treatment programs (Arntz, 1999; Dreessen & Arntz, 1998).

A number of observations suggest that it may be preferable to defer Axis II assessment: (a) personality pathology at initial evaluation holds little or no prognostic value in many ED samples (e.g., Bulik, Sullivan, Carter, McIntosh, & Joyce, 1999; Grilo, Sanislow, Shea, et al., 2003; Herzog et al., 1999); (b) PD features often remit with successful treatment (e.g., Garner et al., 1990; Kennedy et al., 1990), even in patients with severe, long-standing EDs (Rø, Martinsen, Hoffart, Sexton, et al., 2005); (c) patterns still evident after brief intervention are stronger predictors of follow-up status (e.g., Steiger et al., 1994); and (d) focal therapies produce comparable improvements in ED symptoms for patients with and without PDs, although those with poor overall adjustment may need additional treatment to address their more generalized difficulties (e.g., Sansone & Fine, 1992; Steiger & Stotland, 1996; Wonderlich, Fullerton, Swift, & Klein, 1994). The recommendation to "treat and see" should not be confused with the bad clinical habit of inferring Axis II pathology in patients who fail to improve and then, in tidy circular fashion, attributing treatment failure to the presence of a PD. The common tendency to backfill PD diagnoses to explain disappointing results contributes to inflated estimates of the relationship between these variables (Arntz, 1999; Dreessen & Arntz, 1998; Grilo et al., 1998).

Paradoxically, personality assessment at intake is most beneficial to the extent we recognize we may not be assessing personality. The borderline features seen in Patient A/B were not representative of her pre-ED functioning and did not predict her post-ED future. They did anticipate her reaction patterns in the near term, however, and suggested specific treatment components that proved helpful in addressing them. Validity means "usefulness for a *purpose*"—and if we pick our objectives thoughtfully, the measurement of presumed personality variables can be useful indeed. The data we collect at intake are not always instructive about stable traits or eventual outcome; in most cases, however, they are sensitive indicators of the disruption caused by an active ED.

NOTE

This chapter is a revised version of an article that appeared in *Eating Disorders*. Please address future correspondence to Kelly M. Vitousek, Department of Psychology, University of Hawaii, 2430 Campus Road, Honolulu, HI, 96822; telephone: 808-956-6269; fax: 808-956-4700; e-mail: vitousek@hawaii.edu.

REFERENCES

Allison, D. B. (1993). A note on the selection of control groups and control variables in comorbidity research. *Comprehensive Psychiatry, 34,* 336–339.

American Psychiatric Association. (2000). *Diagnostic and statistical manual of mental disorders* (4th ed., Text Revision). Washington, DC: Author.

Ames-Frankel, J., Devlin, M. J., Walsh, B. T., Strasser, T. J., Sadik, C., Oldham, J. M., et al. (1992). Personality disorder diagnoses in patients with bulimia nervosa: Clinical correlates and changes in treatment. *Journal of Clinical Psychiatry, 53,* 90–96.

Arntz, A. (1999). Do personality disorders exist? On the validity of the concept and its cognitive behavioral formulation and treatment. *Behaviour Research and Therapy, 37,* S97–S134.

Berkson, J. (1946). Limitations of the application of fourfold table analysis to hospital data. *Biometrics Bulletin, 2,* 47–53.

Bernstein, D. P., Cohen, P., Velez, C. N., Schwab-Stone, M., Siever, L. J., & Shinsato, L. (1993). Prevalence and stability of *DSM–III–R* personality disorders in a community-based survey of adolescents. *American Journal of Psychiatry, 150,* 1237–1243.

Beumont, P. J. V., Garner, D. M., & Touyz, S. W. (1994). Diagnoses of eating or dieting disorders: What may we learn from past mistakes? *International Journal of Eating Disorders, 16,* 349–362.

Beumont, P., & Vandereycken, W. (1998). Challenges and risks for health care professionals. In W. Vandereycken & P. J. V. Beumont (Eds.), *Treating eating disorders: Ethical, legal and personal issues* (pp. 1–29). New York: New York University Press.

Bloks, H., Hoek, H. W., Callewaert, I., & van Furth, E. (2004). Stability of personality traits in patients who received intensive treatment for a severe eating disorder. *Journal of Nervous and Mental Disease, 192,* 129–138.

Brotman, A. W., Stern, T. A., & Herzog, D. B. (1984). Emotional reactions of house officers to patients with anorexia nervosa, diabetes, and obesity. *International Journal of Eating Disorders, 3,* 71–77.

Brozek, J. (1953). Semistarvation and nutritional rehabilitation: A qualitative case study, with emphasis on behavior. *Journal of Clinical Nutrition, 1,* 107–118.

Brozek, J., & Erickson, N. K. (1948). Item analysis of the psychoneurotic scales of the Minnesota Multiphasic Personality Inventory in experimental semi-starvation. *Journal of Consulting Psychology, 12,* 403–411.

Bulik, C. M., Sullivan, P. F., Carter, F. A., McIntosh, V. V., & Joyce, P. R. (1999). Predictors of rapid and sustained response to cognitive-behavioral therapy for bulimia nervosa. *International Journal of Eating Disorders, 26,* 137–144.

Bulik, C. M., Sullivan, P. F., Fear, J. L., & Pickering, A. (2000). Outcome of anorexia nervosa: Eating attitudes, personality and parental bonding. *International Journal of Eating Disorders, 28,* 139–147.

Carroll, J. M., Touyz, S. W., & Beumont, P. J. V. (1996). Specific comorbidity between bulimia nervosa and personality disorders. *International Journal of Eating Disorders, 19,* 159–170.

Casper, R. C. (1990). Personality features of women with good outcome from restricting anorexia nervosa. *Psychosomatic Medicine, 52,* 156–170.

Clark, L. A., Livesley, W. J., & Morey, L. (1997). Personality disorder assessment: The challenge of construct validity. *Journal of Personality Disorders, 11,* 205–231.

Cumella, E. J., Wall, A. D., & Kerr-Almeida, N. (2000). MMPI–2 in the inpatient assessment of women with eating disorders. *Journal of Personality Assessment, 75,* 387–403.

Daws, G. (1994). *Prisoners of the Japanese.* New York: William Morrow.

Diaz-Marsa, M., Carrasco, J. L., & Saiz, J. (2000). A study of temperament and personality in anorexia and bulimia nervosa. *Journal of Personality Disorders, 14,* 352–359.

Dreessen, L., & Arntz, A. (1998). The impact of personality disorders on treatment outcome of anxiety disorders: Best-evidence synthesis. *Behaviour Research and Therapy, 36*, 483–504.

Fairburn, C. G., Cooper, Z., Doll, H. A., & Welch, S. L. (1999). Risk factors for anorexia nervosa: Three integrated case-control comparisons. *Archives of General Psychiatry, 56*, 468–476.

Fairburn, C. G., Cooper, Z., & Shafran, R. (2003). Cognitive behaviour therapy for eating disorders: A "transdiagnostic" theory and treatment. *Behaviour Research and Therapy, 41*, 509–528.

Fairburn, C. G., Shafran, R., & Cooper, Z. (1999). A cognitive behavioural theory of anorexia nervosa. *Behaviour Research and Therapy, 37*, 1–13.

Fairburn, C. G., Welch, S. L., Doll, H. A., Davies, B. A., & O'Connor, M. E. (1997). Risk factors for bulimia nervosa: A community-based case-control study. *Archives of General Psychiatry, 54*, 509–517.

Fessler, D. M. T. (2002). Pseudoparadoxical impulsivity in restrictive anorexia nervosa: A consequence of the logic of scarcity. *International Journal of Eating Disorders, 31*, 376–388.

Galbaud du Fort, G. G., Newman, S. C., & Bland, R. C. (1993). Psychiatric comorbidity and treatment seeking: Sources of selection bias in the study of clinical populations. *Journal of Nervous and Mental Disease, 181*, 467–474.

Garner, D. M. (1997). Psychoeducational principles in treatment. In D. M. Garner & P. E. Garfinkel (Eds.), *Handbook of treatment for eating disorders* (2nd ed., pp. 145–177). New York: Guilford.

Garner, D. M., Olmsted, M. P., Davis, R., Rockert, W., Goldbloom, D., & Eagle, M. (1990). The association between bulimic symptoms and reported psychopathology. *International Journal of Eating Disorders, 9*, 1–15.

Garnet, K. E., Levy, K. N., Mattanah, J. J. F., Edell, W. S., & McGlashan, T. H. (1994). Borderline personality disorder in adolescents: Ubiquitous or specific? *American Journal of Psychiatry, 151*, 1380–1382.

Gillberg, I. C., Rastam, M., & Gillberg, C. (1995). Anorexia nervosa 6 years after onset: Part I; Personality disorders. *Comprehensive Psychiatry, 36*, 61–69.

Godt, K. (2002). Personality disorders and eating disorders: The prevalence of personality disorders in 176 female outpatients with eating disorders. *European Eating Disorders Review, 10*, 102–109.

Grilo, C. M. (2002). Recent research of relationships among eating disorders and personality disorders. *Current Psychiatry Reports, 4*, 18–24.

Grilo, C. M. (2004). Diagnostic efficiency of *DSM–IV* criteria for obsessive compulsive personality disorder in patients with binge eating disorder. *Behaviour Research and Therapy, 42*, 57–65.

Grilo, C. M., McGlashan, T. H., & Oldham, J. M. (1998). Course and stability of personality disorders. *Journal of Practical Psychiatry and Behavioral Health, 4*, 61–75.

Grilo, C. M., McGlashan, T. H., & Skodol, A. E. (2000). Stability and course of personality disorders: The need to consider comorbidities and continuities between Axis I psychiatric disorders and Axis II personality disorders. *Psychiatric Quarterly, 71*, 291–307.

Grilo, C. M., Sanislow, C. A., Shea, M. T., Skodol, A. E., Stout, R. L., Pagano, M. E., et al. (2003). The natural course of bulimia nervosa and eating disorder not otherwise specified is not influenced by personality disorders. *International Journal of Eating Disorders, 34,* 319–330.

Grilo, C. M., Sanislow, C. A., Skodol, A. E., Gunderson, J. G., Stout, R. L., Shea, M. T., et al. (2003). Do eating disorders co-occur with personality disorders? Comparison groups matter. *International Journal of Eating Disorders, 33,* 155–164.

Grilo, C. M., Shea, M. T., Sanislow, C. A., Skodol, A. E., Gunderson, J. G., Stout, R. L., et al. (2004). Two-year stability and change of schizotypal, borderline, avoidant, and obsessive-compulsive personality disorders. *Journal of Consulting and Clinical Psychology, 72,* 767–775.

Guetzkow, H. S., & Bowman, P. H. (1946). *Men and hunger: A psychological manual for relief workers.* Elgin, IL: Brethren.

Halmi, K. A. (2005). Obsessive-compulsive personality disorder and eating disorders. *Eating Disorders, 13,* 85–92.

Halmi, K. A., Kleifield, E. I., Braun, D. L., & Sunday, S. R. (1999). Personality correlates of ED subtypes. In C. R. Cloninger (Ed.), *Personality and psychopathology* (pp. 67–82). Washington, DC: American Psychiatric Press.

Herpertz-Dahlmann, B., Muller, B., Herpertz, S., Heussen, N., Hebebrand, J., & Remschmidt, H. (2001). Prospective 10-year follow-up in adolescent anorexia nervosa—Course, outcome, psychiatric comorbidity, and psychosocial adaptation. *Journal of Child Psychology and Psychiatry, 42,* 603–612.

Herzog, D. B., Dorer, D. J., Keel, P. K., Selwyn, S. E., Ekeblad, E. R., Flores, A. T., et al. (1999). Recovery and relapse in anorexia and bulimia nervosa: A 7.5-year follow-up study. *Journal of the American Academy of Child and Adolescent Psychiatry, 38,* 829–837.

Kaplan, A. S., & Garfinkel, P. E. (1999). Difficulties in treating patients with eating disorders: A review of patient and clinician variables. *Canadian Journal of Psychiatry, 44,* 665–670.

Karwautz, A., Troop, T. A., Rabe-Hesketh, S., Collier, D. A., & Treasure, J. L. (2003). Personality disorders and personality dimensions in anorexia nervosa. *Journal of Personality Disorders, 17,* 73–85.

Kasen, S., Cohen, P., Skodol, A. E., Johnson, J. G., & Brook, J. S. (1999). Influence of child and adolescent psychiatric disorders on young adult personality disorders. *American Journal of Psychiatry, 156,* 1529–1535.

Keel, P. K., Fichter, M., Quadflieg, N., Bulik, C. M., Baxter, M. G., Thornton, L., et al. (2004). Application of a latent class analysis to empirically define eating disorder phenotypes. *Archives of General Psychiatry, 61,* 192–200.

Kennedy, S. H., McVey, G., & Katz, R. (1990). Personality disorders in anorexia nervosa and bulimia nervosa. *Journal of Psychiatric Research, 24,* 259–269.

Keys, A., Brozek, J., Henschel, A., Mickelsen, O., & Taylor, H. L. (1950). *The biology of human starvation* (2 vols.). Minneapolis: University of Minnesota Press.

Kleifield, E. I., Sunday, S., Hurt, S., & Halmi, K. A. (1994). The effects of depression and treatment on the Tridimensional Personality Questionnaire. *Biological Psychiatry, 36,* 68–70.

Korenblum, M., Marton, P., Golombeck, H., & Stein, B. (1990). Personality status: Changes through adolescence. *Psychiatric Clinics of North America, 13*, 389–399.

Lenzenweger, M. F. (1999). Stability and change in personality disorder features: A longitudinal study of personality disorders. *Archives of General Psychiatry, 56*, 1009–1015.

Leon, G. R., Lucas, A. R., Colligan, R. C., Ferdinande, R. J., & Kamp, J. (1985). Sexual, body-image and personality attitudes in anorexia nervosa. *Journal of Abnormal Child Psychology, 13*, 245–258.

Levi, P. (1958/1996). *Survival in Auschwitz: The Nazi assault on humanity.* New York: Touchstone.

Levy, K. N., Becker, D. F., Grilo, C. M., Mattanah, J. J. F., Garnet, K. E., Quinlan, D. M., et al. (1999). Concurrent and predictive validity of the personality disorder diagnosis in adolescent inpatients. *American Journal of Psychiatry, 156*, 1522–1528.

Leyton, G. B. (1946). Effects of slow starvation. *Lancet, 2*, 73–79.

Lilenfeld, L. R. R., Stein, D., Bulik, C. M., Strober, M., Plotnicov, K., Pollice, C., et al. (2000). Personality traits among currently eating disordered, recovered and never ill first-degree female relatives of bulimic and control women. *Psychological Medicine, 30*, 1399–1410.

Linehan, M. M. (1993). *Cognitive-behavioral treatment of borderline personality disorder.* New York: Guilford.

Livesley, W. J., Schroeder, M. L., Jackson, D. N., & Jang, K. L. (1994). Categorical distinctions in the study of personality disorder: Implications for classification. *Journal of Abnormal Psychology, 103*, 6–17.

Loranger, A. W., Lenzenweger, M. F., Gartner, A. F., Susman, V. L., Herzig, J., Zammit, G. K., et al. (1991). Trait-state artifacts and the diagnosis of personality disorders. *Archives of General Psychiatry, 48*, 720–728.

Ludolph, P. S., Westen, D., Misle, B., Jackson, A., Wixom, J., & Wiss, F. C. (1990). The borderline diagnosis in adolescents: Symptoms and developmental history. *American Journal of Psychiatry, 147*, 470–476.

Mattanah, J. J. F., Becker, D. F., Levy, K. N., Edell, W. S., & McGlashan, T. H. (1995). Diagnostic stability in adolescents followed up 2 years after hospitalization. *American Journal of Psychiatry, 152*, 889–894.

McDavid, J. D., & Pilkonis, P. A. (1996). The stability of personality disorder diagnoses. *Journal of Personality Disorders, 10*, 1–15.

Meijer, M., Goedhart, A. W., & Treffers, P. D. A. (1998). The persistence of borderline personality disorder in adolescence. *Journal of Personality Disorders, 12*, 13–22.

O'Brien, K. M., & Vincent, N. K. (2003). Psychiatric comorbidity in anorexia and bulimia nervosa: Nature, prevalence, and causal relationships. *Clinical Psychology Review, 23*, 57–74.

Oldham, J. M., & Skodol, A. E. (2000). Charting the future of Axis II. *Journal of Personality Disorders, 14*, 17–29.

Perkins, P. S., Klump, K. L., Iacono, W. G., & McGue, M. (2005). Personality traits in women with anorexia nervosa: Evidence for a treatment-seeking bias? *International Journal of Eating Disorders, 37*, 32–37.

Perry, J. C. (1992). Problems and considerations in the valid assessment of personality disorders. *American Journal of Psychiatry, 149*, 1645–1653.

Pinto, A., Grapentine, W. L., Francis, G., & Picariello, C. M. (1996). Borderline personality disorder in adolescents: Affective and cognitive features. *Journal of the American Academy of Child and Adolescent Psychiatry, 34,* 1338–1343.

Pollice, C., Kaye, W. H., Greeno, C. G., & Weltzin, T. E. (1997). Relationship of depression, anxiety, and obsessionality to state of illness in anorexia nervosa. *International Journal of Eating Disorders, 21,* 367–376.

Pope, H. G., Jr., Frankenburg, F. R., Hudson, J. I., Jonas, J. M., & Yurgelun-Todd, D. (1987). Is bulimia associated with borderline personality disorder? A controlled study. *Journal of Clinical Psychiatry, 48,* 181–184.

Pryor, T., & Wiederman, M. W. (1996). Use of the MMPI-2 in the outpatient assessment of women with anorexia nervosa or bulimia nervosa. *Journal of Personality Assessment, 66,* 363–373.

Reich, J. H., & Green, A. I. (1991). Effect of personality disorders on outcome of treatment. *Journal of Nervous and Mental Disease, 179,* 74–82.

Rø, Ø., Martinsen, E. W., Hoffart, A., & Rosenvinge, J. H. (2005). Two-year prospective study of personality disorders in adults with longstanding eating disorders. *International Journal of Eating Disorders, 37,* 112–118.

Rø, Ø., Martinsen, E. W., Hoffart, A., Sexton, H., & Rosenvinge, J. H. (2005). The interactions of personality disorders and eating disorders: A two-year prospective study of patients with longstanding eating disorders. *International Journal of Eating Disorders, 38,* 106–111.

Rosen, K. V., & Tallis, F. (1995). Investigation into the relationship between personality traits and OCD. *Behaviour Research and Therapy, 33,* 445–450.

Rosenvinge, J. H., Martinussen, M., & Ostensen, E. (2000). The comorbidity of eating disorders and personality disorders: A meta-analytic review of studies published between 1983 and 1998. *Eating and Weight Disorders, 5,* 52–61.

Sansone, R. A., & Fine, M. A. (1992). Borderline personality as a predictor of outcome in women with eating disorders. *Journal of Personality Disorders, 6,* 176–186.

Sansone, R. A., & Levitt, J. L. (2005). Borderline personality and eating disorders. *Eating Disorders, 13,* 71–83.

Sansone, R. A., Wiederman, M. W., & Sansone, L. A. (2000). The prevalence of borderline personality disorder among individuals with obesity: A critical review of the literature. *Eating Behaviors, 1,* 93–104.

Serpell, L., Livingstone, A., Neiderman, M., & Lask, B. (2002). Anorexia nervosa: Obsessive-compulsive disorder, obsessive-compulsive personality disorder, or neither? *Clinical Psychology Review, 22,* 647–669.

Shafran, R., Cooper, Z., & Fairburn, C. G. (2002). Clinical perfectionism: A cognitive behavioral analysis. *Behaviour Research and Therapy, 40,* 773–791.

Shafran, R., & Mansell, W. (2001). Perfectionism and psychopathology: A review of research and treatment. *Clinical Psychology Review, 21,* 879–906.

Shea, M. T., Stout, R. L., Gunderson, J. G., Morey, L. C., Grilo, C. M., McGlashan, T. H., et al. (2002). Short-term stability of schizotypal, borderline, avoidant, and obsessive compulsive personality disorders. *American Journal of Psychiatry, 159,* 2036–2041.

Shea, M. T., & Yen, S. (2003). Stability as a distinction between Axis I and Axis II disorders. *Journal of Personality Disorders, 17,* 373–386.

Skodol, A. E., Oldham, J. M., Hyler, S. E., Kellman, H. D., Doidge, N., & Davies, M. (1993). Comorbidity of *DSM–III–R* eating disorders and personality disorders. *International Journal of Eating Disorders, 14*, 403–416.

Skoog, D. K., Andersen, A. E., & Laufer, W. S. (1984). Personality and treatment effectiveness in anorexia nervosa. *Journal of Clinical Psychology, 40*, 955–961.

Speranza, M., Corcos, M., Godart, N., Loas, G., Guilbaud, O., Jeammet, P., et al. (2001). Obsessive compulsive disorders in eating disorders. *Eating Behaviors, 2*, 193–207.

Steiger, H., Leung, F., Thibaudeau, J., Houle, L., & Ghadirian, A. M. (1993). Comorbid features in bulimics before and after therapy: Are they explained by Axis II diagnoses, secondary effects of bulimia, or both? *Comprehensive Psychiatry, 34*, 45–53.

Steiger, H., & Stotland, S. (1996). Prospective study of outcome in bulimics as a function of Axis-II comorbidity: Long-term responses on eating and psychiatric symptoms. *International Journal of Eating Disorders, 20*, 149–161.

Steiger, H., Stotland, S., & Houle, L. (1994). Prognostic implications of stable versus transient "borderline features" in bulimic patients. *Journal of Clinical Psychiatry, 55*, 206–214.

Stonehill, E., & Crisp, A. H. (1977). Psychoneurotic characteristics of patients with anorexia nervosa before and after treatment and at follow-up 4–7 years later. *Journal of Psychosomatic Research, 21*, 187–193.

Sunday, S. R., Peterson, C. B., Andreyka, K., Crow, S. J., Mitchell, J. E., & Halmi, K. A. (2001). Differences in *DSM–III–R* and *DSM–IV* diagnoses in eating disorder patients. *Comprehensive Psychiatry, 42*, 448–455.

Thornton, C., & Russell, J. (1997). Obsessive compulsive comorbidity in the dieting disorders. *International Journal of Eating Disorders, 21*, 83–87.

Tozzi, F., Thornton, L. M., Klump, K. L., Fichter, M. M., Halmi, K. A., Kaplan, A. S., et al. (2005). Symptom fluctuation in eating disorders: Correlates of diagnostic crossover. *American Journal of Psychiatry, 162*, 732–740.

Tyrer, P. (1995). Are personality disorders well classified in *DSM–IV*? In W. J. Livesley (Ed.), *The DSM–IV personality disorders* (pp. 29–42). New York: Guilford.

van Velzen, C. J. M., & Emmelkamp, P. M. G. (1996). The assessment of personality disorders: Implications for cognitive and behavior therapy. *Behaviour Research and Therapy, 34*, 655–668.

Vitousek, K. M. (2004). The case for semi-starvation. *European Eating Disorders Review, 12*, 275–278.

Vitousek, K., Daly, J., & Heiser, C. (1991). Reconstructing the internal world of the eating disordered individual: Overcoming denial and distortion in self-report. *International Journal of Eating Disorders, 10*, 647–666.

Vitousek, K. M., Gray, J. A., & Grubbs, K. M. (2004). Caloric restriction for longevity, I: Paradigm, protocols, and physiological findings in animal research. *European Eating Disorders Review, 12*, 279–299.

Vitousek, K. M., Gray, J. A., & Talesfore, C. (in press). Caloric restriction for longevity in humans: A new rationale for semi-starvation. *European Eating Disorders Review, 12*.

Vitousek, K., & Manke, F. (1994). Personality variables and disorders in anorexia nervosa and bulimia nervosa. *Journal of Abnormal Psychology, 103*, 137–147.

Vitousek, K. M., Manke, F. M., Gray, J. A., & Vitousek, M. N. (2004). Caloric restriction for longevity, II: The systematic neglect of behavioral and psychological outcomes in animal research. *European Eating Disorders Review, 12,* 338–360.

Vitousek, K., Watson, S., & Wilson, G. T. (1998). Enhancing motivation for change in treatment-resistant eating disorders. *Clinical Psychology Review, 18,* 391–420.

von Ranson, K. M., Kaye, W. H., Weltzin, T. E., Rao, R., & Matsunaga, H. (1999). Obsessive-compulsive disorder symptoms before and after recovery from bulimia nervosa. *American Journal of Psychiatry, 156,* 1703–1708.

Walsh, T. (2002, September). *Pharmacotherapy for anorexia nervosa.* Paper presented at the NIMH Conference on Anorexia Nervosa, Rockville, MD.

Walters, P., Moran, P., Choudhury, P., Lee, T., & Mann, A. (2004). Screening for personality disorder: A comparison of personality disorder assessment by patients and informants. *International Journal of Methods in Psychiatric Research, 13,* 34–49.

Weindruch, R., & Walford, R. L. (1988). *The retardation of aging and disease by dietary restriction.* Springfield, IL: Charles C. Thomas.

Wentz Nilsson, E., Gillberg, C., Gillberg, I. C., & Rastam, M. (1999). Ten-year follow-up of adolescent onset anorexia nervosa: Personality disorders. *Journal of the American Academy of Child and Adolescent Psychiatry, 38,* 1389–1395.

Westen, D., & Chang, C. (2000). Personality pathology in adolescence: A review. In A. H. Esman & L. T. Flaherty (Eds.), *Adolescent psychiatry: Developmental and clinical studies; The Annals of the American Society for Adolescent Psychiatry* (Vol. 25, pp. 61–100). Hillsdale, NJ: Analytic Press.

Westen, D., & Harnden-Fischer, J. (2001). Personality profiles in eating disorders: Rethinking the distinction between Axis I and Axis II. *American Journal of Psychiatry, 158,* 547–562.

Westen, D., Shedler, J., Durrett, C., Glass, S., & Martens, A. (2003). Personality diagnoses in adolescence: *DSM–IV* Axis II diagnoses and an empirically derived alternative. *American Journal of Psychiatry, 160,* 952–966.

Widiger, T. A. (2000). Personality disorders in the 21st century. *Journal of Personality Disorders, 14,* 3–16.

Widiger, T. A., & Costa, P. T., Jr. (1994). Personality and personality disorders. *Journal of Abnormal Psychology, 103,* 78–91.

Widiger, T. A., & Sanderson, C. J. (2000). Toward a dimensional model of personality disorders. In W. J. Livesley (Ed.), *The DSM–IV personality disorders* (pp. 433–458). New York: Guilford.

Wilson, G. T. (1998). The clinical utility of randomized controlled trials. *International Journal of Eating Disorders, 24,* 13–29.

Wonderlich, S. A. (2002). Personality and eating disorders. In C. G. Fairburn & K. D. Brownell (Eds.), *Eating disorders and obesity: A comprehensive handbook* (pp. 204–209). New York: Guilford.

Wonderlich, S. A., Fullerton, D., Swift, W. J., & Klein, M. H. (1994). Five-year outcome from eating disorders: Relevance of personality disorders. *International Journal of Eating Disorders, 15,* 233–243.

Wonderlich, S. A., Lilenfeld, L. R., Riso, L. P., Engel, S., & Mitchell, J. E. (2005). Personality and anorexia nervosa. *International Journal of Eating Disorders, 37,* S68–S71.

Wonderlich, S. A., & Mitchell, J. E. (1997). Eating disorders and comorbidity: Empirical, conceptual, and clinical implications. *Psychopharmacology Bulletin, 33,* 381–390.

Wonderlich, S., & Mitchell, J. E. (2001). The role of personality in the onset of eating disorders and treatment implications. *Psychiatric Clinics of North America, 24,* 249–258.

Zanarini, M. C., Frankenburg, F. R., Hennen, J., Reich, D. B., & Silk, K. R. (2004). Axis I comorbidity in patients with borderline personality disorder: 6-year follow-up and prediction of time to remission. *American Journal of Psychiatry, 161,* 2108–2114.

Zanarini, M. C., Frankenburg, F. R., Pope, H. G., Hudson, J. I., Yurgelun-Todd, D., & Cicchetti, C. J. (1990). Axis II comorbidity of normal-weight bulimia. *Comprehensive Psychiatry, 31,* 20–24.

Zimmerman, M. (1994). Diagnosing personality disorders: A review of issues and research methods. *Archives of General Psychiatry, 51,* 225–245.

Zimmerman, M., & Mattia, J. I. (1999). Differences between clinical and research practices in diagnosing borderline personality disorder. *American Journal of Psychiatry, 156,* 1570–1574.

Personality Disorders Most Relevant to Eating Disorders

7

Obsessive-Compulsive Personality and Eating Disorders

PARINDA PARIKH, MD
KATHARINE HALMI, MD

The eating disorders anorexia nervosa, bulimia nervosa, binge eating disorder, and their variants have been documented in the history of Western civilization for the past 15 centuries. Clinicians are often challenged with frequent relapse and poor prognoses when treating patients with eating disorders. This can be attributed to the multifactorial etiology and comorbid Axis I and/or Axis II disorders. Hence, a clear understanding of the various facets of eating disorders may help in clinical management. One such facet found in those with eating disorders is obsessive-compulsive personality disorder (OCPD) and an associated disorder, obsessive-compulsive disorder (OCD).

The differentiation between OCPD, an Axis II disorder, and OCD, an Axis I disorder, can be subtle and often confusing, especially in the literature describing the characteristics of patients with eating disorders. OCPD has a cluster of characteristics, but perfectionism is the aspect most thoroughly studied in eating disorders. Perfectionism is an aspect of personality, which, described from a psychobiological viewpoint, is an extreme (high) variant of the temperament dimension of persistence (Kaplan & Sadock, 2000). Several researchers are searching for links between common genetic factors, neurobiological changes, and

TABLE 7.1   The Diagnostic Criteria for Anorexia Nervosa
(American Psychiatric Association, 2000)

A. Refusal to maintain a body weight at or above a minimally normal
   weight for age and height (e.g., weight loss leading to maintenance of
   body weight less than 85% of that expected, or failure to make expected
   weight gain during a period of growth, leading to body weight less than
   85% of that expected)
B. Intense fear of gaining weight or becoming fat, even though underweight
C. Disturbance in the way in which one's body weight or shape is
   experienced, undue influence of body weight or shape on self-evaluation,
   or denial of the seriousness of the current low body weight
D. In postmenarcheal females, amenorrhea, that is, the absence of at least
   three consecutive menstrual cycles (a woman is considered to have
   amenorrhea if her periods occur only following hormone, for example,
   estrogen, administration)

   Restricting type: During the current episode of anorexia nervosa, the
       person has not regularly engaged in binge eating or purging behavior
       (i.e., self-induced vomiting or the misuse of laxatives, diuretics, or
       enemas).
   Binge eating/purging type: During the current episode of anorexia nervosa,
       the person has regularly engaged in binge eating or purging behavior
       (i.e., self-induced vomiting or the misuse of laxatives, diuretics, or
       enemas).

psychological factors to explain the overlap of perfectionism and other
traits of OCPD and OCD in eating disorders. This chapter will attempt
to clarify the personality disorder traits of perfectionism and the concepts of obsessions and compulsions, as presented in the eating disorder
research literature.

DEFINITIONS

According to the *Diagnostic and Statistical Manual of Mental Disorders–
Text Revision (DSM–IV–TR)* (American Psychiatric Association, 2000),
there are several criteria for anorexia nervosa and bulimia nervosa,
which are shown in Tables 7.1 and 7.2, respectively.

The *DSM–IV–TR* definition of OCPD is as follows: "a pervasive pattern of preoccupation with orderliness, perfectionism, [and] mental and
interpersonal control at the expense of flexibility, openness and efficiency." This is demonstrated by (a) a preoccupation with details, lists,
and order; (b) perfectionism that interferes with task completion; (c)
excessive devotion to a task, exclusive of leisure activities and friends;
and (d) an inflexible, rigid, and stubborn mental set (American Psychiatric Association, 2000, p. 729). Although OCPD has a cluster of
characteristics, perfectionism is the aspect most thoroughly studied in

TABLE 7.2   The Diagnostic Criteria for Bulimia Nervosa (American Psychiatric Association, 2000)

A. Recurrent episodes of binge eating; an episode of binge eating is characterized by both of the following:

   1. eating, in a discrete period of time (e.g., within any 2-hour period), an amount of food that is definitely larger than most people would eat during a similar period of time and under similar circumstances

   2. a sense of lack of control over eating during the episode (e.g., a feeling that one cannot stop eating or control what or how much one is eating)

B. Recurrent inappropriate compensatory behavior to prevent weight gain, such as self-induced vomiting; misuse of laxatives, diuretics, enemas, or other medications; fasts; or excessive exercise

C. The binge eating and inappropriate compensatory behaviors both occur, on average, at least twice a week for 3 months

D. Self-evaluation is unduly influenced by body shape and weight

E. The disturbance does not occur exclusively during episodes of anorexia nervosa

   Purging type: During the current episode of bulimia nervosa, the person has regularly engaged in self-induced vomiting or the misuse of laxatives, diuretics, or enemas.

   Nonpurging type: During the current episode of bulimia nervosa, the person has used other inappropriate compensatory behaviors, such as fasting or excessively exercising, but has not regularly engaged in self-induced vomiting or the misuse of laxatives, diuretics, or enemas.

eating disorders. The prevalence of OCPD is about 1% in community samples, about 3% to 10% in psychiatric populations, and anywhere from 3% to 60% in patients with eating disorders.

In contrast to OCPD, OCD is characterized by recurrent obsessions and compulsions. The diagnostic criteria according to the *DSM–IV–TR* for OCPD and OCD are shown in Tables 7.3 and 7.4, respectively.

OCPD AND EATING DISORDERS

References to obstinacy, the inability to pardon, inflexibility, rigidity, and stubbornness are recurrent in the descriptions of the personality characteristics encountered in patients with anorexia nervosa. Marcé (1860), for example, referred to the anorectic individual's obstinate refusal of food. Laseque (1873) stated that anorectics never pardon. Perfectionistic, rigid, and inflexible personality traits were described in patients with anorexia nervosa in publications from as long ago as 30 to 50 years (DuBois, 1949; Kaye & Leigh, 1954; King, 1963; Palmer & Jones, 1939).

TABLE 7.3   The Diagnostic Criteria for Obsessive-Compulsive Personality
Disorder (American Psychiatric Association, 2000)

The individual has a pervasive pattern of preoccupation with orderliness,
perfectionism, and mental and interpersonal control, at the expense of
flexibility, openness, and efficiency, beginning by early adulthood and
present in a variety of contexts, as indicated by four (or more) of the
following. The individual

1. is preoccupied with details, rules, lists, order, organization, or
   schedules to the extent that the major point of the activity is lost;
2. shows perfectionism that interferes with task completion (e.g., is
   unable to complete a project because his or her own overly strict
   standards are not met);
3. is excessively devoted to work and productivity to the exclusion
   of leisure activities and friendships (not accounted for by obvious
   economic necessity);
4. is overconscientious, scrupulous, and inflexible about matters of
   morality, ethics, or values (not accounted for by cultural or religious
   identification);
5. is unable to discard worn-out or worthless objects even when they
   have no sentimental value;
6. is reluctant to delegate tasks or to work with others unless they
   submit to exactly his or her way of doing things;
7. adopts a miserly spending style toward both self and others; money is
   viewed as something to be hoarded for future catastrophes;
8. shows rigidity and stubbornness.

PREVALENCE OF OCPD IN EATING DISORDERS

Despite these preceding common descriptors, the actual prevalence of
OCPD in patients with eating disorders appears to be low. Using the
Structured Clinical Interview for the *DSM* (American Psychiatric Association, 1994), Braun, Sunday, and Halmi (1994) explored the prevalence
of OCPD in various eating disorder diagnostic groups. They found that
only 9% of 105 patients met the criteria for OCPD. An interesting finding in this study was that only 6% of anorectic restrictors met this diagnosis, compared with 13% of the binge/purge type anorectics. Because
patients who binge and purge tend to be more impulsive, it was surprising to find that they had OCPD at twice the prevalence of that found
in the restrictors. Another finding in this study was that subthreshold
OCPD was diagnosed in 18% of the patients with anorexia nervosa. In
other words, these patients had several characteristics associated with
the diagnosis of OCPD but not enough to fulfill the actual requirements
for diagnosis. In addition, none of the patients with normal-weight bulimia nervosa in this study met the threshold criteria for the diagnosis of
OCPD; however, 6 met the subthreshold diagnostic criteria. This finding suggests that patients with bulimia nervosa may have some, but not
all, of the characteristics of OCPD, along with impulsivity. In this study,

TABLE 7.4   The Diagnostic Criteria for Obsessive-Compulsive Disorder (American Psychiatric Association, 2000)

A. Either obsessions or compulsions

Obsessions as defined by Items 1, 2, 3, and 4:

1. Recurrent and persistent thoughts, impulses, or images that are experienced, at some time during the disturbance, as intrusive and inappropriate and that cause marked anxiety or distress.
2. The thoughts, impulses, or images are not simply excessive worries about real-life problems.
3. The person attempts to ignore or suppress such thoughts, impulses, or images or to neutralize them with some other thought or action.
4. The person recognizes that the obsessional thoughts, impulses, or images are a product of his or her own mind (not imposed from without as in thought insertion).

Compulsions as defined by Items 1 and 2:

1. The person feels driven to perform repetitive behaviors (e.g., hand washing, ordering, checking) or mental acts (e.g., praying, counting, repeating words silently) in response to an obsession or according to rules that must be applied rigidly.
2. The behaviors or mental acts are aimed at preventing or reducing distress or preventing some dreaded event or situation; however, these behaviors or mental acts either are not connected in a realistic way with what they are designed to neutralize or prevent or are clearly excessive.

B. At some point during the course of the disorder, the person has recognized that the obsessions or compulsions are excessive or unreasonable. *Note:* This does not apply to children.
C. The obsessions or compulsions cause marked distress, are time-consuming (take more than 1 hour a day), or significantly interfere with the person's normal routine, occupational (or academic) functioning, or usual social activities or relationships.
D. If another Axis I disorder is present, the content of the obsessions or compulsions is not restricted to it (e.g., preoccupation with food in the presence of an eating disorder; hair pulling in the presence of trichotillomania; concern with appearance in the presence of body dysmorphic disorder; preoccupation with drugs in the presence of a substance-use disorder; preoccupation with having a serious illness in the presence of hypochondriasis; preoccupation with sexual urges or fantasies in the presence of a paraphilia; or guilty ruminations in the presence of major depressive disorder).
E. The disturbance is not due to the direct physiological effects of a substance (e.g., a drug of abuse, a medication) or a general medical condition.

in another diagnostic subsample of patients with normal-weight bulimia who had a history of anorexia nervosa ($n = 18$), 2 met the threshold, and 5 met the subthreshold, criteria for OCPD.

Bellodi et al. (1992) used the Structured Interview for *DSM* Personality Disorders–Revised (American Psychiatric Association, 1994) for personality disorder assessment and found that 22% of an eating disorder sample of mixed anorectics and bulimics met the criteria for the diagnosis of OCPD. (It is interesting that this was similar to prevalence rates of OCPD found in patients with OCD in the same study.) Using structured interviews for diagnosis, other studies have found the prevalence rate of OCPD to vary between 3% and 60% (Herzog, Keller, Lavori, Kenny, & Sachs, 1992; Piran, Lerner, Garfinkel, Kennedy, & Brouillette, 1988; Wonderlich, Swift, Slotnick, & Goodman, 1990). This wide range in findings may be attributed to the general difficulty in diagnosing personality disorders (Arntz, 1999) as well as the various measures used to diagnose personality disorders (Serpell, Livingstone, Neiderman, & Lask, 2002). Suggesting possible genetic influences, family studies have reported an increased prevalence of OCPD in the relatives of individuals with eating disorders (Wonderlich et al., 1990).

Practice Point

The complete *DSM–IV–TR* diagnosis of OCPD is not highly prevalent in eating disorders; however, many components of this diagnosis, such as perfectionism, persistence, control, and rigidity, are present to varying degrees.

RELATIONSHIPS AMONG PERFECTIONISM, OCD, AND OCPD

There is a significant correlation between perfectionism and obsessive-compulsive traits as measured by perfectionism subscales (Frost, Marten, Lahart, & Rosenblate, 1990; Frost & Steketee, 1997; Tozzi, Jacobson, Neale, Kendler, & Bulik, 2004). This relationship was studied in individuals with anorexia and bulimia nervosa who were participating in the International Price Foundation Genetic Study (Halmi & Price Foundation Collaborative Group, 2003). The participants were assessed for perfectionism, OCD, and OCPD. No differences were found in the prevalence of OCD, OCPD, or their combination across eating disorder subtypes. Those who had neither OCD nor OCPD had the lowest perfectionism scores, whereas those who had both OCD and OCPD had the highest perfectionism scores. A stronger relationship was found between perfectionism and OCPD, compared to the relationship of perfectionism with OCD. However, perfectionism was exacerbated by the presence of both OCD and OCPD (Halmi & Price Foundation Collaborative Group, 2003).

Strober (1980) described certain patients with anorexia as "obsessional with inflexible thinking," suggesting that OCPD traits persist even after the individual recovers from anorexia nervosa. Findings by Matsunaga et al. (1999) and Matsunaga et al. (2000) indicate that 15% of patients in their study who recovered from anorexia nervosa continued to meet strict diagnostic criteria for OCPD, even after 1 year of full remission of their eating disorder. The following case report illustrates the intertwining relationship between OCPD and OCD in a clinical patient, supporting these research findings.

Case Report

Sue (not her real name), a 37-year-old single, White female, just completed her fifth hospitalization for anorexia nervosa. She was first hospitalized at age 22. Prior to this initial hospitalization, Sue had finished college and was in the initial year of her first job when her relationship with a young man ended. After this event, she began to restrict her food intake and, over the subsequent year, lost 20 pounds. At a height of 5'4", she maintained a weight of 90 pounds for the next 6 years. She denied binging, purging, or using laxatives or diet pills. She was extremely perfectionistic at her job, and as a result, her career advanced quickly. After her mother died, 3 years before her admission to the current program, she began to lose more weight. She continued to rapidly lose weight to the point that she could no longer adequately perform her job, which she lost a year prior to her last hospitalization. In the few months before admission, she rapidly lost weight until she reached 50 pounds. Sue had been amenorrheic for 15 years.

Sue was regarded as very perfectionistic throughout her childhood and college career. She always obtained the highest grades. Two years prior to her first hospitalization, she developed obsessive-compulsive rituals that appeared unrelated to her eating disorder. These rituals, which included checking doors, the stove, and lights, began to take up so much time that they began interfering with her functioning. As these rituals continued, she became more socially withdrawn, and during the last 2 years, she suffered from anhedonia, decreased concentration, decreased attention, and sleep disturbances. She denied being depressed but admitted to feeling bored. Sue denied drug, nicotine, or alcohol use. Sue had a maternal grandfather who had anorexia nervosa and OCD. After 6 months of intensive medical treatment and psychotherapy, she was able to obtain a normal weight and be discharged to an outpatient program.

It is interesting to note that this patient's OCD symptoms did not occur until her anorexia nervosa was well advanced. However, prior to the onset of anorexia nervosa, Sue did have pronounced perfectionistic tendencies. During the period of her extreme emaciation, the OCD symptoms that were unrelated to her eating disorder were the most severe. With nutritional rehabilitation, both the OCD symptomatology and the rituals and preoccupations associated with her eating disorder decreased. Her rigid, inflexible, and perfectionistic nature still prevailed after weight restoration and undoubtedly will be a factor that will interfere with her personal relationships.

Practice Point
The major difference between OCPD and OCD is that OCPD is not characterized by the presence of obsessions and compulsions but presents as a pervasive pattern of inflexibility.

CONCLUSION

Studies of obsessions and compulsions as well as obsessive-compulsive personality features in patients with eating disorders have surprisingly shown that perfectionistic features can exist in patients with bulimia nervosa as well as with anorexia nervosa. Thus, the seemingly contradictory traits of impulsivity and perfectionism are present in some patients with bulimia nervosa. No study has directly examined the effect of obsessions and compulsions on the trait of perfectionism. The latter is usually conceptualized as a trait and thus little influenced by Axis I symptomatology. It is likely that a common genetic link exists in the expression of obsessions, compulsions, and features of OCPD. This may be one of several biological vulnerabilities for the development of an eating disorder.

NOTE

Please address correspondence to Dr. Parinda Parikh, MD, New York Presbyterian Hospital, 21 Bloomingdale Road, White Plains, NY, 10605; telephone: 914-997-8677; fax: 914-682-6988; e-mail: pap9014@med.cornell.edu.

REFERENCES

American Psychiatric Association. (1994). *Diagnostic and statistical manual of mental disorders* (4th ed.). Washington, DC: Author.

American Psychiatric Association. (2000). *Diagnostic and statistical manual of mental disorders* (4th ed., Text Revision). Washington, DC: Author.

Arntz, A. (1999). Do personality disorders exist? On the validity of the concept and its cognitive-behavioral formulation and treatment. *Behaviour Research and Therapy, 37*, S97–S134.

Bellodi, L., Pasquali, L., Diaferia, G., Scuito, G., Bernardeschi, L., & Coccji, S. (1992). Do eating, mood and obsessive-compulsive patients share a common personality profile? *New Trends in Experimental and Clinical Psychiatry, 8*, 87–92.

Braun, D. L., Sunday, S. R., & Halmi, K. A. (1994). Psychiatric comorbidity in patients with eating disorders. *Psychological Medicine, 24*, 859–867.

DuBois, F. S. (1949). Compulsion neuroses with cachexia. *American Journal of Psychiatry, 106*, 107–110.

Frost, R. O., Marten, P., Lahart, C., & Rosenblate, R. (1990). The dimensions of perfectionism. *Cognitive Therapy and Research, 14*, 449–468.

Frost, R., & Steketee, G. (1997). Perfectionism in obsessive-compulsive disorder patients. *Behaviour Research and Therapy, 35*, 291–296.

Halmi, K. A., & Price Foundation Collaborative Group. (2003, September 16–19). *The relationship of perfectionism to OCPD and OCD.* Paper presented at the Eating Disorder Research Society meeting, Ravello, Italy.

Herzog, D. B., Keller, M. B., Lavori, P. W., Kenny, G. M., & Sachs, N. R. (1992). The prevalence of personality disorders in 210 women with eating disorders. *Journal of Clinical Psychiatry, 53*, 147–152.

Kaplan, H. I., & Sadock, B. J. (Eds.). (2000). *Comprehensive textbook of psychiatry* (7th ed.). Baltimore: Lippincott, Willliams, and Wilkins.

Kaye, D. W., & Leigh, D. (1954). The natural history, treatment and prognosis of anorexia nervosa. *Journal of Mental Science, 100*, 411–416.

King, A. (1963). Primary and secondary anorexia nervosa syndrome. *British Journal of Psychiatry, 109*, 470–475.

Laseque, S. (1873). De L'Anorexie Hystrique. *Archives of General Medicine, 1*, 385–403.

Marcé, L. V. (1860). On a form of hypochondriacal delirium occurring consecutive to dyspepsia and characterized by refusal of food. *Journal of Psychological Medicine and Mental Pathology, 13*, 264–266.

Matsunaga, H., Kaye, W. H., McConaha, C., Plotnicov, K., Pollice, C., & Rao, R. (2000). Personality disorders among subjects recovered from eating disorders. *International Journal of Eating Disorders, 27*, 353–357.

Matsunaga, H., Kiriike, N., Iwasaki, Y., Miyata, A., Yamagami, S., & Kaye, W. H. (1999). Clinical characteristics in patients with anorexia nervosa and obsessive-compulsive disorder. *Psychological Medicine, 29*, 407–414.

Palmer, H. D., & Jones, M. S. (1939). Anorexia nervosa as a manifestation of compulsion neuroses. *Archives of Neurology and Psychiatry, 41*, 856–866.

Piran, N., Lerner, P., Garfinkel, P. E., Kennedy, S. H., & Brouillette, C. (1988). Personality disorders in anorexic patients. *International Journal of Eating Disorders, 7*, 589–599.

Serpell, L., Livingstone, A., Neiderman, M., & Lask, B. (2002). Anorexia nervosa: Obsessive-compulsive disorder, obsessive-compulsive personality disorder, or neither? *Clinical Psychology Review, 22*, 647–669.

Strober, M. (1980). Personality and symptomatological features in young, nonchronic anorexia nervosa patients. *Journal of Psychosomatic Research, 24*, 353–359.

Tozzi, F., Jacobson, K., Neale, B. M., Kendler, K. S., & Bulik, C. M. (2004). Genetic and environmental influences on the relation between perfectionism and obsessionality. *Behavior Genetics, 34*, 483–493.

Wonderlich, S. A., Swift, W. J., Slotnick, H. B., & Goodman, S. (1990). DSM–III–R personality disorders in eating-disorders subtypes. *International Journal of Eating Disorders, 9*, 607–616.

CHAPTER

8

Borderline Personality and Eating Disorders

RANDY A. SANSONE, MD
JOHN L. LEVITT, PHD

Borderline personality disorder (BPD) is a complex Axis II phenomenon that is categorized in the *Diagnostic and Statistical Manual of Mental Disorder—Fourth Edition (DSM-IV)* (American Psychiatric Association, 1994) as a Cluster B disorder (i.e., dramatic, erratic characteristics). Most affected individuals sustain a remarkably intact (albeit transient) social façade, which appears in stark contrast to their long-standing self-regulation difficulties and self-harm behavior, chaotic interpersonal relationships, and chronic dysphoria. This polar combination of features (intact façade, internal chaos) is intriguing and has been the inspiration for several movies, including *Play Misty for Me, Fatal Attraction, Misery, Looking for Mr. Goodbar, The Crush*, and *Single White Female*.

THE EPIDEMIOLOGY OF BPD

Prevalence Rates in the United States

The overall prevalence of personality disorders in the general population is around 5% to 10% (Ellison & Shader, 2003). According to the *DSM–IV* (American Psychiatric Association, 1994), the prevalence of BPD in the general population is around 2%. Stone (1986), however, believed that the prevalence of BPD may be as high as 10%, suggesting that it might be one of the more common Axis II disorders in the general population.

Although recent data is sparse, BPD appears to be one of the more frequent Axis II disorders encountered in both psychiatric inpatients and outpatients (Quigley, 2005). According to findings by Widiger and Rogers (1989), the prevalence of BPD in inpatient and outpatient psychiatric settings is 15% and 27%, respectively. In addition, up to 50% of inpatients with personality disorders suffer from BPD (Widiger & Weissman, 1991). In an inpatient psychiatric sample, we determined the prevalence of BPD to be nearly 47% on clinical interview and nearly 55% on assessment with a *DSM–IV* criteria checklist (Sansone, Songer, & Gaither, 2001). In a retrospective review of medical records in a university-based outpatient psychotherapy clinic, we found the prevalence of BPD traits or disorder to be nearly 22% (Sansone, Rytwinski, & Gaither, 2003). We caution that these differing prevalence rates, which have been determined during different eras in various treatment settings, may in part reflect changes in the management of mental health services.

Practice Point
Clinicians are quite likely to find themselves treating patients with BPD in either inpatient or outpatient settings.

Gender Distribution

According to the *DSM–IV* (American Psychiatric Association, 1994), more women than men suffer from BPD. However, this deduction may not be accurate. There appear to be distinct gender patterns in BPD symptom presentations. In clinical settings, women with BPD tend to demonstrate histrionic features, self-directed self-harm behavior (e.g., cutting or scratching self), and Axis I diagnoses of eating disorders and post-traumatic stress disorder (Johnson et al., 2003). In contrast, men tend to demonstrate antisocial features (Johnson et al., 2003), externally directed self-harm behavior (i.e., bar fights, high-risk behaviors), and Axis I diagnoses of substance abuse (Johnson et al., 2003). Why these gender differences in symptom presentation occur remains unknown, but they may relate to cultural, genetic, and neurohormonal factors. It is important that, as a result of these symptom differences, women with BPD tend to amass in mental health settings whereas men with BPD tend to congregate in prison settings. Therefore, in our opinion, investigator bias and study setting may contribute to the misleading impression of a female predominance in BPD (Skodol & Bender, 2003).

Practice Point
Women patients with BPD appear to exhibit symptom patterns characterized by "acting in," whereas men with BPD tend to exhibit symptom patterns characterized by "acting out."

Cultural and Racial Differences

Few empirical studies have explored cultural or racial patterns in BPD. According to Paris (1996), BPD is more likely to be encountered in Western cultures, but some data indicate that there may be high variability. For example, in a Norwegian community sample, investigators (Torgersen, Kringlen, & Cramer, 2001) found BPD to be relatively infrequent, particularly when compared to other personality disorders. In contrast, in a study of French high school students, Chabrol, Montovany, Chouicha, Callahan, and Mullet (2001) found a substantially high prevalence rate for BPD, between 10% and 18%.

Prevalence studies of BPD among subcultures within the same country are rare. However, one such study exists. In a U.S. sample, Chavira et al. (2003) found that, compared with Whites and Blacks, Hispanics evidenced higher rates of BPD.

Is there really cultural variation in the development and presentation of BPD? If so, then theoretically, non-Western cultures must have some protective influences with respect to the suspected prime causative factors of BPD, which include genetics, early developmental trauma, and/or parental dysfunction. This premise could be possible if a given population had an inherent genetic resilience, refrained from childhood maltreatment, and/or maintained extended family networks that might dilute the negative effects of parental pathology. On the other hand, if the proposed etiological variables are fairly consistent worldwide, it is possible that local culture tempers the expression of the features of BPD (e.g., less overt self-harm behavior but the accentuation of other features such as somatic preoccupation and/or medically self-defeating behaviors); these latter behaviors are not even identified in the *DSM*. Given the possibility of cultural tempering of BPD symptoms, such patients in particular societies might go underdetected and the prevalence rate might appear misleadingly low.

The Prevalence of BPD Among Individuals With Eating Disorders

Among individuals with eating disorders, the explicit prevalence of BPD remains unknown. However, in a recent literature review (Sansone, Levitt, & Sansone, 2005), we found that BPD prevalence rates among individuals with eating disorders varied according to diagnosis. In restricting anorexia nervosa, binge eating/purging anorexia nervosa, and bulimia nervosa, the prevalence rates were 10%, 25%, and 28%, respectively. The prevalence of BPD among those with binge eating disorder was around 12% (Sansone et al., 2005). These data substantiate the clinical impression that the intersection of eating disorders and BPD is not uncommon.

TABLE 8.1 "The Criteria for Borderline Personality Disorder", According to the *Diagnostic and Statistical Manual of Mental Disorders, Fourth Edition, Text Revision* (American Psychiatric Association, 2000)

Borderline personality disorder is indicated by a pervasive pattern of instability of interpersonal relationships, self-image, and affects, and a marked impulsivity beginning by early adulthood and present in a variety of contexts, as indicated by five (or more) of the following:

1. frantic efforts to avoid real or imagined abandonment;
2. a pattern of unstable and intense interpersonal relationships characterized by alternating between extremes of idealization and devaluation;
3. identity disturbance: markedly and persistently unstable self-image or sense of self;
4. impulsivity in at least two areas that are potentially self-damaging (e.g., spending, sex, substance abuse, reckless driving, binge eating);
5. recurrent suicidal behavior, gestures, or threats, or self-mutilating behavior;
6. affective instability due to a marked reactivity of mood (e.g., intense episodic dysphoria, irritability, or anxiety usually lasting a few hours and only rarely more than a few days);
7. chronic feelings of emptiness;
8. inappropriate, intense anger or difficulty controlling anger (e.g., frequent displays of temper, constant anger, recurrent physical fights); and
9. transient, stress-related paranoid ideation or severe dissociative symptoms.

THE DIAGNOSIS OF BPD

The Diagnostic and Statistical Manual of Mental Disorders–Text Revision *Criteria*

The *Diagnostic and Statistical Manual of Mental Disorders–Text Revision* (*DSM–IV–TR*) (American Psychiatric Association, 2000) criteria are the current benchmark for psychiatric diagnosis. The *DSM–IV–TR* lists nine criteria for BPD; five are required for diagnostic confirmation (see Table 8.1).

Self-Report Assessments

In addition to the *DSM–IV–TR* criteria, there are self-report assessment tools for the diagnosis of BPD. Several self-report measures are particularly well adapted for use in clinical settings because of their ease of administration, brevity, and minimal to no cost. These include the borderline personality subscale of the Personality Diagnostic Questionnaire–4 (Hyler, 1994), the Self-Harm Inventory (Sansone, Wiederman, & Sansone, 1998) (see Table 8.2), and the McLean Screening Instrument

TABLE 8.2 The Self-Harm Inventory (Sansone, Wiederman, & Sansone, 1998)

Instructions: Please answer the following questions by checking either "Yes" or "No." Check "Yes" *only* to those items that you have done intentionally, or *on purpose,* to hurt yourself.

Yes	No	Have you ever intentionally, or on purpose, ...
___	___	1. overdosed? (If yes, indicate number of times: ___ .)
___	___	2. cut yourself on purpose? (If yes, indicate number of times: ___ .)
___	___	3. burned yourself on purpose? (If yes, indicate number of times: ___ .)
___	___	4. hit yourself? (If yes, indicate number of times: ___ .)
___	___	5. banged your head on purpose? (If yes, indicate number of times: ___ .)
___	___	6. abused alcohol?
___	___	7. driven recklessly on purpose? (If yes, indicate number of times: ___ .)
___	___	8. scratched yourself on purpose? (If yes, indicate number of times: ___ .)
___	___	9. prevented wounds from healing?
___	___	10. made medical situations worse, on purpose (e.g., skipped medication)?
___	___	11. been promiscuous (i.e., had many sexual partners)? (If yes, indicate how many ___ .)
___	___	12. set yourself up in a relationship to be rejected?
___	___	13. abused prescription medication?
___	___	14. distanced yourself from God as punishment?
___	___	15. engaged in emotionally abusive relationships? (If yes, indicate number of relationships: ___ .)
___	___	16. engaged in sexually abusive relationships? (If yes, indicate number of relationships: ___ .)
___	___	17. lost a job on purpose? (If yes, indicate number of times: ___ .)
___	___	18. attempted suicide? (If yes, indicate number of times: ___ .)
___	___	19. exercised an injury on purpose?
___	___	20. tortured yourself with self-defeating thoughts?
___	___	21. starved yourself to hurt yourself?
___	___	22. abused laxatives to hurt yourself? (If yes, indicate number of times: ___ .)

Have you engaged in any other self-destructive behaviors not asked about in this inventory? If so, please describe below.

© 1995: Sansone, Sansone, and Wiederman

for Borderline Personality Disorder (Zanarini et al., 2003). Each of these measures is one page in length, easily scored, and available for clinician use. In addition to diagnosing BPD (scores of five "yes" responses or higher), the Self-Harm Inventory also elicits the respondent's history of self-harm behavior, which may help to focus the clinician's initial intervention strategies. A potential limitation of all self-report measures is their tendency to be diagnostically overinclusive. As with any assessment tool, each requires clinical substantiation to confirm the diagnosis of BPD.

Semistructured Interviews

Several semistructured interviews for BPD are available for clinician use. However, these are more commonly used in research settings because of cost, administration time, and/or required training for use. Examples include the Diagnostic Interview for Borderlines–Revised (Zanarini, Gunderson, Frankenburg, & Chauncey, 1989), the Personality Disorder Examination (Loranger, 1988), the Structured Clinical Interview for *DSM–III–R* Personality Disorders (Spitzer, Williams, Gibbon, & First, 1990), and the Diagnostic Interview for Personality Disorders (Zanarini, 1983).

Clinical Adaptation of the Diagnostic Interview for Borderlines: PISIA

For diagnosis in clinical practice, we have used a clinical adaptation of the original Diagnostic Interview for Borderlines (Kolb & Gunderson, 1980). In contrast to the *DSM*, these criteria are much easier to recall because the five core diagnostic areas can be organized around the abbreviation PISIA. The acronym stands for psychotic/quasi-psychotic episodes, impulsivity, social adaptation, interpersonal relationships, and affect (see Table 8.3). In using this approach, the clinician must verify one type of psychotic/quasi-psychotic phenomenon, both long-standing self-regulation difficulties and self-harm behavior (impulsivity), a socially intact façade (i.e., social adaptation), chaotic and unfulfilling interpersonal relationships, and a chronically dysphoric affect. For the evaluation of impulsivity, we explicitly ask about specific behaviors. For example, for self-regulation difficulties, we explicitly ask, "Have you ever had any drug or alcohol problems . . . prescription abuse problems . . . difficulties regulating money?" For self-harm behavior, we explicitly ask, "Have you ever cut, burned, or scratched yourself ... attempted suicide . . . been in an abusive relationship . . . had any high-risk hobbies . . . engaged in any high-risk behaviors?" For patient screening purposes, the Impulsivity and Affect categories are high-yield criteria, probably because these features have been empirically determined to be stable over time (McGlashan et al., 2005). Because of the prevalence of BPD

TABLE 8.3   A Clinical Adaptation of the Diagnostic Interview for Borderlines (Kolb & Gunderson, 1980): PISIA

P	*Psychotic/quasi-psychotic episodes:* transient, fleeting, brief episodes that tend to be recurrent over the patient's lifetime; may include the following: • Depersonalization • Derealization • Dissociation • Rage reactions • Paranoia (patient recognizes the illogical nature of his or her suspiciousness) • Fleeting or isolated hallucinations or delusions • Unusual reactions to drugs
I	*Impulsivity:* long-standing behaviors that may be stable over time, coexist with other behaviors, or replace one another over time (i.e., substitution): • *Self-regulation difficulties* (e.g., eating disorders such as anorexia and bulimia nervosa, binge eating disorder, obesity; drug, alcohol, or prescription abuse; money management difficulties such as bankruptcies, credit card difficulties, uncontrolled gambling; promiscuity; mood regulation difficulties) • *Self-destructive behaviors* (e.g., self-mutilation such as hitting, cutting, burning, or biting oneself; suicide attempts; sadomasochistic relationships; high-risk hobbies such as parachuting or racing; high-risk behaviors such as frequenting dangerous bars or jogging in parks at night)
S	*Social adaptation:* superficially intact social veneer; if the individual demonstrates high academic or professional performance, it is usually inconsistent and erratic.
I	*Interpersonal relationships:* chaotic and unsatisfying relationships; the relationship style is characterized by "dichotomous relatedness," wherein social relationships tend to be very superficial and transient whereas personal relationships tend to be extremely intense, manipulative, and dependent; intense fears of being alone; rage with the primary caretaker.
A	*Affect:* chronically dysphoric or labile; since adolescence, the majority of the mood experience has been dysphoric, with the predominant affects being anxiety, anger, depression, or emptiness.

Note: In using these criteria, the patient must meet criteria in each category (i.e., the patient must have one type of long-standing quasi-psychotic phenomenon, both long-standing self-regulation difficulties and self-destructive behavior, a superficially intact veneer, chronically unsatisfying relationships with others, and chronic mood disturbance with either persistent dysphoria or mood lability).

among individuals with eating disorders, we believe that each should be screened for this Axis II disorder.

Practice Point
All patients with eating disorders should be evaluated for BPD through clinical screening and even a specialized assessment tool.

Difficulties in BPD Diagnosis

Although the diagnostic criteria in the *DSM–IV–TR* are relatively clear, BPD can be difficult to diagnose in the clinical setting. First, there is the elusive, intact social façade, which momentarily obscures the dramatic underlying symptomatology of BPD.

Second, BPD is known to be a polysymptomatic disorder. In this regard, studies in psychiatric settings indicate that BPD is associated with multiple Axis I and Axis II diagnoses (Sansone et al., 2003; Zanarini et al., 1998; Zimmerman & Mattia, 1999). As a result, dramatic comorbid Axis I diagnoses may distract the clinician from exploring or considering a diagnosis of BPD on Axis II, particularly when the Axis I disorder is a life-threatening eating disorder.

Third, BPD may be particularly difficult to diagnose in medical settings. As in mental health settings, there may be a profusion of diagnoses, but these tend to be somatically based and may include extensive somatic preoccupation involving multiple body areas (Sansone & Sansone, 2003), chronic pain syndromes (Sansone, Whitecar, Meier, & Murry, 2001), and even bona fide somatization disorder (Hudziak, Boffeli, Kreisman, & Battaglia, 1996). (Again, note that physical symptoms are not even alluded to as diagnostic criteria in the *DSM*.) In addition, in medical settings, the characteristic self-harm behavior associated with BPD in mental health settings may manifest in more medicalized modes, such as sabotaging one's medical care. Examples of this include engaging in medication noncompliance, exposing oneself to infection in the hopes of getting ill, interfering with wound healing, and/or getting into altercations with health care providers to intentionally precipitate one's dismissal from a medical practice (Sansone, Wiederman, & Sansone, 2000; Sansone, Wiederman, Sansone, & Mehnert-Kay, 1997).

Finally, BPD exists along a functional continuum, from low to high. In contrast to those in state hospitals and community mental health centers, higher functioning patients with BPD tend to experience fewer quasi-psychotic episodes, engage in more socially discreet self-harm behavior (i.e., less self-mutilation), maintain a more durable social façade, sustain more stable interpersonal relationships (e.g., long-standing marriages), and demonstrate less lability in affect. In our experience, patients with BPD and eating disorders, in general, tend to reside in the higher range of this continuum of functionality, compared with other types of patients with BPD. This latter observation appears to support Stone's (1990) finding of a better long-term prognosis for the BPD subgroup with eating disorders, compared to other subgroups of patients with borderline personality.

Practice Point

Compared to patients with BPD in general, patients with eating disorders and BPD tend to reside in the higher end of the functional continuum, which tends to afford a better overall prognosis.

ETIOLOGICAL FACTORS

The etiology of BPD appears to be multidetermined. Although earlier research discounted a genetic contribution (Torgersen, 1994), more recent studies indicate that, as in many of the personality disorders, there may be a nonspecific genetic predisposition to BPD (Skodol et al., 2002). Specifically, core biological vulnerabilities in the areas of affective stability, impulse management, and/or cognitive or perceptual styling may be inherited (Goodman, New, & Siever, 2004).

It is important that the majority of empirical studies in BPD confirm the presence of some type of repetitive early developmental trauma, which may include sexual, physical, and emotional abuse, as well as the witnessing of violence (Sansone & Sansone, 2000). Physical neglect (e.g., insufficient food, lack of medical care) has not been associated with BPD, suggesting the relevance of an intrusive and malignant overtone to the nature of the childhood adversity. In support of the role of childhood adversity, imaging studies in individuals with BPD indicate abnormalities in the hippocampus (Sala et al., 2004), which is known to be fairly sensitive to the effects of repeated stressful episodes.

In addition to genetic predisposition, the transgenerational nature of trauma and maltreatment and the exposure to chaotic family environments may contribute to the tendency of BPD to run in families. Indeed, Zanarini et al. (2004) confirmed a higher rate of the disorder in the families of patients with BPD, compared with other Axis II probands. Other contributory family variables may include biparental failure, or the absence of sufficient and consistent support from both parents (Zanarini et al., 2000); overt parental psychopathology (Bradley, Jenei, & Westen, 2005); and overall family instability (Bradley et al., 2005). These etiological factors do not exclude the possibility of other contributory causes, such as triggering events.

Practice Point

BPD appears to be a multidetermined disorder, with genetic vulnerability, repetitive early developmental trauma, and parental psychopathology being likely contributory substrates.

THE RELATIONSHIP OF BPD TO EATING DISORDERS

Why comorbid eating disorder pathology emerges among some individuals with BPD remains unknown. In the following section, we speculate on a variety of possible relationships between BPD and eating disorders.

Differences and Similarities in Diagnostic Criteria and Areas of Functioning

The eating disorder diagnoses represent syndromes of related behaviors that, at particular thresholds, result in a specific diagnosis. That is, when a certain number of relevant behaviors (e.g., purging, restricting) present together over a specified period of time, an eating disorder diagnosis is indicated and confirmed. Broader aspects of individual functioning are not diagnostically required for eating disorder diagnoses.

In contrast, the criteria for BPD are globally broader and cover a greater number of functional areas than the eating disorder diagnoses. This is, in part, related to the fact that the BPD diagnosis represents a *trait* condition (i.e., an ongoing, integral facet of the individual's general functioning), whereas an eating disorder diagnosis hypothetically represents a *state* condition (i.e., an acute and/or transient condition). From this perspective, we expect the personality disorder to be more fixed, long standing, and resistant to change, whereas the eating disorder would be somewhat more susceptible to change. Yet some patients with eating disorders demonstrate remarkable resistance to change, with resulting symptom longevity that is similar in many ways to personality disorders. Do these resistant cases actually represent personality disorders that have aggregated around eating disorder symptoms? Or is our view of eating disorders as acute phenomena too narrow? Or both?

Table 8.4 compares the eating disorder and BPD diagnostic criteria according to functional dimensions. Note that the BPD diagnosis covers relational, behavioral, cognitive, and affective areas of functioning. In contrast, eating disorder diagnoses generally emphasize behavioral and cognitive processes, with relatively little emphasis on relational (i.e., none) or affective processes (i.e., minimal).

TABLE 8.4   Borderline Personality Disorder Versus Eating Disorder Diagnoses: Criteria Comparison According to the *Diagnostic and Statistical Manual of Mental Disorders–Text Revision* (American Psychiatric Association, 2000)

	Number of Criteria		
	Borderline Personality Disorder	Anorexia Nervosa	Bulimia Nervosa
Relational processes	2		
Behavioral processes	2	1	3
Cognitive processes	2	2	2
Affective processes	3	1	

Despite these seeming differences, the affected areas of functioning in eating disorders may be quite similar to BPD. For example, affective dysfunction is a fundamental characteristic of those with BPD. Similarly, the role of impaired affective functioning in eating disorders is apparent but may be understated in the *DSM*. In this regard, the work of Garner (1997) underscores the concept that starvation predisposes an individual toward affective instability (i.e., emotional distress, mood changes, irritability, outbursts of anger). BPD is associated with relational disturbances. Likewise, the social isolation encountered in patients with eating disorders certainly represents a relational effect of the disorder.

Goodsitt's (1997) description of anorexia and bulimia nervosa seems very compatible with BPD, particularly with regard to the self-regulation and affective difficulties. Goodsitt (1997) described the world of the anorexic as follows:

> Lacking reliable self-soothing, tension regulation, and mood regulation, and feeling restlessly bored, empty, and aimless, the anorexic is driven to constant activity and strenuous physical exertion to drown out these painful internal conditions. By focusing on food and weight, by rigidly counting calories and regulating ingestion, by turning off her needs for others and turning inward to herself, and by filling up her life with rituals that help her feel a sense of predictability and control, she narrows down her world to something she feels she can manage. (pp. 209–210)

Likewise, Goodsitt (1997) described the early world of the young bulimic as "prior to the onset of bulimia is a child who is more tension-ridden, conflicted, and impulsive than the anorexic child. Her self-esteem is unstable. . . . The bulimic enters puberty and adolescence poorly equipped to regulate her moods, tensions, self-esteem, and cohesion" (p. 209).

Finally, Levitt and Sansone (Levitt & Sansone, 2002; Sansone & Levitt, 2002) indicated that impulsivity (e.g., self-harm behavior and suicide attempts) and dissociation are common phenomena in patients with eating disorders, particularly among bulimics. Given that patients with eating disorders often appear to have difficulty modulating moods and behavior, maintaining self-esteem, sustaining successful relationships, and constructing an identity, there may be fewer genuine differences in areas of functioning with BPD than indicated by the *DSM–IV–TR* (American Psychiatric Association, 2000).

Possible Relationships Between Eating Disorders and BPD

Eating disorders and BPD are frequently encountered in the same patients. The notion of co-occurrence simply states that the two disorders exist in the same individual, but it does not clarify the relationship.

Dolan-Sewell, Krueger, and Shea (2001) provided useful theoretical models that explore how Axis I and Axis II disorders might co-occur.

TABLE 8.5   Comparison of Theoretical Models That Might Explain the
Co-occurrence of Borderline Personality Disorder and Eating Disorders

Models	Shared Etiology	Shared Mechanism of Action
Independence	No	No
Common cause	Yes	No
Spectrum/subclinical	Yes	Yes
Predisposition/vulnerability	No	Yes
Complication/scar	No	Yes
Pathoplasty/exacerbation	No	Yes
Psychobiological	Maybe	Yes

Note: Based on the work by Dolan-Sewell, Krueger, and Shea (2001).

The following briefly reviews these models as they apply to BPD and
eating disorders. We limit our focus to two broad categories for examining the relationship between eating disorders and BPD: *etiology* (i.e.,
origin or cause) and *mechanisms of action* (i.e., the ways that disease processes affect the patient). A summary and comparison of these models,
in terms of etiology and mechanisms of action, are found in Table 8.5.

Independence model. The independence model assumes that BPD and
eating disorders have no actual relationship to one another except co-
occurrence. This approach assumes that the co-occurrence is primarily
due to chance and that the disorders do not share an etiology, disease
process, or symptom presentation.

Common cause model. The common cause model assumes that eating
disorders and BPD share a common etiology (i.e., the same cause) but
have different presentations and disease processes. Thus, from this perspective, eating disorders and BPD originate from the same cause but
later may become very different diseases with different mechanisms of
action (i.e., affect the patient in quite varied ways).

Spectrum/subclinical model. This model assumes that eating disorders
and BPD share similar etiologies and mechanisms of action. Consequently, from this perspective, the two disorders are not really distinct
from each other; one is actually a milder version of the other. In this
case, the eating disorder would likely represent a subclinical variant, or
an attenuated form, of BPD. This would appear more likely than BPD
representing a variant of an eating disorder.

Predisposition/vulnerability model. This model assumes that one of the
disorders occurs before the other disorder and increases the likelihood,
or risk, that the second disorder will occur. For this approach, etiologies
are generally quite distinct but the mechanism of action, or disease processes, of one of the disorders increases the risk of the second. In addition,

the second disorder (in this case, the eating disorder) is not necessarily dependent on the presence of the first (i.e., BPD). To summarize, the disease processes associated with BPD may increase the vulnerability of a patient to develop an eating disorder.

Complication/scar models. This model assumes that the two disorders are distinct entities. The second disorder develops in the environment caused by the first, but then the second disorder continues after the first disorder remits. Thus, the second disorder could be construed as a scar, or even a remnant, of the first disease condition. This model suggests that BPD and eating disorders have distinct etiologies but their disease processes are related. This model posits that eating disorders occur in the environment caused by BPD but continue as an aftereffect or scar of BPD as some, many, or all of the symptoms dissipate.

Pathoplasty/exacerbation model. In this model, the two disorders occur randomly (i.e., their etiologies are independent), but one of the disorders affects the presence and disease course of the other, either additively (i.e., pathoplasty) or synergistically (i.e., exacerbation). This model suggests that the presence of an eating disorder affects the course of BPD or that the presence of BPD affects the course of an eating disorder, or both. Thus, the presence of both BPD and an eating disorder, together, can have quite severe interactive effects on the patient. Whether the effects of the disorders are additive or synergistic is an empirical question and requires further exploration.

Psychobiological models. Psychobiological models focus on biology and genetics and assume that these have a significant role in the development and interaction between disorders. In this case, BPD and eating disorders are manifestations of these underlying biological systems. The notion of etiology is relatively unclear in this approach, because rather than viewing eating disorders and BPD as being generated from the same cause, these disorders are seen as representations of biological and/ or genetic predispositions. Their disease processes, however, are shared as a result of biological and genetic factors.

From an intuitive perspective, it seems that a personality disorder such as BPD would tend to precipitate or to predispose an individual to an Axis I disorder such as an eating disorder. This relationship would entail one of the following models: spectrum, predisposition/vulnerability, complication/scar, exacerbation, or psychobiological models. As an example, in the psychobiological model, it might be possible that BPD is genetically programmed and that the eating disorder actually exacerbates the BPD potential (i.e., the BPD potential would actually be present but lying relatively dormant). In this example, as the eating disorder symptoms become more pronounced, various BPD symptoms also become stimulated, as in a cascade effect, with the BPD symptoms evolving to diagnostic proportions.

As a second example, in the predisposition/vulnerability model, the BPD symptoms could be already present within the individual but, again, not be evident. As the patient begins to manifest the eating disorder symptoms, adjunctive symptoms associated with BPD might be stimulated. As a pragmatic example, a patient who had been abused and who was having difficulty with repetitive relationship failures might turn to employing eating disorder symptoms. As the eating disorder symptoms increase in intensity, other symptoms associated with BPD might become activated, such as depersonalization, anger, fears of abandonment, and so forth.

Practice Point
At the present time, the explicit relationship between BPD and eating disorders remains unclear, although a variety of theoretical models might explain such a relationship.

Self-Injury Equivalents

Another interesting relationship might exist between BPD and eating disorders in terms of the meanings of a given behavior. For example, rather than serving the purposes of food and weight regulation, a given eating disorder behavior may be solely used for self-harm (i.e., a self-injury equivalent). An example might be the use of self-induced vomiting that was not preceded by any food ingestion, in which the behavior is strictly engaged in to hurt oneself. From a clinical perspective, self-damaging eating pathology *generally* appears to fulfill both missions in the patient with BPD and an eating disorder—that of self-harm as well as food and weight regulation.

Practice Point
In patients with both BPD and eating disorders, self-damaging eating pathology may function as self-harm behavior as well as an attempt to regulate food intake and weight.

CONCLUSIONS

BPD, which appears to be a multidetermined disorder, is a relatively common Axis II disorder in general treatment settings. This complex disorder also co-occurs with some frequency among those with eating disorders, most often among those with binge eating and purging behaviors. All patients with eating disorders should be screened for BPD, and there are a variety of ways to confirm diagnosis. Although the precise relationship between the two disorders remains unknown, we have presented, through models, some possibilities. Although BPD remains an intriguing comorbidity among the eating disorders, we have much to learn about the relationship between the two disorders. Only additional research will clarify the intriguing association of BPD and eating disorders.

Resources

The Borderline Personality Disorder Resource Center (www.bpdresourcecenter.com).

Gunderson, J. G. (2005). *Understanding and treating borderline personality disorder: A guide for professionals and families.* Washington, DC: American Psychiatric Press.

NOTE

Please address all correspondence to Randy A. Sansone, MD, Sycamore Primary Care Center, 2115 Leiter Road, Miamisburg, OH, 45342; telephone: 937-384-6850; fax: 937-384-6938; e-mail: Randy.sansone @kmcnetwork.org.

REFERENCES

American Psychiatric Association. (1994). *Diagnostic and statistical manual of mental disorders* (4th ed.). Washington, DC: Author.

American Psychiatric Association. (2000). *Diagnostic and statistical manual of mental disorders* (4th ed., Text Revision). Washington, DC: Author.

Bradley, R., Jenei, J., & Westen, D. (2005). Etiology of borderline personality: Disentangling the contributions of intercorrelated antecedents. *Journal of Nervous and Mental Disease, 193,* 24–31.

Chabrol, H., Montovany, A., Chouicha, K., Callahan, S., & Mullet, E. (2001). Frequency of borderline personality disorder in a sample of French high school students. *Canadian Journal of Psychiatry, 46,* 847–849.

Chavira, D. A., Grilo, C. M., Shea, M. T., Yen, S., Gunderson, J. G., Morey, L. C., et al. (2003). Ethnicity and four personality disorders. *Comprehensive Psychiatry, 44,* 483–491.

Dolan-Sewell, R. T., Krueger, R. F., & Shea, M. T. (2001). Co-occurrence with syndrome disorders. In W. J. Livesley (Ed.), *Handbook of personality disorders: Theory, research and treatment* (pp. 84–104). New York: Guilford.

Ellison, J. M., & Shader, R. I. (2003). Pharmacologic treatment of personality disorders: A dimensional approach. In R. I. Shader (Ed.), *Manual of psychiatric therapeutics* (pp. 169–183). Philadelphia: Lippincott, Williams, & Wilkins.

Garner, D. M. (1997). Psychoeducational principles in treatment. In D. M. Garner & P. E. Garfinkel (Eds.), *Handbook of treatment for eating disorders* (2nd ed., pp. 145–177). New York: Guilford.

Goodman, M., New, A., & Siever, L. (2004). Trauma, genes, and the neurobiology of personality disorders. In R. Yehuda & B. McEwen (Eds.), *Biobehavioral stress response: Protective and damaging effects* (pp. 104–116). New York: New York Academy of Sciences.

Goodsitt, A. (1997). Eating disorders: A self-psychological perspective. In D. M. Garner & P. E. Garfinkel (Eds.), *Handbook of treatment for eating disorders* (2nd ed., pp. 205–228). New York: Guilford.

Hudziak, J. J., Boffeli, T. J., Kreisman, J. J., & Battaglia, M. M. (1996). Clinical study of the relation of borderline personality disorder to Briquet's Syndrome (hysteria), somatization disorder, antisocial personality disorder, and substance abuse disorders. *American Journal of Psychiatry, 153,* 1598–1606.

Hyler, S. E. (1994). *Personality Diagnostic Questionnaire–4.* New York: New York State Psychiatric Institute, Author.

Johnson, D. M., Shea, M. T., Yen, S., Battle, C. L., Zlotnick, C., Sanislow, C. A., et al. (2003). Gender differences in borderline personality disorder: Findings from the Collaborative Longitudinal Personality Disorders Study. *Comprehensive Psychiatry, 44,* 284–292.

Kolb, J. E., & Gunderson, J. G. (1980). Diagnosing borderline patients with a semi-structured interview. *Archives of General Psychiatry, 37,* 37–41.

Levitt, J. L., & Sansone, R. A. (2002). Searching for the answers: Eating disorders and self-harm. *Eating Disorders: The Journal of Treatment and Prevention, 10,* 189–191.

Loranger, A. W. (1988). *Personality disorder examination manual.* Yonkers, NY: DV Communications.

McGlashan, T. H., Grilo, C. M., Sanislow, C. A., Ralevski, E., Morey, L. S., Gunderson, J. G., et al. (2005). Two-year prevalence and stability of individual *DSM–IV* criteria for schizotypal, borderline, avoidant, and obsessive-compulsive personality disorders: Toward a hybrid model of Axis II disorders. *American Journal of Psychiatry, 162,* 883–889.

Paris, J. (1996). Cultural factors in the emergence of borderline pathology. *Psychiatry, 59,* 185–192.

Quigley, B. D. (2005). Diagnostic relapse in borderline personality: Risk and protective factors. *Dissertation Abstracts International, 65,* 3721B.

Sala, M., Perez, J., Soloff, P., di Nemi, S. U., Caverzasi, E., Soares, J. C., et al. (2004). Stress and hippocampal abnormalities in psychiatric disorders. *European Neuropsychopharmacology, 14,* 393–405.

Sansone, R. A., & Levitt, J. L. (2002). Self-harm behaviors among those with eating disorders: An overview. *Eating Disorders: The Journal of Treatment and Prevention, 10,* 205–213.

Sansone, R. A., Levitt, J. L., & Sansone, L. A. (2005). The prevalence of personality disorders among those with eating disorders. *Eating Disorders: The Journal of Treatment and Prevention, 13,* 7–21.

Sansone, R. A., Rytwinski, D. R., & Gaither, G. A. (2003). Borderline personality and psychotropic medication prescription in an outpatient psychiatry clinic. *Comprehensive Psychiatry, 44,* 454–458.

Sansone, R. A., & Sansone, L. A. (2000). Borderline personality disorder: The enigma. *Primary Care Reports, 6,* 219–226.

Sansone, R. A., & Sansone, L. A. (2003). Borderline personality: Different symptoms in different settings? *International Journal of Psychiatry in Clinical Practice, 7,* 187–191.

Sansone, R. A., Songer, D. A., & Gaither, G. A. (2001). Diagnostic approaches to borderline personality and their relationship to self-harm behavior. *International Journal of Psychiatry in Clinical Practice, 5,* 273–277.

Sansone, R. A., Whitecar, P., Meier, B. P., & Murry, A. (2001). The prevalence of borderline personality among primary care patients with chronic pain. *General Hospital Psychiatry, 23,* 193–197.

Sansone, R. A., Wiederman, M. W., & Sansone, L. A. (1998). The Self-Harm Inventory (SHI): Development of a scale for identifying self-destructive behaviors and borderline personality disorder. *Journal of Clinical Psychology, 54,* 973–983.

Sansone, R. A., Wiederman, M. W., & Sansone, L. A. (2000). Medically self-harming behavior and its relationship to borderline personality symptoms and somatic preoccupation among internal medicine patients. *Journal of Nervous and Mental Disease, 188,* 45–47.

Sansone, R. A., Wiederman, M. W., Sansone, L. A., & Mehnert-Kay, S. (1997). Sabotaging one's own medical care: Prevalence in a primary care setting. *Archives of Family Medicine, 6,* 583–586.

Skodol, A. E., & Bender, D. S. (2003). Why are women diagnosed borderline more than men? *Psychiatric Quarterly, 74,* 349–360.

Skodol, A. E., Siever, L. J., Livesley, W. J., Gunderson, J. G., Pfohl, B., & Widiger, T. A. (2002). The borderline diagnosis II: Biology, genetics, and clinical course. *Biological Psychiatry, 51,* 951–963.

Spitzer, R. L., Williams, J. B. W., Gibbon, M., & First, M. B. (1990). *Structured Clinical Interview for* DSM–III–R *Personality Disorders (SCID-II).* Washington, DC: American Psychiatric Press.

Stone, M. H. (1986). Borderline personality disorder. In R. Michels & J. O. Cavenar (Eds.), *Psychiatry* (2nd ed., pp. 1–15). Philadelphia: Lippincott.

Stone, M. H. (1990). *The fate of borderline patients.* New York: Guilford.

Torgersen, S. (1994). Genetics in borderline conditions. *Acta Psychiatrica Scandanavica, 379,* 19–25.

Torgersen, S., Kringlen, E., & Cramer, V. (2001). The prevalence of personality disorders in a community sample. *Archives of General Psychiatry, 58,* 590–596.

Widiger, T. A., & Rogers, J. H. (1989). Prevalence and comorbidity of personality disorders. *Psychiatric Annals, 19,* 132–136.

Widiger, T. A., & Weissman, M. M. (1991). Epidemiology of borderline personality disorder. *Hospital and Community Psychiatry, 42,* 1015–1021.

Zanarini, M. C. (1983). *Diagnostic interview for personality disorders.* Belmont, MA: Author.

Zanarini, M. C., Frankenburg, F. R., Dubo, E. D., Sickel, A. E., Trikha, A., Levin, A., et al. (1998). Axis I comorbidity of borderline personality disorder. *American Journal of Psychiatry, 155,* 1733–1739.

Zanarini, M. C., Frankenburg, F. R., Reich, D. B., Marino, J. F., Lewis, R. E., Williams, A. A., et al. (2000). Biparental failure in the childhood experiences of borderline patients. *Journal of Personality Disorders, 14,* 264–273.

Zanarini, M. C., Frankenburg, F. R., Yong, L., Raviola, G., Reich, D. B., Hennen, J., et al. (2004). Borderline psychopathology in the first-degree relatives of borderline and Axis II comparison probands. *Journal of Personality Disorders, 18,* 449–447.

Zanarini, M. C., Gunderson, J. G., Frankenburg, F. R., & Chauncey, D. L. (1989). The revised diagnostic interview for borderlines: Discriminating BPD from other Axis II disorders. *Journal of Personality Disorders, 3,* 10–18.

Avoidant Personality Disorder and Eating Disorders

JOHN L. LEVITT, PHD
RANDY A. SANSONE, MD

Eating disorders (EDs) have become increasingly common, and clinical experience suggests that these patients are presenting with complex symptom constellations (e.g., Garner & Garfinkel, 1997; Levitt, 1998, 2000; Levitt & Sansone, 2002). Indeed, multisymptomatic presentations have become so prevalent in the ED population (e.g., self-harm behavior) that assessment instruments and treatment approaches are often insufficient in meeting the needs of these patients (Sansone & Levitt, 2005b; Sansone & Sansone, 2004; Vitousek & Stumpf, 2005).

These polysymptomatic presentations suggest a number of clinical conclusions. First, the fact that an individual has an ED, in itself, tells us relatively little about the person. That is, what is this individual's personality really like? The other types of psychological problems, which may have predated or surfaced during the ED, remain essentially unknown (Brownell & Fairburn, 1995; Garner & Garfinkel, 1997). Indeed, heterogeneity in the presentation of patients with EDs appears to be the rule rather than the exception (Cooper, 1995; Garner & Garfinkel, 1997).

Second, as previously stated, patients who present with ED symptoms are typically presenting with complex comorbid, or coexisting, symptom clusters that interface with the ED in a variety of ways (Levitt, Sansone, & Cohn, 2004). Comorbid disorders may include a host of psychological problems (e.g., Edelstein & Yager, 1992; Strober & Katz, 1988), such as impulse difficulties and substance abuse (Johnson & Connors, 1987; Mitchell, Pyle, Specker, & Hanson, 1992), personality disorders (Sansone & Levitt, 2005a, 2005b; Sansone, Levitt, & Sansone, 2005; Wonderlich & Mitchell, 1997), and symptoms related to abuse and trauma (e.g., Vanderlinden & Vandereycken, 1997), as well as medical complications (e.g., Mehler & Andersen, 1999). These comorbid factors may significantly "influence" the course of treatment (American Psychiatric Association, 2000) and appear to be increasingly prevalent in certain high-risk populations such as children (Lask & Bryant-Waugh, 2000) and in previously underrepresented groups such as males (Andersen, Cohn, & Holbrook, 2000).

Finally, factors involved in the development and maintenance of EDs, as well as some of the other related conditions mentioned, are multifactorial and not currently clearly established: "It is a combination of these influences that determine whether an individual follows a path from exposure to a risk factor to the onset of the disorder, and whether this disorder then becomes established or even chronic" (Cooper, 1995, p. 199).

Practice Point
Patients presenting with EDs are frequently symptomatically complex.

In this chapter, we focus on the role of comorbid avoidant personality disorder (AVPD) in the assessment of EDs. AVPD was elected because of its relatively common frequency of presentation within the ED population (Sansone et al., 2005). In the literature, there has been relatively little discussion of the impact of this disorder on those with EDs.

PERSONALITY DISORDERS AND EDS: A COMPLEX RELATIONSHIP

The concept of "personality disorder" refers to an identifiable "style" (i.e., pattern) of behavior, thought, relating, and affectivity that deviates from cultural expectations and that causes significant impairment or distress in some aspect of psychosocial functioning (American Psychiatric Association, 1994; Sansone et al., 2005). Rates of personality comorbidity with EDs have been reported from 21% to 97% (Westen & Harnden-Fischer, 2001) but can be as high as 100% when self-report measures are used (Maranon, Echeburua, & Grijalvo, 2004). Conversely, data suggest that those with personality disorders may have a higher than normal prevalence rate for EDs (Westen & Harnden-Fischer, 2001). Grilo et al. (2003), for example, reported that personality disorders occur more frequently in patients with EDs than in patient controls without EDs, and that EDs occur more frequently with patients diagnosed with borderline personality disorder than with other personality disorders. Indeed, certain personality features, including negative emotionality, poor interoceptive awareness, low self-esteem, obsessive-compulsive symptoms, and perfectionism have been described as likely precursors to the development of ED symptoms (Zaider, Johnson, & Cockell, 2002, p. 319).

For the purposes of better diagnostic understanding, the *Diagnostic and Statistical Manual of Mental Disorders–Fourth Edition* (*DSM–IV*) (American Psychiatric Association, 1994) divided the various personality disorders into three general clusters. Cluster A refers to those personality disorders characterized by odd and/or eccentric features; Cluster B refers to those personality disorders characterized by dramatic and/or erratic features; and Cluster C refers to those personality disorders characterized by anxious and/or inhibited features.

Attempting to highlight the prevalence of personality disorders in EDs, the *Practice Guideline for the Treatment of Patients With Eating Disorders* (American Psychiatric Association, 2000) reports that, in general, anorexia nervosa tends to be accompanied primarily by Cluster C disorders, whereas normal-weight individuals with bulimia nervosa tend to be characterized by Cluster B features. These patterns have been confirmed in several studies of various ED patient populations, including outpatients (e.g., Godt, 2002). However, note that Grilo et al. (2003) found inconsistent support for these associations.

OVERVIEW OF AVPD

Epidemiology

According to the *DSM–IV* (American Psychiatric Association, 1994), the prevalence of AVPD in the general population is between 0.5% and 1.0%. The *DSM–IV* does not clarify any differences in prevalence rates according to gender, ethnic, or cultural origins. The onset of the disorder is typically in infancy or childhood, with the emergence of shyness, social withdrawal, stranger anxiety, and fearfulness of novel situations. There may be an exacerbation of AVPD symptoms during adolescence and early adulthood. From a developmental perspective, Rettew and colleagues (2003) found that in childhood and adolescence, those with AVPD evidenced poorer athletic performance, less involvement with hobbies, and less adolescent popularity.

Etiology

Although the explicit etiology of AVPD remains unknown, there appear to be a variety of potential contributory factors. These may include a shy and/or anxious temperament (Joyce et al., 2003), parental neglect (Joyce

TABLE 9.1   The Criteria for Avoidant Personality Disorder According to the
Diagnostic and Statistical Manual of Mental Disorders, Fourth Edition
(American Psychiatric Association, 1994)

The individual has a pervasive pattern of social inhibition, feelings of inadequacy, and hypersensitivity to negative evaluation, beginning by early adulthood and present in a variety of contexts, as indicated by four (or more) of the following. The individual

1. avoids occupational activities that involve significant interpersonal contact, because of fears of criticism, disapproval, or rejection;
2. is unwilling to get involved with people unless certain of being liked;
3. shows restraint within intimate relationships because of the fear of being shamed or ridiculed;
4. is preoccupied with being criticized or rejected in social situations;
5. is inhibited in new interpersonal situations because of feelings of inadequacy;
6. views self as socially inept, personally unappealing, or inferior to others;
7. is unusually reluctant to take personal risks or to engage in any new activities because they may prove embarrassing.

et al., 2003), and possibly physical and/or emotional abuse (Rettew et al., 2003). In addition, Meyer, Pilkonis, and Beevers (2004) empirically determined an attachment style in those with AVPD characterized by anxious and avoidant features. With regard to family influences, Tillfors, Furmark, Ekselius, and Fredrikson (2001) found that having a family member with AVPD resulted in a twofold to threefold risk for the development of the disorder, which strongly suggests a genetic predisposition to the disorder.

Diagnostic Criteria for AVPD

According to the *DSM–IV* (American Psychiatric Association, 1994), the current benchmark for psychiatric diagnosis, there are seven criteria for AVPD (see Table 9.1). Four of these criteria are necessary for one to make the diagnosis of AVPD. According to recent research by Morey et al. (2004), the current criteria for AVPD are valid and confirm a coherent psychiatric syndrome. In examining the most time-stable clinical features over a 2-year period, McGlashan and colleagues (2005) empirically confirmed the feature "feeling inadequate and feeling socially inept."

In terms of other psychiatric diagnoses, AVPD is oftentimes comorbid with childhood and adolescent anxiety disorders (Joyce et al., 2003). In addition, Tillfors, Furmark, Ekselius, and Fredrikson (2004) indicated that AVPD appears to be very diagnostically similar to social phobia and that the two may actually represent different points along

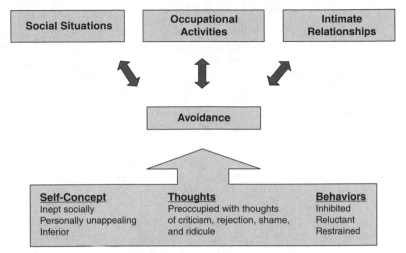

Figure 9.1   The relationship process between the individual with avoidant personality disorder and his or her environment.

a functional continuum; likewise, both may represent a dimension of social anxiety rather than separate disorders.

Dynamics of AVPD

As suggested by the general criteria for AVPD in Table 9.1, the individual with this particular Axis II disorder exhibits a number of psychological qualities and behavioral patterns that result in avoiding significant interpersonal and occupational interactions. These qualities and patterns result in a complex, multifaceted process of limiting general contact with the environment. The transactional process that an individual with AVPD has with his or her environment might be "mapped," as shown in Figure 9.1.

The interactional processes illustrated in Figure 9.1 suggest that the individual with AVPD is characterized by active detachment from involvement with others across a number of psychosocial settings. Three general areas are specifically interrelated and affected by AVPD.

First, the individual's self-concept is significantly negative. These individuals perceive that they are inherently undesirable both personally and socially and therefore unappealing and incompetent. Second, as a result of this negative self-concept, individuals with AVPD tend to be cognitively preoccupied with the anticipation of shame and rejection, which causes intense fear. That is, their cognitive emphasis tends to center on thoughts of potential criticism, shame, ridicule, and rejection. Thus, with an inherently poor and inaccurate self-concept and low self-esteem, the thought processes of the individual with AVPD echo over and over with the same concerns—the anticipated social resonation of negative self-worth. The primal emotions of fear and anxiety are stimulated to varying degrees by both their negative self-concept and negativistic thinking. Finally, these individuals tend to develop anticipatory behavioral processes (i.e., anticipate negative outcomes) that reflect or mirror the self-concept and cognitive styles described previously.

Practice Point
Patients with AVPD have a very negative self-concept and tend to ruminate about their personal and interpersonal deficiencies.

Reluctant to get involved in social interactions, occupational activities, or personal relationships, individuals with AVPD tend to avoid or limit interaction within these contexts, and they generally inhibit themselves from any but the most minimal or required interaction. Having limited interactions within these contexts, and experiencing these contexts with much anticipated fear and anxiety, individuals with AVPD tend to have transient and superficial contacts, at best, thus reinforcing their underlying tendency to avoid. The ultimate result is a pervasive pattern of avoidance across social, intimate, and occupational settings. Of course, each individual is different, and each presents along a continuum of the features described.

Practice Point
Along with their negative self-concept and self-deprecating ruminative style, patients with AVPD tend to experience their interpersonal interactions with fear and anxiety.

AVPD AND EDS

The Prevalence of AVPD in EDs

Sansone et al. (2005) found that among those with anorexia nervosa, restricting type, the top four personality disorders, represented in descending order of frequency, were obsessive-compulsive personality disorder, followed by AVPD, borderline personality disorder, and dependent personality disorder. The top four personality disorders for those with anorexia nervosa, binge-purge type were, in descending order, borderline personality disorder, AVPD, dependent personality disorder, and obsessive-compulsive personality disorder. For bulimia nervosa, the top four personality disorder diagnoses in descending order were borderline personality disorder, dependent personality disorder, histrionic personality disorder, and AVPD. Finally, the top three descending personality disorder diagnoses for those with binge eating disorder were obsessive-compulsive personality disorder, AVPD, and borderline personality disorder.

In summary, Cluster C personality disorders including AVPD were significantly represented among all ED diagnoses. These relationships are illustrated in Figure 9.2. Figure 9.2 shows that, of the top four personality

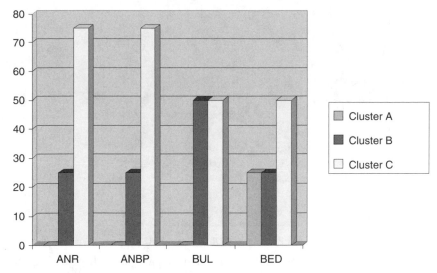

Figure 9.2 The relative contribution of each personality disorder cluster to each eating disorder diagnosis.

Note: Based on the work by Sansone, Levitt, and Sansone (2005). ANR = anorexia nervosa, restricting type; ANBP = anorexia nervosa, binge-purge type; BUL = bulimia nervosa; BED = binge eating disorder.

disorders in each ED diagnostic cluster, Cluster C personality disorders are almost twice as likely to be represented, except in bulimia nervosa, where they are likely to be equally represented. Godt (2002) and Maranon, Echeburua, and Grijalvo (2004) reported similar results.

These findings suggest that Cluster C personality disorders are associated with all ED diagnoses and that obsessive-compulsive personality disorder and AVPD are the most frequently represented Cluster C diagnoses. From another perspective, AVPD represents one of the top four diagnoses in every ED category, whereas obsessive-compulsive personality disorder is represented only in the top four of three ED categories. (Note that obsessive-compulsive personality disorder made the most significant personality disorder contribution in the anorexia nervosa restricting type and binge eating disorder categories.) Clearly, AVPD plays a significant role among those with EDs and requires further study.

Practice Point
Cluster C personality diagnoses are common in all patient diagnostic groups but especially in anorexia nervosa restricting type and binge eating disorder.

Previously, Sansone et al. (2005) summed percentages of each personality disorder for each category of ED diagnosis to get a comparative sense of the extent of personality pathology exhibited within each

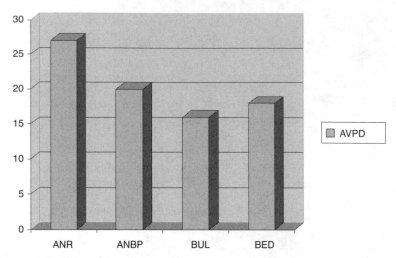

Figure 9.3 The relative contribution of avoidant personality disorder to overall personality disorder psychopathology, by eating disorder diagnosis.

Note: Based on the work by Sansone, Levitt, and Sansone (2005). ANR = anorexia nervosa, restricting type; ANBP = anorexia nervosa, binge-purge type; BUL = bulimia nervosa; BED = binge eating disorder.

diagnosis. Taking this one step further, we can derive an approximate "loading" that the contribution of AVPD might have to the overall psychopathology within each ED diagnosis by taking the AVPD percentages and dividing them by the total personality disorder percentage contribution per diagnostic grouping. (We are aware of the limitations of this approach, but we use this data only as an approximation of the AVPD contribution to total Axis II psychopathology per diagnosis.) This data is summarized in Figure 9.3. The data show that AVPD ranges from 16% to 27% of the personality disorder psychopathology across ED diagnoses, with AVPD playing a seemingly greater role in both subtypes of anorexia nervosa, followed by binge eating disorder and then bulimia nervosa. Thus, it appears that anxiety, fear, and avoidance are common to all ED diagnostic categories but especially to the anorexic diagnoses.

Practice Point
Anxiety, fear, and avoidance play an important role in the EDs, particularly in the anorexic diagnoses.

Possible Relationships Between AVPD and EDs

Given the frequency of comorbidity between AVPD and EDs, is there a potential relationship between the disorders? Empirical data are scant, but we suspect that the potential relationships between AVPD and EDs are complex and highly variable. Indeed, as previously indicated,

TABLE 9.2   Avoidant Personality Disorder Versus Eating Disorder
Diagnoses: Criteria Comparison According to the *Diagnostic and Statistical
Manual of Mental Disorders, Fourth Edition* (American Psychiatric Association,
1994)

	Number of Diagnostic Criteria			
	Avoidant Personality Disorder	Anorexia Nervosa	Bulimia Nervosa	Binge Eating Disorder
Relational processes	2			1
Behavioral processes	1	1	3	4
Cognitive processes	2	2	2	1
Affective processes	2	1		2

AVPD tends to be significantly represented among those with EDs, yet
this Axis II disorder appears to be relatively underrepresented in discussions in the ED literature. Dennis and Sansone (1997) are two of
the few authors in the ED field to discuss AVPD in the context of its
relationship to EDs. They described AVPD as "characterized by the
active but ambivalent detachment from social involvement with others"
(p. 443). They stated that these individuals tend to want involvement in
relationships because, like others, they desire affection, attention, and
social interaction. But, because they "deeply fear" being shamed and
rejected by others, sufferers will opt to lead isolated and quite unhappy
lives. The individual with AVPD and an ED tends to exhibit a hypervigilant cognitive style (i.e., scanning the environment for any negativity),
an inhibited withdrawn interpersonal style (i.e., underinvolved), and a
hypersensitive affective style (i.e., apprehensive) (Sperry, 1999). Except
for general clinical suggestions (e.g., Dennis & Sansone, 1997), clinical
models for treating those with both AVPD and EDs appear currently
unavailable in the ED literature.

Practice Point
The relationship between EDs and AVPD is complex and highly variable,
and limited treatment information is available.

Comparison of areas of functioning. Table 9.2 reflects a functional comparison between AVPD and the various EDs. EDs represent syndromes
of related behaviors but, as seen in Table 9.2, tend to be somewhat limited in providing a broad view of the individual's overall functioning.
The criteria for AVPD (see Table 9.1) appear to be broader and to more
evenly cover a greater number of functional areas than the ED diagnoses (see Table 9.2). Specifically, AVPD diagnosis covers relational,
behavioral, cognitive, and affective processes or areas of functioning,
whereas ED diagnosis generally emphasizes behavioral and cognitive
processes, with minimal emphasis on relational or affective processes.

The only exception appears to be the ED diagnosis of binge eating disorder, but even here, broad-based functional criteria are relatively limited. The limitations of the comparisons presented in Table 9.2 may be due to the fact that AVPD represents a broader view of individual functioning based on ongoing and relatively stable characteristics over time (i.e., traits), whereas an ED diagnosis hypothetically represents more transient characteristics (i.e., states) according to the *DSM–IV* (American Psychiatric Association, 1994). *However, the areas that these disorders might share most in common involve fear, anxiety, and avoidance.*

Models of interaction. According to the models of interaction proposed by Dolan-Sewell, Krueger, and Shea (2001), one might compare two disorders, in this case AVPD and EDs, in two general ways: (a) etiology or developmental origins and (b) mechanisms of action (Sansone & Levitt, 2005a). In analyzing the relationship between these two disorders in terms of etiology (see Sansone & Levitt, 2005a), the extent to which an ED can lead to AVPD or whether AVPD can cause an ED is currently unclear. So associations between the two and speculations about their interaction are not readily available (Dolan-Sewell et al., 2001; Sansone & Levitt, 2005a).

In examining mechanism of action, we might examine the ways that AVPD and EDs follow similar pathways or organizations, share similar psychological features, or have common or similar outcomes. From this perspective, mechanisms of action refer to associative, versus causative, relationships. Thus, we are interested in the ways in which there might be a goodness of fit between AVPD and EDs. These associations are briefly outlined next.

AVPD is commonly observed in patients who present with anorexia nervosa. Patients with anorexia nervosa are generally characterized by anxious, fearful, and avoidant processes (e.g., Strober, 2004). Bruch (1973) suggested long ago that anorexics were characterized by social isolation and a "paralyzing sense of ineffectiveness" (p. 254). She suggested, "The essential underlying disturbances in [anorexia nervosa] are related to the patient's defective self-awareness and their distorted interpersonal experiences" (Bruch, 1973, p. 222). Clearly, the processes described in the "typical" anorexic are similar to those previously described for the individual with AVPD. Indeed, Bruch (1973) concluded, "It will be noted that all these explanations of eating and noneating are related to problems in the interpersonal field and to doubts about personal adequacy and self-respect" (p. 270).

As for bulimia nervosa, Swift and Wonderlich (1988) described the personality traits of individuals with bulimia as depressed, impulsive, anxious, alienated, obsessive, and interpersonally sensitive, with low self-esteem. Johnson and Connors (1987) described individuals with bulimia as having difficulties in interoceptive awareness (i.e., the awareness and ability to identify internal states), body dissatisfaction, interpersonal ineffectiveness, interpersonal distrust, a relentless drive for thinness, maturity fears (again higher for anorexics), and perfectionistic personality features. Although the composite of many of these features is similar to that encountered in borderline personality disorder, particularly the impulsivity (Johnson & Connors, 1987; Sansone & Levitt, 2005a), these individuals may also become afraid of eating in certain places, having their binge-purge behaviors "found out," and so forth. Guilt, fears of discovery, and interpersonal ineffectiveness often appear to be common characteristics of those with bulimia nervosa (Swift & Wonderlich, 1988), which suggests that fear, anxiety, and avoidance behaviors are frequently found in those who have bulimia—features that are associated with AVPD.

The adaptive context. The adaptive context refers to the possible ways that psychopathology may "benefit" the individual—in this case, the possible ways that an ED might benefit the individual with AVPD. Strober (2004) acknowledged the association between anorexia nervosa and anxious personality traits characterized by harm avoidance, reduced novelty seeking, caution, perfectionism, restraint, and regimentation (p. 505). He suggested that *weight fears and compulsive dieting might represent fear-based learning and phobic avoidance responses.* This description generally suggests that some of the psychopathology in AVPD may be shifted or "housed" in anorexia nervosa.

Dennis and Sansone (1997) suggested that EDs may be extremely adaptive in those with AVPD. From a very pragmatic perspective, *those who relentlessly pursue weight loss may yearn to disappear from society, thus reducing the opportunity for criticism.* In addition, *through the vicissitudes of starvation, individuals with anorexia nervosa are able to avoid the terrifying feelings of interpersonal vulnerability through numbness.* This emotional indifference, in turn, establishes the necessary physical and psychological distance between those with anorexia nervosa and others. Finally, in some individuals with anorexia nervosa, *the ED might replace intimate relationships by providing an important life focus for time, energy, and emotions* (Dennis & Sansone, 1997, p. 443).

An ED may play another vital adaptive role in those with AVPD. Clearly, EDs are culturally driven disorders that encompass a societal ideal of perfection. It may be that *some individuals with AVPD gravitate toward an ED to obtain the ideal body shape and thereby achieve the societal ideal. By doing so, they avoid criticism from others and sustain the possibility that weight loss may resolve some of their social difficulties.* After all, in AVPD, beneath the façade of avoidance lies the desire to connect with others.

CONCLUSION

In this chapter, we noted the significant and potential roles that AVPD plays in our understanding and treatment of EDs. Indeed, AVPD is a relatively common Axis II disorder, appears to be multidetermined, and co-occurs among those with EDs with some frequency. Although the precise relationship between AVPD and EDs is unknown, we explored some possible relationships between the two. There is little question that fear, anxiety, and avoidance play a significant role across EDs and AVPD. Clinical models will need to incorporate treatment approaches for both disorders. Only further research and discussion can clarify and increase our understanding of the various relationships between and treatment approaches to these challenging disorders.

NOTE

Please address all correspondence to John L. Levitt, PhD, 1650 Moon Lake Blvd., Hoffman Estates, IL, 60194; telephone: 847-832-2610; fax: 847-991-9645; e-mail: levittj@aol.com.

REFERENCES

American Psychiatric Association. (1994). *Diagnostic and statistical manual of mental disorders* (4th ed.). Washington, DC: Author.

American Psychiatric Association. (2000). *Practice guideline for the treatment of patients with eating disorders* (2nd ed.). Arlington, VA: Author.

Andersen, A. E., Cohn, L., & Holbrook, T. (2000). *Making weight: Men's conflicts with food, weight, shape, and appearance.* Carlsbad, CA: Gurze Books.

Brownell, K. D., & Fairburn, C. G. (Eds.). (1995). *Eating disorders and obesity: A comprehensive handbook.* New York: Guilford.

Bruch, H. (1973). *Eating disorders: Obesity, anorexia nervosa, and the person within.* New York: Basic Books.

Cooper, Z. (1995). The development and maintenance of eating disorders. In K. D. Brownell & C. G. Fairburn (Eds.), *Eating disorders and obesity: A comprehensive handbook* (pp. 199–206). New York: Guilford.

Dennis, A. B., & Sansone, R. A. (1997). Treatment of patients with personality disorders. In D. M. Garner & P. E. Garfinkel (Eds.), *Handbook of treatment for eating disorders* (2nd ed., pp. 437–449). New York: Guilford.

Dolan-Sewell, R. T., Krueger, R. F., & Shea, M. T. (2001). Co-occurrence with syndrome disorders. In W. J. Livesley (Ed.), *Handbook of personality disorders: Theory, research and treatment* (pp. 84–104). New York: Guilford.

Edelstein, C. K., & Yager, J. (1992). Eating disorders and affective disorders. In J. Yager, H. E. Swordsman, & C. K. Edelstein (Eds.), *Special problems in managing eating disorders* (pp. 15–50). Washington, DC: American Psychiatric Press.

Garner, D. M., & Garfinkel, P. E. (Eds.). (1997). *Handbook of treatment for eating disorders* (2nd ed.). New York: Guilford.

Godt, K. (2002). Personality disorders and eating disorders: The prevalence of personality disorders in 176 female outpatients with eating disorders. *European Eating Disorder Review, 10,* 102–109.

Grilo, C. M., Sanislow, C. A., Skodol, A. E., Gunderson, J. G., Stout, R. L., Shea, M. T., et al. (2003). Do eating disorders co-occur with personality disorders? Comparison groups matter. *International Journal of Eating Disorders, 33,* 155–164.

Johnson, C., & Connors, M. E. (1987). *The etiology and treatment of bulimia nervosa: A biopsychosocial perspective.* New York: Basic Books.

Joyce, P. R., McKenzie, J. M., Luty, S. E., Mulder, R. T., Carter, J. D., Sullivan, P. F., et al. (2003). Temperament, childhood environment and psychopathology as risk factors for avoidant and borderline personality disorders. *Australian and New Zealand Journal of Psychiatry, 37,* 756–764.

Lask, B., & Bryant-Waugh, R. (Eds.). (2000). *Anorexia nervosa and related disorders in childhood and adolescence* (2nd ed.). East Sussex, UK: Psychology Press.

Levitt, J. L. (1998). The disorganized client: New management strategies. *Paradigm, 2,* 20.

Levitt, J. L. (2000, August). *Surviving the storm: Treating the complex eating disordered client.* Paper presented at the International Association of Eating Disorder Professional, Annual Conference, Orlando, FL.

Levitt, J. L., & Sansone, R. A. (2002). Searching for the answers: Eating disorders and self-harm. *Eating Disorders: The Journal of Treatment and Prevention, 10,* 189–191.

Levitt, J. L., Sansone, R. A., & Cohn, L. (Eds.). (2004). *Self-harm behavior and eating disorders: Dynamics, assessment, and treatment.* New York: Brunner-Routledge.

Maranon, I., Echeburua, E., & Grijalvo, J. (2004). Prevalence of personality disorders in patients with eating disorders: A pilot study using the IPDE. *European Eating Disorder Review, 12,* 217–222.

McGlashan, T. H., Grilo, C. M., Sanislow, C. A., Ralevski, E., Morey, L. C., Gunderson, J. G., et al. (2005). Two-year prevalence and stability of individual *DSM–IV* criteria for schizotypal, borderline, avoidant, and obsessive-compulsive personality disorders: Toward a hybrid model of Axis II disorders. *American Journal of Psychiatry, 162,* 883–889.

Mehler, P. S., & Andersen, A. E. (Eds.). (1999). *Eating disorders: A guide to medical care and complications.* Baltimore: John Hopkins University Press.

Meyer, B., Pilkonis, P. A., & Beevers, C. G. (2004). What's in a (neutral) face? Personality disorders, attachment styles, and the appraisal of ambiguous social cues. *Journal of Personality Disorders, 18,* 320–336.

Mitchell, J. E., Pyle, R. L., Specker, S., & Hanson, K. (1992). Eating disorders and chemical dependency. In J. Yager, H. E. Gwirtsman, & C. K. Edelstein (Eds.), *Special problems in managing eating disorders* (pp. 1–14). Washington, DC: American Psychiatric Press.

Morey, L. C., Skodol, A. E., Grilo, C. M., Sanislow, C. A., Zanarini, M. C., Shea, M. T., et al. (2004). Temporal coherence of criteria for four personality disorders. *Journal of Personality Disorders, 18,* 394–398.

Rettew, D. C., Zanarini, M. C., Yen, S., Grilo, C. M., Skodol, A. E., Shea, M. T., et al. (2003). Childhood antecedents of avoidant personality disorder: A retrospective study. *Journal of the American Academy of Child and Adolescent Psychiatry, 42,* 1122–1130.

Sansone, R. A., & Levitt, J. L. (2005a). Borderline personality and eating disorders. *Eating Disorders: The Journal of Treatment and Prevention, 13,* 71–84.

Sansone, R. A., & Levitt, J. L. (2005b). Personality and eating disorders: Exploring the frontier. *Eating Disorders: The Journal of Treatment and Prevention, 13,* 3–6.

Sansone, R. A., Levitt, J. L., & Sansone, L. A. (2005). The prevalence of personality disorders among those with eating disorders. *Eating Disorders: The Journal of Treatment and Prevention, 13,* 7–22.

Sansone, R. A., & Sansone, L. A. (2004). Assessment tools: Eating disorder symptoms and self-harm behavior. In J. L. Levitt, R. A. Sansone, & L. Cohn (Eds.), *Self-harm behavior and eating disorders: Dynamics, assessment, and treatment* (pp. 93–104). New York: Brunner-Routledge,.

Sperry, L. (1999). *Cognitive behavior therapy of* DSM–IV *personality disorders.* New York: Brunner-Routledge.

Strober, M. (2004). Pathologic fear conditioning and anorexia nervosa: On the search for novel paradigms. *International Journal of Eating Disorders, 35,* 504–508.

Strober, M., & Katz, J. L. (1988). Depression in the eating disorders: A review and analysis of descriptive, family, and biological findings. In D. M. Garner & P. E. Garfinkel (Eds.), *Diagnostic issues in anorexia nervosa and bulimia nervosa* (pp. 80–111). New York: Brunner/Mazel.

Swift, W. J., & Wonderlich, S. A. (1988). Personality factors and diagnosis in eating disorders: Traits, disorders, and structures. In D. M. Garner & P. E. Garfinkel (Eds.), *Diagnostic issues in anorexia nervosa and bulimia nervosa* (112-165). New York: Brunner/Mazel.

Tillfors, M., Furmark, T., Ekselius, L., & Fredrikson, M. (2001). Social phobia and avoidant personality disorder as related to parental history of social anxiety: A general population study. *Behaviour Research and Therapy, 39,* 289–298.

Tillfors, M., Furmark, T., Ekselius, L., & Fredrikson, M. (2004). Social phobia and avoidant personality disorder: One spectrum disorder? *Nordic Journal of Psychiatry, 58,* 147–152.

Vanderlinden, J., & Vandereycken, W. (1997). *Trauma, dissociation, and impulse dyscontrol in eating disorders.* Bristol, PA: Brunner/Mazel.

Vitousek, K. M., & Stumpf, R. E. (2005). Difficulties in the assessment of personality traits and disorders in eating-disordered individuals. *Eating Disorders: The Journal of Treatment and Prevention, 13,* 37–60.

Westen, D., & Harnden-Fischer, J. (2001). Personality profiles in eating disorders: Rethinking the distinction between Axis I and Axis II. *American Journal of Psychiatry, 158,* 547–562.

Wonderlich, S. A., & Mitchell, J. E. (1997). Eating disorders and co-morbidity: Empirical, conceptual, and clinical implications. *Psychopharmacological Bulletin, 33,* 381–390.

Zaider, T. I., Johnson, J. G., & Cockell, S. J. (2002). Psychiatric disorders associated with the onset and persistence of bulimia nervosa and binge eating disorder during adolescence. *Journal of Youth and Adolescence, 31,* 318–329.

Treatment Approaches

10

Treatment Strategies in the Obsessive-Compulsive Individual With an Eating Disorder

JANICE RUSSELL, MD, FRACP, FRANZCP, MFCP

To the clinician, the *absence* of obsessive-compulsive symptomatology in individuals with eating disorders (EDs), particularly those toward the anorexic (i.e., anorexia nervosa [AN]) end of the spectrum, seems more noteworthy than its presence (Bruce & Steiger, 2005; Kaye, Bailer, Frank, Wagner, & Henry 2005). Obsessions, compulsive behaviors, and ruminative thinking, as well as the personality traits of perfectionism, inflexibility, conformity, high personal standards, and a need for control, characterize many who present for treatment. These features inevitably challenge clinicians as they develop treatment modalities for patients with EDs—especially interventions pertaining to weight, shape, and food. As a result, obsessive-compulsive features often need to be addressed in those patients with EDs who are exhibiting full or partial comorbid obsessive-compulsive disorder (OCD) or obsessive-compulsive personality disorder (OCPD).

Historically, discriminating ED symptomatology from obsessive-compulsive symptoms has been problematic. Originally, AN was proposed to be a form of obsessive-compulsive neurosis. In fact, earlier psychoanalytic thinking portrayed AN to be on a continuum of OCPD (Hsu, Kaye, & Weltzin, 1993; Serpell, Livingstone, Neiderman, & Lask, 2002). More recently Maj (2005) suggested that comorbidity may be an artifact created by shortcomings in the prevailing nosological systems. However, although obsessive-compulsive features may emerge in the context of disordered eating, nutritional deprivation, and/or weight loss, they frequently predate the ED in a more generalized form. In addition, although obsessive-compulsive symptoms may subside with clinical improvement, they often remain after recovery as a chronic anxiety disorder, a distinctive cognitive style, enduring personality traits, or as a frank personality disorder (Anderluh, Tchanturia, Rabe-Hesketh, & Treasure, 2003; Godart, Flament, Lecrubier, & Jeammet, 2000; Kaye, Bailer, et al., 2005; Thornton & Russell, 1997).

OCD and OCPD are often comorbid in the course of an ED (Bruce & Steiger, 2005; Cavedini, Erzegovesi, Ronchi, & Bellodi, 1997; Halmi, 2005; Shea et al., 2004). Although estimates of prevalence and comorbidity vary widely, the association of OCD and OCPD is strongest in AN (Binford & le Grange, 2005; Grilo, 2002; Halmi, 2005; Picot & Lilenfeld, 2003; Sansone & Levitt, 2005; Thornton & Russell, 1997). Indeed, as either cause or effect, obsessive-compulsive comorbidity tends to be more closely related to the ED behaviors, per se (e.g., dietary restriction).

Effective assessment of obsessive-compulsive symptoms in the individual with an ED can be fraught with difficulties (Vitousek & Stumpf, 2005). In the clinical setting, a primary therapeutic objective is to focus treatment on specific goals. Therefore, for treatment to be effective, it is vital to clearly identify the level of disability caused by obsessive-compulsive symptoms and their potential impact on ED treatment, in general. Indeed, most obsessive-compulsive symptoms tend to improve, and some remit, with successful treatment of the ED (Baer & Jenike, 1992; Bruce & Steiger, 2005; Godart et al., 2000).

Practice Point

The clinical aim should be to identify which, if any, of the obsessive-compulsive symptoms should be the focus of specific treatment.

Treatment strategies for patients with EDs, whether physical, behavioral, psychodynamic, or pharmacological, need to target obsessive-compulsive symptoms, which can impinge on the general treatment of the ED (i.e., influence effectiveness, and patient compliance and response) (AuBuchon & Malatesta, 1994; Bruce & Steiger, 2005; Cavedini et al., 1997; Dreessen, Hoekstra, & Arntz, 1997; Halmi et al., 2005). Directly addressing the obsessive-compulsive symptomatology would be expected to accelerate the ED treatment progress with effective nutritional rehabilitation. This chapter examines various treatment strategies for working with patients who exhibit both EDs and comorbid obsessive-compulsive traits or OCPD.

ASSESSMENT

The diagnostic assessment of obsessive-compulsive symptoms and behaviors can be a difficult undertaking because of (a) the early age of onset in many patients with EDs, (b) the effect of nutritional deprivation in predisposing individuals to obsessive and perseverative thought patterns around food and eating, and (c) the common ED psychological characteristics of rigid self-evaluation, secrecy, and distorted thinking. The interaction of these factors is made even more complex by fluctuations in both ED psychopathology and personality functioning as effects of time, treatment, and maturation (Vitousek & Stumpf, 2005). In the clinical setting, diagnostic judgments around symptoms must be made with due caution while considering these factors.

Diagnostic instruments for obsessive-compulsive symptoms and personality disorder are routinely used in research and treatment settings and can be useful to confirm clinical impressions (Halmi, 2005; Thornton & Russell, 1997). Many items in these instruments target perfectionism, which is often viewed as a proxy for OCPD, a predisposing risk factor, and a core symptom of EDs (e.g., particularly in AN) (Franco-Paredes, Mancilla-Diaz, Vazquez-Arevalo, Lopez-Aguilar, & Alvarez-Rayon, 2005; Kaye, Frank, Bailer, & Henry, 2005; Shafran, Lee, & Fairburn, 2004; Shafran & Mansell, 2001).

Although various assessment tools are available, clinicians need to *inquire* about obsessive-compulsive symptoms, including their severity and associated effects. In many cases, the ED appears so problematic as to deflect attention away from assessment of the obsessive-compulsive symptoms. Therefore, an effort must be made to understand the role of the patient's obsessive-compulsive symptoms in the development and maintenance of the ED, including the obstacles these symptoms might present to therapeutic engagement and collaboration.

One important aspect of clinical assessment is whether the obsessive-compulsive symptoms are more weight, shape, and food focused (i.e., limited to the ED) or whether they represent something more generalized. In the initial stages, however, this differentiation may be of little consequence because, in most cases, the ED must be addressed as a matter of priority. Still, obsessive-compulsive symptoms should be regularly taken into account in the treatment process.

Practice Point

In the assessment process, specific inquiry must be made to examine the effects of obsessive-compulsive symptoms on the individual's functioning and their role in the ED.

TREATMENT SETTING

The treatment setting is of great importance when managing patients with EDs and comorbid obsessive-compulsive symptoms. The ED program, whether residential or inpatient, partial or day patient, outpatient, or even virtual, will provide varying degrees of medical support, nutritional rehabilitation, psychoeducation, behavioral containment, and therapeutic engagement in some form of a "holding environment." Structure and predictability make these milieus relatively tolerable for these individuals.

At the outset, particular features seen in association with obsessive-compulsive symptoms, namely, negative emotionality, stress reactivity, and alienation, need to be promptly contained before they impede treatment participation (Perkins, Klump, Iacono, & McGue, 2005). Other obsessive-compulsive personality characteristics, such as perfectionism, may need to be tempered so as not to interfere with behavioral strategies. Next I discuss the components of treatment in the context of a number of treatment modalities: physical or medical, behavioral (general and specific), motivational, psychodynamic, and pharmacological. I also present two illustrative case histories.

TREATMENT STRATEGIES

Physical or Medical Approach

Obsessive-compulsive patients can oftentimes be engaged around medical issues. They may display great interest in the results of their blood tests and other *physical* investigations, which should be carefully discussed. Some patients with EDs appear to be competent amateur scientists with interests in health, nutrition, and metabolism. For these individuals, a psychoeducational approach is often well accepted. The use of hypothetical or deductive reasoning, augmented with research findings, may help explain the rationale behind treatment rules and limits and increase patient motivation and participation.

Practice Point
A scientific approach can aid in patient engagement. It may be useful to carefully discuss the patient's laboratory studies and the medical basis of treatment.

Nutritional rehabilitation is likely to bring about some reduction in distorted and perseverative thinking. However, one particular issue—exercise and its management—should be addressed early on. For this patient population, an exercise therapist may be particularly helpful. The therapist can assess activity levels, educate patients about healthy exercise, and formulate and update an exercise program suitable to the patient's recovery status (Beumont, Arthur, Russell, & Touyz, 1994).

In addition, pilates, tai chi, yoga, and massage also help with general anxiety management and improve body appraisal (Hart et al., 2001). Modulating obsessive-compulsive overdrive with these endeavors (i.e., exercise and related activities) is of key importance.

General Behavioral Techniques

Obsessive-compulsive symptoms will naturally emerge in the context of nutritional rehabilitation. Such symptoms can be evaluated during nutritional assessment and counseling, when the patient is exposed to food, and when the patient is faced with the obligation to eat appropriately and regularly. Two aims of normalizing food and eating patterns are desensitization and habituation. In addition, better nutrition promotes better judgment and cognitive processing.

One specific technique is the use of a Mandometer, which is a computerized biofeedback technique for monitoring the speed of eating (Sodersten, Bergh, & Ammar, 2003). The Mandometer, for example, can be helpful for pacing obsessionally slow eaters. An advantage to this approach is that a computer may be better accepted than a tired parent, overworked nurse, or other patients exhorting the patient to eat more quickly. However, whether the Mandometer is helpful for *other* patients with EDs is conjectural (Schmidt, 2003).

Practice Point
The ED must be addressed concomitantly with the obsessive-compulsive symptoms (e.g., around exercise and nutritional rehabilitation).

With weight gain, there is often an expected increase in anxiety. Therapeutic coaching can be helpful and should include assisting the patient to being more open in one's thinking and/or being prepared to try something new. Perfectionistic tendencies (i.e., those that might lead patients to set themselves up for failure by aiming for too much too quickly) need to be addressed. Patients should be reassured that challenging goals will be *progressively* tackled.

As treatment continues, obsessive-compulsive traits such as stubbornness, inflexibility, impossible personal standards, guilt, and fear of failure are likely to be encountered. These can be gently confronted and examined with nonjudgmental encouragement. Bear in mind that patients may be easier to train and educate than to reassure or reason with, particularly if they are still emaciated. The analogy of working with a sensible athletics coach with one's best interests at heart versus "the coach from hell" can be useful, particularly in exercise-driven individuals.

Practice Point
Obsessive-compulsive patients with EDs may be more amenable to training and education than to reassurance or reason.

Specific Behavioral Techniques

Cognitive behavioral therapy (CBT). CBT (Fairburn, Jones, Peveler, Hope, & O'Connor, 1993) and interpersonal psychotherapy (IPT) have been shown to be efficacious in bulimia nervosa; CBT is recommended as the "gold standard" for evidence-based treatment (Palmer, 2004). The focus of CBT is on identifying and changing faulty cognitions that underlie ED behaviors; IPT focuses on aspects of interpersonal interaction such as assertiveness, role transition, grief, and interpersonal deficits. Prior to a recent comparison of treatment modalities in AN and the anorexia spectrum (McIntosh et al., 2005), there had been little research using CBT and IPT in EDs other than bulimia nervosa. In obsessive-compulsive individuals with EDs, CBT, with its reliance on coaching in diligent self-examination and application to homework, might be expected to be more easily accepted than IPT, which focuses on anxiety-provoking social interactions—particularly in the earlier stages of treatment. Note that not all patients are helped by CBT, and other psychopathological issues may need to be addressed in different ways (e.g., long-term psychodynamic psychotherapy).

Standard cognitive-behavioral strategies, beginning with self-monitoring, can be used to address the characteristic "tyranny of the shoulds" found in many patients with EDs. Such "shoulds" are often associated with neurotic or disabling perfectionism (Shafran & Mansell, 2001). Specifically, the therapist can set up in vivo experiments and have the patient observe what happens when he or she is ignoring automatic thoughts or does not carry out rigidly set rules (Shafran et al., 2004). This should be preceded by a discussion of the kinds of emotions that might emerge, along with instruction in their management. The latter might include, for example, ways of managing anxiety (i.e., slow breathing and counting, progressive muscular relaxation, visualization, exercise in keeping with the patient's nutritional state).

Anger may emerge with therapeutic challenges. Therefore, anger management may be relevant and can be undertaken in stronger, medically stable patients, with the use of a punching bag, kickboxing classes, or martial arts training. Other anger-management techniques include journaling; venting to a family member, trusted friend, or member of the treatment team; and/or getting assertiveness training.

Practice Point
Anxiety and anger management techniques should precede experimentation with challenges to obsessive-compulsive symptoms.

Dialectical behavior therapy (DBT). DBT (Linehan, 1993) affect and behavioral management techniques center on the dialectical tension between change and the acceptance "of what is." The latter, paradoxically, represents the desired change, and each interaction between patient and therapist is focused on achieving balance without recourse to behavioral excesses. Skills training includes meditation, mindfulness, radical acceptance, and avoidance of self-harm. Although these might be more relevant for individuals with Cluster B personality pathology (Sansone & Sansone, 2005; Thompson-Brenner & Westen, 2005), the Eastern relaxation and meditation techniques integral to DBT may be quite applicable to anxious and obsessional patients in general. Although the context of a strong, positive, and validating therapeutic relationship is a necessary prerequisite, DBT and CBT techniques can be taught in group settings with amplification and reinforcement in individual sessions.

Specific Techniques for Perfectionism and Cognitive Rigidity

Apart from the usual encouragement for patients to be more flexible in their thinking, less rigid in their standards, and less critical of themselves and others, some other techniques may also be helpful. Management begins with monitoring, and using records and diaries to examine the evidence in support of maintaining or changing perfectionistic assumptions. Experiments can then be set up to challenge these conclusions, broaden thinking, and increase the adoption of different perspectives—all of which might allow for different standards of self-appraisal. Other techniques include graded exposure to feared situations, such as untidiness, along with learning response prevention (i.e., not tidying up), getting communications training, and prioritizing and dealing with procrastination. Depending on their urgency, ED issues can be tackled pari passu, left to the ED program, or temporarily put aside (with regular review) in the expectation of improvement secondary to the amelioration of perfectionism.

Shafran, Teachman, Kerry, and Rachman (1999) described two specific cognitive distortions in OCD, OCPD, and EDs. One cognitive distortion is thought-action fusion, where simply entertaining a negative thought is as bad as carrying it out. This appears to be the forerunner of the second cognitive distortion, thought-shape fusion, where merely thinking about a forbidden food is tantamount to eating it. The identification and challenge of these cognitive distortions have been empirically associated with a reduction in anorexic and obsessive psychopathology (Serpell et al., 2002).

Cognitive remediation therapy (CRT). Davies and Tchanturia (2005) described a novel set of interventions aimed at reducing cognitive inflexibility, a vulnerability and maintaining factor for EDs. This concept relates to difficulties with certain forms of executive function such as set shifting (Tchanturia et al., 2004) and has been shown to improve little, if at all, with weight gain and nutritional rehabilitation. CRT consists of card and sorting games and hand and approximation exercises conducted on an individual basis with a therapist. The aim is to improve thinking skills and the capacity to shift conceptual sets. One would expect this technique, originally used to remedy cognitive deficits in schizophrenia, to be readily acceptable to emaciated patients with AN, as it provides engagement in a positive mental activity without the need to address distressing issues around the ED. A simplified form of this therapy is engaging the patient in simple card games such as solitaire or patience.

Practice Point
CRT might be useful for very ill patients with anorexia and marked cognitive inflexibility.

Motivational enhancement therapy (MET). MET confronts issues related to ambivalence and inflexibility, as exemplified by the pros and cons of giving up or holding on to the ED and/or impossible personal standards. This approach is highlighted by the externalizing technique of separating oneself from the ED and attempting to give it a name and identity. This approach includes writing letters to the ED, or the associated rigid rules, and imagining life in 10 years with and without the symptoms. A letter is written to a hated body part followed by the patient's imagined response, followed by the patient's reply, and so forth, and can be an engaging way of dealing with these symptoms. In addition, assessing the patient's "stages of change" can be useful in determining an individual's readiness to work in therapy, though these often fluctuate (Rieger et al., 2000). One advantage of MET is that it can be used in individual and group settings.

Cognitive analytical therapy (CAT). CAT is a relatively short-term, highly collaborative form of therapy that uses letter writing to define the patient's disparate states of mind, particularly as the content relates to change. CAT has important similarities to motivational enhancement techniques and can be readily applied to the treatment of both obsessive-compulsive and ED symptoms (Ryle & Kerr, 2002). CAT enables the clinician to reframe and transform experiences of therapeutic impotence and negativity and may have a particular place in the management of treatment-resistant patients who seem to have reached an impasse (Treasure & Ward, 1997). However, CAT is technologically complicated, requires extensive supervision, and is likely to be limited in use.

Practice Point
CAT may help therapists and resistant patients who have reached a therapeutic impasse.

Psychodynamic or Psychotherapeutic Approaches

Milieu support. The milieu of an ED program should be therapeutic and supportive. In this regard, the processes of refeeding and behavioral containment need to be repeatedly reframed, drawing on scientific reasoning, medical facts, and research by way of explanation. Somewhat to our surprise, our patients say the most beneficial aspects of the ward milieu are meal supervision and support followed by talks with nurses and other patients in a nonjudgmental, hope-generating atmosphere

(Russell, Poland, & Abraham, 2004). One patient described this as "a safe place to change."

Supportive psychotherapy. Supportive psychotherapy (Buckley, 1994), a somewhat underrated treatment modality, was recently shown to achieve better outcomes than standard CBT and IPT in patients recovering from AN (McIntosh et al., 2005). The supportive psychotherapy used in this study was patient directed and focused on nutrition and the ED as required—unlike the other two modalities, which focused solely on changing cognitions or dealing with interpersonal difficulties, respectively.

Other therapeutic approaches. A self-psychological approach has been suggested in the literature, and one of its goals is to ultimately nurture the sense of self so as to obviate the need to engage in ED behaviors (Russell & Meares, 1997).

Behavioral versus psychodynamic approaches. Interestingly, a naturalistic study by Thompson-Brenner and Westen (2005) in female patients with bulimia nervosa suggests that patients with constricted and perfectionistic personality types tend to be treated more with behavioral rather than psychodynamic techniques. The latter approach was preferred for patients with bulimia and disinhibited personality styles. This might have related to compliance, a necessary prerequisite for success with behavioral techniques and something that is difficult to secure in disinhibited patients who might adhere more readily to a psychodynamic approach.

Practice Point

A psychotherapy approach should provide the matrix for symptom-targeted behavioral therapies.

Medications

Antidepressants. Kaye, Frank, Bailer, Henry, et al. (2005) described persisting serotonergic perturbations in patients with EDs, even after recovery. Serotonin modulates mood, feeding, and impulse control, and medications influencing serotonin have been observed to have at least some effect on these symptoms. The clinical question is whether these agents are modifying the ED, an associated depressive mood state, an OCD-like component, or a personality disorder (Sansone & Sansone, 2005). As mentioned earlier, obsessive-compulsive symptoms may persist after recovery from an ED. Therefore, the notion of endophenotypes such as those of constrained eating, compulsivity, and cognitive inflexibility is relevant, here (Collier & Treasure, 2004).

Research findings indicate that the use of selective serotonin reuptake inhibitor (SSRI) antidepressants in various types of EDs offers some benefit (Attia & Schroeder, 2005; Halmi, 1997; Sansone & Sansone, 2005). In addition, the use of these medications, as well as the use of other types of antidepressants, in the management of maladaptive perfectionism, anxiety, OCD, and depression may be helpful. Unfortunately, emaciation compromises the efficacy of *any* antidepressant. Also, anti-depressants, used alone, are markedly less effective than when used in conjunction with psychological and behavioral interventions.

Practice Point
Any medication is optimally effective when used in conjunction with psy-chological intervention and in the context of a therapeutic relationship.

In contrast to the inconsistent literature implicating serotonin in the genetic basis of EDs (Kaye, Frank, Bailer, Henry, et al., 2005), a recent study demonstrated polymorphism of the noradrenergic transporter gene in patients with restricting AN and their parents, compared to healthy controls. This finding might provide indirect support for using selective noradrenergic reuptake inhibitor (SNRI) antidepressants in depressed and unmotivated patients with AN (Russell, 2004; Urwin et al., 2002; Urwin et al., 2003). However, SSRIs still seem to be of value in managing obsessive symptomatology; theoretically, a combina-tion of these drugs may be efficacious, as well.

Practice Point
Although SSRI and SNRI antidepressants can be useful in AN, SSRIs appear to improve obsessive symptoms and prevent relapse.

Antipsychotic agents. In keeping with a postulated abnormality in central dopamine regulation, early studies in the treatment of AN examined the use of chlorpromazine to promote weight gain and reduce obsessive quasi-psychotic thinking. However, side effects (e.g., hypo-tension, sedation, extrapyramidal symptoms, binge eating) limited and finally curtailed the use of conventional antipsychotic agents (Attia & Schroeder, 2005; Halmi, 1997).

However, the atypical antipsychotics, with their more acceptable side-effect profile, may be of particular value in AN. Despite a paucity of data from double-blind randomly controlled trials, which can be a dif-ficult undertaking in patients who actively resist randomization (Rus-sell, 2004), atypical antipsychotics have been shown to be of benefit. Specifically, they appear to cause a reduction in rumination with regard to weight, shape, and food preoccupation (Mondraty et al., 2005; Pow-ers & Santana, 2004). These agents, which affect both dopaminergic and serotonergic receptors, may also be beneficial for OCD and body dysmorphic disorder (BDD), obsessional thinking, compulsive behav-iors, quasi-psychotic symptoms, anxiety, insomnia, and hyperactivity (Phillips & McElroy, 1993; Sareen et al., 2004). The latter use is sup-ported by findings from animal work (Hillebrand, van Elburg, Kas, van Engeland, & Adan, 2005).

In small doses, weight gain is probably not a major effect of atypical antipsychotics in low-weight patients. In normal-weight EDs, the use of particular atypical antipsychotics is cautioned because of their metabolic effects (e.g., increase in body weight, glucose, cholesterol, triglycerides) and the risk of a distressing increase in binge eating (exceptions may be amisulpride and aripiprazole). Diabetes mellitus, if it occurs, can be ketoacidotic and is not always dose or weight related, so the mechanism remains unclear (Cavazzoni, Mukhopadhyay, Carlson, Breier, & Buse, 2004). Also, partly weight-restored patients with AN have been shown to be more sensitive to insulin than lean age-matched female controls (Russell, Kriketos, Milner, & Campbell, 2005), so it seems that atypical antipsychotics can be used in these cases with impunity—at least until a minimum healthy weight is reached.

Practice Point
Atypical antipsychotic drugs may cause weight gain and metabolic effects and are best avoided or used with caution except in low doses in patients with AN at low weight.

General Commentary About the Use of Medication

It should be stressed that medication is likely to achieve lasting success only when used in the context of psychological treatment and, more important, a supportive therapeutic alliance. Many obsessive-compulsive individuals are wary of medication. They may have obtained large amounts of information, both accurate and inaccurate, which may be compounded by misinterpretation. Obviously, these issues need to be carefully discussed.

Patients may express resistance to medication as not wanting to put substances into their bodies (no matter how unhealthy their weight-losing behaviors might be). A common refrain is, "I just want to do it myself," particularly from those emaciated by anorexia and troubled by obsessive and intrusive thoughts about food, shape, or weight, or quasi-psychotic exhortations to eat or not eat. Short of instituting mandatory treatment (which might be indicated for the mortally ill but usually does not improve the therapeutic alliance), the clinician has little option but to accept the refusal graciously, urging the patient to think about what was suggested and emphasizing that medication can be made available whenever he or she feels ready to try it.

OCD AND BDD

BDD manifests when a minor imperfection in appearance, often facial, becomes the focus of disabling obsessions and accompanying avoidance behaviors. This preoccupation can have either an obsessive or delusional quality and often occurs in patients with EDs—particularly in those with obsessive-compulsive personality traits. Although the focus is oftentimes a certain body part, it may generalize to the whole body or the general musculature as in muscle dysmorphophobia (Phillips &

McElroy, 1993; Rabe-Jablonska & Sobow, 2000). In an attempt to remedy the defect, individuals might pursue weight-losing behaviors, body building to a pathological degree, and/or inappropriate cosmetic surgery. BDD is easily missed, as patients have become used to living with their concerns, do not expect others to understand, feel embarrassed about their predicament, and/or may go to great lengths to avoid scrutiny.

Inquiry as to attitudes about the entire body, certain body parts, or the general musculature is often and easily overlooked, but the patient may respond positively to the clinician's interest. Supervised mirror exposure (Serpell et al., 2002), response prevention to the urge to check in a mirror at other times, and a medication regimen (usually of the SSRI type) are often indicated. The addition of antipsychotic agents may be undertaken if the symptoms have a delusional quality (Phillips & McElroy, 1993) or if containment of self-mutilation (including injurious cosmetic surgery) becomes a concern.

Practice Point
It is important to inquire as to whether patients with EDs have symptoms of BDD. Excessive cosmetic surgery should raise concerns in this regard.

OUTCOME

Personality disorders in general have a propensity to improve with time, and a reduction in personality pathology has been reported with recovery from the associated ED (Lenzenweger, Johnson, & Willett, 2004; Rø, Martinsen, Hoffart, & Rosenvinge, 2005). Although there is disagreement in the literature about whether OCD or Axis II psychopathology including OCPD prejudices the outcome of behavioral or pharmacological treatment (AuBuchon & Malatesta, 1994; Dreessen et al., 1997; Thiel, Zuger, Jacoby, & Schussler, 1998), personality comorbidity has been found to be associated with longer treatment, more frequent hospitalizations, and more negative treatment experiences (Milos, Spindler, Buddeberg, & Crameri, 2003). An interesting finding is that obsessive-compulsive traits may be an advantage in treatment. In evaluating fluoxetine and CBT, alone and in combination, to assess relapse prevention in AN, Halmi et al. (2005) found that although acceptance of medication was low, obsessive symptomatology predicted acceptance of CBT and combined therapy.

Practice Point
OCPD tends to improve with time and recovery from the ED; indeed, obsessionality may even be a positive factor in treatment.

CASE HISTORIES

Case 1

Kristine was a 27-year-old woman who lived with her parents and younger brother. She worked as a cosmetic saleswoman in the same department store for several years, and her work was very important to her. She would travel across the city by public transport to arrive unnecessarily early each morning, obsess about the efficiency of her coworkers, argue with and criticize them (although she was not their supervisor), think incessantly about her sales figures, and stay late to finish her work in which she was obsessionally slow. Upon arriving home, she would engage in elaborate rituals while undressing and removing her makeup. She ate little during the day, would not eat with the family, and was highly irritable. Around midnight, she would go into the backyard and sweep up leaves. She would then fold and put away any wet or soiled towels she found—much to their owners' annoyance. Following her "chores," she would pick at leftover food and eat a number of bowls of dessert and a large quantity of fruit before going to bed. Her weight was very low on occasions, and, when Kristine refused treatment, her mother would take her to an emergency department and try to have her involuntarily admitted.

Nine years ago, Kristine was admitted to an ED residential program for 3 weeks. She rapidly gained weight but attained no insight, left precipitously, and reluctantly continued in outpatient treatment only at her mother's insistence. She would not talk about her rituals, minimized her symptoms, and denied her ED. Her mother would express her concern and describe her observations, which Kristine would refute. Following her mother's last attempt to have mandatory treatment instituted (Kristine had all but ceased to eat, lost several pounds, collapsed on one occasion, was amenorrheic, and was becoming even more extreme in her behaviors to the point where her job was in jeopardy), Kristine agreed to resume taking medications. During her early 20s, she had taken these with good effect during a period when she was relatively well. Kristine resumed taking citalopram 40 mg in the morning and olanzapine 7.5 mg at night, with the support of her general practitioner and psychiatrist. There was a prompt resolution of the irritability and the nightly rituals of sweeping leaves and folding towels. She slept better, ate evening meals with her family, experienced a weight gain of 10 pounds in 2 months, and resumed menstruation. She reported feeling better and was less argumentative but would not be confronted about her obsessive symptoms. Kristine continued to have no social life and be extraordinarily focused on and punctilious in her work.

Case 2

Anne was a talented 15-year-old ballet student who was told by her ballet teacher that, at a BMI of 21.5, she was too heavy. She restricted her eating, induced vomiting, and increased her level of exercise. At school, she was regarded as a perfectionistic high achiever. She lost 22 pounds in 6 months and developed amenorrhea, and her BMI fell to 18. She was admitted to a residential facility for the treatment of EDs after outpatient treatment had failed.

Initially, Anne was ostensibly pleasant and compliant, but she became inordinately angry when she gained any weight, insisting that she still wished to lose weight. A history of childhood sexual abuse was disclosed, major conflicts between Anne and her mother came to light, and Anne threatened to leave both home and school. When Anne was permitted to attend an outside ballet class, she declined on the grounds that she believed she would be the "fattest person there." She acknowledged that her perception of her weight and body shape was distorted and agreed to work with the clinical psychologist on challenging her inflexible attitudes. Depression emerged as she became aware of her shattered dreams—a conclusion based on an unrealistic conviction that she would be too heavy to professionally dance at a BMI of 19. An antidepressant was commenced, following which she self-harmed and required a temporary increase in containment until the crisis passed. Anne was then discharged to continue outpatient treatment with a clinical psychologist, a dietitian, and a DBT program.

CONCLUSION

When they occur together, obsessive-compulsive symptomatology—whether related to OCD, BDD, OCPD, or obsessional personality traits—can be difficult to separate from EDs. Their relationship is a complex one. Symptom-based treatment can be difficult and rewarding. There are general and specific behavioral strategies, ongoing psychotherapy in a variety of modalities, and psychoactive medications that are helpful, particularly within a supportive therapeutic alliance and appropriate treatment milieu. Patience, meticulous diligence, and perseverance will be required of the clinician, who would do well to mirror the more adaptive qualities of the obsessive-compulsive individual with an ED.

NOTE

Please direct correspondence to Janice Russell, MD, Northside Clinic, 2 Greenwich Road, Greenwich, NSW 2063, Australia; telephone: 612-9433-3555; fax: 612-9433-3599; e-mail: JRUSSEL1@mail.usyd.edu.au.

REFERENCES

Anderluh, M. B., Tchanturia, K., Rabe-Hesketh, S., & Treasure, J. (2003). Childhood obsessive-compulsive personality traits in adult women with eating disorders: Defining a broader eating disorder phenotype. *American Journal of Psychiatry, 160*, 242–247.

Attia, E., & Schroeder, L. (2005). Pharmacologic treatment of anorexia nervosa: Where do we go from here? *International Journal of Eating Disorders, 37*, S60–S63.

AuBuchon, P. G., & Malatesta, V. J. (1994). Obsessive compulsive patients with comorbid personality disorder: Associated problems and response to a comprehensive behavior therapy. *Journal of Clinical Psychiatry, 55*, 448–453.

Baer, L., & Jenike, M. A. (1992). Personality disorders in obsessive compulsive disorder. *Psychiatric Clinics of North America, 15*, 803–812.

Beumont, P. J., Arthur, B., Russell, J. D., & Touyz, S. W. (1994). Excessive physical activity in dieting disorder patients: Proposals for a supervised exercise program. *International Journal of Eating Disorders, 15*, 21–36.

Binford, R. B., & le Grange, D. (2005). Adolescents with bulimia nervosa and eating disorder not otherwise specified-purging only. *International Journal of Eating Disorders, 38*, 157–161.

Bruce, K. R., & Steiger, H. (2005). Treatment implications of Axis-II comorbidity in eating disorders. *Eating Disorders: The Journal of Treatment and Prevention, 13*, 93–108.

Buckley, P. (1994). Self psychology, object relations theory and supportive psychotherapy. *American Journal of Psychotherapy, 48*, 519–529.

Cavazzoni, P., Mukhopadhyay, N., Carlson, C., Breier, A., & Buse, J. (2004). Retrospective analysis of risk factors in patients with treatment-emergent diabetes during clinical trials of antipsychotic medications. *British Journal of Psychiatry—Supplementum, 47*, S94–S101.

Cavedini, P., Erzegovesi, S., Ronchi, P., & Bellodi, L. (1997). Predictive value of obsessive-compulsive personality disorder in antiobsessional pharmacological treatment. *European Neuropsychopharmacology, 7*, 45–49.

Collier, D. A., & Treasure, J. L. (2004). The aetiology of eating disorders. *British Journal of Psychiatry, 185*, 363–365.

Davies, H., & Tchanturia, K. (2005). Cognitive remediation therapy as an intervention for acute anorexia nervosa: A case report. *International Eating Disorders Review, 13*, 311–316.

Dreessen, L., Hoekstra, R., & Arntz, A. (1997). Personality disorders do not influence the results of cognitive and behavior therapy for obsessive compulsive disorder. *Journal of Anxiety Disorders, 11*, 503–521.

Fairburn, C. G., Jones, R., Peveler, R. C., Hope, R. A., & O'Connor, M. (1993). Psychotherapy and bulimia nervosa: Longer-term effects of interpersonal psychotherapy, behavior therapy, and cognitive behavior therapy. *Archives of General Psychiatry, 50*, 419–428.

Franco-Paredes, K., Mancilla-Diaz, J. M., Vazquez-Arevalo, R., Lopez-Aguilar, X., & Alvarez-Rayon, G. (2005). Perfectionism and eating disorders: A review of the literature. *European Eating Disorders Review, 13*, 61–70.

Godart, N. T., Flament, M. F., Lecrubier, Y., & Jeammet, P. (2000). Anxiety disorders in anorexia nervosa and bulimia nervosa: Comorbidity and chronology of appearance. *European Psychiatry: The Journal of the Association of European Psychiatrists, 15*, 38–45.

Grilo, C. M. (2002). Recent research of relationships among eating disorders and personality disorders. *Current Psychiatry Reports, 4*, 18–24.

Halmi, K. A. (1997). Biological basis for treatment of anorexia nervosa. *European Neuropsychopharmacology, 7*(Suppl. 2), 115–116.

Halmi, K. A. (2005). Obsessive-compulsive personality disorder and eating disorders. *Eating Disorders: The Journal of Treatment and Prevention, 13*, 85–92.

Halmi, K. A., Agras, W. S., Crow, S., Mitchell, J., Wilson, G. T., Bryson, S. W., et al. (2005). Predictors of treatment acceptance and completion in anorexia nervosa: Implications for future study designs. *Archives of General Psychiatry, 62*, 776–781.

Hart, S., Field, T., Hernandez-Reif, M., Nearing, G., Shaw, S., Schanberg, S., et al. (2001). Anorexia nervosa symptoms are reduced by massage therapy. *Eating Disorders: The Journal of Treatment and Prevention, 9*, 289–299.

Hillebrand, J. J., van Elburg, A. A., Kas, M. J., van Engeland, H., & Adan, R. A. (2005). Olanzapine reduces physical activity in rats exposed to activity-based anorexia: Possible implications for treatment of anorexia nervosa? *Biological Psychiatry, 58*, 651–657.

Hsu, L. K., Kaye, W., & Weltzin, T. (1993). Are the eating disorders related to obsessive compulsive disorder? *International Journal of Eating Disorders, 14*, 305–318.

Kaye, W. H., Bailer, U. F., Frank, G. K., Wagner, A., & Henry, S. E. (2005). Brain imaging of serotonin after recovery from anorexia and bulimia nervosa. *Physiology and Behavior, 86*, 15–17.

Kaye, W. H., Frank, G. K., Bailer, U. F., & Henry, S. E. (2005). Neurobiology of anorexia nervosa: Clinical implications of alterations of the function of serotonin and other neuronal systems. *International Journal of Eating Disorders, 37*, S15–S19.

Kaye, W. H., Frank, G. K., Bailer, U. F., Henry, S. E., Meltzer, C. C., Price, J. C., et al. (2005). Serotonin alterations in anorexia and bulimia nervosa: New insights from imaging studies. *Physiology and Behavior, 85*, 73–81.

Lenzenweger, M. F., Johnson, M. D., & Willett, J. B. (2004). Individual growth curve analysis illuminates stability and change in personality disorder features: The longitudinal study of personality disorders. *Archives of General Psychiatry, 61*, 1015–1024.

Linehan, M. M. (1993). *Cognitive-behavioral treatment of borderline personality disorder*. New York: Guilford.

Maj, M. (2005). "Psychiatric comorbidity": An artefact of current diagnostic systems? *British Journal of Psychiatry, 186*, 182–184.

McIntosh, V. V., Jordan, J., Carter, F. A., Luty, S. E., McKenzie, J. M., Bulik, C. M., et al. (2005). Three psychotherapies for anorexia nervosa: A randomized, controlled trial. *American Journal of Psychiatry, 162,* 741–747.

Milos, G. F., Spindler, A. M., Buddeberg, C., & Crameri, A. (2003). Axes I and II comorbidity and treatment experiences in eating disorder subjects. *Psychotherapy and Psychosomatics, 72,* 276–285.

Mondraty, N., Birmingham, C. L., Touyz, S., Sundakov, V., Chapman, L., & Beumont, P. (2005). Randomized controlled trial of olanzapine in the treatment of cognitions in anorexia nervosa. *Australasian Psychiatry, 13,* 72–75.

Palmer, R. (2004). Bulimia nervosa: 25 years on. *British Journal of Psychiatry, 185,* 447–448.

Perkins, P. S., Klump, K. L., Iacono, W. G., & McGue, M. (2005). Personality traits in women with anorexia nervosa: Evidence for a treatment-seeking bias? *International Journal of Eating Disorders, 37,* 32–37.

Phillips, K. A., & McElroy, S. L. (1993). Insight, overvalued ideation, and delusional thinking in body dysmorphic disorder: Theoretical and treatment implications. *Journal of Nervous and Mental Disease, 181,* 699–702.

Picot, A. K., & Lilenfeld, L. R. (2003). The relationship among binge severity, personality psychopathology, and body mass index. *International Journal of Eating Disorders, 34,* 98–107.

Powers, P. S., & Santana, C. (2004). Available pharmacological treatments for anorexia nervosa. *Expert Opinion on Pharmacotherapy, 5,* 2287–2292.

Rabe-Jablonska, J. J., & Sobow, T. M. (2000). The links between body dysmorphic disorder and eating disorders. *European Psychiatry: The Journal of the Association of European Psychiatrists, 15,* 302–305.

Rieger, E., Touyz, S., Schotte, D., Beumont, P., Russell, J., Clarke, S., et al. (2000). Development of an instrument to assess readiness to recover in anorexia nervosa. *International Journal of Eating Disorders, 28,* 387–396.

Rø, Ø., Martinsen, E. W., Hoffart, A., & Rosenvinge, J. (2005). Two-year prospective study of personality disorders in adults with longstanding eating disorders. *International Journal of Eating Disorders, 37,* 112–118.

Russell, J. (2004). Management of anorexia nervosa revisited. *British Medical Journal, 328,* 479–480.

Russell, J., Kriketos, A. D., Milner, K. D., & Campbell, L. (2005). Adiponectin and insulin sensitivity in anorexia nervosa patients: Effect of weight recovery. *World Psychiatry, 3*(Suppl. 1), S63.

Russell, J., & Meares, R. (1997). Paradox, persecution and the double game: Psychotherapy in anorexia nervosa. *Australian and New Zealand Journal of Psychiatry, 31,* 691–699.

Russell, J., Poland, T., & Abraham, S. (2004). Importance of the milieu in treatment of eating disorders. Paper presented at 39th Royal Australian and New Zealand College of Psychiatry Congress, Christchurch, New Zealand.

Ryle, A., & Kerr, I. B. (2002). *Introducing cognitive analytic therapy.* New York: John Wiley and Sons.

Sansone, R. A., & Levitt, J. L. (2005). Personality disorders and eating disorders: Exploring the frontier. *Eating Disorders: The Journal of Treatment and Prevention, 13,* 3–5.

Sansone, R. A., & Sansone, L. A. (2005). The use of psychotropic medications in eating disorder patients with personality disorders. *Eating Disorders: The Journal of Treatment and Prevention, 13,* 123–134.

Sareen, J., Kirshner, A., Lander, M., Kjernisted, K. D., Eleff, M. K., & Reiss, J. P. (2004). Do antipsychotics ameliorate or exacerbate obsessive compulsive disorder symptoms? A systematic review. *Journal of Affective Disorders, 82,* 167–174.

Schmidt, U. (2003). Mandometer musings. *European Eating Disorders Review, 11,* 1–6.

Serpell, L., Livingstone, A., Neiderman, M., & Lask, B. (2002). Anorexia nervosa: Obsessive-compulsive disorder, obsessive-compulsive personality disorder, or neither? *Clinical Psychology Review, 22,* 647–669.

Shafran, R., Lee, M., & Fairburn, C. G. (2004). Clinical perfectionism: A case report. *Behavioural and Cognitive Psychotherapy, 32,* 353–357.

Shafran, R., & Mansell, W. (2001). Perfectionism and psychopathology: A review of research and treatment. *Clinical Psychology Review, 21,* 879–906.

Shafran, R., Teachman, B. A., Kerry, S., & Rachman, S. (1999). A cognitive distortion associated with eating disorders: Thought-shape fusion. *British Journal of Clinical Psychology, 38,* 167–179.

Shea, M. T., Stout, R. L., Yen, S., Pagano, M. E., Skodol, A. E., Morey, L. C., et al. (2004). Associations in the course of personality disorders and Axis I disorders over time. *Journal of Abnormal Psychology, 113,* 499–508.

Sodersten, P., Bergh, C., & Ammar, A. (2003). Anorexia nervosa: Towards a neurobiologically based therapy. *European Journal of Pharmacology, 480,* 67–74.

Tchanturia, K., Morris, R. G., Anderluh, M. B., Collier, D. A., Nikolaou, V., & Treasure, J. (2004). Set shifting in anorexia nervosa: An examination before and after weight gain, in full recovery and relationship to childhood and adult OCPD traits. *Journal of Psychiatric Research, 38,* 545–552.

Thiel, A., Zuger, M., Jacoby, G. E., & Schussler, G. (1998). Thirty-month outcome in patients with anorexia or bulimia nervosa and concomitant obsessive-compulsive disorder. *American Journal of Psychiatry, 155,* 244–249.

Thompson-Brenner, H., & Westen, D. (2005). Personality subtypes in eating disorders: Validation of a classification in a naturalistic sample. *British Journal of Psychiatry, 186,* 516–524.

Thornton, C., & Russell, J. (1997). Obsessive compulsive comorbidity in the dieting disorders. *International Journal of Eating Disorders, 21,* 83–87.

Treasure, J., & Ward, A. (1997). Cognitive analytical therapy in the treatment of anorexia nervosa. *Clinical Psychology and Psychotherapy, 4,* 62–71.

Urwin, R. E., Bennetts, B. H., Wilcken, B., Beumont, P. J., Russell, J. D., & Nunn, K. P. (2003). Investigation of epistasis between the serotonin transporter and norepinephrine transporter genes in anorexia nervosa. *Neuropsychopharmacology, 28,* 1351–1355.

Urwin, R. E., Bennetts, B., Wilcken, B., Lampropoulos, B., Beumont, P., Clarke, S., et al. (2002). Anorexia nervosa (restrictive subtype) is associated with a polymorphism in the novel norepinephrine transporter gene promoter polymorphic region. *Molecular Psychiatry, 7,* 652–657.

Vitousek, K. M., & Stumpf, R. E. (2005). Difficulties in the assessment of personality traits and disorders in eating-disordered individuals. *Eating Disorders: The Journal of Treatment and Prevention, 13,* 37–60.

CHAPTER
11

A Self-Regulation Treatment Approach for the Patient With an Eating Disorder and Borderline Personality Disorder

JOHN L. LEVITT, PHD

The treatment of patients with eating disorders (EDs) is renowned for its challenges, complexities, and inherent risks. For psychological and emotional reasons, patients with EDs deny their body's need for food and nutrition by restricting, purging, or losing control over their nutritional intake through binging. Indeed, clinicians are faced with few other psychiatric populations represented by such psychologically and physically high-risk individuals.

These patients often exhibit a treatment course that is prolonged, eventful, and highly demanding of therapists' skills, talents, and professional resources (Garner & Garfinkel, 1997). When patients with EDs also exhibit concomitant personality disorders, such as borderline personality disorder (BPD), treatment may become extraordinarily difficult (Dennis & Sansone, 1991, 1997; Johnson & Connors, 1987; Linnehan, 1993a).

The prevalence of BPD among patients with EDs is not explicitly known. Estimates, however, suggest that prevalence rates range from 10% to 28%, depending on the type of ED (Sansone & Levitt, 2005; Sansone, Sansone, & Levitt 2004). Clearly, the eating disorder/borderline personality disorder (EDBPD) subgroup is appreciably represented in the general ED population. For treatment to be successful, specific approaches need to be engaged and undertaken.

Few authors in the ED literature have addressed this population. Some authors have recognized the inherent difficulties in working with patients with EDs and BPD (e.g., such as in males) (Andersen, 1990). Others have briefly discussed this issue in only slightly more detail, as it applies to the clinical issues among the broader ED population (e.g., Tobin, 1993; Vanderlinden & Vandereycken, 1997). Dennis and Sansone (1991, 1997) identified specific stages of treatment, which they found useful in treating the patient with EDBPD. Using a primarily psychodynamic approach referred to as "direct, confrontational, and interpretive, coupled with cognitive-behavioral techniques designed to improve self-esteem and contain self-destructive behaviors" (Dennis & Sansone, 1997, p. 439), these authors described four stages of clinical treatment for the patient with EDBPD. Stage I is "establishing the therapeutic milieu," Stage II is the "stabilization of transference," Stage III is "resolving internal themes," and, finally, Stage IV refers to "preparing for termination." In a related area, Sansone and Levitt (2005) discussed the treatment of the self-harming patient with EDBPD and identified several of the therapeutic obstacles that are likely to be encountered in this group.

In contrast to the ED literature, and its references to BPD, the BPD treatment literature tends to minimally address the issues of the ED population (e.g., Linehan, 1993a; Yeomans, Selzer, & Clarkin, 1992). So, with few exceptions, there appears to be little discussion of the treatment of the patient with EDBPD in either the ED or BPD literature.

Practice Point
There is limited information on the treatment of the patient with EDBPD.

Given the relative importance of this subgroup of patients, and the somewhat limited available information to address their particular needs, further clinical exploration is needed. In the following sections, I outline the relevant characteristics of EDBPD (i.e., potential targets for initial treatment) and provide a multiphase conceptual format for working with the patient with EDBPD.

Relational Dimensions	2 criteria
Behavioral Dimensions	6 criteria
Cognitive Dimensions	6 criteria
Affective Dimensions	4 criteria

Figure 11.1　The dimensions of impaired functioning for the patient with an eating disorder/borderline personality disorder, according to combined criteria found in the *Diagnostic and Statistical Manual of Mental Disorders–Fourth Edition* (American Psychiatric Association, 1994).

CLINICAL PRESENTATION OF THE PATIENT WITH EDBPD

The patient with EDBPD has been described in various ways (e.g., Sansone & Levitt, 2005; Sansone et al., 2004), making the diagnosis of BDP potentially fraught with difficulties (Sansone et al., 2004). The patient with EDBPD exhibits potential difficulties in functioning across a wide spectrum of areas. For example, by examining the criteria for both ED and BPD diagnoses found in the *Diagnostic and Statistical Manual of Mental Disorders–Fourth Edition* (American Psychiatric Association, 1994) and summarizing them according to dimensions of impaired functioning, one can develop some perspective on the broad range of potential dysfunction found in a typical patient with EDBPD (see Figure 11.1).

From a clinical perspective, these patients present in quite varied and challenging ways, with impairments over broad dimensions of functioning, and they require intensive and thoughtful treatment services. Examples of presentation characteristics that clinicians might possibly encounter are illustrated in Table 11.1. Of course, there may be extreme variations in presentation styles across these patients, but the characteristics noted in Table 11.1 provide a general overview of the patients' "symptom picture."

In general, these individuals are frequently seen as difficult patients— the ones who appear to derive power and/or accomplishments through their symptoms, who often portray themselves as effective and accomplished while maintaining a helpless position of relating, who meet the minimal expectations for limits to solicit approval but may do so in an unhealthy or indirect manner, and who often engage in a conflict between wanting to be rescued versus wanting to be independent (Levitt, 2000a, 2000b). Levitt (1998) previously described patients who exhibit these patterns as "disorganized" and emphasized using a clear treatment framework (Levitt, 2000a, 2000b).

TABLE 11.1   Examples of Clinical Characteristics Commonly Encountered
in the EDBPD Patient Population

- Poor social skills with pseudomaturity
- Feelings of being out of place, time, and context
- Faster physical development than psychological readiness
- Inability to cope with the demands of life
- Ongoing attempts to be in control, perfectionistic, and performance based
- Narrow psychological and interpersonal experiences (i.e., limited amount of information taken in)
- Chaotic and frequent acting-out behaviors
- Predominant affects of shame, guilt, and rage
- Extreme attention-seeking behavior in a passive-aggressive to aggressive interactional style
- Loss of control
- Wide range of concomitant impulsive and compulsive behaviors
- Symptom substitution with multiple Axis I and Axis II diagnoses
- History of multiple hospitalizations
- History of extensive therapy without significant change
- Long-term symptomatology
- High relapse rate
- Tendency toward life-threatening and pseudo-life-threatening behaviors
- Extensive psychiatric comorbidity

Note: EDBPD = eating disorder/borderline personality disorder.

Practice Point
The typical patient with EDBPD often presents as disorganized and "difficult," and is frequently challenging for clinicians.

THE TREATMENT FRAMEWORK

Given the preceding descriptions of the patient with EDBPD, it is relatively easy to see how difficult and challenging the patient and treatment programs might be for clinicians. In this section I present and discuss various phases of treatment that have been found useful for working with these patients.

There are two major concepts that underlie treatment in this approach. First, the treatment approach acknowledges the importance of each set of symptom clusters, and their interactions (i.e., EDBPD), and addresses the symptoms of both the ED and the BPD. Although relative emphasis may be placed on one set of symptoms at different times (e.g., the ED), the other relevant interacting symptoms (i.e., the BPD) are kept in clear view on the "therapeutic map" at all times.

Practice Point
This treatment framework addresses both the ED and the BPD symptoms.

Second, our treatment framework *deliberately* employs the concepts of "phases." Emphasizing phases embodies the concepts that treatment is composed of a variety of components that are interrelated, that treatment needs to be individually tailored for each patient and relevant patient condition(s) (i.e., it is not static), and that the treatment framework is multifaceted. Treatment phases in the treatment framework are highly interrelated. Indeed, the patient may need to revisit a particular phase more than once as he or she moves toward the treatment goal(s).

The treatment framework presented here is consistent with others described elsewhere (e.g., Dennis & Sansone, 1997; Levitt, 2004). It is organized around five general phases: assessment and evaluation, organizing the treatment structure, psychotherapy, transition, and termination.

Practice Point
Treatment for the EDBPD may be usefully conceptualized as a sequence of phases.

Assessment and Evaluation Phase

Accurately assessing and evaluating these patients is of critical importance. Because of their often chronic, severe, and high-risk presentations, it is vital to assess and evaluate these patients in an ongoing manner. At the beginning of treatment, it is important to accurately determine the nature of their ED and their presenting personality characteristics. Examples of useful assessment tools for conducting these evaluations have been discussed elsewhere (e.g., Garner & Garkinkel, 1997; Sansone & Sansone, 2004). The key point is that assessment tools and processes need to be adopted and implemented for the long term and for patient-relevant conditions (Sansone & Sansone, 2004). In other words, because these patients often tend to be chronically symptomatic, the clinician needs to anticipate regularly evaluating the patient's symptom status (e.g., ED, related compulsive symptomatology, personality dimensions, and so forth) throughout treatment. Tools such as the Eating Attitudes Test (Garner & Garfinkel, 1979), the Self-Harm Inventory (Sansone, Wiederman, & Sansone, 1998), and the Borderline Personality scale of the Personality Diagnostic Questionnaire–4 (Hyler, 1994) are examples of instruments that may be used repeatedly to explore patient conditions over time. (For additional examples of instruments, see Sansone and Sansone [2004].) Using these tools, as well as regularly eliciting clinical information from the patient, represents the foundation of continual assessment and evaluation.

Practice Point
Careful evaluation of both the ED and the BPD symptom picture is essential not only at the beginning of treatment but also in an ongoing manner. Clinicians need to consider a variety of assessment tools and processes, which need to be adopted and regularly employed over the long term.

Organizing a Treatment Structure Phase

Organizing the therapeutic milieu (i.e., the treatment structure), and maintaining it, represents one of the greatest challenges to clinicians working with these patients. As described earlier, these patients tend to be multisymptomatic (Levitt, 2000a). It is vital that clinicians have a clear way of organizing treatment that is understandable and useful to both the clinician and the patient. From this perspective, it is important that the patient and the therapist understand and agree to how treatment will be conducted. This includes the overall structure of treatment as well as the identified goals. In this way, the patient, along with the therapist, is able to evaluate progress. Thus, the patient's buy-in is essential. This type of engagement tends to empower the patient from the onset.

Practice Point
It is necessary that both the patient and the therapist understand and agree to how treatment will be conducted.

The structural-process model (SPM). One useful approach for organizing treatment is the SPM, which is derived from the concepts of self-regulation (Levitt, 2004). The SPM is made up of three broad components: Basics, Foundation Skills, and Actions. These components were designed to be easily understood and applied to treatment by both patients and therapists.

The Basics refers to those skills and processes that focus on self-care. The term *Basics* is employed to remind the treatment team that effective self-care and the reduction of self-destructive symptoms is essential for effective recovery. Foundation Skills refer to those skills and processes that are typically thought of as therapy interventions, such as cognitive behavior treatments, interpersonal therapy, and so forth (see Garner & Garfinkel, 1997, for a review). That is, the patient's personal patterns of thinking (i.e., "information" used for managing self) and relating (i.e., "information" used to manage interactions) are identified, and ways of addressing these to enhance effective recovery are focused on in the Foundation Skills. These skills also address the ways that information is selected, focused on, and employed within the therapeutic relationship for the purpose(s) of recovery. The Actions part of the SPM refers to skills and processes associated with motivation. The Actions provide a way of teaching and learning the skill elements of motivation, and monitoring the components of motivation, so that these may be identified and assessed over time. Patients are taught the SPM and how to employ it. The goal of the SPM is to teach and empower patients to more effectively regulate themselves such that reliance on their clinical symptoms (e.g., ED, self-harm behavior) may decrease.

There are several advantages to employing the SPM with the patient with EDBPD. First, the SPM provides a relatively clear organizational structure for conducting treatment. Second, the SPM is relatively therapeutically neutral (i.e., flexible and accepting) in terms of the techniques employed. Third, the SPM provides a consistent and clear perspective on the presence and function(s) of the presenting symptoms (i.e., the SPM provides the patient and therapist a feedback mechanism for monitoring self-regulation). Finally, the SPM encourages the patient to take, and maintain, an active role in his or her recovery. For a more thorough discussion of the SPM, see Levitt (2004). The following sections, based on the SPM, focus on the role of symptoms, the role of the therapist, the role of the patient, the treatment relationship, and the Skills Base that may be taught to the patient with EDBPD. Again, for the effective treatment of the patient with EDBPD, clinicians must employ a clear and structured approach, especially at the beginning of therapy (Dennis & Sansone, 1997).

Practice Point

A clear and structured approach is useful for working with the patient with EDBPD, especially at the beginning of treatment. The SPM is a useful way for organizing the treatment of the patient with EDBPD.

Identification of symptoms. Initially, the patient with EDBPD seeks help either for problems related to the ED or for other problems in functioning related to BPD (e.g., self-harm behavior, relationship difficulties, depression, anxiety) and then the ED becomes apparent. In either case, the primary presenting problem(s), along with the ED symptoms, needs to be targeted with the patient's understanding and agreement.

For the patient to learn effective self-regulation, it is important that the ED symptoms be addressed, even if they appear to be related to the personality pathology or represent underlying psychological issues. In the SPM, it is important from the onset to address, assess, and teach the patient the Basics and to assist the patient in acknowledging that the ED symptoms need to be addressed, because of either their severity or their ability to interfere with treatment. Throughout the course of treatment, there is a continuing focus on containing and stabilizing the ED and related symptoms. Similarly, as other related problems (e.g., self-harm behavior) and features of BPD emerge and affect the patient's life functioning, they will be directly focused on. In the SPM, the context for focusing on these symptoms is the repeated emphasis to the patient to learn and apply the skills and processes that are inherent within the SPM.

Improved self-concept and self-efficacy tend to emerge through an organized and structured approach to symptoms that engages the patient in a positive and thoughtful way, is designed to assist the patient to function effectively, and helps the patient to achieve some initial successes. Thus, low self-worth, a key dynamic encountered in many patients with EDs and BPD, begins to be enhanced. A general Skills Base, to be discussed later, is also employed to teach patients how to more efficiently self-regulate and is useful, along with the SPM, in assisting the patient to interrupt his or her symptom patterns.

Practice Point

By carefully and thoughtfully applying the SPM, the patient may enhance his or her self-concept and sense of self-efficacy.

Role of the therapist. The therapist's role in the SPM approach is to be teacher, guide, and mentor for the patient. The therapist outlines the expectations of treatment, teaches the SPM, and teaches new skills or engages necessary skills that already exist in the patient's repertoire (i.e., Skills Base). The therapist also guides the patient as he or she tries to apply the SPM, explains or normalizes the ups and downs of treatment, and supports the patient's efforts in recovery.

In the beginning of treatment, the primary relational elements that the therapist focuses on relate to teaching the SPM and the ways that therapy will be conducted. An important tool for clearly addressing the role of symptoms and the therapist's expectation(s) for therapy, especially for the patient with BPD, is a therapeutic contract (Yeomans et al., 1992). The contract provides a means for identifying tolerances in therapy and setting limits. Regarding the former, the extent to which the therapy can tolerate certain behaviors needs to be specified; this sets some initial boundaries for the patient to self-regulate in therapy (see Figure 11.2).

In addition to providing the contract, the therapist reviews the importance of learning the Basics and emphasizes the ways that *symptoms* will be focused on. Expectations about changing a specific ED, or other symptoms, as well as learning new ways of managing oneself, are clarified and explained. Later, as the patient's functioning improves, the therapist will guide the patient to focus more specifically on relationship elements (i.e., the phase of psychotherapy).

Practice Point

At the beginning of therapy with the patient with EDBPD, a therapeutic contract is a useful tool for clarifying expectations and teaching therapy.

Role of the patient. The patient's role throughout therapy is to be a "student of oneself." Patients are initially responsible for learning and practicing how to contain self-destructive symptoms and developing the skills to manage themselves (i.e., self-regulate). The patient is responsible for learning the SPM and the elements of the Skills Base to practice self-management.

The patient works with the therapist to become a self-observer and data collector to identify skill areas that are necessary to enhance daily functioning. Then, along with the therapist, the patient practices the new skills both within and outside of sessions. The specific Skills Base is individualized for each patient.

The patient's essential responsibility is to remain an expert on himself or herself and to provide as specific and clear information as possible for both the therapist and the patient to respond to and plan together. The emphasis throughout this form of treatment is for the patient to be

I understand that my treatment is designed to promote my recovery by helping me to learn how to live without relying on, or using, my eating disorder or other self-destructive symptoms or patterns. I am committed to my recovery and am aware that participation in treatment is beneficial for my recovery. I agree to the following guidelines for participation in treatment.

1. I will pay a fee of $_____ per session.

2. I will attend all sessions that meet at_____(time) and understand that they will last ____minutes.

3. I agree to arrive on time and be ready.

4. I will leave a message at least 24 hours ahead if I am going to be absent.

5. I agree to not involving other individuals, including therapy professionals, in my treatment without the expressed agreement
   from my therapist.

6. I agree to be open-minded and be a student of myself.

7. I agree to talk respectfully in treatment.

8. I agree to stay for the entire session and not leave until it is over.

9. I agree to be honest.

10. I agree to have a safety plan in case I have a crisis outside of therapy.

11. I agree to not come to therapy under the influence of drugs or alcohol or other self-destructive conditions.

12. I agree to turn off my cell phone or pager during therapy.

13. I agree to do my homework outside of therapy.

14. I agree to consistently work on learning to manage myself in my recovery.

15. I agree to openly discuss and address any and all self-destructive symptoms and work to keep them from interfering in my
    therapy.

17. I agree to discuss any problems or concerns with my therapist openly and honestly.

18. I agree that if I do not follow these guidelines, my ability to continue to participate in therapy may be re-evaluated. This
    includes termination and/or referral to another level of care (such as hospitalization) or to another treatment provider.

_____   _____   _____   _____
Patient's signature   Date   Therapist's signature   Date

Figure 11.2   An example of an initial eating disorder/borderline personality disorder contract.

in charge of himself or herself and to make as many of the treatment decisions as possible.

Practice Point
The patient's role throughout therapy is to be a "student of oneself."

The treatment relationship. The treatment relationship is vital to the patient's recovery. It is the therapist's primary tool for teaching, guiding, and mentoring. It is also the vehicle for the patient to learn and practice self-regulating behaviors that are designed to enhance functioning and to obtain new information about himself or herself. In this way, the therapeutic relationship represents a laboratory for new efforts at self-management.

In this approach, the most important function within the relationship is genuineness. That is, the therapist interacts as much as possible with his or her true self in the professional context. This allows the patient to develop a sense of safety and trust in the therapist and spend less time trying to out-psyche the therapist. It also encourages the patient to be genuine. The concept of being responsible to the relationship is important because it allows considerable latitude for teaching the patient about relationships, identifying relationship distortions, and holding the patient accountable to a relationship in which the patient agrees to participate. This tends to reduce acting-out behaviors and provides a neutral way of setting limits.

In this approach, a major area of focus in the therapeutic relationship is managing the intensity of affect. Unlike other approaches (see Garner & Garfinkel, 1997, for a review), affect is *not encouraged* in the SPM. Rather, affect is identified as an extremely important emotional facet that, initially, must be managed and contained. The reason for this is that many patients with BPD tend to have an extremely difficult time managing affect (e.g., Linehan, 1993a). Models that emphasize the increased identification and expression of affect may tend to inadvertently increase affect before the patient has the skills to manage it. Generally, the patient with EDBPD is already struggling with affect management. In the SPM, one initial goal of the relationship is to assist the patient in learning the skills to manage and contain affect (see Table 11.2). Managing affect is in keeping with being a *thoughtful* student of oneself. With the patient's developing capability for maintaining a consistent pattern of managing himself or herself, there is less focus on the SPM and Skills Base and there is a gradually more intense emphasis on the phase of psychotherapy, which includes more focus on affect.

Practice Point
The therapeutic relationship is an important tool for helping the patient to manage and contain affect.

The Skills Base. The patient is taught the SPM, engaged in a treatment relationship where appropriate expectations for both the therapist and the patient are detailed and specified, and taught the necessary skills for being able to achieve improved life functioning and stability. The Skills Base represents various skills that are associated with the ability to manage oneself across various areas of functioning. General skill areas are management, problem solving, pattern recognition, relationship management, cognitive processing, and educational resourcing skills. These skill areas are consistent with the EDBPD diagnostic symptom clusters. The therapist, with the patient, selects specific skills to learn and practice. These skills are briefly described in Table 11.2.

Psychotherapy Phase

With the successful learning of the SPM, and the application of relevant skills within the Skills Base, the patient gradually moves to the next phase of treatment—psychotherapy. Psychotherapy is defined as

TABLE 11.2 Skills Base Areas to Enhance Self-Regulation in the Treatment of the Patient With EDBPD

Skill Area 1: Management Skills
- Management Skills refer to the ability to regulate oneself across a variety of areas given the supports, limitations, and demands of the environment.
- Affect Management, as a subset of management skills, refers to the ability to contain and manage affect across situations and settings.

Skill Area 2: Problem-Solving Skills
- Problem-solving skills refer to the ability to use an organized framework for approaching difficult problematic situations and for arriving at new solutions.

Skill Area 3: Pattern Recognition Skills
- Pattern recognition skills refer to the ability to identify and use repeated sequences of cognitive (thoughts), affective (feelings), and behavioral interactions that are contextually interdependent. Recognition "makes the unseen accessible."

Skill Area 4: Relationship Management Skills
- Relationship management refers to the ability to be able to maintain a "steady psychological state" given the requirements and circumstances of the relationship situation or setting.

Skill Area 5: Cognitive Processing Skills
- Cognitive processing skills refer to the ability to identify and use one's thoughts and thought processes and the ways in which they interact with feelings and behaviors to improve functioning.

Skill Area 6: Educational Resourcing Skills
- Educational resourcing skills refer to the ability to apply learning and learning resources to enhance recovery.

Note: EDBPD = eating disorder/borderline personality disorder.

the exploration and use of the patient's personal material, including the characteristics of relationship styles (i.e., transference), the role of affect, and the interaction between them. Structuring therapy and psychotherapy are not mutually exclusive. Indeed, the focus and emphasis on therapy structure versus general psychotherapy is a matter of emphasis and timing. Instead of focusing on the Basics and the Actions of the SPM, treatment turns to the Foundation Skills, or the patient's personal internal information. Instead of the emphasis being primarily on self-management (i.e., the emphasis on containing and reducing symptoms), the emphasis is on a broader exploration of the individual and his or her interpersonal functioning, both with the therapist and with the broader relational environment. The approach used here is based on the style and training of the therapist. For example, relationship areas might be explored from a dialectal model (Linehan, 1993a, 1993b), a systemic-relational approach (Levitt, 2000a, 2000b), or a more traditional psychodynamic approach (e.g., Dennis & Sansone, 1997).

It is important, however, that one does not move totally from the organized treatment structure, or SPM, to psychotherapy (i.e., discontinue the SPM). Indeed, even during the psychotherapy phase, the SPM is monitored to ensure that when relationships and their meanings are explored, and/or when affect and its identification and expression are encouraged, the patient continues to self-regulate and does not return to relying on symptoms.

Practice Point
As the patient is able to more effectively and efficiently self-regulate, the treatment emphasis is placed on the Foundation Skills component of the SPM.

Transition Phase

Although transition is often considered to be a part of the termination phase, it is important to view this as a separate phase of therapy because of the tendency for patients with EDs and BPD to struggle with changes. Transition is that phase of treatment in which the patient moves from his or her current therapy relationship to other forms of support and life experience. These supports might include the use of community support groups or other resources (e.g., educational opportunities) in which the patient might invest himself or herself. As for the time of transitioning, regardless of who suggests it, it is important that the patient take an active role.

Transition, like termination, needs to be planned well in advance and not delayed until therapy appears to be reaching a close. Indeed, as in other phases, it is important for the therapist to work with the patient so he or she can successfully make the linkages to new experiences and develop some investment in these experiences.

It is also important to note that patients with EDs and BPD will likely struggle with termination, and transition may be necessary for an extended period of time. Indeed, for many of these patients, official termination may not be sustained, and some contact with the therapist may be necessary for the patient to maintain his or her gains. The therapist might see the patient every other week or once a month or even build in booster sessions in which the patient attends a course of treatment, for example, for 4 weeks, every 6 months.

Termination Phase

Termination is inherent in all relationships. For patients with EDs and BPD, the therapist should introduce the idea of termination at the beginning of treatment. Treatment endings are likely to be difficult, particularly for this patient subgroup. Presenting the notion that the therapeutic relationship is designed to improve their life functioning and will, someday, be less necessary for them is an important discussion when the SPM is first being taught. Thus, the patient is taught from the beginning that termination is a mutual decision as long as the conditions of the therapeutic contract are being maintained. Experience using the SPM has demonstrated that those patients who use the SPM generally address termination appropriately, especially if care is made with transitioning them to other important life experiences.

Practice Point

Transition and termination are important components of therapy and need to be planned for from the start of therapy, addressed throughout, and carefully tended to as they become the focus during later treatment phases.

CONCLUSION

Patients with EDs and BPD are challenging to work with. Yet these patients provide an excellent opportunity for therapists to develop rewarding and successful treatment experiences. Experience has demonstrated that when therapy is constructed thoughtfully, attention is placed on developing a clear organizational structure, and psychotherapy is gradually introduced in a condition of self-regulation, the patient often flourishes in recovery. Of course, this is not to suggest that therapy with these patients will not be difficult. However, improved life functioning and enhanced self-esteem are indeed possible with most patients with EDs and BPD.

NOTE

Please address all correspondence to John L. Levitt, PhD, 1650 Moon Lake Blvd., Hoffman Estates, IL, 60194; telephone: (847) 241-5922; fax: (847) 991-9645; e-mail: levittj@aol.com.

REFERENCES

American Psychiatric Association. (1994). *Diagnostic and statistical manual of mental disorders* (4th ed.). Washington, DC: Author.

Andersen, A. E. (1990). Diagnosis and treatment of males with eating disorders. In A. E. Andersen (Ed.), *Males with eating disorders* (pp. 133–162). New York: Brunner/Mazel.

Dennis, A. B., & Sansone, R. A. (1991). The clinical stages of treatment for the eating disorder patient with borderline personality disorder. In C. Johnson (Ed.), *Psychodynamic treatment of anorexia nervosa and bulimia* (pp. 128–164). New York: Guilford.

Dennis, A. B., & Sansone, R. A. (1997). Treatment of patients with personality disorders. In D. M. Garner & P. E. Garfinkel (Eds.), *Handbook of treatment for eating disorders* (2nd ed., pp. 437–449). New York: Guilford.

Garner, D. M., & Garfinkel, P. E. (1979). The Eating Attitudes Test: An index of the symptoms of anorexia. *Psychological Medicine, 9,* 273–279.

Garner, D. M., & Garfinkel, P. E. (Eds.). (1997). *Handbook of treatment for eating disorders* (2nd ed.). New York: Guilford.

Hyler, S. E. (1994). *Personality Diagnostic Questionnaire–4.* New York: New York State Psychiatric Institute, Author.

Johnson, C., & Connors, M. E. (1987). *The etiology and treatment of bulimia nervosa: A biopsychosocial perspective.* New York: Basic Books.

Levitt, J. L. (1998). The disorganized client: New management strategies. *Paradigm, 2,* 20.

Levitt, J. L. (2000a, March). *Nature and treatment of the symptomatically complex eating disordered clients: Trauma, self-injury, and dual diagnosis.* Invited workshop given at Pinecrest Christian Hospital, Professional Lecture Series, Grand Rapids, MI.

Levitt, J. L. (2000b, August). *Surviving the storm: Treating the complex eating disordered client.* Paper presented at the International Association of Eating Disorder Professionals, annual conference, Orlando, FL.

Levitt, J. L. (2004). A self-regulatory approach to the treatment of eating disorders and self-injury. In J. L. Levitt, R. A. Sansone, & L. Cohn (Eds.), *Self-harm and eating disorders: Dynamics, assessment and treatment* (pp. 211–229). New York: Brunner-Routledge.

Linehan, M. M. (1993a). *Cognitive behavioral treatment of borderline personality disorder.* New York: Guilford.

Linehan, M. M. (1993b). *Skills training manual for treating borderline personality disorder.* New York: Guilford.

Sansone, R. A., & Levitt, J. L. (2005). Borderline personality and eating disorders. *Eating Disorders: The Journal of Treatment and Prevention, 13,* 71–83.

Sansone, R. A., & Sansone, L. A. (2004). Assessment tools: Eating disorder symptoms and self-harm behavior. In J. L. Levitt, R. A. Sansone, & L. Cohn (Eds.), *Self-harm and eating disorders: Dynamics, assessment and treatment* (pp. 93–104). New York: Brunner-Routledge.

Sansone, R. A., Sansone, L. A., & Levitt, J. L. (2004). Borderline personality disorder: Self-harm and eating disorders. In J. L. Levitt, R. A. Sansone, & L. Cohn (Eds.), *Self-harm and eating disorders: Dynamics, assessment and treatment* (pp. 61–74). New York: Brunner-Routledge.

Sansone, R. A., Wiederman, M. W., & Sansone, L. A. (1998). The Self-Harm Inventory (SHI): Development of a scale for identifying self-destructive behaviors and borderline personality disorder. *Journal of Clinical Psychology, 54,* 973–983.

Tobin, D. L. (1993). Psychodynamic psychotherapy and binge eating. In C. G. Fairburn & G. T. Wilson (Eds.), *Binge eating: Nature, assessment, and treatment* (pp. 287–313). New York: Guilford.

Vanderlinden, J., & Vandereycken, W. (1997). *Trauma, dissociation, and impulse dyscontrol in eating disorders.* Bristol, PA: Brunner/Mazel.

Yeomans, F. E., Selzer, M. A., & Clarkin, J. F. (1992). *Treating the borderline patient: A contract-based approach.* New York: Basic Books.

CHAPTER

12

Borderline Personality and Eating Disorders: An Eclectic Approach to Treatment

RANDY A. SANSONE, MD
LORI A. SANSONE, MD

The treatment of individuals who present with both borderline personality disorder (BPD) and an eating disorder is a complicated and challenging undertaking. The symptoms of these patients are oftentimes prolific, dramatic, and self-injurious. To complicate matters, the relationship issues between the therapist and patient are often intense and volatile and anchored in complicated interactions (i.e., transferences), often resulting from the patient's historic and chaotic relationships with early caretakers. Treatment continuity is frequently challenged by a variety of factors, including the patient's erratic motivation and compliance, the limited availability of financial resources for long-term treatment, and the need for varying levels of care (e.g., brief inpatient hospitalization, residential treatment). In addition, there is no empirically proven intervention for borderline personality, with or without eating disorder comorbidity.

Given the preceding concerns, why master a therapeutic approach to patients with BPD? About a quarter of binge/purging patients harbor BPD, which makes the avoidance of this Axis II disorder clinically

197

impossible. In addition, many of the techniques used in BPD treatment can be incorporated into the treatment of patients with other types of psychiatric disorders.

Before beginning a description of our approach, we wish to carefully acknowledge several caveats. First, in this short chapter, we are able to cover only the skeletal structure of treatment, which necessarily undergoes modification with each patient to meet his or her unique needs. Second, there are many effective ways to treat these patients; we do not mean to suggest in any way that our approach is the only or best approach. Indeed, our approach continues to undergo modification. Third, our approach is an eclectic one with elements of contracting, psychoeducation, transference work, psychodynamic psychotherapy, and cognitive-behavioral intervention. We believe that most approaches to BPD consist of various titrations of these treatment elements. Having a treatment menu is necessary, as the heterogeneous nature of BPD requires highly individualized treatment. Even though the composition of and approach to BPD treatment varies, one fundamental principle appears to transcend all successful treatments—*consistency*. Indeed, we believe that *consistency is more integral to treatment success than a specific approach or philosophy*.

Practice Point
Consistency is a fundamental treatment principle in the treatment of BPD.

TREATMENT ENTRY

Treatment entry entails a variety of therapeutic tasks, including the establishment of a consistent treatment environment, proper assessment, and contracting.

Establishing a Consistent Treatment Environment

Patients with BPD are keenly hypervigilant, which for many likely relates to their earlier histories of childhood trauma and adversity. Because of this, it is essential to maintain an office environment that emphasizes stability and continuity, so as not to distract the patient from therapy work. This entails *consistent* office staff, office location, furniture and decorations, appointment times, and billing procedures. Irregularities in the office rhythm tend to precipitate mistrust in these patients and disruptions in the therapy relationship.

Assessment and Treatment Determination

During the eating disorder assessment, we routinely evaluate each and every patient for BPD because of the substantially high frequency of

TABLE 12.1   The PISIA Criteria for the Diagnosis of Borderline
Personality Disorder

P	*Psychotic, quasi-psychotic episodes,* which are transient and fleeting (e.g., depersonalization, derealization)
I	*Impulsivity,* which is characterized by long-standing self-regulation difficulties (e.g., drug and/or alcohol abuse, eating disorder pathology, promiscuity) and self-harm behavior (e.g., self-mutilating, attempting suicide, being in abusive relationships)
S	*Social adaptation,* which manifests as an intact social façade
I	*Interpersonal relationships,* which are chaotic and unfulfilling
A	*Affect,* which is chronically dysphoric or labile

Note: Adapted from the Diagnostic Interview for Borderlines (Kolb & Gunderson, 1980).

this disorder. We rely on the PISIA criteria for diagnosis (see Table 12.1; see also the descriptive chapter on borderline personality in this book). Using these criteria, we not only diagnose BPD but also determine where the patient is positioned on a functional continuum. Mid- to high-functioning patients can be readily considered for a psychotherapy treatment. Very low-functioning patients may be limited to a supportive or maintenance approach that emphasizes the grooming of successful life skills rather than psychodynamic work.

Contracting: the Containment of High-Lethal Behavior

If the patient is a candidate for psychotherapy treatment (i.e., in the mid- to high range of the functional continuum), the next task is to broach a psychotherapy treatment contract. At the outset, we attempt to limit the risks of this psychologically rigorous type of intervention. Specifically, psychodynamic work inherently entails an element of patient regression. If the patient is vulnerable to suicide, the regressive pull of a psychological treatment may precipitate a serious attempt. Although this is an alarming and unnerving event, from a treatment perspective, the suicide attempt functions as a distracter for both the patient and the therapist—distracting away from psychotherapeutic work to crisis management. If such behavior continues, repeated suicide gestures and attempts can slowly erode the psychological work and refocus the treatment to putting out fires. This unproductive cycle of treatment may be avoided, or at least curtailed, through contracting at treatment entry.

How does one contract for suicide containment? We candidly explain to new patients that psychotherapy treatment is not without risk—it may cause patient regression. Specifically, if the patient is vulnerable to suicide, then a regressive treatment may precipitate an attempt. The therapist, in turn, has an obligation to minimize risks, and this type of treatment risk is not practical or feasible (i.e., the issue of safety is essentially a nonnegotiable process). If the patient is able to contract for personal safety, then a treatment may be considered and initiated. If safety cannot be agreed to by the patient, then other forms of treatment may be entertained in another provider venue, such as medication management, supportive or maintenance treatment, and so on.

Practice Point
Contracting for safety at treatment entry may provide a safety net for an intervention that, by nature, is regressive.

Once the contract is agreed to, the patient may experience slippage. At the outset, we emphasize that suicidal thoughts, gestures, and attempts will result in the reexamination of the *feasibility* of the treatment "at this time."

> Patient: "I am beginning to feel like I'm going to hurt myself—like overdose or something."
> Therapist: "I am really glad that you told me this. I am worried that this treatment is getting too stressful for you. Remember, we discussed the regressive nature of treatment. Are you really sure that you are *ready* to take on this type of treatment?"

Essentially, the therapist challenges the patient around his or her readiness for treatment, offers to temporarily or permanently suspend the treatment, and in most cases leaves the door open to future treatment—"Please follow up with me when you believe that you are able to weather this type of treatment." In our experience, the majority of patients will sincerely work to contain high-lethal behaviors to initiate a recovery and to maintain an attachment to the therapist.

Contracting: the Containment of Low-Lethal Behavior

After contracting around suicidal ideation, the next task is to contract for a reasonable reduction in any behaviors that may potentially impede the treatment. Most of these behaviors are self-sabotaging or self-harm behaviors (SHB) and not all will disturb the treatment. For example, self-cutting may deter some therapists and not others. On the other hand, acute intoxication at sessions is not acceptable. When treatment-disruptive behaviors are identified, the therapist next contracts or negotiates for a reasonable reduction of such behaviors.

> Therapist: "You mentioned that you use marijuana."
> Patient: "Yes, sometimes I do."
> Therapist: "I can't have you coming to sessions high."
> Patient: "Huh?"

Therapist: "We can't do the work we need to do if you are intoxicated with pot. I need an 80% reassurance that you will not come to sessions high."

If the patient exceeds the 20% allowable rate, the treatment feasibility is again challenged and resolved with either recontracting or terminating because of the lack of *readiness*. Note that with low-lethal behaviors, we allow some room for slippage, because to contain all SHB at the outset of treatment might ultimately precipitate a serious suicide attempt (i.e., an unacceptable risk).

Practice Point
Contracting for disruptive low-lethal behaviors entails more flexibility.

Relationship Focus

Following the successful negotiation of a treatment-entry contract, we begin treatment by emphasizing the importance of the therapeutic relationship. We actively discuss boundaries (e.g., experiences with boundaries in prior therapy relationships; therapist availability in terms of office hours, telephone calls, and emergency appointments), the importance of a good fit between the patient and therapist (e.g., "Fit is really important—please let me know if you are having any problems with our relationship"), the role of honesty (e.g., "You can decide *not* to tell me something if it's not related to suicide, but you cannot lie to me—I will do the same with you"), and the management of future potential conflict (e.g., "If you are upset about something, will you be able to tell me?"; "What's the best way to confront you so that you don't feel attacked or demeaned?").

Practice Point
It is vital to openly discuss the therapeutic relationship and how the therapist and patient will work together.

Throughout treatment, we emphasize with the patient the importance of the continued monitoring and processing of the therapeutic relationship. We believe that this is essential for patients who are borderline, whether this is session-to-session checking in or active transference work.

With regard to transference work, this entails the examination of the dynamics not only in session but also out of session. For example, the patient may describe a supervisor at work who is perceived as angry and withholding. These perceptions can be actively pulled into session and examined in terms of how the patient sees the therapist (e.g., "You really get angry with your supervisor—I was wondering if you ever have these same feelings about me, as well?"). Again, we emphasize this "relationship checking" aspect of treatment at the outset.

We have found that without a strong relationship focus, many patients with BPD do not hook into treatment. Most yearn for psychological intimacy and attachment yet are petrified by it. We have found that treatments that sidestep a relationship focus (e.g., purely cognitive-behavioral approaches) tend to leave patients with BPD emotionally adrift.

Practice Point
Ongoing monitoring of the therapeutic relationship, particularly transference elements, is necessary to develop and maintain a therapeutically healthy relationship in working with patients with BPD.

THE BEGINNING OF TREATMENT
Treatment Emphasis

During the early phases of treatment, we tend to emphasize treating the borderline features over eating disorder pathology. We elect to do this because (a) of the overriding importance of the relationship focus in BPD treatment and (b) in many patients the eating disorder symptoms are often dually functioning as SHB (i.e., self-injury equivalents), therefore they are less likely to respond to eating disorder intervention, alone. This does not mean that we discount the components of eating disorder treatment. On the contrary, we actively offer psychoeducation, examine a week's worth of food records to confirm eating patterns, encourage and participate in the development of menu plans, reinforce the normalization of eating patterns, offer suggestions for nutrition management (e.g., typically to increase protein and dairy intake), and suggest techniques for deterring binge eating and purging behavior. However, we tend to lower our expectations with regard to the time frames for eating disorder recovery and emphasize to the struggling patient with BPD that "It's two steps forward, and one step backward."

We have noted that demoralization tends to occur when patients with BPD compare themselves with patients with eating disorders but not BPD, who tend to make significant gains more rapidly in treatment. We actively underscore the importance of recognizing that "You are far more complicated than other patients, and it's important to realize that your recovery will be more challenging—hang in there."

Tackling SHB

During the early phase of treatment, we actively confront the issue of SHB. In our opinion, chronic SHB is characteristic of the borderline disorder—a perspective that is not shared by all authorities in the field. We also believe that SHB fulfills a variety of complex functions beyond affect management—another perspective that is not shared by all authorities in the field. Regardless of these incongruent perspectives, SHB has the influential role of demoralizing and devaluing patients and reinforcing a self-destructive identity. In addition, SHB literally frightens away those who are attempting to engage in relationships with the patient (e.g., recall Michael Douglas's distancing response to Glenn Close's wrist cutting in *Fatal Attraction*). This suggests that self-concept and relationship work cannot effectively proceed while the patient is actively assaulting himself or herself.

There are many techniques for the management of SHB. We have discussed these techniques in our previous work (Dennis & Sansone, 1989, 1990; Sansone & Johnson, 1995; Sansone, Levitt, & Sansone, 2004; Sansone & Sansone, in press) and review them briefly in this chapter. Again, the heterogeneous nature of BPD suggests that these techniques will need to be individualized in a given patient.

Establishing dialogue. In most cases, we have found that few patients ever really openly talk about the functional meaning of their SHB. Those who are socially connected to the patient (e.g., friends, family, teachers) are oftentimes too frightened or intimidated by the behaviors to broach any dialogue around their function and meaning. For this reason, we emphasize at the outset of treatment that SHB will be an important and routine focus of the treatment. Many patients find this very uncomfortable—they seem to prefer to act out the behavior rather than process it. In response, it is important to anticipate this reaction and validate the patient (e.g., "I sincerely recognize that talking about your SHB is pretty novel for you").

Psychoeducation. We believe that patients need to understand the detrimental psychological effects of SHB on themselves and others. We promote this by repeatedly expressing sincere concern about the disastrous consequences of such behavior to the patient and to relationships with others. It is critical that this discussion does not come across as pedantic, parental, or judgmental. Sincerity, caring, and candor are paramount. For example, it is important to underscore that healthy self-esteem cannot be developed and sustained in the presence of SHB. SHB, by its nature, devalues self. Therefore, SHB need to be strategically contained to promote self-value.

Lately, we also have been educating patients, in a rudimentary way, about the complex neurohormonal effects of trauma. We essentially emphasize that some of the symptoms that they are experiencing (e.g., hypervigilance, affective regulation difficulties, sleep disturbance) may, in part, be sustained by the physiological changes related to trauma—that their symptoms are not related simply to being "inadequate people."

Cognitive restructuring. Patients with BPD typically legitimize their self-destructive patterns through a series of false beliefs or faulty cognitions. In our experience, these faulty cognitions often provide insight into their early developmental experiences. Examples of faulty cognitions include the following: (a) "It doesn't matter if I hurt myself" (therapist response: "SHB denigrates the self and distances other people—it *does* matter that you hurt yourself"), (b) "My sister's worse than me and so is my dad" (therapist response: "Just because other people close to you engage in SHB does not make it normative"), (c) "If I didn't cut myself, I wouldn't be able to control my feelings" (therapist response: "Cutting yourself actually prevents you from developing healthier, alternative coping mechanisms"), and (d) "Hurting myself physically is the only way that you will believe that I am in pain" (therapist response: "Although this may be the only way to be heard by unhealthy people, you don't need to do this behavior to grab my attention").

Psychodynamic intervention. SHB plays some vital functional role in the patient's psychology. Although psychodynamic themes vary from patient to patient, common ones include the need to (a) manage frightening or overwhelming feelings, (b) construct and continually reinforce an identity whose foundation is based on self-destructive behavior (e.g., "I may be nothing, but I'm the only patient on this unit who was ever tube fed for 2 months"), (c) engage others without being personally vulnerable (e.g., "I don't have to build a relationship, I just cut myself and he responds!"), (d) contain anger that would otherwise be directed toward someone else (i.e., displacement), (e) reorganize oneself from a quasi-psychotic episode, and (f) indirectly acknowledge the underlying trump card of suicide (e.g., "I'm not afraid to hurt myself")—that this card is actively present without being played. Therefore, in a given patient, the therapist must consistently unravel the meaning or function of SHB. Doing so sets the stage for the treatment dyad to dialogue less costly coping strategies.

Interpersonal restructuring. Interpersonal restructuring refers to various psychological approaches that reshape the meaning and function of SHB in the interpersonal relationship. Many authors have suggested strategies, but the approach by Gunderson (1984) is one of our favorites. In this approach, at the time of acute SHB, the therapist (a) explores the underlying meaning of the intended SHB (therapist: "You are threatening to cut yourself; I need to understand what you are *really* trying to communicate with this behavior"), (b) explains that action by the therapist (e.g., hospitalization, a prompt follow-up outpatient appointment) is governed by legal and ethical reasons—that therapists choose to show caring in healthier ways than rescuing patients, and (c) clarifies that SHB heightens the therapist's anxiety, rendering him or her less effective as a treatment provider (i.e., it challenges the viability of the treatment). In the aftermath of the crisis, the therapist (a) clarifies the ongoing importance of understanding the patient's SHB, (b) reviews the recent intervention and troubleshoots for effective solutions in the future, and (c) acknowledges that the therapist is not always available for crises.

Sublimation. One effective technique in containing SHB is to literally divert the patient to more socially acceptable means of expression. These diversions may include journaling, drawing, and doing other expressive endeavors. In this way, the deeper meaning of SHB may be understood through a creative means, rather than by trying to unravel the significance of a nondescript cut on the forearm.

Medications. Although medications may be effective in reducing some specific symptom domains such as affect dysregulation or in diminishing the intensifying effects of an Axis I disorder on Axis II symptomatology, they are not, in our experience, highly successful for the long-term management of SHB. This is not to imply that they are not useful as tempering adjuncts to treatment, but the effects tend to be modest, probably because of the consolidated self and interpersonal functions of SHB.

Integration of coping skills. Although the preceding interventions help to contain SHB, some also function as coping skills (e.g., sublimation). As the containment of SHB develops, the concomitant introduction and grooming of coping skills must occur as replacement strategies. The development of coping skills usually entails psychoeducation (e.g., in the area of relationships and conflict management), assertiveness training (e.g., the negotiation of feelings and needs with others), the strengthening of the patient's social network (e.g., enhancement of social and family bonds, when feasible), delay techniques (e.g., a refocus on identifying feelings, thoughts, and behaviors prior to acting; relaxation training; use of soothers or a soothing box that literally contains objects that promote a sense of well-being; mindfulness training), diversion or life structure (e.g., physical activity, school, employment), and the development of a higher tolerance for negative feelings (i.e., weathering or white-knuckling negative affective states—therapist: "I guarantee that this will pass"). These approaches are augmented by acute problem solving, which can smooth out some of the psychosocial rough spots.

Realistic life perspectives. We also believe that it is important to give patients a realistic view of the road of life. That road, unfortunately, is fraught with bumps for everyone. At times, the road is bumpier. Planning and strategizing will, it is hoped, reduce the bumps in the life road, but it never fully eliminates them. This perspective is designed to make life's frustrations more normative and to curb self-sabotaging beliefs, such as, "This always happens to me! I always get screwed! Nothing good ever happens!"

Practice Point
SHB should be directly and openly discussed in treatment as soon as possible. There are a variety of techniques for the management of SHB; these must be integrated into the treatment on an individual basis.

THE MIDDLE OF TREATMENT

Following the reasonable stabilization of SHB and the therapeutic relationship, which typically takes about 6 to 18 months, the focus of treatment centers on psychological growth. Key areas of therapeutic work are (a) an improvement in the primitive defense of splitting, (b) the enhancement of self-regulation skills, and (c) improved interpersonal connectedness.

Splitting

As a by-product of ongoing trauma, specific areas of the personality structure seem to literally get stuck in particular developmental phases, whereas others appear to progress and mature. The overall effect of repetitive early trauma seems to be an uneven personality structure, hampered by inconsistencies and seemingly paradoxical thoughts and behaviors (i.e., poor self-integration). In our opinion, splitting is most likely caused by repetitive trauma (it may also be related to poor parental mentoring) and, therefore, an early developmental arrest.

By definition, splitting is the active separation of thoughts and feelings into the extremes of good and bad. Essentially, individuals who engage in splitting tend to come across as extreme in their thinking—that is, black and white. This tendency to think in absolutes has the advantage of simplifying the world (i.e., digesting life's complexities into simple portions, in a childlike way). However, in actuality, splitting compromises reality. For example, most individuals are not absolutely good or bad but rather mixtures of good and bad features, and everything in-between.

In addition to intrapsychic splitting, splitting may manifest in interpersonal relationships, as well. Unconsciously, the patient creates a relationship game board in which there are white tokens and black tokens. In doing so, systems (e.g., inpatient staffs) are positioned to seemingly act out their roles as either white or black tokens, which results in team conflict and dissention. This amazing dynamic is perhaps not so unique when we think of healthy adolescents who routinely engage in splitting with their mom and dad.

Resolving splitting to a reasonable degree is important, as it facilitates the use of others for soothing. If others are seen strictly as good or bad, and during times of stress, if negative feelings color everyone as bad, then there is no relationship that is available for soothing during times of stress.

The prevalence of splitting has undergone little empirical study. In addition, we are not aware of any explicit assessment measures for this phenomenon or any empirically proven treatment techniques. We recommend the following: (a) defining splitting for the patient; (b) pointing out its emergence, when this can be tactfully done; (c) illustrating the compromises to "split thinking"; (d) modeling integrated thinking by contemplating aloud when making decisions; and (e) developing specific exercises to foster better perceptual integration (e.g., therapist: "I understand that you see your supervisor as horrible and abusive; however, for our upcoming session, I would like you to write out some of his positive features").

Self-Regulation

In our opinion, enhancing self-regulation is a monumental challenge. We strongly suspect that there may be a developmental milestone with regard to self-regulation, as there is with the acquisition of language or reading skills. For various reasons (e.g., trauma, poor parental mentoring, genetic predisposition), patients with BPD pass this developmental milestone without achieving the fundamentals or essentials of self-regulation. As a result, they grow into adults with global self-regulation difficulties that may manifest as drug and alcohol misuse, promiscuity, money problems (e.g., bankruptcies, credit card debt, gambling), recalcitrant pain syndromes, and/or eating disorders, including obesity.

We approach self-regulation issues by initially identifying and labeling them. By labeling them as "self-regulation problems," our intent is to neutralize problematic behaviors. Specifically, introducing a label for these types of difficulties also enables the therapist to veer away from constantly focusing on a specific symptom area (e.g., purging), which can sometimes come across to the patient as scrutiny or judgment. For example, rather than saying, "So, how's the purge control progressing?" one might more tactfully query, "How are you doing with self-regulation?"

In addition to identifying self-regulation as a phenomenon, we provide some psychoeducation around the difficulties in enhancing self-regulation. We clearly emphasize that containing SHB and the development of healthier coping strategies are steps toward enhanced self-regulation, but that self-regulation will not come easily and that it tends to be a lifelong issue. We also emphasize that improvement in one area (e.g., eating disorder symptoms) may result in slippage in some other area (e.g., alcohol misuse).

We actively reinforce patient gains with self-regulation through positive commentary and affect. In contrast, we tend to be emotionally neutral with self-regulatory setbacks. The idea is to groom healthy behavior and not reinforce slippage. Indeed, with slippage, we respond with cognitive coaching by emphasizing that setbacks are normal in the course of recovery and that we should not overreact to them.

We also try to incorporate the perspective of "taking care of oneself." Self-care is repeatedly established as a core value in the treatment. As the therapist "tries to take care of you, you must learn to take care of you, as well." This also applies to learning to self-regulate better—mastery is a means of "taking better care of you." We emphasize this as an important responsibility to oneself.

Practice Point
Reducing splitting and enhancing self-regulation are important treatment foci during the middle phase of treatment.

Enhancement of Interpersonal Relationships

Many of the preceding interventions (e.g., relationship building, skills
building such as assertiveness, reasonable resolution of splitting, containment of SHB through improved self-regulation) contribute to the
culmination of enhanced interpersonal relatedness. These various processes are fine-tuned during the middle phase of treatment and, it is
hoped, exercised in a relationship outside of therapy.

THE END OF TREATMENT

The middle portion of treatment may take anywhere from 6 months to
several years, depending on the particular case. The end of treatment,
or termination, should last at least several months. The reason for this
is that the issues around attachment and loss in patients with BPD are
bound to resurface at this time, which intensifies the dynamics in the
therapeutic relationship. Rather than viewing this as pretermination
decompensation, perhaps a more realistic way to view this is the active
rechallenge of old beliefs and an opportunity for the therapist to consolidate the treatment experience.

The timing of termination can be difficult to define. We generally
look for (a) a reasonable reduction in overall SHB, (b) generally enhanced
self-regulation as evidenced through the normalization of food patterns
and body weight, (c) the development of healthier interpersonal relationships outside of the therapeutic relationship, and (d) a healthier self-
concept. In general, we believe that with treatment, these patients shift
to a higher level in the BPD functional continuum. Although according
to some studies, the BPD diagnosis may be no longer be evident, we suggest that these individuals may have shifted to subthreshold or subclinical symptoms and now reside in the upper functional continuum.

One particular dilemma with termination is the patient's confrontation of his or her abandonment fear—"If I get better, you will leave me,
so I better stay sick." This is a complicated issue, because it does have
some veracity. Healing and growing result in independence from the
therapist. However, the patient must come to understand that although
termination functionally feels like abandonment, the context is substantially different. Rather than being abandoned, the patient is making
a successful movement toward independence. Termination represents
achievement rather than punishment.

As termination unfolds, the patient may voice the fear that "I'll never
find anyone to be close to like you." At this juncture, it is important to

emphasize that the individual has proved his or her ability to form a successful attachment in the therapy relationship and that this attachment success can transcend the therapy relationship to other relationships. In reality, most successful patients have already begun to build successful relationships outside of therapy, and this process can be actively acknowledged. Indeed, we use healthier connections with others as a measure of how well the treatment is faring.

Unless contraindicated, at the end of a treatment course, we tend to leave the door open to future treatment, after a consolidation period of 6 to 12 months. We do not want to foster patient dependence, but we want to be available for brief therapy work for expediency's sake (we *know* the patient).

Practice Point
The final phase of treatment in BPD is an active and robust period in which the therapist consolidates the overall treatment experience.

GROUP TREATMENT

Many of the preceding techniques can be undertaken in a group-treatment format. Such formats are less expensive, demystify these disorders, promote universality, enhance connections with others, and are empirically effective. However, with patients with BPD, there are several risks to group intervention, including contagion phenomenon (i.e., patients with BPD assimilating the SHB of other group members), competition (i.e., who can be the most provocative patient), and immobilization (e.g., group gridlock). These hazards may be lessened by maintaining effective group sizes of six to eight patients, excluding patients without BPD, integrating patients with BPD at different levels of recovery, and excluding patients with BPD with incompatible features (e.g., suicidal ideation, substance-abuse problems, antisocial features).

TREATMENT PITFALLS

Poor Patient Selection

One common pitfall that we encounter in psychotherapy supervision is the therapist's prior decision to take into psychotherapy treatment a patient with BPD who is in the lower functional continuum—that is, a patient who is genuinely a candidate for supportive or maintenance treatment. Such low-functioning patients tend to fill therapy hours, effectively limiting the ability of genuine psychotherapy candidates to enter into psychotherapy treatment. This phenomenon seems to be more common in community mental health settings, because for various political, philosophical, and supervisory reasons, clinicians are not able to triage patients with BPD to specific treatment tracks (i.e., supportive or maintenance tracks).

The Patient With Malignant BPD

Another pitfall is the patient with malignant BPD (perhaps 5% of all patients with BPD) who continually challenges any treatment through repeated and severe suicide attempts. Through the recommended treatment-entry contracting, such patients will be screened out; if they manage to slip through, they will eventually flunk the contract. These patients are not candidly discussed in the BPD literature, and we are not aware of any specific treatment approaches to this subgroup.

Confrontation of Perpetrators

Therapeutic confrontation of those who perpetrated on our adult patients as children is somewhat controversial. In our experience, this type of intervention seems to have far more risks than benefits. Some of these risks include the following: (a) revictimization of the patient through reexposure to the perpetrator; (b) retraumatization of the patient through indifferent or discrediting responses from the perpetrator; (c) overwhelming patient affects in the aftermath of confrontation, which heightens the risk of SHB; and (d) damage to the therapeutic relationship because of a negative outcome (patient: "You said this would be helpful!"). We do not mean to suggest that this type of intervention is proscriptive, but we believe that it should be employed only in rare cases, after careful analysis of risks and benefits. In our experience, in the years following perpetration, psychological growth in adult perpetrators tends to be nil for most.

Disability

Disability status is another potential treatment quagmire in the treatment of patients with BPD. In our experience, employment disability tends to disable patients, such that there is the unintentional but realistic impairment of recovery. This is not to say that there are not exceptions, but life structure through employment is always encouraged, rather than the unintentional therapeutic reinforcement of a disabled, or victim, role.

Comorbid Substance Abuse

Comorbid substance abuse is a substantial deterrent to successful treatment. Most studies in this area indicate that comorbid substance abuse in BPD is associated with a poorer prognosis and a heightened risk of suicide. Therefore, substance abuse needs to be scrutinized with keen concern. We have typically recommended that a patient candidate enter into a substance-abuse treatment program and maintain sobriety for at least 6 months before entering into psychotherapy treatment. Again, there are always exceptions.

Practice Point
When evaluating patients for psychotherapy treatment, be mindful of the potential pitfalls of poor patient selection, disability, and substance abuse.

Manualized or Institutional Approaches Versus Individual Psychotherapy

Some clinicians have voiced their concerns about taking on BPD treatment without an institutional treatment approach such as dialectical behavior therapy. In our opinion, such programs offer very similar components as the individual approach described in this chapter; however, the advantage of a packaged approach is institutional consistency. Although consistency can be maintained at the individual level, it can be more difficult to sustain if the patient is attending other treatment programming. It is interesting that institutional programs such as dialectical behavior therapy are actively undergoing adaptation for patients with eating disorders and BPD. On a cautionary note, the outcomes for patients in manualized programs remain largely unknown because of the small numbers of participants in empirical studies and the relatively short follow-up periods, given disorders such as BPD and eating disorders.

CONCLUSION

The treatment of the patient with both BPD and an eating disorder can be effectively undertaken in an individual psychotherapy setting. Following contracting at entry, we believe that creating a consistent treatment structure is critical to the successful management of such patients. A variety of therapeutic techniques are available, and these can be titrated into the treatment on an individualized basis. The initial stage of treatment is stabilization of SHB and the therapeutic relationship; the second stage is reasonably resolving splitting, enhancing self-regulation, and fostering interpersonal connectedness; and the final stage is termination, which is a distinct treatment period in itself. Most of the suggested techniques can be undertaken in group format, although there are distinct hazards with the group treatment of patients with BPD. Finally, there are traditional pitfalls that most therapists encounter at some point in their careers, including poor patient selection for a given treatment.

How do patients with eating disorders and BPD fare with treatment? Research findings support the notion that among those with BPD, patients with eating disorders manage relatively well (Stone, 1990). This finding echoes our clinical experience, which indicates that although the Axis II disorder may be slower to respond to treatment, the eating disorder symptoms may respond fairly well. Although these are patients who are challenging and difficult to treat, we wish to emphasize that they are definitely treatable.

NOTE

Please address all correspondence to Randy A. Sansone, MD, Sycamore Primary Care Center, 2115 Leiter Road, Miamisburg, OH, 45342; telephone: 937-384-6850; fax: 937-384-6938; e-mail: Randy.sansone@kmcnetwork.org.

REFERENCES

Dennis, A. B., & Sansone, R. A. (1989). Treating the bulimic patient with borderline personality disorder. In W. Johnson (Ed.), *Advances in eating disorders* (pp. 239–266). Greenwich, CT: JAI Press.
Dennis, A. B., & Sansone, R. A. (1990). The clinical stages of treatment of the eating disorder patient with borderline personality disorder. In C. Johnson (Ed.), *Psychodynamic treatment for anorexia and bulimia nervosa* (pp. 128–164). New York: Guilford.
Gunderson, J. G. (1984). *Borderline personality disorder.* Washington, DC: American Psychiatric Press.
Kolb, J. E., & Gunderson, J. G. (1980). Diagnosing borderline patients with a semistructured interview. *Archives of General Psychiatry, 37,* 37–41.
Sansone, R. A., & Johnson, C. L. (1995). Treating the eating disorder patient with borderline personality: Theory and technique. In J. Barber & P. Crits-Christoph (Eds.), *Dynamic therapies for psychiatric disorders (Axis I)* (pp. 230–266). New York: Basic Books.
Sansone, R. A., Levitt, J. L., & Sansone, L. A. (2004). Psychotherapy strategies and self-harm behavior. In J. L. Levitt, R. A. Sansone, & L. Cohen (Eds.), *Self-harm behavior and eating disorders: Dynamics, assessment, and treatment* (pp. 121–133). New York: Brunner-Routledge.
Sansone, R. A., & Sansone, L. A. (in press). Self-harm behavior and eating disorders. In P. I. McSwain (Ed.), *Trends in eating disorder research.* Hauppauge, NY: Nova Science Publishers.
Stone, M. H. (1990). *The fate of borderline patients: Successful outcome and psychiatric practice.* New York: Guilford.

13

The Treatment of Avoidant Personality Disorder in Patients With Eating Disorders

HENDRIK HINRICHSEN, DCLINPSY
GLENN WALLER, DPHIL

A significant proportion of patients with eating disorders fulfill the diagnostic criteria for avoidant personality disorder (e.g., Sansone, Levitt, & Sansone 2005; van Hanswijck de Jonge, van Furth, Lacey, & Waller, 2003). Levitt and Sansone (this volume) estimate the prevalence at between 16% and 27%, depending on the subtype of eating disorder. This contrasts markedly with the general population prevalence of 0.5% to 1% for avoidant personality disorder (American Psychiatric Association, 2000). This comorbidity, however, often goes unnoticed by clinicians, and there are currently no available studies describing treatment effectiveness with patients experiencing both of these disorders. Therefore, it is important to consider the psychological factors that might explain the comorbidity between the eating disorders and avoidant personality disorder and then develop ideas from that knowledge base. Our clinical experience suggests that we have the most to learn from studying the current knowledge base regarding social anxiety and social phobia, and their association with the eating disorders.

THE ROLE OF SOCIAL ANXIETY AND SOCIAL PHOBIA

Patients with eating disorders and comorbid avoidant personality disorder are clinically frequently similar to those with a diagnosis of generalized social phobia (i.e., patients who are socially phobic and fear most social situations, rather than just one or two specific types). There is a substantial overlap between generalized social phobia and avoidant personality disorder (e.g., Heimberg, 1996; Schneier, Spitzer, Gibbon, Fyer, & Liebowitz, 1991), leading to questions regarding the use of maintaining two distinct diagnostic categories on two separate axes of the *Diagnostic and Statistical Manual of Mental Disorders–Fourth Edition* (*DSM–IV*) (American Psychiatric Association, 1994; Hofmann, Heinrichs, & Moscovitch, 2004). We find that it is best to understand social anxiety, generalized social phobia, and avoidant personality disorder as lying along a continuum, with social anxiety and avoidant personality disorder being at the extremes of that continuum. The key differences between generalized social phobia and avoidant personality disorder tend to be in the behavioral manifestations of the disorders. Those with social phobia make efforts to overcome their fears, even if those efforts are maladaptive (e.g., drinking alcohol to be able to go out and socialize). In contrast, those with avoidant personality disorder are more likely to avoid social interactions altogether.

Practice Point
Patients with social phobia attempt to overcome their fears, whereas those with avoidant personality disorder avoid social interaction altogether.

Although many controlled outcome trials have demonstrated the effectiveness of cognitive-behavioral therapy (CBT) for generalized social phobia (with effect sizes higher than 2.0) (Rodebaugh, Holaway, & Heimberg, 2004), there has been less research investigating the effectiveness of treatments for avoidant personality disorder. The literature on avoidant personality disorder is characterized by a number of uncontrolled clinical reports and single-case studies (e.g., Alden, 1989; Gradman, Thompson, & Gallagher-Thompson, 1999; Newman, 1999), all of which support the effectiveness of CBT for avoidant personality disorder (see A. T. Beck, Freeman, & Davis, 2004, Chapter 1). In addition, a large outcome trial for generalized social phobia found CBT to be effective in the treatment of avoidant personality disorder, although the treatment gains were not as significant for this group as for patients presenting without avoidant personality disorder (Felske, Perry, Chambless, Renneberg, & Goldstein, 1996).

To our knowledge, no studies so far have looked at the treatment of avoidant personality disorder or generalized social phobia in the context of an eating disorder, despite research showing that generalized social phobia is a common problem in those with eating disorders (e.g., Brewerton, Lydiard, Ballenger, & Herzog, 1993; Bulik, Sullivan,

Fear, & Joyce, 1997; Godart, Flament, Lecrubier, & Jeammet, 2000). This is particularly surprising in light of recent clinical evidence that suggests that similar factors may be involved in the development and maintenance of both avoidant personality disorder (or social phobia) and unhealthy eating attitudes and behaviors (e.g., Bulik, 2003; Steiger, Gauvin, Jabalpurwala, Seguin, & Stotland, 1999). When such common factors each have an impact on both aspects of pathology, they can be thought of as providing "links of meaning." Given that the evidence seems to indicate that CBT is a singularly effective intervention for treatment of the eating disorders (e.g., Fairburn & Harrison, 2003; National Institute for Clinical Excellence, 2004), as well as for social phobia and avoidant personality disorder (Clark et al., 2003; Felske et al., 1996), we focus on cognitive-behavioral factors and their social-developmental context.

LINKS OF MEANING BETWEEN THE EATING DISORDERS AND AVOIDANT PERSONALITY DISORDER

Common factors between avoidant personality disorder and the eating disorders are best illustrated by considering their developmental pathways. For example, a person who is shy or avoidant by temperament might find it hard in early life to engage in social interactions. As a result, he or she might find it harder to make friends in school. Negative life experiences (e.g., being criticized by a parent or a teacher, or teased by peers) could lead to a loss of confidence in one's abilities and personal value. Such a loss of confidence might intensify concerns about physical appearance, due to either being teased about appearance or being criticized about other aspects of life. This may leave the individual feeling that the body is the only domain where he or she has any true control. In turn, such experiences may increase the person's tendency to avoid any social situations that could possibly lead to criticism or humiliation. The resulting combination of low self-esteem, feelings of social isolation, and concerns about appearance constitute the typical risk factors for the development of an eating disorder (e.g., Garner, 1991; Slade, 1982).

Practice Point
Combinations of low self-esteem, concerns about appearance, and feelings of social isolation constitute typical risk factors for the development of an eating disorder.

Once social anxiety has taken root, the individual might try to compensate for his or her lack of social confidence by losing weight. The experience of control over one's weight is often experienced as a feeling of success, though in a limited domain (e.g., "If I can't be as likeable/funny/intelligent/attractive as other people, at least I can be the thinnest"). Initially, weight loss might trigger positive reactions from others, thus reinforcing restrictive tendencies. However, over time, continued attempts to maintain weight below healthy requirements may lead to uncontrollable episodes of binging, culminating in repetitive cycles of restricting, binging, and/or purging or excessively exercising to counter feared weight gain.

This example highlights two links of meaning between avoidant personality disorder and eating disorders. First, social factors often *trigger* a patient's initial decision to lose weight (e.g., Slade, 1982). Second, social factors are frequently involved in the *maintenance* of eating pathology (e.g., Steiger et al., 1999). Our clinical experience suggests that social factors can trigger and maintain both restrictive and bulimic behaviors. Although some patients report using bulimic behaviors to regulate negative emotional states (Fairburn, Cooper, & Shafran, 2003; Meyer, Waller, & Waters, 1998), others use restriction (and associated weight loss) as a means of enhancing their perceived social attractiveness and likeability (Waller, Kennerley, & Ohanian, in press).

Practice Point
Social factors play a significant role in triggering and maintaining both restrictive and bulimic behaviors.

In line with these observations, recent evidence suggests that patients with eating disorders and social phobia or avoidant personality disorder may be less likely to benefit from standard CBT for eating disorders (Ghaderi, in press). Indeed, it is our experience that patients with eating disorders whose social concerns have not been addressed adequately in treatment have a higher risk of relapse at follow-up than those who have dealt with such concerns. Thus, effective treatment for patients with eating disorders and comorbid avoidant personality disorder needs to address both their personality pathology and their eating difficulties. This approach should accompany all stages of work with such patients (i.e., assessment, formulation, and treatment).

Practice Point
Effective treatment for comorbid eating disorders and avoidant personality disorder needs to address both the personality pathology and the eating difficulties.

ASSESSMENT AND FORMULATION FOR CBT

To construct a useful cognitive formulation of avoidant personality disorder in the context of an eating disorder, the initial assessment should identify the main cognitive structures and behavioral coping strategies that maintain the patient's problems. In addition to a structured clinical assessment for eating disorders (e.g., Waller, Cordery, et al., in press), the Structured Clinical Interview for *DSM–IV* module for avoidant personality disorder is useful for establishing a diagnosis of avoidant personality disorder (First, Spitzer, Gibbon, & Williams, 1995). Moreover, patients can be asked to complete a number of self-report questionnaires that will supplement and corroborate the information gathered during the interview (see following list). Taken together, these assessment tools should provide the clinician with the essential building blocks for developing an initial cognitive-behavioral formulation.

Practice Point

We recommend using the following questionnaires when assessing comorbid avoidant personality disorder in the eating disorders:

1. Brief Fear of Negative Evaluation Scale (Leary, 2001)
2. Young Schema Questionnaire–Short Version (Young & Brown, 2003)
3. Personality Belief Questionnaire (A. T. Beck & Beck, 1991)
4. Distress Tolerance Scale (Corstorphine, Mountford, Tomlinson, Waller, & Meyer, 2005)
5. Testable Assumptions Questionnaire–Eating Disorders (Hinrichsen, Garry, & Waller, in press)

Figure 13.1 outlines a formulation of the early experiences, core beliefs, dysfunctional assumptions, and behavioral processes involved in the development and maintenance of avoidant personality disorder in the context of an eating disorder. This model is divided into two parts. The first part describes the development of social avoidance and eating difficulties, while the second part describes how these problems are maintained.

Early Life Experiences and Negative Core Beliefs

Patients with eating disorders and comorbid avoidant personality disorder or severe social phobia often have unconditional, negative core beliefs about themselves (e.g., "I'm unlikable," "I'm different," "I'm defective") and others (e.g., "Nobody cares about me," "Ultimately, other people will always abandon or reject me"). These beliefs are frequently related to themes of (a) *defectiveness* (the belief that one is flawed or defective in important respects that makes one unlovable), (b) *abandonment* (the belief that significant others will discontinue providing emotional support), and/or (c) *emotional inhibition* (the belief that the expression of spontaneous feelings must be inhibited to avoid disapproval by others) (Hinrichsen, Waller, & Emanuelli, 2004; Waller, Ohanian, Meyer, & Osman, 2000). In most cases, the development of these core beliefs goes back to childhood experiences of being rejected or severely criticized by significant others (e.g., parents, teachers, siblings, or peers).

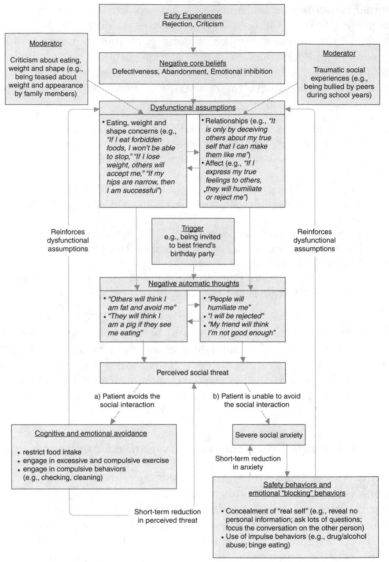

Figure 13.1 The general formulation of the links between avoidant personality disorder and eating disorder pathology.

Dysfunctional Assumptions

Once the patient's core beliefs have taken root, specific life experiences (moderators) will determine which specific psychopathologies patients will develop. Although adverse life experiences (e.g., recurrent criticism by family members about the patient's eating, shape, and weight) are associated with the development of eating-related dysfunctional assumptions, socially traumatic experiences (e.g., being teased or humiliated in front of others) are likely to contribute to the development of socially related dysfunctional assumptions (e.g., Hackmann, Clark, & McManus, 2000). A. T. Beck et al. (2004) proposed that two types of dysfunctional assumptions ("If ... then ..." beliefs) are at the core of avoidant personality disorder—assumptions about relationships and assumptions about negative affect.

First, although a patient believes that his or her real self cannot be liked by other people, there is the belief that by hiding one's true nature, he or she will be able to deceive others and get them to at least like him or her superficially (e.g., "If I always agree with others, they might think I'm OK"). As a relationship with another person becomes more intimate, the patient with avoidant personality disorder experiences strong fears of abandonment, leading him or her to subjugate personal needs to those of the other person to minimize the potential for conflict or disagreement (e.g., being nonassertive). Second, a patient fears that his or her negative feelings will get out of control and that he or she will not be able to cope (e.g., "If I allow myself to feel down, the feeling will overwhelm me and I won't be able to cope"). As a result, the patient constantly strives to avoid experiencing negative affect. Thus, a central characteristic of patients with eating disorders and comorbid avoidant personality disorder is their tendency to block or avoid negative cognitions and affect (i.e., cognitive and emotional avoidance).

Negative Automatic Thoughts, Behaviors, and Maintenance

Figure 13.1 illustrates the example of a patient who has been invited to her best friend's birthday party and is experiencing negative thoughts about eating, weight, shape, and the possibility of social rejection. The resulting sense of social threat might lead the patient either to avoid the party altogether or to attend the party despite experiencing severe social anxiety. In the weeks and days leading up to the event, the patient is likely to engage in cognitive and emotional avoidance (e.g., restricting, excessively exercising, sleeping, watching television) to minimize the sense of perceived social threat. In the majority of cases, the avoidance becomes so pervasive that the patient ends up avoiding the social interaction altogether (route *a* in Figure 13.1). Although this behavior temporarily reduces one's sense of perceived social threat, it ultimately serves to confirm the dysfunctional assumptions (e.g., "Others will accept me only if I lose weight," "If I reveal my true self to others, they will reject me").

If the patient is unable to avoid the social interaction (e.g., the friend insists that he or she come to the party; route *b* in Figure 13.1), he or she is likely to experience severe social anxiety. This social anxiety will lead him or her to engage in safety behaviors and emotional blocking behaviors during the event (e.g., revealing nothing of himself or herself, keeping the conversation focused on the other person, binge eating, getting drunk) to manage anxiety and minimize the risk of being disliked or rejected. In addition, because of their core beliefs, avoidant personality disorder patients tend to misinterpret any perceived disapproval during social interactions as a sign of rejection (e.g., "He doesn't like me because I'm boring/weird/odd/unintelligent"). Conversely, positive reactions or compliments are reinterpreted as resulting from the individual not having revealed the real self, thereby also confirming the core beliefs (e.g., "She likes me only because we didn't talk about me/I agreed with her/I presented myself as strong and in control," "As soon as he gets to know the real me, he will see what a boring/inferior/defective/damaged person I am"). The result is that patients end up avoiding both negative and positive social interactions, for fear that their real self will be revealed and they will be rejected or abandoned. Again, the patient's use of safety and subtle avoidance behaviors during social interactions leads to a reinforcement of dysfunctional assumptions, thereby maintaining the social anxiety (see Figure 13.1).

CBT FOR AVOIDANT PERSONALITY DISORDER IN THE EATING DISORDERS

Effective treatment for comorbid avoidant personality disorder in patients with eating disorders requires the skillful integration of treatment strategies for the eating disorders (e.g., Cooper, Whitehead, & Boughton, 2004; Fairburn, Marcus, & Wilson, 1993; Waller, Kennerley et al., in press) with those for avoidant personality disorder (e.g., A. T. Beck et al., 2004; Butler & Surawy, 2004) and generalized social phobia (e.g., Butler & Hackmann, 2004; Clark, 2005; Hinrichsen & Clark, 2003). In cases of moderate social anxiety or social phobia, the principle of parsimony leads us to address the eating pathology first, addressing the social concerns only later. Our experience is that this approach is likely to result in changes in both aspects of pathology from an early point in treatment. However, the findings of the case series by Ghaderi (in press) suggest that this outcome is less likely among patients who report severe social phobia or avoidant personality disorder.

In such cases, it makes sense to assume that the two disorders are linked rather than coincidental. As the formulation in Figure 13.1 indicates, the two disorders are capable of maintaining each other. Thus, we find it most useful to work on the eating disorder and the avoidant personality disorder simultaneously, in keeping with the fact that CBT needs to address emotional avoidance and eating-related cognitions (e.g., Fairburn et al., 2003). Therefore, our treatment strategies for such cases are integrative rather than additive.

Practice Point

Effective treatment for comorbid avoidant personality requires the skill-ful integration of treatment strategies for the eating disorders with those for avoidant personality disorder and generalized social phobia.

Although standard CBT for the eating disorders is often relatively brief (15 to 20 sessions), the treatment of an eating disorder in a patient with avoidant personality disorder can take considerably longer. This is mainly because of patients' extensive use of avoidance and blocking behaviors in and out of sessions, which takes time to address. We have found that most patients require between 30 and 40 sessions to make significant progress.

Stages of CBT for Comorbid Avoidant Personality Disorder in the Eating Disorders

This treatment can be broadly divided into five stages, although these stages overlap rather than exist exclusively. As avoidant personality disorder is characterized by the patient's extensive use of cognitive and emotional avoidance, and his or her fear of rejection, the initial focus in treatment is the establishment of a close working alliance (Stage 1). Thereafter (Stage 2), it is important to help the patient overcome his or her tendency to manage negative affect through the use of avoidance (e.g., restriction, excessive exercise, compulsive behaviors) or emotional blocking behaviors (e.g., alcohol abuse, binge eating). This work forms the basis for the identification and modification of the patient's core beliefs and the development of alternative, more positive beliefs (Stage 3). Next, the patient and therapist jointly set up a series of behavioral experiments to test the patient's dysfunctional assumptions that are specific to his or her eating disorder and avoidant personality disorder (Stage 4). The final stage involves ensuring that the patient maintains the progress he or she has made following the end of treatment (Stage 5). The clinical techniques used during each stage are outlined next.

Given the differences in patient presentation and speed of progress, it is important that these treatment stages are used flexibly and that they are allowed to overlap. For example, the identification and modification of negative core beliefs may occur at an early stage in therapy or at the end, depending on whether the therapist feels that the patient's core beliefs are getting in the way of his or her progress in treatment. However, we have found that the first two stages (establishing a close working alliance, and overcoming cognitive and emotional avoidance) must be addressed from an early point in the treatment of such cases, as both of these factors can be responsible for patients dropping out at an early stage.

Practice Point

The following five treatment stages should be used flexibly in the treatment of comorbid avoidant personality disorder in the eating disorders:

Stage 1: Establishing a close working alliance
Stage 2: Tackling cognitive and emotional avoidance
Stage 3: Identifying and challenging negative core beliefs
Stage 4: Using behavioral experiments to test dysfunctional
       assumptions
Stage 5: Maintaining progress after treatment

Stage 1: Establishing a close working alliance. The basis of successful treatment for avoidant personality disorder in the context of an eating disorder is the establishment of a trusting relationship between the patient and therapist. Initially, the patient is likely to find it difficult to reveal his or her true self to the therapist, as the usual concerns about being rejected will also apply in this relationship. The patient should be encouraged to identify and express fears of rejection openly so that they can be discussed in the session. By making it clear that the therapist understands the patient's concerns, the risks of early disengagement and dropout can be reduced. Once a trusting relationship has been established, the therapy sessions provide an ideal environment in which the patient can try out alternative social behaviors through interactions with the therapist (e.g., expressing an opinion, making eye contact, revealing difficult personal experiences) and thereby explore their effects on the social interaction before experimenting with them outside the session.

Stage 2: Tackling cognitive and emotional avoidance. The second step is to address the patient's extensive use of avoidance behaviors (e.g., restriction, excessive exercise, compulsive behaviors) and to increase his or her tolerance of negative cognitions and affect. The construction of a joint formulation (based on the model outlined earlier) can help the patient to understand how he or she is using avoidance to manage anxiety in anticipation of social events. For example, a patient who has been invited to a dinner party might feel unable to change the social demands of attending but might exercise and restrict excessively prior to the event because of concerns about being judged about physical appearance. However, as this activity does not address the patient's core concerns, it is likely that the social anxiety will return, leading ultimately to the avoidance of the event. Once the patient has been made aware of this connection, he or she can be asked to track the use of avoidance behaviors with the help of a diary (see Leahy, 2005). Using the information the patient has collected, the patient and therapist can then consider the use of more adaptive behaviors in anticipation of social events (e.g., meeting up with a close friend before going into a party).

The patient's pattern of avoidance can be further explored through identifying negative cognitions and emotions in the session. For example, following a discussion of an incident at work, the therapist may notice a significant drop in the patient's mood. However, the patient may fail to express any negative thoughts or suddenly move on to a different subject. The therapist should take note of such behavior and point it out to the patient so that the process can be jointly formulated. The therapist can explain that the drop in mood is not random but a secondary emotional state, consequent on emotional inhibition strategies and behaviors that are used in response to the patient's primary emotion (social anxiety) (see Corstorphine & Mountford, 2005). For homework, the therapist can then encourage the patient to watch out for similar patterns during the week and make note of possible triggers that set off avoidant behavior. For example, the therapist may discuss experiences that the patient typically avoids (e.g., dating, completing the "thoughts and feelings" column on the food record) and the associated primary and secondary emotions. By encouraging the patient to stay with the negative feelings in session (rather than using blocking or avoidance behaviors), the therapist can teach the patient to build tolerance for such emotions so that he or she can become more skilled at identifying avoidant reactions and the underlying emotions and cognitions. This allows the patient to challenge his or her underlying beliefs in real-life settings.

Stage 3: Identifying and challenging negative core beliefs. The majority of patients with eating disorders and avoidant personality disorder exhibit negative core beliefs regarding the self and others—particularly defectiveness, abandonment, and emotional inhibition beliefs. Such core beliefs should be identified at assessment and monitored thereafter.

When starting to address core beliefs, the therapist may find it helpful initially to discuss with the patient the results from the Young Schema Questionnaire–Short Version and the Personality Belief Questionnaire. This involves educating the patient about the nature of core beliefs (particularly those they have identified) and clarifying the personal meaning of these beliefs to them (e.g., defectiveness: "I am not worthy of love"; abandonment: "Ultimately, people I care about will leave me"). The therapist should emphasize that the patient's core beliefs are likely to have been adaptive at an earlier stage of life (e.g., the patient as a child may have experienced rejection and criticism by parents, and at that time it may have been appropriate to expect such treatment) but that they are no longer valid now (e.g., in relationships with a partner or friends). The therapist can start challenging the patient's core beliefs by carrying out a historical review of one of the most central beliefs (e.g., "I'm unlikable," "I'm different," "Nobody cares about me"). This usually allows the patient to obtain a better understanding of the belief's developmental origins. The historical review should be followed up with the joint construction and subsequent testing of alternative beliefs that better explain the patient's life experiences (e.g., "I am as likeable as most other people, but I grew up in an environment where others could not deal with my needs"). These new beliefs can then be considered as "alternative hypotheses," to be tested using positive experience diaries and behavioral experiments (for more details see J. S. Beck, 2005; A. T. Beck et al., 2004; Fennell & Jenkins, 2004).

Although cognitive restructuring is an important element of core belief work in CBT, we find it vital to ensure that the behavioral element of the treatment is integrated into such treatment, in the form of behavioral experiments. The key targets for change in core belief work are the patient's attributional patterns. Most patients attribute negative life experiences to themselves in a global and consistent way, and schema-focused CBT is most effective when the individual learns to attribute such events in less self-critical ways (e.g., understanding that his or her childhood experiences were not his or her fault or that they no longer apply).

Occasionally, the patient will find it difficult to shift the meaning of negative experiences through the use of positive experience diaries and behavioral experiments alone. In such cases, the therapist may consider the use of imagery rescripting exercises (see Arntz & Weertman, 1999). These strategies allow the patient to explore and reinterpret early childhood experiences (e.g., bullying by peers in childhood, teasing about weight and shape by family members) that may have played a significant role in the development of negative assumptions and core beliefs.

Stage 4: Using behavioral experiments to test dysfunctional assumptions. Patients with avoidant personality disorder have a number of dysfunctional assumptions and conditional beliefs about the world, which can be addressed with the help of behavioral experiments (Hinrichsen et al., in press). For example, the dysfunctional assumption "It is only by deceiving others about my true self that I can make them like me" might be tested by setting up an experiment in which the patient discloses important personal information (e.g., the fact that he or she has an eating disorder) to those closest to them (e.g., parents, partner). In follow-up experiments, this might be extended to the patient's three best friends. By gradually disclosing more information about the self, the patient usually discovers that the result is not rejection but the development of a closer connection with friends and family. Another typical experiment involves the patient expressing his or her opinions with friends or at work. By comparing the patient's negative predictions with actual outcomes, it can be established that others' reactions to this change in behavior are more positive than anticipated.

Patients' use of safety behaviors and emotional blocking behaviors within social situations also needs to be addressed. Butler and Hackmann (2004) and Clark (2005) proposed a series of behavioral experiments to help patients explore the consequences of using safety behaviors (i.e., behaviors that the patient uses to conceal the real self) during social interactions. Each experiment involves a conversation with a stooge, during which the patient either uses or drops safety behaviors. The conversations usually help patients to discover that, contrary to their belief, safety behaviors significantly *increase* their social anxiety. By reviewing a video recording of these conversations, it can usually be established that the patient comes across better than he or she thought and that the negative self-impression is misleading (i.e., the patient does not look as anxious/odd/strange as he or she thinks). Once these points have been established, they can be followed up with a series of behavioral experiments, where the patient drops safety behaviors in a variety of social situations and focuses attention on the other person, instead. In this way, the patient can learn that revealing more personal information about oneself does not result in rejection or humiliation (for further details of such experiments, see Bennett-Levy et al., 2004; Waller, Cordery et al., in press).

Patients' use of emotional blocking behaviors (e.g., alcohol, drugs, binging) in social situations is often related to the underlying assumption that these behaviors are effective in reducing social anxiety. By carrying out a pros-and-cons analysis (see Leahy & Holland, 2000), the therapist can often establish that, over the longer term, these behaviors pose significant health risks (e.g., alcohol and drug dependency, increased use of binging to cope with negative emotional states) and increase the risk of humiliation or rejection by others (e.g., acting out when drunk). Moreover, by asking the patient to track the effects of using these coping strategies on his or her levels of anxiety (see Kennerley, 2000), the therapist can often establish that the benefits are short-lived or nonexistent (i.e., the patient feels no better after using the blocking behavior). The patient should be encouraged to use alternative, more adaptive, behaviors during social interactions (e.g., making contributions to conversations, keeping track of and limiting the amount of food and alcohol consumed).

Stage 5: Maintaining progress after treatment. Toward the end of therapy, the therapist and patient must develop a plan for maintaining progress. Patients will often be tempted to become avoidant again as they start facing new social challenges. Therefore, the patient and therapist should jointly set goals, such as establishing new friendships and deepening existing relationships, expressing opinions more openly, becoming more assertive with others at work or in social settings, or starting a new course. As the patient will feel anxious about setting up such challenges, the therapist must emphasize that being proactive is essential for further progress. When the patient does experience feelings of anxiety on encountering new situations, the therapist should stress that such an emotional reaction is normal rather than pathological and that it is a necessary (but transient) stage in learning new skills to overcome fears. Finally, the therapist should encourage the patient to continue a log of positive experiences and to regularly review the evidence for and against fears and alternative beliefs.

Further Considerations

A number of considerations apply when treating avoidant personality disorder in the context of an eating disorder. First, many patients find it difficult to eat in the presence of others. The underlying fear in these situations is usually that others will judge or humiliate the patient for eating too much or being greedy. Such fears can be addressed by setting up graded behavioral experiments, starting with the patient's eating small amounts of food (e.g., a snack) in the company of others, and closely self-monitoring his or her reactions.

Second, some patients present with body image concerns or report a tendency to engage in social comparisons when they are in social situations. These concerns are usually driven by the process of rumination or worry, focus on the patient's perceived shortcomings compared to others, and significantly lower mood. By educating patients about the negative effects of worry and rumination, and asking them to keep a "worry diary" (see Leahy, 2005), the therapist can establish that these behaviors contribute to (rather than reduce) the patient's anxiety and have a significant negative impact on mood. The patient is then asked to practice focusing attention on others in social situations, rather than on the self.

Third, a patient with avoidant personality disorder may feel that he or she lacks the knowledge of how to act in certain social situations (e.g., he or she may never have developed a close friendship or been out on a date). In these cases, the therapist should consider the use of social skills training (e.g., maintaining eye contact, asking open-ended questions during a conversation) to help widen the patient's repertoire of socially engaging and appropriate behaviors. For example, the therapist and patient may role play a scenario in which the patient asks a friend to have a chat over coffee. Through the use of video feedback, the therapist can help the patient to understand the effects of different behaviors on the social interaction.

CONCLUSIONS

About a fifth of patients with eating disorders fulfill the diagnostic criteria for avoidant personality disorder. Conceptually, avoidant personality disorder can be thought of as lying on a continuum with social phobia, representing the most severe end of the social anxiety spectrum. Although CBT is an effective treatment for avoidant personality disorders, no studies have so far looked at the effectiveness of this treatment when combined with CBT for the eating disorders. However, recent research indicates that patients with eating disorders whose extreme social concerns have not been addressed in treatment may have a poorer outcome. Thus, effective treatment needs to address patients' personality pathology and the eating difficulties.

Effective treatment of avoidant personality disorder in the context of an eating disorder requires the skillful integration of treatment strategies for the eating disorder with those for avoidant personality disorder and generalized social phobia. Treatment can be broadly divided into five stages, starting with the establishment of a close working alliance and a reduction in patients' use of avoidance or emotional blocking behaviors in anticipation of social events. This work forms the basis for the identification and modification of core beliefs and the implementation of behavioral experiments to test dysfunctional assumptions that are specific to patients' eating disorder and extreme social concerns. Additional issues (e.g., difficulties eating in the presence of others, body image concerns, social skills deficits) may also need to be addressed.

Further research is required to determine the effectiveness of these treatment techniques in this comorbid group. Thus far, we know comparatively little about the nature of social phobia and avoidant personality in the eating disorders. However, it is increasingly apparent that both disorders are driven by similar core beliefs and comparable dysfunctional assumptions. Further research is currently underway to help determine these assumptions and core beliefs, and we hope to be able to refine the present treatment in the years to come.

NOTE

Please address correspondence to Dr. Hendrik Hinrichsen, Eating Disorders Section, Division of Psychological Medicine, Institute of Psychiatry, De Crespigny Park, London SE5 8AF; telephone: +44 208 682 6747; fax: +44 208 682 6724; e-mail: hendrik.hinrichsen@gmx.net.

REFERENCES

Alden, L. E. (1989). Short-term structured treatment for avoidant personality disorder. *Journal of Consulting and Clinical Psychology, 57,* 756–764.

American Psychiatric Association. (1994). *Diagnostic and statistical manual of mental disorders* (4th ed.). Washington, DC: Author.

American Psychiatric Association. (2000). *Diagnostic and statistical manual of mental disorders* (4th ed., Text Revision). Washington, DC: Author.

Arntz, A., & Weertman, A. (1999). Treatment of childhood memories: Theory and practice. *Behaviour Research and Therapy, 37,* 715–740.

Beck, A. T., & Beck, J. S. (1991). *The Personality Belief Questionnaire.* Bala Cynwyd, PA: Beck Institute for Cognitive Therapy and Research.

Beck, A. T., Freeman, A., & Davis, D. D. (2004). *Cognitive therapy of personality disorders* (2nd ed.). New York: Guilford.

Beck, J. S. (2005). *Cognitive therapy for challenging problems: What to do when the basics don't work.* New York: Guilford.

Bennett-Levy, J., Butler, G., Fennell, M., Hackmann, A., Mueller, M., & Westbrook, D. (2004). *Oxford guide to behavioural experiments in cognitive therapy.* Oxford, UK: Oxford University Press.

Brewerton, T. D., Lydiard, R. B., Ballenger, J. C., & Herzog, D. B. (1993). Eating disorders and social phobia. *Archives of General Psychiatry, 50,* 70.

Bulik, C. (2003). Anxiety, depression, and eating disorders. In J. Treasure, U. Schmidt, & E. van Furth (Eds.), *Handbook of eating disorders* (pp. 193–198). Chichester, UK: Wiley.

Bulik, C. M., Sullivan, P. F., Fear, J. L., & Joyce, P. R. (1997). Eating disorders and antecedent anxiety disorders: A controlled study. *Acta Psychiatrica Scandinavica, 96,* 101–107.

Butler, G., & Hackmann, A. (2004). Social anxiety. In J. Bennett-Levy, G. Butler, M. Fennell, A. Hackmann, M. Mueller, & D. Westbrook (Eds.), *Oxford guide to behavioural experiments in cognitive therapy* (pp. 141–158). Oxford, UK: Oxford University Press.

Butler, G., & Surawy, C. (2004). Avoidance of affect. In J. Bennett-Levy, G. Butler, M. Fennell, A. Hackmann, M. Mueller, & D. Westbrook (Eds.), *Oxford guide to behavioural experiments in cognitive therapy* (pp. 351–369). Oxford, UK: Oxford University Press.

Clark, D. M. (2005). A cognitive perspective on social phobia. In W. R. Crozier & L. E. Alden (Eds.), *The essential handbook of social anxiety for clinicians* (pp. 193–218). Chichester, UK: Wiley.

Clark, D. M., Ehlers, A., McManus, F., Hackmann, A., Fennell, M., Campbell, H., et al. (2003). Cognitive therapy vs fluoxetine plus self-exposure in the treatment of generalised social phobia (social anxiety disorder): A randomised placebo controlled trial. *Journal of Consulting and Clinical Psychology, 71,* 1058–1067.

Cooper, M. J., Whitehead, L., & Boughton, N. (2004). Eating disorders. In J. Bennett-Levy, G. Butler, M. Fennell, A. Hackmann, M. Mueller, & D. Westbrook (Eds.), *Oxford guide to behavioural experiments in cognitive therapy* (pp. 267–284). Oxford, UK: Oxford University Press.

Corstorphine, E., & Mountford, V. (2005, April). *Addressing affect regulation problems in the eating disorders.* Paper presented at the Seventh London International Eating Disorders Conference, London.

Corstorphine, E., Mountford, V., Tomlinson, S., Waller, G., & Meyer, C. (2005, April). *Distress tolerance in the eating disorders.* Paper presented at the Seventh London International Eating Disorders Conference, London.

Fairburn, C. G., Cooper, Z., & Shafran, R. (2003). Cognitive behaviour therapy for eating disorders: A "transdiagnostic" theory and treatment. *Behaviour Research and Therapy, 41,* 509–528.

Fairburn, C. G., & Harrison, P. J. (2003). Eating disorders. *Lancet, 361,* 407–416.

Fairburn, C. G., Marcus, M. D., & Wilson, G. T. (1993). Cognitive behaviour therapy for binge eating and bulimia nervosa: A comprehensive treatment manual. In C. G. Fairburn & G. T. Wilson (Eds.), *Binge eating: Nature, assessment and treatment* (pp. 361–404). New York: Guilford.

Felske, U., Perry, K. J., Chambless, D. L., Renneberg, B., & Goldstein, A. J. (1996). Avoidant personality disorder as a predictor for treatment outcome among generalised social phobics. *Journal of Personality Disorders, 10*, 174–184.

Fennell, M., & Jenkins, H. (2004). Low self-esteem. In J. Bennett-Levy, G. Butler, M. Fennell, A. Hackmann, M. Mueller, & D. Westbrook (Eds.), *Oxford guide to behavioural experiments in cognitive therapy* (pp. 413–430). Oxford, UK: Oxford University Press.

First, M. B., Spitzer, R. L., Gibbon, M., & Williams, J. B. W. (1995). *Structured clinical interview for DSM–IV (SCID–I; January 1995 final)*. New York: Biometrics Research.

Garner, D. M. (1991). *Eating Disorder Inventory–2 professional manual*. Odessa, FL: Psychological Assessment Resources.

Ghaderi, A. (in press). Does individualization matter? A randomized trial of standardized (focused) versus individualized (broad) cognitive behavior therapy for bulimia nervosa. *Behaviour Research and Therapy*.

Godart, N. T., Flament, M. F., Lecrubier, Y., & Jeammet, P. (2000). Anxiety disorders in anorexia nervosa and bulimia nervosa: Comorbidity and chronology of appearance. *European Psychiatry, 15*, 38–45.

Gradman, T. J., Thompson, L. W., & Gallagher-Thompson, D. (1999). Personality disorders and treatment outcome. In E. Rosowsky, R. C. Abrams, & R. A. Zweig (Eds.), *Personality disorders in older adults: Emerging issues in diagnosis and treatment* (pp. 69–94). Mahwah, NJ: Lawrence Erlbaum.

Hackmann, A., Clark, D. M., & McManus, F. (2000). Recurrent images and early memories in social phobia. *Behaviour Research and Therapy, 38*, 601–610.

Heimberg, R. G. (1996). Social phobia, avoidant personality disorder, and the multiaxial conceptualization of interpersonal anxiety. In P. M. Salkovskis (Ed.), *Trends in cognitive and behavioural therapies* (pp. 43–62). Chichester, UK: Wiley.

Hinrichsen, H., & Clark, D. M. (2003). Anticipatory processing in social anxiety: Two pilot studies. *Journal of Behavior Therapy and Experimental Psychiatry, 34*, 205–218.

Hinrichsen, H., Garry, J., & Waller, G. (in press). Development and preliminary validation of the Testable Assumptions Questionnaire–Eating Disorders (TAQ–ED). *Eating Behaviors*.

Hinrichsen, H., Waller, G., & Emanuelli, F. (2004). Social anxiety and agoraphobia in the eating disorders: Associations with core beliefs. *Journal of Nervous and Mental Disease, 192*, 784–787.

Hofmann, S. G., Heinrichs, N., & Moscovitch, D. A. (2004). The nature and expression of social phobia: Toward a new classification. *Clinical Psychology Review, 24*, 769–797.

Kennerley, H. (2000). *Overcoming childhood trauma*. New York: New York University Press.

Leahy, R. L. (2005). *The worry cure: Seven steps to stop worry from stopping you*. New York: Harmony.

Leahy, R. L., & Holland, S. J. (2000). *Treatment plans and interventions for depression and anxiety disorders*. New York: Guilford.

Leary, M. R. (2001). Brief Fear of Negative Evaluation Scale. In M. Sajatovic & L. F. Ramirez (Eds.), *Rating scales in mental health* (pp. 47–48). Hudson, OH: Lexi-Comp.

Levitt, J. L., & Sansone, R. A. (2006). Avoidant personality disorder and the eating disorders. In R. A. Sansone & J. L. Levitt (Eds.), *Personality disorders and eating disorders: Exploring the frontier* (pp. 149–162) New York: Routledge.

Meyer, C., Waller, G., & Waters, A. (1998). Emotional states and bulimic psychopathology. In H. W. Hoek, J. L. Treasure, & M. A. Katzman (Eds.), *Neurobiology in the treatment of eating disorders* (pp. 271–289). Chichester, UK: Wiley.

National Institute for Clinical Excellence. (2004). *Eating disorders: Core interventions in the treatment and management of anorexia nervosa, bulimia nervosa and related eating disorders (Clinical Guideline 9).* London: National Collaborating Centre for Mental Health.

Newman, C. F. (1999). Showing up for your own life: Cognitive therapy of avoidant personality disorder. *In Session: Psychotherapy in Practice, 4,* 55–71.

Rodebaugh, T. L., Holaway, R. M., & Heimberg, R. G. (2004). The treatment of social anxiety disorder. *Clinical Psychology Review, 24,* 883–908.

Sansone, R. A., Levitt, J. L., & Sansone, L. A. (2005). The prevalence of personality disorders among those with eating disorders. *Eating Disorders: The Journal of Treatment and Prevention, 13,* 7–22.

Schneier, F. R., Spitzer, R. L., Gibbon, M., Fyer, A. J., & Liebowitz, M. R. (1991). The relationship of social phobia subtypes and avoidant personality disorder. *Comprehensive Psychiatry, 32,* 496–502.

Slade, P. D. (1982). Towards a functional analysis of anorexia nervosa and bulimia nervosa. *British Journal of Clinical Psychology, 21,* 167–179.

Steiger, H., Gauvin, L., Jabalpurwala, S., Seguin, J. R., & Stotland, S. (1999). Hypersensitivity to social interactions in bulimic syndromes: Relationship to binge eating. *Journal of Consulting and Clinical Psychology, 67,* 765–775.

van Hanswijck de Jonge, P., van Furth, E. F., Lacey, J. H., & Waller, G. (2003). The prevalence of *DSM–IV* personality pathology among individuals with bulimia nervosa, binge-eating disorder and obesity. *Psychological Medicine, 33,* 1311–1317.

Waller, G., Cordery, H., Corstorphine, E., Hinrichsen, H., Lawson, R., Mountford, V., et al. (in press). *Cognitive-behavioural therapy for the eating disorders.* Cambridge, UK: Cambridge University Press.

Waller, G., Kennerley, H., & Ohanian, V. (in press). Schema-focused cognitive behaviour therapy with eating disorders. In L. P. Riso, P. T. du Toit, & J. E. Young (Eds.), *Cognitive schemas and core beliefs in psychiatric disorders: A scientist-practitioner guide.* New York: American Psychiatric Association.

Waller, G., Ohanian, V., Meyer, C., & Osman, S. (2000). Cognitive content among bulimic women: The role of schemas. *International Journal of Eating Disorders, 28,* 235–241.

Young, J. E., & Brown, G. (2003). *Young Schema Questionnaire–short version.* Cognitive Therapy Center of New York. Retrieved November 15, 2005, from http://www.schematherapy.com/id54.htm

14

The Use of Psychotropic Medications in Patients With Eating Disorders and Personality Disorders

RANDY A. SANSONE, MD
LORI A. SANSONE, MD

Personality disorders affect between 5% and 10% of the general population (Ellison & Shader, 2003). Among those with eating disorders, the explicit prevalence of Axis II disorders remains unknown (see Sansone, Levitt, & Sansone, 2005), although these types of comorbidities appear common (Sansone et al., 2005). Personality disorders may be more prevalent among patients with eating disorders in inpatient settings and residential and tertiary-care facilities compared with those in outpatient settings. In these more intensive settings, patients tend to have more complex psychiatric comorbidity. Although these patients, who are challenging to treat, may seem to be the very population in most need of pharmacological intervention, studies of medications specifically designed for patients with eating disorders and personality disorders are virtually nonexistent.

In approaching this complex topic, we decided to restrict the content of this chapter to philosophical issues and the broader principles of psychotropic medication management, rather than to review the available studies of individual drugs and their efficacy in specific

Axis II populations. We elected this approach for two reasons. First, the overall data on medications in Axis II disorders is sparse, particularly with regard to studies of patients with eating disorders. Second, summaries of these studies are available, elsewhere (Kapfhammer & Hippius, 1998; Koenigsberg, Woo-Ming, & Siever, 2002; Markovitz, 2001; Rivas-Vazquez & Blais, 2002; Trestman, Woo-Ming, de Vegvar, & Siever, 2001). As a preamble to the material that follows, there is no medication to date that has been specifically approved by the Food and Drug Administration for the treatment of any personality disorder.

A GENERAL CONSTRUCT OF PERSONALITY AND PERSONALITY PATHOLOGY

The consolidation of personality, including personality disorders, appears to be influenced by a number of variables (see Figure 14.1). As much as 50% of the variance in personality traits may be attributable to genetics (Ellison & Shader, 2003). Genetic predisposition, which is supported by twin, adoptive, and family studies (Trestman et al., 2001), appears to then create the rudimentary biological framework for the individual's neurohormonal physiology and temperament (Ellison & Shader, 2003; Markovitz, 2001; Trestman et al., 2001). Subsequently, the external environment, which is known to influence personality development (Demetriou, 2003; Siever, Koenigsberg, & Reynolds, 2003; Uzuncan, 2003), appears to modify this primal neurohormonal environment during early development through various external experiences, including learning (Ellison & Shader, 2003). Eventually, this evolving internal environment appears to gradually consolidate into ongoing cognitive, affective, and behavioral patterns, which constitute the individual's hardwiring, or personality structure. How these various factors (i.e., genetics, environment, stressors) explicitly contribute to personality disorder symptomatology, however, remains unknown. During times of stress, and in the presence of Axis I symptomatology including eating disorders, personality symptoms appear to undergo exacerbation (Chick, Martin, Nevels, & Cotton, 1994).

Although the preceding conceptual model is appealing, it is important to acknowledge the possibility that disordered personality may also lead to, or reinforce, underlying neurochemical changes (Markovitz, 2001).

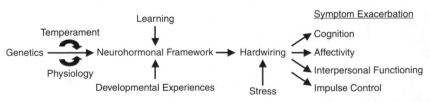

Figure 14.1 A general construct of personality and personality disorder symptomatology.

This possibility introduces the classic chicken–egg dilemma regarding which comes first—the neurochemical changes or the personality disorder (or does each reinforce the other?).

HOW MEDICATIONS MIGHT WORK IN PERSONALITY DISORDERS

How psychotropic medications exert their effects in those with personality disorders is unknown. There are several theories (e.g., Kapfhammer & Hippius, 1998; Rivas-Vazquez & Blais, 2002). First, it may be that medications exert a direct effect on the personality disorder. Second, it may be that the medication exerts an effect on the predominant or core symptoms of a personality disorder. Finally, it may be that medications exert a direct effect on a comorbid Axis I disorder, which alleviates, to some degree, the symptomatology of the Axis II disorder. This phenomenon has been confirmed in at least one study (Black & Sheline, 1997).

Although the last theory (i.e., Axis I treatment influencing Axis II functioning) is intriguing, some authors (Koenisberg et al., 2002; Soloff, 1998) question altogether the distinct separateness of Axis I and Axis II disorders. Rather than existing as separate diagnostic entities, some Axis I and Axis II disorders might actually overlap and exist on a continuum of psychopathology. A classic example of this symptom blending across axes might be social phobia and avoidant personality disorder. If the two exist on a continuum, it may be that medication treatment simultaneously affects disorders on both axes.

Practice Point
How medications work in the treatment of personality disorders is unknown.

POTENTIAL PROBLEMS IN EVALUATING STUDIES OF MEDICATIONS IN PERSONALITY DISORDERS

Empirical studies are the foundation of evidence-based medicine. However, in examining the empirical efficacy of psychotropic medications in those with personality disorders, a number of methodological challenges emerge.

First, a given individual may manifest several different personality disorders (Ellison & Shader, 2003; Gitlin, 1993). For example, among those with eating disorders, it is not uncommon to encounter both borderline and obsessive-compulsive personality symptoms. The phenomenon of multiple Axis II diagnoses in a single individual is particularly evident when using assessment measures for personality disorders such as the Personality Diagnostic Questionnaire–4 (Hyler, 1994), the Millon Clinical Multiaxial Inventory–III (Millon, Davis, & Millon, 1997), and the Structured Clinical Interview for *DSM* Personality Disorders (Spitzer, Williams, Gibbon, & First, 1990). Multiple personality disorder diagnoses tend to blur diagnostic clarity and cloud the interpretation of findings (i.e., which Axis II disorders is the medication affecting?).

Second, explicit criteria for personality disorder diagnosis have emerged only recently. Prior to 1980 (i.e., the publication year of the third revision of the *Diagnostic and Statistical Manual of Mental Disorders* [*DSM*]), there were no specific or reliable criteria for personality disorder diagnoses, and therefore there was a lack of consistency.

Third, the classification of personality disorders has evolved over time, with the use of different diagnoses during different eras (i.e., each version of the *DSM* has a different collection of personality disorders). The second edition of the *DSM* contains 11 distinct personality disorders, including the now-defunct disorders of cyclothymic, explosive, asthenic, passive-aggressive, and inadequate personality disorders. The third edition contains 11 distinct personality disorders, including the now-defunct disorder, passive-aggressive personality. The revised third edition contains 15 personality disorders, including the now-defunct disorders of multiple, organic, passive-aggressive, sadistic, and self-defeating personalities. The fourth edition (*DSM–IV*) (American Psychiatric Association, 1994) and text revision (*DSM–IV–TR*) (American Psychiatric Association, 2000a) contain 10 personality disorders. So, depending on the date of the pharmacological study, various personality disorders might have been under study, and others excluded, because of *DSM* nosology.

Fourth, for any given personality disorder, there appear to be heterogeneous symptoms or subtypes among individuals (Gitlin, 1993; Koenigsberg et al., 2002). This is most evident in borderline personality (e.g., obsessive-compulsive features, antisocial features, histrionic features). It is possible that these different personality disorder subtypes respond to different medications. Therefore, some studies may have obtained inconsistent results because of the unintentional incorporation of various subtypes of individuals with the "same" general personality disorder. This phenomenon may explain why several authorities cautiously emphasize that no single pharmacological agent is consistently effective for a specific personality disorder (Coccaro, 1993; Ellison & Shader, 2003).

In addition to the preceding issues, there are other potential difficulties with empirical studies of medications in those with personality disorders. These include large placebo effects (Moleman, van Dam, & Dings, 1999), difficulties in measuring the response of specific target symptoms (e.g., affective lability) due to the lack of objective measures, and indeterminate time frames for medication response (i.e., how long should drug trials be for those with personality disorders?). In addition, longer term studies (e.g., months to years) are virtually nonexistent in this area.

Practice Point
The concept of the "personality disorder" has been changing, and thus how we treat it is also in a state of flux.

SELECTING A MEDICATION: THE TARGET-SYMPTOM APPROACH

We are not aware of any sources that espouse the belief that a given personality disorder diagnosis reliably propels the selection of a particular medication or medication class (e.g., antipsychotics). In the literature, the most commonly recommended approach to the pharmacological treatment of patients with personality disorders appears to be the *target-symptom approach* (Ellison & Shader, 2003; Ewing, Falk, & Otto, 1996; Kapfhammer & Hippius, 1998; Koenigsberg et al., 2002; Markovitz, 2001; Rivas-Vazquez & Blais, 2002; Trestman et al., 2001). In this approach, the predominant personality disorder symptoms or symptom domains are identified, and then the corresponding psychotropic agents that are known to be effective for these symptoms are prescribed.

As for the delineation of symptom domains, various authors (Ellison & Shader, 2003; Kapfhammer & Hippius, 1998; Koenigsberg et al., 2002; Rivas-Vazquez & Blais, 2002) have commonly described (a) cognitive or perceptual symptoms (e.g., transient psychotic episodes, paranoia, ideas of reference, dissociation, magical thinking, unusual perceptual experiences), (b) impulsive or aggressive symptoms (e.g., anger, self-harm behavior, homicidal ideation), (c) affective instability (e.g., chronic dysphoria, depression, mood lability), and/or (d) anxiety or inhibition symptoms (e.g., fear, nervousness, behavioral inhibition with novel stimuli). Others (Gillig, 2000) have identified additional symptom domains, which may include compulsivity, slow habituation to new stimuli, and the use of primitive defenses. It is possible that these target symptoms reflect underlying disturbances in specific neurotransmitters. For example, serotonin dysfunction has been associated with impulsivity and noradrenaline dysfunction with mood disorders (Kavoussi & Coccaro, 1999; Koenigsberg et al., 2002).

The target-symptom approach is inherently appealing to clinicians. The identification of a target symptom and the use of corresponding medication appear simple (i.e., if the patient is depressed, prescribe an antidepressant; if the patient is psychotic, prescribe an antipsychotic). However, it is not necessarily a straightforward or predictable approach.

First, compared with the many studies of this approach in Axis I disorders such as mood and anxiety disorders, the target-symptom approach to the treatment of personality disorders has limited empirical support (Ellison & Shader, 2003). Second, although identifying a particular target symptom appears straightforward, it may not be. For example, identified target symptoms might be naturally transient (e.g., quasi-psychotic episodes in a patient with borderline personality disorder). Likewise, there may be multiple target symptoms or target symptoms that fluctuate from day to day—which of these will require treatment?

Third, a specific medication may treat multiple types of symptoms, complicating the interpretation of findings. The best example of this might be selective serotonin reuptake inhibitors, which are effective in the treatment of depression, anxiety, impulsivity, post-traumatic stress disorder symptoms, and panic attacks. What symptom complex is the medication affecting?

Fourth, positive empirical findings in a given study (i.e., evidence based) may result in the clinical exclusion of other, effective medications. Most important, the "absence of evidence" (e.g., the absence of studies that support a particular drug's efficacy) does not equate with "evidence of absence" (i.e., the inability of the studied drug to be efficacious). This dilemma is best illustrated with the use of anticonvulsants in borderline personality. Only particular anticonvulsants have been studied and therefore empirically sanctioned. Yet prescribers may elect to use gabapentin (Neurontin), which has inconsistent empirical support but several advantages over other anticonvulsants (i.e., no laboratory studies or serum levels, safety in overdose, few drug interactions due to renal excretion). Should gabapentin be excluded from clinical consideration because of the lack of rigorous empirical trials, particularly given the methodological issues associated with drug studies in those with personality disorders?

In addition to the preceding concerns, there is empirical evidence that the target-symptom approach is not always predictable in terms of treatment response. Markovitz (2001) described a group of patients with schizotypal personality, who were depicted as "schizophrenic-like" (i.e., the target symptoms being cognitive and perceptual disturbances). Yet the use of fluoxetine (Prozac) was of clear benefit to these patients. In retrospect, a rigid target-symptom approach in this particular population would have overlooked the use of this effective antidepressant in favor of antipsychotics. In the aftermath of this experience, Markovitz concluded, "No single behavior can predict responsivity to a medication group."

Finally, the target-symptom approach may not be a feasible strategy with all personality disorders. It may be that one particular category of medication, regardless of presenting symptoms, is effective for multiple symptoms found in various domains. For example, borderline personality is highlighted by a seemingly unending array of symptoms; yet according to Moleman et al. (1999), low-dose antipsychotics are effective "beyond a doubt."

Practice Point
The target-symptom approach to medication selection in personality disorders is widely espoused but has a variety of inherent limitations.

The preceding discussion is not intended to summarily dismiss the value of the target-symptom approach or to diminish its current status in clinical settings. Indeed, this is the approach that is suggested by most authorities. However, patients and prescribers need to be aware of its potential limitations.

ESSENTIAL ELEMENTS OF THE PRESCRIBING CONTEXT FOR PERSONALITY DISORDERS

We believe that the effective use of psychotropic medications in those with personality disorders requires a specific therapeutic context. For both the prescriber and the patient, this context sets the stage for successful prescription. The following are suggested guidelines for psychotropic medication management in the eating disorder and personality disorder population:

- identify specific target symptoms and explain to the patient the anticipated role of the medication;
- explore the patient's interpretation or understanding of the medication (Silk, 1999);
- prepare the patient for possible side effects (e.g., known weight effects of the medication);
- anticipate drug sensitivity, which may be more prevalent in those patients with histories of early developmental trauma and/or metabolic disturbances (e.g., low potassium);
- begin medications at low test doses and gradually increase the doses to standard levels;
- explain to patients the importance of an orderly approach to medications (Trestman et al., 2001) and the need for reasonable drug-trial durations (e.g., 6 to 12 weeks);
- develop a consistent approach for measuring symptom response over extended periods of time (e.g., assessing symptom change "over the past 4 weeks" according to a rating scale of A, B, C, D, F, or the overall percentage reduction of symptoms);
- avoid benzodiazepines in patients with Axis II disorders—not only are they physiologically addicting, synergistic with other sedating medications including alcohol, and liable to cause cognitive impairment (e.g., driving accidents, falls) but in some cases benzodiazepines may paradoxically disinhibit the patient's behavior;
- avoid whenever possible medications that may pose serious risks in overdose, such as tricyclic antidepressants and lithium;
- avoid dramatic polypharmacy (e.g., three antidepressants) or excessive dosing (e.g., Zoloft 800 mg per day)—the potential benefits of such extreme interventions may not outweigh the potential risks

of harmful side effects, drug synergism, and/or iatrogenic overdose in a physically debilitated patient with an eating disorder; and

- anticipate that the more severe the personality disorder is, the poorer the response will be to medications (Friis, Wilberg, Dammen, & Urnes, 1999).

One recurrent dilemma with medications in patients with Axis II disorders is the anticipation of an immediate response. Lack of a robust response may prompt the discontinuation of a drug, with the very quick exhaustion of multiple drugs. Likewise, overt noncompliance is always a potential issue (Spitz, 1999), particularly among self-defeating patients. It is also important to recognize the environmental responsiveness of the patient's symptoms (Koenigsberg et al., 2002) and to avoid reflex changes in medications with psychosocial crises.

Practice Point

The following are reasonable expectations of psychotropic medications in patients with Axis II disorders:

1. Medications are meaningful to the overall treatment.
2. Responses may be modest and possibly dissipate over time.
3. Residual symptomatology tends to be the rule.
4. No single medication can be expected to resolve all symptoms in a given patient.
5. How medications work in the treatment of personality disorders is currently unknown.

BORDERLINE PERSONALITY DISORDER AND MEDICATIONS

Among the personality disorders, borderline personality is the most studied with regard to psychotropic medication. Because of this, as well as its prevalence among those with eating disorders, we highlight several issues with regard to this specific disorder.

First, virtually every class of psychotropic medication has been explored in the treatment of borderline personality (e.g., antidepressants, anxiolytics, anticonvulsants, lithium, antipsychotics, opiate antagonists). No single medication is consistently effective (Coccaro, 1998; Soloff, 1994), and a large placebo effect is observed in most studies (Moleman et al., 1999). Second, study samples of patients with borderline personality have been small (Soloff, 2000), yet ironically these have functioned as the basis for treatment recommendations such as those proposed by the American Psychiatric Association (2001). Third, there is virtually no information on the efficacy of drug combinations (e.g., combination of antidepressant and anticonvulsant drugs) (Grossman, 2002). Fourth, there are no known bona fide predictors of drug response in patients with borderline personality (Bagby, Ryder, & Cristi, 2002; Gardner & Cowdry, 1986). Fifth, although most medications have had varying degrees of success in patients with borderline personality (Brinkley, 1993), most treatment effects are modest, and residual symptoms tend to be the rule rather than the exception (Soloff, 2000).

Other important issues relating to medication management in patients with borderline personality are (a) the assessment of treatment response and (b) the duration of medication treatment. Regarding the assessment of the treatment response, target symptoms may be difficult to measure as they may tend to wax and wane in the natural course of the disorder. In addition, patients with borderline personality may unintentionally overstate the severity of some symptoms while under-reporting other symptoms despite their severity or actual impact on the individual's functioning.

In terms of the duration of medication treatment, there is no current empirical data to guide the prescriber (i.e., there are no long-term studies of medications in borderline personality). Should the prescriber use medications briefly for acute symptoms or continuously as prophylaxis against symptom recurrence? Essentially, the role of extended pharmacotherapy remains unknown (Ellison & Shader, 2003).

We have previously described a pharmacological approach to borderline personality (Sansone, Levitt, & Sansone, 2004). We suggest beginning with at least two back-to-back trials of selective serotonin reuptake inhibitors (SSRIs)—for example, sertraline (Zoloft), citalopram (Celexa), escitalopram (Lexapro), or fluoxetine (Prozac)—and, if these are ineffective, following with a trial of venlafaxine extended release (Effexor XR). We support the use of SSRIs as first-line medications in those with borderline personality because these patients are generally polysymptomatic and tend to have multiple Axis I diagnoses (Sansone, Rytwinski, & Gaither, 2003; Zanarini et al., 1998; Zimmerman & Mattia, 1999); in turn, SSRIs are broad spectrum in their clinical action (e.g., effective for depression, anxiety, obsessive-compulsive disorder, premenstrual dysphoric disorder, social anxiety disorder, post-traumatic stress disorder, panic disorder). In adolescent patients, the use of these medications entails careful monitoring, especially for suicidal ideation.

If partially effective, antidepressant therapy may then be augmented by an anticonvulsant such as gabapentin (Neurontin), topiramate (Topamax), or valproate (Depakote). If further augmentation is indicated, the antidepressant and anticonvulsant may subsequently be supplemented with a low-dose, weight-neutral, atypical antipsychotic such as risperidone (Risperdal), ziprasidone (Geodon), or aripiprazole (Abilify). These recommendations do not exclude the use of other types of medications but rather provide an initial clinical framework or strategy for prescribing.

Practice Point

The suggested initial medication approach for patients with eating disorders and borderline personality disorder is as follows:

1. The prescriber should begin with at least two back-to-back trials of SSRIs.
2. If the SSRIs are ineffective, the prescriber should follow these medications with a trial of venlafaxine extended release.
3. The prescriber may then augment antidepressant therapy, if partially effective, with anticonvulsant medications.
4. The prescriber may consider low-dose, weight-neutral, atypical antipsychotics in refractory patients.
5. The prescriber needs to closely monitor all patients, especially adolescents.

The prescription of psychotropic medications in the treatment of patients with borderline personality may precipitate a variety of behaviors and dynamics. Medication misuse, abuse, and dependence are all potential risks in these patients, as well as the emergence of suicide attempts or low-lethal self-harm behavior through medication overdoses. Given the potential for splitting, patients with borderline personality may polarize therapists and prescribers (when different). Patients with borderline personality may also take an all-or-none approach to the assessment of the therapeutic effects of medication, resulting in very high and unrealistic expectations of drug treatment. Because of impulsivity, some patients may abruptly curtail drug trials and promptly demand new and different medications, a process that can drain medication options very quickly. Patients with borderline personality may also use medication crises to repetitively establish contact with the prescriber or to maintain their status as "the unique and untreatable patient." These crises may relate to exquisite side-effect sensitivity, idiosyncratic responses to medications, medication allergies (Sansone, Gentile, & Markert, 2000), and/or surreptitious noncompliance. Despite these risks, a substantial number of patients with borderline personality experience modest yet meaningful improvements with medication intervention.

SPECIAL CONSIDERATIONS WITH MEDICATIONS IN PATIENTS WITH EATING DISORDERS

Anorexia Nervosa

In the treatment of low-weight patients with eating disorders, medications have been found somewhat ineffective, in comparison to their use following weight restoration (American Psychiatric Association, 2000b; Powers, 2000). Following weight recovery, antidepressants have been found to protect against relapse in anorexia nervosa (Kaye et al., 2001). Whether this experience translates to the medication treatment of personality disorder symptoms in low-weight patients is unknown, as no research is available.

Bulimia Nervosa

The only medication approved by the Food and Drug Administration for the treatment of eating disorders is fluoxetine (Prozac), which is indicated for the treatment of bulimia nervosa. Despite the implication that fluoxetine may be unique in this regard, other SSRIs and non-SSRI antidepressants (Brewerton, 1999; Peterson & Mitchell, 1999), and anticonvulsants (Marx, Kotwal, McElroy, & Malhotra, 2003), have been successful in the treatment of bulimia. Again, empirical evidence does not exclude the potential value of other types of medications in particular patients or subpopulations. The only medication that is contraindicated in the treatment of eating disorders is bupropion (Wellbutrin) because of the enhanced risk of seizures.

Prescribing Suggestions

Because patients with eating disorders are highly sensitive to weight status and body issues, we advocate the use of medications that are relatively weight neutral (Sansone et al., 2004). These may include sertraline (Zoloft), fluoxetine (Prozac), venlafaxine (Effexor XR), low-dose gabapentin (Neurontin), topiramate (Topamax), buspirone (Buspar), low-dose risperidone (Risperdal), ziprasidone (Geodon), and aripiprazole (Abilify) (Sansone et al., 2004). Medications associated with high frequencies of weight gain include most tricyclic antidepressants, paroxetine (Paxil), lithium, several anticonvulsants (e.g., valproate [Depakote], and most typical and several atypical (e.g., olanzapine [Zyprexa], clozapine [Clozaril]) (Sansone et al., 2004) antipsychotics.

Practice Point

Weight-neutral medications are advised in prescribing psychotropic drugs to patients with eating disorders and personality disorders.

CONCLUSIONS

The role of medications in individuals with both eating disorders and personality disorders has undergone very little study. Medications have been examined among individuals with personality disorders, but these empirical studies are fraught with a variety of potential complications. It is not precisely known how medications actually work in personality disorders, although the current approach to prescription is based on a target-symptom approach, which has inherent limitations. Prior to prescribing medications in patients with eating disorders and personality disorders, establishing a prescriptive context tends to set the stage for successful intervention. For patients with borderline personality, the risks and benefits of prescription are complicated, and for individuals with eating disorders, the effects of medications on body weight are particularly relevant. Clearly, a considerable amount of research remains to be done on the intersection of eating disorders, personality disorders, and medications.

NOTE

Please address all correspondence to Randy A. Sansone, MD, Sycamore Primary Care Center, 2115 Leiter Road, Miamisburg, OH, 45342; telephone: 937-384-6850; fax: 937-384-6938; e-mail: Randy.sansone@ kmcnetwork.org.

REFERENCES

American Psychiatric Association. (1994). *Diagnostic and statistical manual of mental disorders* (4th ed.). Washington, DC: Author.

American Psychiatric Association. (2000a). *Diagnostic and statistical manual of mental disorders* (4th ed., Text Revision). Washington, DC: Author.

American Psychiatric Association. (2000b). *Practice guideline for the treatment of patients with eating disorders* (Rev. ed.). Washington, DC: Author.

American Psychiatric Association. (2001). Practice guideline for the treatment of patients with borderline personality disorder. *American Journal of Psychiatry, 158*, S1–S52.

Bagby, R. M., Ryder, A. G., & Cristi, D. (2002). Psychosocial and clinical predictors of response to pharmacotherapy for depression. *Journal of Psychiatry and Neuroscience, 27*, 250–257.

Black, K. J., & Sheline, Y. I. (1997). Personality disorder scores improve with effective pharmacotherapy of depression. *Journal of Affective Disorders, 43*, 11–18.

Brewerton, T. D. (1999). Binge eating disorder: Diagnosis and treatment options. *CNS Drugs, 11*, 351–361.

Brinkley, J. R. (1993). Pharmacotherapy of borderline states. *Psychiatric Clinics of North America, 16*, 853–884.

Chick, D., Martin, S. K., Nevels, R., & Cotton, C. R. (1994). Relationship between personality disorders and clinical symptoms in psychiatric inpatients as measured by the Millon Clinical Multiaxial Inventory. *Psychological Reports, 74*, 331–336.

Coccaro, E. F. (1993). Psychopharmacological studies in patients with personality disorders. *Journal of Personality Disorders* (Suppl. 1), 181–192.

Coccaro, E. F. (1998). Clinical outcome of psychopharmacologic treatment of borderline and schizotypal personality disordered subjects. *Journal of Clinical Psychiatry, 59*, 30–35.

Demetriou, A. (2003). Mind, self, and personality: Dynamic interactions from late childhood to early adulthood. *Journal of Adult Development, 10*, 151–171.

Ellison, J. M., & Shader, R. I. (2003). Pharmacologic treatment of personality disorders: A dimensional approach. In R. I. Shader (Ed.), *Manual of psychiatric therapeutics* (pp. 169–183). Philadelphia: Lippincott, Williams, and Wilkins.

Ewing, S. E., Falk, W. E., & Otto, M. W. (1996). The recalcitrant patient: Treating disorders of personality. In M. H. Pollack, M. W. Otto, & J. F. Rosenbaum (Eds.), *Challenges in clinical practice: Pharmacologic and psychosocial strategies* (pp. 355–379). New York: Guilford.

Friis, S., Wilberg, T., Dammen, T., & Urnes, O. (1999). Pharmacotherapy for patients with personality disorders: Experiences from a group analytic treatment program. In J. Derksen & C. Maffei (Eds.), *Treatment of personality disorders* (pp. 255–268). The Netherlands: Kluwer.

Gardner, D. L., & Cowdry, R. W. (1986). Positive effects of carbamazepine on behavioral dyscontrol in borderline personality disorder. *American Journal of Psychiatry, 143*, 519–522.

Gillig, P. M. (2000). Integration of psychotherapy and medication in the treatment of severe personality disorders. In L. VandeCreek (Ed.), *Innovations in clinical practice: A source book* (pp. 73–84). Sarasota, FL: Professional Resource Press.

Gitlin, M. J. (1993). Pharmacotherapy of personality disorders: Conceptual framework and clinical strategies. *Journal of Clinical Psychopharmacology, 13*, 343–353.

Grossman, R. (2002). Psychopharmacologic treatment of patients with borderline personality disorder. *Psychiatric Annals, 32*, 357–370.

Hyler, S. E. (1994). *The Personality Diagnostic Questionnaire–4 (PDQ–4)*. New York: New York State Psychiatric Institute, Author.

Kapfhammer, H. P., & Hippius, H. (1998). Special feature: Pharmacotherapy in personality disorders. *Journal of Personality Disorders, 12*, 277–288.

Kavoussi, R., & Coccaro, E. F. (1999). Pharmacotherapy. In M. Hersen & A. S. Bellack (Eds.), *Handbook of comparative interventions for adult disorders* (2nd ed., pp. 584–600). New York: John Wiley and Sons.

Kaye, W. H., Nagata, T., Weltzin, T. E., Hsu, L. K., Sokol, M. S., McConaha, C., et al. (2001). Double-blind, placebo-controlled administration of fluoxetine in restricting- and restricting-purging-type anorexia nervosa. *Biological Psychiatry, 52*, 464–471.

Koenigsberg, H. W., Woo-Ming, A. M., & Siever, L. J. (2002). Pharmacological treatments for personality disorders. In P. E. Nathan & J. M. Gorman (Eds.), *A guide to treatments that work* (pp. 625–641). London: Oxford Press.

Markovitz, P. (2001). Pharmacotherapy. In W. J. Livesley (Ed.), *Handbook of personality disorders: Theory, research, and treatment* (pp. 475–493). New York: Guilford.

Marx, R., Kotwal, R., McElroy, S. L., & Malhotra, S. (2003). What treatment data support topiramate in bulimia nervosa and binge eating disorder? What is the drug's safety profile? How is it used in these conditions? *Eating Disorders: The Journal of Treatment and Prevention, 11*, 71–75.

Millon, T., Davis, R., & Millon, C. (1997). *Millon Clinical Multiaxial Inventory–III (MCMI–III) manual* (2nd ed.). Minneapolis, MN: National Computer Systems.

Moleman, P., van Dam, K., & Dings, V. (1999). Psychopharmacological treatment of personality disorders: A review. In J. Derkson & C. Maffei (Eds.), *Treatment of personality disorders* (pp. 207–227). The Netherlands: Kluwer.

Peterson, C. B., & Mitchell, J. E. (1999). Psychosocial and pharmacological treatment of eating disorders: A review of research findings. *Journal of Clinical Psychology, 55*, 685–697.

Powers, P. S. (2000). Psychopharmacological approaches to eating disorders. *Academy for Eating Disorders Newsletter, 16*, 2, 7.

Rivas-Vazquez, R. A., & Blais, M. A. (2002). Pharmacologic treatment of personality disorders. *Professional Psychology: Research and Practice, 33*, 104–107.

Sansone, R. A., Gentile, J., & Markert, R. J. (2000). Drug allergies among patients with borderline personality disorder. *General Hospital Psychiatry, 22*, 289–293.

Sansone, R. A., Levitt, J. L., & Sansone, L. A. (2004). Psychotropic medications, self-harm behavior, and eating disorders. In J. L. Levitt, R. A. Sansone, & L. Cohn (Eds.), *Self-harm behavior and eating disorders: Dynamics, assessment, and treatment* (pp. 245–262). New York: Brunner-Routledge.

Sansone, R. A., Levitt, J. L., & Sansone, L. A. (2005). The prevalence of personality disorders among those with eating disorders. *Eating Disorders: The Journal of Treatment and Prevention, 13*, 7–21.

Sansone, R. A., Rytwinski, D. R., & Gaither, G. A. (2003). Borderline personality and psychotropic medication prescription in an outpatient psychiatry clinic. *Comprehensive Psychiatry, 44*, 454–458.

Siever, L. J., Koenigsberg, H. W., & Reynolds, D. (2003). Neurobiology of personality disorders: Implications for a neurodevelopmental model. In D. Cicchetti & E. Walker (Eds.), *Neurodevelopmental mechanisms in psychopathology* (pp. 405–427). New York: Cambridge University Press.

Silk, K. R. (1999). Collaborative treatment for patients with personality disorders. In R. B. Riba & R. Balon (Eds.), *Psychopharmacology and psychotherapy: A collaborative approach* (pp. 221–277). Washington, DC: American Psychiatric Press.

Soloff, P. H. (1994). Is there any drug treatment of choice for the borderline patient? *Acta Psychiatrica Scandinavica, 89*, 50–55.

Soloff, P. H. (1998). Algorithms for pharmacological treatment of personality dimensions: Symptom-specific treatments for cognitive-perceptual, affective, and impulsive-behavioral dysregulation. *Bulletin of the Meninger Clinic, 62*, 195–214.

Soloff, P. H. (2000). Psychopharmacology of borderline personality disorder. *Psychiatric Clinics of North America, 23*, 169–192.

Spitz, R. T. (1999). Treatment noncompliance among hospitalized forensic patients. *Dissertation Abstracts International, 60*, 815B.

Spitzer, R. L., Williams, J. B. W., Gibbon, M., & First, M. B. (1990). *Structured Clinical Interview for DSM–III–R Personality Disorders (SCID–II)*. Washington, DC: American Psychiatric Press.

Trestman, R. L., Woo-Ming, A. M., de Vegvar, M., & Siever, L. J. (2001). Treatment of personality disorders. In A. F. Schatzberg & C. B. Nemeroff (Eds.), *Essentials of clinical psychopharmacology* (pp. 571–587). Washington, DC: American Psychiatric Publishing.

Uzuncan, T. A. (2003). The maternal environment: Facilitating the emotional foundations of the mind. *Dissertation Abstracts International, 64*, 1528B.

Zanarini, M. C., Frankenburg, F. R., Dubo, E. D., Sickel, A. E., Trikha, A., Levin, A., et al. (1998). Axis I comorbidity of borderline personality disorder. *American Journal of Psychiatry, 155*, 1733–1739.

Zimmerman, M., & Mattia, J. I. (1999). Axis I diagnostic comorbidity and borderline personality disorder. *Comprehensive Psychiatry, 40*, 245–252.

SECTION
VII

Outcome

15

Prognostic Implications of Personality Disorders in Eating Disorders

KENNETH R. BRUCE, PHD
HOWARD STEIGER, PHD

Personality characteristics are thought to have various etiological and clinical implications in the eating disorders (EDs), and have, consequently, intrigued ED specialists for years. We have previously reviewed the complex issues pertaining to the role of personality traits and pathology in the etiology of EDs (Bruce & Steiger, 2005; Steiger, 2004; Steiger & Bruce, 2004). In the present chapter, we focus on the prognostic implications of personality pathology for the EDs—that is, personality disorders (PDs) and pathological personality traits. Our chapter covers the implications of personality pathology for ED symptom status, development and onset, natural course, and treatment response. We highlight findings, where available, on the importance of personality pathology with regard to symptoms and treatment of anorexia nervosa (AN), bulimia nervosa (BN), and eating disorder not otherwise specified (EDNOS)—including binge eating disorder (BED). Our aim is to provide a practice-oriented overview and synthesis of the literature.

COMORBID PERSONALITY PATHOLOGY IN THE EDS

Clinical intuition suggests that PDs and EDs go together, and this impression is largely borne out by empirical findings. Compared to healthy controls, individuals with any type of ED (i.e., AN, BN, and EDNOS) are noted to have higher rates of Cluster C PDs (e.g., avoidant, obsessive-compulsive, dependent personalities) as noted in the *Diagnostic and Statistical Manual of Mental Disorders–Fourth Edition* (*DSM–IV*) (American Psychiatric Association, 1994) or related personality traits, such as perfectionism and compulsivity (e.g., Devlin et al., 2002; Herzog, Keller, Lavori, Kenny, & Sacks, 1992; Karwautz, Troop, Rabe-Hesketh, Collier, & Treasure, 2003; Klump et al., 2004; Mitchell & Mussell, 1995; O'Brien & Vincent, 2003; Pratt, Telch, Labouvie, Wilson, & Agras, 2001; Vitousek & Manke, 1994; Wonderlich & Mitchell, 1992). Furthermore, perfectionism, specifically concern over mistakes, appears to differentiate patients with EDs from patients with mood, anxiety, and substance-use disorders (Bulik et al., 2003), indicating that this dimension of perfectionism is relatively unique to the EDs.

In a related vein, patients with "bulimic" ED variants (i.e., BN, AN binge eating/purging type, and binge-purge variants of EDNOS, like BED) often show higher rates of Cluster B PDs (e.g., borderline, histrionic, or narcissistic personalities) and related traits of impulsivity and behavioral, affective, and interpersonal instability (Grilo, 2002; Herzog, Keller, Lavori, et al., 1992; Karwautz et al., 2003; Mitchell & Mussell, 1995; O'Brien & Vincent, 2003; Steiger, Thibaudeau, Ghadirian, & Houle, 1992). In terms of percentage overlap, a recent quantitative review found Cluster C PDs in roughly 45% of individuals with AN and 44% of individuals with BN, whereas Cluster B PDs were found in 44% of individuals with BN (Rosenvinge, Martinussen, & Ostensen, 2000). As for specific PD subtypes, a recent review by Cassin and von Ranson (2005) determined the most common PD diagnoses, assessed by structured clinical interview, to be (a) obsessive-compulsive PD (15%) and avoidant PD (14%) for AN, (b) borderline PD (21%) and avoidant PD (19%) for BN, and (c) avoidant PD (11%), obsessive-compulsive PD (10%), and borderline PD (9%) for BED. Comorbidity rates are variable across studies, but it remains clear that PDs are more common in individuals with, rather than without, an ED. In other words, EDs and PDs co-occur at greater-than-chance levels.

Practice Point

EDs and pathological personality traits co-occur at greater-than-chance levels.

IMPACT OF MALADAPTIVE EATING PRACTICES ON EXPRESSION OF PERSONALITY PATHOLOGY

Because malnutrition can adversely affect personality functioning (Keys, Brozek, Henschel, Mickelson, & Taylor, 1950), apparent personality problems seen in sufferers of EDs can be attributed to the state sequelae of an active ED. Consistent with this, various findings show that EDs exacerbate features with a "characterological coloring" (Ames-Frankel et al., 1992; Bulik, Sullivan, Fear, & Pickering, 2000; Garner et al., 1990; Steiger, Leung, Thibaudeau, Houle, & Ghadirian, 1993). In keeping with this notion, results of very recent studies by Rø and colleagues (Rø, Martinsen, Hoffart, & Rosenvinge, 2005; Rø, Martinsen, Hoffart, Sexton, & Rosenvinge, 2005) indicate that the remission of an ED precedes remission of a PD in a sizable proportion of cases—suggesting substantial secondary effects owing to an active ED. However, we note that Rø and colleagues' studies indicate that changes in PD status do not predict changes in ED symptoms.

THE EFFECT OF PERSONALITY PATHOLOGY ON CURRENT ED SYMPTOMS

EDs have traditionally been construed as expressions of underlying personality disturbances (Bruch, 1973; Johnson & Connors, 1987). Consequently, there has been an implicit assumption that personality pathology should confer an increased risk for ED development and more severe ED symptomatology. Appealing as this notion is, empirical studies provide only limited support. For example, studies that compare individuals with BN with and without severe personality pathology do indeed document more severe general psychiatric symptoms (e.g., depression, self-mutilation, drug abuse), interpersonal problems, social maladjustment, and histories of sexual abuse in more "characterologically disturbed" individuals—but not more marked binge/purge frequencies or other ED-specific symptoms (Johnson, Tobin, & Dennis, 1990; Steiger, Thibaudeau, Leung, Houle, & Ghadirian, 1994; Wonderlich & Swift, 1990). Such findings support the conclusion that PDs are associated with greater generalized psychopathology and poorer social functioning but may have negligible implications for the severity of ED symptoms, as may have once been believed (Gonzalez-Pinto et al., 2004; Grilo et al., 2003). In a similar vein, some studies have suggested that personality pathology may be more relevant to generalized psychopathology in BED patients than to disturbances in specific areas of eating (Fichter, Quadflieg, & Rehm, 2003). Other studies, however, have associated personality pathology with more severe binge eating in BED (e.g., Stice et al., 2001; Wilfley et al., 2000).

Practice Point
Although associated with greater generalized psychopathology, personality pathology does not appear to be systematically associated with increased severity of ED symptoms.

INFLUENCE OF PERSONALITY PATHOLOGY ON THE DEVELOPMENT OR ONSET OF EDS

Many studies have examined the hypothesis that personality pathology precedes the onset of ED symptoms. Rastam (1992) estimated that 67% of a sample of adolescents with AN had a PD prior to the ED onset, the most frequent of which was obsessive-compulsive PD (35% of cases). Similarly, Nagata, Kawarada, Kiriike, and Iketani (2000) estimated that parasuicidality, a feature associated with borderline PD, predated the onset of ED symptoms in 80% of patients with EDs showing such self-destructiveness. Such results imply that personality pathology likely precedes the onset of EDs and might therefore confer risk for ED development.

Other research corroborates this notion that personality pathology exists independently of active eating disturbances. For example, various findings indicate that personality problems may be relatively persistent in patients who recovered, or are recovering, from EDs. For example, Matsunaga et al. (1999) reported that 26% of patients who recovered from AN or BN show an ongoing PD, more often a dramatic-erratic cluster PD (i.e., Cluster B) in the case of BN. In patients with AN, after weight recovery, other investigators have reported persistent harm avoidance (Bloks, Hoek, Callewaert, & van Furth, 2004; Klump et al., 2004); obsessions, compulsions, social-interaction problems (Nilsson, Gillberg, Gillberg, & Rastam, 1999); and perfectionism (Pla & Toro, 1999; Srinivasagam et al., 1995)—although some studies have indicated that these features in recovered patients are still lower than those of active ones (e.g., Bizeul, Sadowsky, & Rigaud, 2001; Sutandar-Pinnock, Woodside, Carter, Olmsted, & Kaplan, 2003). In a related vein, Stein and colleagues (2002) found higher perfectionism to be associated with higher eating-related cognitions in women who recovered from BN.

Prospective data examining whether PDs actually heighten the risk of developing an ED are relatively rare. However, based on limited available data, two recent reviews have reached similar conclusions: (a) perfectionism appears to be an antecedent factor for later AN and BN, and (b) obsessive-compulsive PD is a risk factor for the development of AN but not for BN (Jacobi, Hayward, de Zwaan, Kraemer, & Agras, 2004; Stice, 2002). The same two reviews noted that trait impulsivity does not emerge as a consistent factor for the subsequent development of an ED. Possible explanations might be that impulsivity is characteristic of only a subgroup of individuals with EDs or that it emerges more robustly after ED onset. Alternately, as suggested by Wonderlich, Connolly, and Stice (2004), it may be that impulsivity is multifaceted and that some of its component facets (e.g., specific behaviors such as delinquency) confer risk for BN and BED whereas others (e.g., self-reported impulsiveness) do not.

Practice Point

Perfectionism appears to be a risk factor for the onset or development of ED symptoms. Impulsivity may be characteristic of only a subgroup of patients with EDs, or only some components of the impulsivity construct (e.g., self-destructive behaviors) may be associated with ED development.

INFLUENCE OF PERSONALITY PATHOLOGY ON THE NATURAL COURSE OF ED SYMPTOMS

Comprehensive reviews by Jacobi and her colleagues (2004) and Stice (2002) concluded that obsessive-compulsive PD and trait perfectionism predict poorer natural course outcome for patients with AN. Recent studies continue to bear out this notion (e.g., Bloks et al., 2004; Klump et al., 2004). In contrast, in the Jacobi et al. and Stice reviews, no personality trait was found to reliably influence the natural course of BN symptoms. Other reviews have, however, concluded that the dramatic-erratic (Cluster B) PDs, even if having only weak predictive value for the course of bulimic symptoms, have stronger value as predictors of the course of ongoing, general psychopathology (e.g., symptoms such as anxiety or depression) and social maladjustment (Cassin & von Ranson, 2005; Grilo, 2002; Steiger & Bruce, 2004; Wonderlich & Mitchell, 2001). This pattern suggests that, in BN, personality pathology may have more direct relevance to the course of generalized psychopathology symptoms than to eating-specific pathology.

As for the stability of ED syndrome manifestations, Tozzi et al. (2005) showed that self-directedness was associated with crossover in both directions between AN and BN, whereas crossover from AN to BN was associated with parental criticism and crossover from BN to AN was associated with low novelty seeking. These findings imply that there are few trait factors that predict crossover from AN to BN but that low impulsiveness may be associated with risk for AN development in individuals with BN.

Practice Point

Obsessive-compulsive PDs and associated traits (e.g., perfectionism) appear to be associated with a poorer course in AN; Cluster B PDs (and associated traits) appear to predict a less favorable course of general psychopathological symptoms in BN.

IMPLICATIONS OF PDS (AND ASSOCIATED TRAITS) FOR ED TREATMENT OUTCOME

Treatment guidelines based on expert consensus from the American Psychiatric Association (2000) and the United Kingdom National Institute for Clinical Excellence (NICE, 2004) support the idea that, in patients with EDs, comorbid PDs require specific clinical attention. The American Psychiatric Association guidelines state, "[The] presence of a comorbid PD, particularly borderline PD, dictates the need for longer-term therapy that focuses on the underlying personality structure and dealing with interpersonal relationships in addition to the symptoms of the eating disorder (p. 27)." Similarly, the NICE guidelines state that impulsive patients with BN "may be less likely to respond to a standard program of treatment. As a consequence, treatment should be adapted to the problems presented (p. 70)." Together, these guidelines corroborate the traditionally held notion that comorbid PDs require more elaborate treatments than those described in typical ED-focused treatment packages. A recent survey of community clinicians has indicated that therapists, regardless of theoretical orientation, offer lengthier treatments to patients with EDs and comorbid PDs (particularly those with borderline and avoidant PDs) and rate these patients as having poorer outcomes on eating symptoms (Thompson-Brenner & Westen, 2005), suggesting that these concepts already influence clinical practice.

The preceding suggests that comorbid PDs, in general, negatively affect ED outcome. However, a careful review of findings on the impact of comorbid PDs for treatment response in different ED subtypes suggests that this conclusion may need to be nuanced.

Anorexia Nervosa

Following an extensive review, encompassing 119 treatment outcome studies and a total of 5,590 patients, Steinhausen (2002) concluded that obsessive-compulsive PD is associated with an unfavorable prognosis in AN. It is intriguing that he noted that hysterical personality traits (somewhat the antithesis of obsessive-compulsive traits) coincided with a favorable prognosis. These findings may reflect the intuitive notion that greater or lesser degrees of emotional and interpersonal constriction may negatively (or favorably) affect the ability of patients with AN to benefit from treatment. In keeping with this notion, three studies that have emerged since Steinhausen's review have found that traits consistent with the obsessive-compulsive PD spectrum (namely, perfectionism, harm avoidance, and preference for sameness) predict poorer outcome in AN (Bulik et al., 2000; Fassino et al., 2001; Fichter et al., 2003). In a related vein, Woodside, Carter, and Blackmore (2004) and Zeeck, Hartmann, Buchholz, and Herzog (2005) found that intense maturity fears predicted early termination from inpatient treatment for AN. The idea that anxious/fearful PDs and related traits are associated with a poorer outcome in AN is corroborated by the findings of two other studies that used posttreatment measures of personality pathology to reduce the potentially confounding effects of malnutrition (Herpertz-Dahlmann et al., 2001; Saccomani, Savoini, Cirrincione, Vercellino, & Ravera, 1998). In other words, obsessive-compulsive PD and associated Cluster C personality traits appear to be associated with poorer treatment outcome in AN.

We note two recent findings that contradict the association of elevated PD traits with poorer treatment response in AN. Halmi and colleagues (2005) found initial willingness to participate in a clinical trial offering cognitive-behavioral therapy (CBT) or CBT plus medication to be *higher* in patients with AN and high obsessive preoccupation—although obsessionality did not predict treatment completion. Similarly, Zeeck and colleagues (2005) found that PDs were not associated with completion of an inpatient treatment for AN. However, a recent review by Finfgeld (2002) noted the particularly negative impact of borderline PD on treatment response in the binge eating/purging type of AN. In summary, the evidence generally supports the association between PDs in the obsessive-compulsive and borderline spectra and the poorer outcome in AN.

Bulimia Nervosa

Few studies are available that deal with the effects of Cluster C PDs (or related traits such as perfectionism and harm avoidance) as prognostic indicators for treatment response in BN. One study by Anderson, Joyce, Carter, McIntosh, and Bulik (2002), however, found that CBT-induced improvements in binge and purge frequencies were independent of changes in harm avoidance and self-directedness.

The majority of available studies on BN have explored Cluster B PDs and, most often, borderline PD. Some findings have suggested that patients with BN and borderline PD (Fassino, Abbate-Daga, Piero, Leombruni, & Rovera, 2003) or marked trait impulsivity (Agras et al., 2000) appear more likely to prematurely discontinue therapy, perhaps indicating an association between impulsive personality characteristics and negative treatment outcome. Among treatment completers, however, data on the observed impact of Axis II disorders on BN treatment are equivocal (Bell, 2002; Grilo, 2002; Keel & Mitchell, 1997; Quadflieg & Fichter, 2003; Steiger & Bruce, 2004; Vaz, 1998). Various studies have reported that Cluster B PDs (or traits) negatively influence the response of BN symptoms (e.g., binge eating and vomiting) to treatment (Herzog, Keller, Sacks, Yeh, & Lavori, 1992; Johnson et al., 1990; Rossiter, Agras, Telch, & Schneider, 1993; Steiger, Stotland, & Houle, 1994). In contrast, other reports have failed to strongly link Cluster B PDs or traits to the response of bulimic symptoms to treatment. For example, Wonderlich, Fullerton, Swift, and Klein (1994) reported that PD comorbidity predicted poorer global response but only weak differences on indices of bulimic symptoms. Our group found that during treatment and at follow-up, individuals with BN and comorbid borderline PD show greater psychiatric symptoms than do individuals with BN who do not have comorbid borderline PD; however, there were limited differences on measures reflecting the course of ED symptoms (Steiger & Stotland, 1996; Steiger, Thibaudeau, et al., 1994). Norring (1993) reported similar findings in heterogeneous ED cases; patients showing a "borderline organization" showed the poorest response after 2 and 3 years, but differences were more pronounced on comorbid psychiatric symptoms rather than on eating-specific ones. Furthermore, in an elegantly designed analysis, Fichter et al. (2003) found the severity of bulimic and personality symptoms to be unrelated throughout the course of treatment. After an extensive review of the literature on the effects of Axis II comorbidity for BN treatment response, Grilo (2002) concluded that PD is more closely linked to the longitudinal course of general psychiatric symptoms (or psychosocial functioning) than with fluctuations in the course of the ED symptoms.

Despite the preceding conclusion, it is possible that trait impulsivity may yield more reliable prognostic effects. After an extensive literature review, Keel and Mitchell (1997) concluded that impulsivity was foremost among the prognostic indices for BN, with PD having inconsistent effects. Contradictory findings may, therefore, be attributable to the fact that a trait dimension (impulsivity), and not general personality organization (e.g., borderline PD), accounts substantially for the variance in outcome.

EDNOS and BED

So far, there are only a few available studies examining the effects of PD on treatment outcome for BED. We found two reports showing that comorbid PD may worsen treatment response among those with BED. Wilfley and colleagues (2000) found that the presence of a Cluster B PD at pretreatment predicted significantly fewer improvements in binge eating symptoms in patients with BED at 1 year after treatment. Likewise, Stice and colleagues (2001) documented poorer treatment response in patients with BED and a concurrent PD. By contrast, a study by Fichter and colleagues (2003) suggested that improvements in ED symptoms in BED were not associated with Axis II symptomatology.

Practice Point
Perfectionism appears to be associated with poorer treatment response in patients with AN, and impulsivity appears, at least variably, to be associated with worsened treatment response in all ED subtypes.

CONCLUSIONS

Findings on the clinical and prognostic implications of comorbid personality pathology in those suffering from EDs are at times inconsistent, and it is therefore challenging for research-minded clinicians to develop evidence-based practice principles for the treatment of personality pathology in their patients with EDs. Available findings, portraying eating and personality disturbances as "independent" and "interdependent" entities (e.g., for a theoretical discussion and comment, see Steiger & Bruce, 2004; Wonderlich, Lilenfeld, Riso, Engel, & Mitchell, 2005), are quite difficult to translate into clinical practice. As a limited first step, we offer the following general guidelines.

1. ED symptoms often exaggerate personality problems—particularly perfectionism and impulsivity. Improving nutritional status with ED-focused interventions will normally help to improve general adaptation and personality functioning. In other words, it is *not* best clinical practice to focus exclusively on personality functioning on the assumption that eating symptoms will remit when deeper causes are addressed. However, it is perhaps equally important not to construe personality functioning as being only secondary in the treatment of the ED; clinicians who regard personality pathology as a "nonspecific factor" and focus exclusively on changing eating behaviors are ignoring a large body of research that demonstrates the pathoplastic contributions from personality factors and negative prognostic treatment implications of personality pathology.

2. Eating and personality problems, at least in terms of natural course and treatment response, seem to have mutual effects (e.g., Steiger, Bruce, & Israel, 2003; Wonderlich & Mitchell, 1997). Logically, purging behaviors (vomiting, laxative misuse, etc.) may be exacerbated by impulsivity and intolerance of anxiety, body dissatisfaction may arise from core low self-esteem, and compulsive dieting may be a reflection of generalized perfectionistic tendencies. Therefore, therapeutic work aimed at generalized behavioral or self-image problems can have indirect benefits in reducing eating symptoms, when used along with eating-specific interventions. As patients learn to tolerate emotional distress and to process social experiences more adaptively, they may become less reliant on eating symptoms to soothe anxiety, diffuse angry affects, or regulate negative self experiences (Steiger, Gauvin, Jabalpurwala, Séguin, & Stotland, 1999). These considerations have led various authors to advocate the use of more person-specific, integrated, multimodal treatment approaches that address ED symptoms and personality pathology concurrently (Fairburn, Cooper, & Shafran,

2003; Steiger & Bruce, 2004; Steiger & Israel, 1999; Wonderlich, Peterson, Mitchell, & Crow, 2000).

3. Personality functioning affects the therapeutic relationship. For this reason, it is unlikely that individuals with EDs and personality pathology can be fully treated without attending to the therapeutic relationship experience. The therapeutic relationship is vital as the vehicle of alliance, of course. But more so, it may also be an essential and direct ingredient of change, especially for patients with personality disturbances (see Steiger & Israel, 1999). When patients have dysfunctional attitudes and expectancies about their internal and external worlds (true by definition in the case of individuals with comorbid personality pathology), they may pull for complementary behaviors from others—including their therapists. When such reactions are elicited, it is important for therapists to master the forces that inevitably draw them into an antitherapeutic stance, in which they confirm patients' dysfunctional relationship expectancies by evoking negative interpersonal experiences. For example, therapists' overzealous attempts to cure sometimes entice them to be overbearing or intrusive, their fears of rejection or failure cause them to withdraw from needed levels of involvement, their desire to avoid being controlling lure them into an overly conciliatory stance, and so on. We believe that ED specialists can draw many useful concepts and techniques from an existing literature on relationship factors in general psychotherapy (see Safran, Muran, Samstag, & Stevens, 2001; Samstag, Muran, & Safran, 2004).

4. Finally, whether viewed as etiologically independent or interdependent, personality pathology can be understood, in clinical terms, as an integral part of the active ED syndrome, tightly woven into its symptoms, and relevant as both an expression of and influence on the presentation and evolution of the ED. Indeed, some researchers have already argued for more attention to personality-trait variations in the development of ED diagnostic classifications (Steiger & Bruce, 2004; Steiger et al., 2003; Westen & Harnden-Fischer, 2001; Wonderlich & Mitchell, 1997). This concept, applied to treatment considerations, urges that clinicians and researchers begin to standardize and evaluate interventions aimed at personality components in the EDs.

NOTE

For correspondence, please contact Kenneth R. Bruce, PhD, Eating Disorders Program, Douglas Hospital, 6875 LaSalle Blvd., Montreal, Quebec, Canada, H4H 1R3; telephone: 514-761-6131, loc. 2895; fax: 514-888-4085; e-mail: bruken@douglas.mcgill.ca.

REFERENCES

Agras, W. S., Crow, S. J., Halmi, K. A., Mitchell, J. E., Wilson, G. T., & Kraemer, H. C. (2000). Outcome predictors for the cognitive behavior treatment of bulimia nervosa: Data from a multisite study. *American Journal of Psychiatry, 157*(8), 1302–1308.

American Psychiatric Association. (1994). *Diagnostic and statistical manual of mental disorders* (4th ed.). Washington, DC: Author.

American Psychiatric Association. (2000). *Practice guideline for the treatment of patients with eating disorders.* Washington, DC: Author.

Ames-Frankel, J., Devlin, M. J., Walsh, B. T., Strasser, T. J., Sadik, C., Oldham, J. M., et al. (1992). Personality disorder diagnoses in patients with bulimia nervosa: Clinical correlates and changes with treatment. *Journal of Clinical Psychiatry, 53*(3), 90–96.

Anderson, C. B., Joyce, P. R., Carter, F. A., McIntosh, V. V., & Bulik, C. M. (2002). The effect of cognitive-behavioral therapy for bulimia nervosa on temperament and character as measured by the temperament and character inventory. *Comprehensive Psychiatry, 43*(3), 182–188.

Bell, L. (2002). Does concurrent psychopathology at presentation influence response to treatment for bulimia nervosa? *Eating and Weight Disorders, 7,* 168–181.

Bizeul, C., Sadowsky, N., & Rigaud, D. (2001). The prognostic value of initial EDI scores in anorexia nervosa patients: A prospective follow-up study of 5–10 years. *European Psychiatry, 16*(4), 232–238.

Bloks, H., Hoek, H. W., Callewaert, I., & van Furth, E. (2004). Stability of personality traits in patients who received intensive treatment for a severe eating disorder. *Journal of Nervous and Mental Disease, 192*(2), 129–138.

Bruce, K. R., & Steiger, H. (2005). Treatment implications of Axis-II comorbidity in eating disorders. *Eating Disorders: The Journal of Treatment and Prevention, 13*(1), 93–108.

Bruch, H. (1973). *Eating disorders.* New York: Basic Books.

Bulik, C. M., Sullivan, P. F., Fear, J. L., & Pickering, A. (2000). Outcome of anorexia nervosa: Eating attitudes, personality, and parental bonding. *International Journal of Eating Disorders, 28,* 139–147.

Bulik, C. M., Tozzi, F., Anderson, C., Mazzeo, S. E., Aggen, S., & Sullivan, P. F. (2003). The relation between eating disorders and components of perfectionism. *American Journal of Psychiatry, 160*(2), 366–368.

Cassin, S. E., & von Ranson, K. M. (2005). Personality and eating disorders: A decade in review. *Clinical Psychology Review, 25*(7), 895–916.

Devlin, B., Bacanu, S. A., Klump, K. L., Bulik, C. M., Fichter, M. M., Halmi, K. A., et al. (2002). Linkage analysis of anorexia nervosa incorporating behavioral covariates. *Human Molecular Genetics, 11,* 689–696.

Fairburn, C. G., Cooper, Z., & Shafran, R. (2003). Cognitive behaviour therapy for eating disorders: A "transdiagnostic" theory and treatment. *Behaviour Research and Therapy, 41,* 509–528.

Fassino, S., Abbate-Dagga, G., Amianto, F., Leombruni, P., Fornas, B., Garzaro, L., et al. (2001). Outcome predictors in anorexic patients after 6 months of multimodal treatment. *Psychotherapy and Psychosomatics, 70,* 201–208.

Fassino, S., Abbate-Daga, G., Piero, A., Leombruni, P., & Rovera, G. G. (2003). Dropout from brief psychotherapy within a combination treatment in bulimia nervosa: Role of personality and anger. *Psychotherapy and Psychosomatics, 72*, 203–210.

Fichter, M. M., Quadflieg, N., & Rehm, J. (2003). Predicting the outcome of eating disorders using structural equation modeling. *International Journal of Eating Disorders, 34*, 292–313.

Finfgeld, D. L. (2002). Anorexia nervosa: Analysis of long-term outcomes and clinical implications. *Archives of Psychiatric Nursing, 16*, 176–186.

Garner, D. M., Olmsted, R., Davis, R., Rockert, W., Goldbloom, D., & Eagle, M. (1990). The association between bulimic symptoms and reported psychopathology. *International Journal of Eating Disorders, 9*, 1–16.

Gonzalez-Pinto, A., Inmaculada, F., Cristina, R., de Corres Blanca, F., Sonsoles, E., Fernando, R., et al. (2004). Purging behaviors and comorbidity as predictive factors of quality of life in anorexia nervosa. *International Journal of Eating Disorders, 36*(4), 445–450.

Grilo, C. M. (2002). Recent research of relationships among eating disorders and personality disorders. *Current Psychiatry Reports, 4*, 18–24.

Grilo, C. M., Sanislow, S. A., Skodol, A. E., Gunderson, J. G., Stout, R. L., Shea, M. T., et al. (2003). Do eating disorders co-occur with personality disorders? Comparison groups matter. *International Journal of Eating Disorders, 33*, 155–164.

Halmi, K. A., Agras, W. S., Crow, S., Mitchell, J., Wilson, G. T., Bryson, S. W., et al. (2005). Predictors of treatment acceptance and completion in anorexia nervosa: Implications for future study designs. *Archives of General Psychiatry, 62*(7), 776–781.

Herpertz-Dahlmann, B., Muller, B., Herpertz, S., Heussen, N., Hebebrand, J., & Remschmidt, H. (2001). Prospective 10-year follow-up in adolescent anorexia nervosa: Course, outcome, psychiatric comorbidity and psychosocial adaptation. *Journal of Child Psychology and Psychiatry, 42*, 603–612.

Herzog, D. B., Keller, M. B., Lavori, P. W., Kenny, G. M., & Sacks, N. R. (1992). The prevalence of personality disorders in 210 women with eating disorders. *Journal of Clinical Psychiatry, 53*, 147–152.

Herzog, D. B., Keller, M. B., Sacks, N. R., Yeh, C. J., & Lavori, P. W. (1992). Psychiatric comorbidity in treatment-seeking anorexics and bulimics. *Journal of the American Academy of Child and Adolescent Psychiatry, 31*, 810–818.

Jacobi, C., Hayward, C., de Zwaan, M., Kraemer, H. C., & Agras, W. S. (2004). Coming to terms with risk factors for eating disorders: Application of risk terminology and suggestions for a general taxonomy. *Psychological Bulletin, 130*, 19–65.

Johnson, C., & Connors, M. (1987). *The etiology and treatment of bulimia nervosa*. New York: Basic Books.

Johnson, C., Tobin, D. L., & Dennis, A. (1990). Differences in treatment outcome between borderline and non-borderline bulimics at one-year follow-up. *International Journal of Eating Disorders, 9*, 617–627.

Karwautz, A., Troop, N. A., Rabe-Hesketh, S., Collier, D. A., & Treasure, J. (2003). Personality disorders and personality dimensions in anorexia nervosa. *Journal of Personality Disorders, 17*, 73–85.

Keel, P. K., & Mitchell, J. E. (1997). Outcome in bulimia nervosa. *American Journal of Psychiatry, 154,* 313–321.

Keys, A., Brozek, J., Henschel, A., Mickelson, O., & Taylor, H. (1950). *The biology of human starvation.* Minneapolis: University of Minnesota Press.

Klump, K. L., Strober, M., Bulik, C. M., Thornton, L., Johnson, C., Devlin, B., et al. (2004). Personality characteristics of women before and after recovery from an eating disorder. *Psychological Medicine, 34*(8), 1407–1418.

Matsunaga, H., Kaye, W. H., McConaha, C., Plotnicov, K., Pollice, C., Rao, R., et al. (1999). Psychopathological characteristics of recovered bulimics who have a history of physical or sexual abuse. *Journal of Nervous and Mental Disease, 187,* 472–477.

Mitchell, J. E., & Mussell, M. P. (1995). Comorbidity and binge eating disorder. *Addictive Behaviors, 20,* 725–732.

Nagata, T., Kawarada, Y., Kiriike, N., & Iketani, T. (2000). Multi-impulsivity of Japanese patients with eating disorders: Primary and secondary impulsivity. *Psychiatry Research, 94,* 239–250.

National Institute for Clinical Excellence. (2004). *Eating disorders: Core interventions in the treatment and management of anorexia nervosa, bulimia nervosa and related eating disorders.* London: British Psychological Society.

Nilsson, E. W., Gillberg, C., Gillberg, I. C., & Rastam, M. (1999). Ten-year follow-up of adolescent onset anorexia nervosa: Personality disorders. *Journal of the American Academy of Child and Adolescent Psychiatry, 38,* 1389–1395.

Norring, C. (1993). Borderline personality organization and prognosis in eating disorders. *Psychoanalytic Psychology, 10,* 551–572.

O'Brien, K. M., & Vincent, N. K. (2003). Psychiatric comorbidity in anorexia and bulimia nervosa: Nature, prevalence and causal relationships. *Clinical Psychology Review, 23,* 57–74.

Pla, C., & Toro, J. (1999). Anorexia nervosa in a Spanish adolescent sample: An 8-year longitudinal study. *Acta Psychiatrica Scandinavica, 100,* 441–446.

Pratt, E. M., Telch, C. F., Labouvie, E. W., Wilson, G. T., & Agras, W. S. (2001). Perfectionism in women with binge eating disorder. *International Journal of Eating Disorders, 29*(2), 177–186.

Quadflieg, N., & Fichter, M. M. (2003). The course and outcome of bulimia nervosa. *European Child and Adolescent Psychiatry, 12*(Suppl. 1), 99–109.

Rastam, M. (1992). Anorexia nervosa in 51 Swedish adolescents: Premorbid problems and comorbidity. *Journal of the American Academy of Child and Adolescent Psychiatry, 31,* 819–829.

Rø, Ø., Martinsen, E. W., Hoffart, A., & Rosenvinge, J. (2005). Two-year prospective study of personality disorders in adults with longstanding eating disorders. *International Journal of Eating Disorders, 37*(2), 112–118.

Rø, Ø., Martinsen, E. W., Hoffart, A., Sexton, H., & Rosenvinge, J. H. (2005). The interaction of personality disorders and eating disorders: A two-year prospective study of patients with longstanding eating disorders. *International Journal of Eating Disorders, 38*(2), 106–111.

Rosenvinge, J. H., Martinussen, M., & Ostensen, E. (2000). The comorbidity of eating disorders and personality disorders: A meta-analytic review of studies published between 1983 and 1998. *Eating and Weight Disorders, 5,* 52–61.

Rossiter, E. M., Agras, W. S., Telch, C. F., & Schneider, J. A. (1993). Cluster B personality disorder characteristics predict outcome in the treatment of bulimia nervosa. *International Journal of Eating Disorders, 13,* 349–357.

Saccomani, L., Savoini, M., Cirrincione, M., Vercellino, F., & Ravera, G. (1998). Long-term outcome of children and adolescents with anorexia nervosa: Study of comorbidity. *Journal of Psychosomatic Research, 44,* 565–571.

Safran, J. D., Muran, J. C., Samstag, L. W., & Stevens, C. (2001). Repairing alliance ruptures. *Psychotherapy, 38,* 406–412.

Samstag, L. W., Muran, J. C., & Safran, J. D. (2004). Defining and identifying alliance ruptures. In D. P. Charman (Ed.), *Core processes in brief psychodynamic psychotherapy: Advancing effective practice.* London: Lawrence Erlbaum.

Srinivasagam, N. M., Kaye, W. H., Plotnicov, K. H., Greeno, C., Weltzin, T. E., & Rao, R. (1995). Persistent perfectionism, symmetry, and exactness after long-term recovery from anorexia nervosa. *American Journal of Psychiatry, 152,* 1630–1634.

Steiger, H. (2004). Eating disorders and the serotonin connection: State, trait and developmental effects. *Journal of Psychiatry and Neuroscience, 29,* 20–29.

Steiger, H., & Bruce, K. (2004). Personality traits and disorders in anorexia nervosa, bulimia nervosa and binge eating disorder. In T. D. Brewerton (Ed.), *Eating disorders* (pp. 207–228). New York: Marcel Dekker.

Steiger, H., Bruce, K. R., & Israel, M. (2003). Eating disorders. In G. Stricker, T. A. Widiger, & I. B. Wiener (Eds.), *Comprehensive handbook of psychology* (pp. 173–194). New York: John Wiley and Sons.

Steiger, H., Gauvin, L., Jabalpurwala, S., Séguin, J. R., & Stotland, S. (1999). Hypersensitivity to social interactions in bulimic eating syndromes: Relationship to binge-eating. *Journal of Consulting and Clinical Psychology, 67,* 765–775.

Steiger, H., & Israel, M. (1999). A psychodynamically informed, integrated psychotherapy for anorexia nervosa. *Journal of Clinical Psychology, 55,* 741–753.

Steiger, H., Leung, F., Thibaudeau, J., Houle, L., & Ghadirian, A. M. (1993). Comorbid features in bulimics before and after therapy: Are they explained by Axis-II diagnoses, secondary effects of bulimia, or both? *Comprehensive Psychiatry, 34,* 45–53.

Steiger, H., & Stotland, S. (1996). Prospective study of outcome in bulimics as a function of Axis-II comorbidity: Long-term responses on eating and psychiatric symptoms. *International Journal of Eating Disorders, 20,* 149–161.

Steiger, H., Stotland, S., & Houle, L. (1994). Prognostic implications of stable versus transient "borderline features" in bulimic patients. *Journal of Clinical Psychiatry, 55,* 206–214.

Steiger, H., Thibaudeau, J., Ghadirian, A. M., & Houle, L. (1992). Psychopathological features in bulimics as a function of Axis-II comorbidity: Isolation of mood-independent differences. *International Journal of Eating Disorders, 12,* 383–395.

Steiger, H., Thibaudeau, J. F., Leung, F., Houle, L., & Ghadirian, A. M. (1994). Eating and psychiatric symptoms as a function of Axis II comorbidity in bulimic patients: Three-month and six-month responses after therapy. *Psychosomatics, 35,* 41–49.

Stein, D., Kaye, W. H., Matsunaga, H., Orbach, I., Har-Even, D., Frank, G., et al. (2002). Eating-related concerns, mood, and personality traits in recovered bulimia nervosa subjects: A replication study. *International Journal of Eating Disorders, 32*(2), 225–229.

Steinhausen, H. C. (2002). The outcome of anorexia nervosa in the 20th century. *American Journal of Psychiatry, 159,* 1284–1293.

Stice, E. (2002). Risk and maintenance factors for eating pathology: A meta-analytic review. *Psychological Bulletin, 128,* 825–848.

Stice, E., Agras, W. S., Telch, C. F., Halmi, K. A., Mitchell, J. E., & Wilson, T. (2001). Subtyping binge eating-disordered women along dieting and negative affect dimensions. *International Journal of Eating Disorders, 30,* 11–27.

Sutandar-Pinnock, K., Woodside, D. B., Carter, J. C., Olmsted, M. P., & Kaplan A. S. (2003). Perfectionism in anorexia nervosa: A 6–24-month follow-up study. *International Journal of Eating Disorders, 33*(2), 225–229.

Thompson-Brenner, H., & Westen, D. (2005). A naturalistic study of psychotherapy for bulimia nervosa, part 1: Comorbidity and therapeutic outcome. *Journal of Nervous and Mental Disease, 193*(9), 573–584.

Tozzi, F., Thornton, L. M., Klump, K. L., Fichter, M. M., Halmi, K. A., Kaplan, A. S., et al. (2005). Symptom fluctuation in eating disorders: Correlates of diagnostic crossover. *American Journal of Psychiatry, 162*(4), 732–740.

Vaz, F. J. (1998). Outcome of bulimia nervosa: Prognostic factors. *Journal of Psychosomatic Research, 45,* 391–400.

Vitousek, K., & Manke, F. (1994). Personality variables and disorders in anorexia nervosa and bulimia nervosa. *Journal of Abnormal Psychology, 103,* 137–147.

Westen, D., & Harnden-Fischer, J. (2001). Personality profiles in eating disorders: Rethinking the distinction between Axis I and Axis II. *American Journal of Psychiatry, 158,* 547–562.

Wilfley, D. E., Friedman, M. A., Dounchis, J. Z., Stein, R. I., Welch, R. R., & Ball, S. A. (2000). Comorbid psychopathology in binge eating disorder: Relation to eating disorder severity at baseline and following treatment. *Journal of Consulting and Clinical Psychology, 68,* 641–649.

Wonderlich, S. A., Connolly, K. M., & Stice, E. (2004). Impulsivity as a risk factor for eating disorder behavior: Assessment implications with adolescents. *International Journal of Eating Disorders, 36,* 172–182.

Wonderlich, S. A., Fullerton, D., Swift, W. J., & Klein, M. H. (1994). Five-year outcome from eating disorders: Relevance of personality disorders. *International Journal of Eating Disorders, 5,* 233–244.

Wonderlich, S. A., Lilenfeld, L. R., Riso, L. P., Engel, S., & Mitchell, J. E. (2005). Personality and anorexia nervosa. *International Journal of Eating Disorders, 37*(Suppl.), S68–S71; discussion S87–S89.

Wonderlich, S. A., & Mitchell, J. E. (1992). Eating disorders and personality disorders. In J. Yager, H. E. Gwirtsman, & C. K. Edelstein (Eds.), *Special problems in managing eating disorders* (pp. 51–86). Washington, DC: American Psychiatric Press.

Wonderlich, S. A., & Mitchell, J. E. (1997). Eating disorders and comorbidity: Empirical, conceptual and clinical implications. *Psychopharmacology Bulletin, 33,* 381–390.

Wonderlich, S., & Mitchell, J. E. (2001). The role of personality in the onset of eating disorders and treatment implications. *Psychiatric Clinics of North America, 24*(2), 249–258.

Wonderlich, S. A., Peterson, C., Mitchell, J. E., & Crow, S. (2000). Integrative approaches to treating eating disorders. In K. J. Miller & J. S. Mizes (Eds.), *Comparative treatments of eating disorders* (pp. 173–195). New York: Springer.

Wonderlich, S. A., & Swift, W. J. (1990). Perceptions of parental relationships in the eating disorders: The relevance of depressed mood. *Journal of Abnormal Psychology, 99*(4), 353–360.

Woodside, D. B., Carter, J. C., & Blackmore, E. (2004). Predictors of premature termination of inpatient treatment for anorexia nervosa. *American Journal of Psychiatry, 161*(12), 2277–2281.

Zeeck, A., Hartmann, A., Buchholz, C., & Herzog, T. (2005). Drop outs from in-patient treatment of anorexia nervosa. *Acta Psychiatrica Scandinavica, 111*(1), 29–37.

Index

INDEX

A

Abandonment
  avoidant personality disorder and,
    217–218, 220
  fear of, 134, 144, 208
Abuse
  during childhood, see Childhood
    trauma
  of diuretics, 51–52
  eating disorders and, 70–71
  emotional, 62–64, 152
  of laxatives, 51–52, 71
  perpetrators of, confrontation of,
    210
  physical, 62–64, 139
  as risk factor
    population sample assessments
      on, 62–64
    sequencing model of, 71–71
  sexual, see Sexual abuse
  of substances, see Alcohol abuse;
    Substance abuse
  verbal, 62–64
  witnessing, as risk factor, 65
Acting out, 192
  self-injurious behavior associated
    with, 53
Actions, for borderline personality
    treatment, 188, 190, 192
Adaptive context, of avoidant
    personality disorder, 159
Addictions
  childhood trauma assessment
    with, 63
  eating disorders and, 26, 34, 46,
    51
  impulsivity in, 46–47
Adolescents
  diagnostic cautions for, 10–11

eating disorders assessment in,
  100–102
Adult victims, of childhood trauma,
  66–67
Affect/affective disorders
  in avoidant personality disorder,
    157
  in borderline personality disorder,
    69, 134, 136–137
  diagnostic applications of,
    140–141
  functional impairment of,
    185–186
  treatment strategies for,
    192–193, 205, 207
  target-symptom approach to, 235
Age/age groups
  childhood trauma assessment
    based on, 62, 66–68, 70
    sequencing model of, 71–72
  in diagnostic criteria, 10–11
  self-injurious behavior associated
    with, 52
Age at onset, of eating disorders
  assessment difficulties related to,
    100–102
  personality pathology influence
    on, 141, 250–251
Aggression, target-symptom
    approach to, 235
Agreeableness, dimensional measures
  of, 86
Alcohol abuse
  childhood trauma assessment
    with, 63
  eating disorders and, 26, 34, 46,
    51
  impulsivity in, 46–47

American Psychiatric Association
(APA), eating disorder
treatment guidelines of, 151
Anger, self-injurious behavior
associated with, 53
Anger management, for obsessive-
compulsive personality
disorder, 170
Anorexia nervosa (AN)
antisocial personality disorder
with, 26–29
avoidant personality disorder
with, 26–29
relevancy of, 149–160,
215–220
treatment strategies for,
220–227
borderline personality disorder
with, 15, 26–29, 34, 109
relevancy of, 131–145
treatment strategies for,
186–195, 197–212
as comorbidity, 13–15; *see also*
specific type
assessment difficulties of,
100–108
binge eating/purging type,
28–29
clinical implications of, 34–35,
46
clinical vignette of, 49–50
diagnostic criteria for, 122
impulsivity/compulsivity risk
for, 46–51
literature review on, 25–26
personality assessment
difficulties with, 93–99
personality characteristics
with, 123
prevalence of, 26–29
prognosis implications of,
247–256
restricting type, 26–27
self-injurious behavior and,
51–52, 71
treatment outcomes of,
252–253
dependent personality disorder
with, 26–29
histrionic personality disorder
with, 26–29

narcissistic personality disorder
with, 26–29
obsessive-compulsive personality
disorder with, 23–24,
26–29, 34, 46, 49
diagnostic assessment of,
104–105, 108, 167
relevancy of, 121–128
symptomatology
discrimination in, 165–166
treatment strategies for,
168–176
psychotropic medications for,
240–241
Anticonvulsants, for borderline
personality disorder, 236,
239–240
Antidepressants
for anorexia nervosa, 240–241
for body dysmorphic disorder, 176
for borderline personality
disorder, 239–240
for bulimia nervosa, 241
for obsessive-compulsive
personality disorder,
173–174
target-symptom approach to,
236–237
Antipsychotics
for body dysmorphic disorder, 176
for obsessive-compulsive
personality disorder,
174–175
target-symptom approach to,
236–237, 241
Antisocial Features (ANT) clinical
scale, of maladaptive
personality traits, 81
Antisocial personality disorder
anorexia nervosa in, 26–29
binge eating in, 32–34
bulimia nervosa in, 28, 30–32
childhood trauma associated with,
62–64, 67
cultural influences on, 11–12
diagnostic concepts for, 5, 8, 11
gender distributions of, 132
Anxiety/anxiousness
in avoidant personality disorder,
153–154, 226

dimensional measures of, 87
eating disorders and, prognosis
    implications of, 248, 252,
    255
psychotropic medications for,
    235–236
self-injurious behavior associated
    with, 52
social
    automatic, 218–220
    in avoidant personality
        disorder, 153–154, 157
    role of, 214–215
    treatment strategies for,
        224–226
Anxious personality disorder,
    152–153
diagnostic concepts for, 5, 87
APA (American Psychiatric
    Association), eating disorder
    treatment guidelines of, 151
Appetite, 108
Aripiprazole (Abilify), 239, 241
Assertiveness training, 205
Assessment
    behavioral vs. biophysical, 16–17
    clinical, 79–88; *see also* Clinical
        assessment
Assumptions, dysfunctional, avoidant
    personality disorder and,
    215, 218–219
    treatment strategies for, 224–225
Attention-deficit/hyperactivity
    disorder, 60, 69
Attention seeking, self-injurious
    behavior associated with, 53
Automatic thoughts, negative,
    avoidant personality
    disorder and, 218–220
    treatment strategies for, 223–224
Avoidant personality disorder
    (AVPD)
    anorexia nervosa in, 26–29
    binge eating in, 32–34
    bulimia nervosa in, 28, 30–32
    childhood trauma associated with,
        62–64, 67
    cognitive-behavioral therapy for,
        220–226
    efficacy of, 213–214, 216,
        226–227

integrative approach to,
    220–221, 226
stages of, 221–225
diagnostic concepts for, 5, 8–9
diagnostic criteria for, 152–153
dynamic characteristics of,
    153–154
eating disorders with, 149–160
    adaptive context of, 159
    functional comparisons,
        157–158
    interaction models for,
        158–159
    possible relationships between,
        156–157
    prevalence of, 154–156
    prognosis of, 248, 250, 252
    theory background for,
        149–151
    treatment strategies for,
        220–227
epidemiology of, 151
etiology of, 151–152, 158
treatment approaches to, 213–227
    cognitive assessment for,
        216–220
    cognitive-behavioral therapy
        as, 220–226
    eating disorders influence on,
        215–216, 218
    efficacy of, 213–214, 216,
        226–227
    social anxiety/phobia role and,
        214–215
Axis I category, of *DSM-IV*
    Axis II comorbidity in, 13–14
    eating disorders and, 35, 44, 94,
        121
        assessment problems with,
            100, 102, 106–107
        gender distribution of, 132
    personality disorders and
        assessment challenges, 94, 97,
            99
        concepts of, 3, 10, 17
        neurobiological construct of,
            232–233
Axis II category, of *DSM-IV*
    Axis I comorbidity in, 13–14
    diagnostic interview for, 83
    eating disorders and, 23–24,
        34–35, 44, 121

assessment problems with,
        100–102, 106–109
    prevalence of, 133, 154–157
    treatment outcomes of,
        253–254
personality disorders and
    assessment challenges of, 61,
        93–94, 99
    challenges to, 5–8, 68
    childhood trauma impact on,
        61, 67–68
    concepts of, 3, 17, 93
    epidemiology of, 131–133
    neurobiological construct of,
        232–233
    psychotropic medications for,
        237–238

B

Bariatric surgery, 95
Basics, for borderline personality
        treatment, 188–189
BED, *see* Binge eating disorder (BED)
Behavioral assessment
    for avoidant personality disorder,
        216–218
    for eating disorders, 103–106
    for personality disorders, 16–17
Behavioral processes
    in avoidant personality disorder,
        157
    in borderline personality disorder,
        140–141
        functional impairment of,
            185–186
Behavioral therapy
    for obsessive-compulsive
        personality disorder
        general techniques, 169
        psychodynamic approaches vs.,
            173
        specific techniques, 170–171,
            176
    for self-injurious behavior, 53–54
Beliefs, *see* Core beliefs
Benzodiazepines, 237
Bias
    clinician, 98–99
    sampling, 95–96

Binge eating disorder (BED)
    antisocial personality disorder
        with, 32–34
    avoidant personality disorder
        with, 32–34
        relevancy of, 149–160,
            215–220
        treatment strategies for,
            220–227
    borderline personality disorder
        with, 32–34
        relevancy of, 131–145
        treatment strategies for,
            186–195, 197–212
    as comorbidity, 14–15
        in anorexia nervosa, 28–29
    childhood trauma associated
        with, 64
    clinical implications of, 34–35
    impulsivity/compulsivity in,
        47–48
    literature review on, 25–26
    personality assessment
        difficulties with, 94
    prevalence of, 32–34
    prognosis implications of,
        247–256
    self-injurious behavior and,
        51–52
    treatment outcomes of, 254
    dependent personality disorder
        with, 32–34
    histrionic personality disorder
        with, 32–34
    narcissistic personality disorder
        with, 32–34
    obsessive-compulsive personality
        disorder with, 32–34
        relevancy of, 121–128
        treatment strategies for,
            168–176
Binge-purge cycle, perfectionism as
        driving, 47
Biofeedback, for obsessive-
        compulsive personality
        disorder, 169
Biological model, of personality
        pathology, 232–233
Biophysical assessment, for
        personality disorder, 17
Biosocial model, of personality, 86

Blended model, of personality
  disorders, 9–10
BN, *see* Bulimia nervosa (BN)
Body building, 176
Body dysmorphic disorder, 167, 175
  treatment strategies for, 174–176,
    226
Borderline Features (BOR) clinical
  scale, 81
Borderline personality disorder
  (BPD)
  anorexia nervosa in, 15, 26–29,
    34, 109
  binge eating in, 32–34
  bulimia nervosa in, 28, 30–32, 34,
    49, 71
  childhood trauma associated with,
    62–64
    adult victims studies, 67
    eating disorders and, 71, 206
    empirical studies review,
      65–66
    intensifying factors of, 67–68
    other personality disorders vs.,
      66
    population studies review,
      62–64
    studies refuting, 68–69
  compulsivity in, 45
  diagnosis of, 134–138
    difficulties in, 138
    interview adaptations for,
      136–137
    self-report assessments for,
      134–136
    semistructured interviews for,
      136
  diagnostic criteria for, 134
    blended model of, 9
    distinctiveness of, 8
    functional, 140–141
    problems with, 94, 97, 102,
      109
  eating disorders with, 131–145
    clinical presentation of,
      185–186
    diagnostic comparisons,
      140–141
    eclectic treatment approach to,
      197–212
    prevalence of, 133, 184
    prognosis of, 248, 253–254

  self-injury equivalents of, 144
  self-regulation treatment
    approach to, 183–195
  theoretical relationship models
    for, 141–144
  eclectic treatment approach to,
    197–212
    beginning tasks, 202–205
    behavior containment
      contracts, 190–191,
      199–201, 210
    ending tasks, 208–209
    entry tasks, 198–202
    for groups, 209
    indications for, 197–198, 211
    middle tasks, 205–208
    pitfalls with, 209–211
  epidemiology of, 131–133
  etiological factors of, 139
  malignant, 210
  memory misrepresentation with,
    60, 69
  nontraumatic childhood pathways
    to, 69
  psychotropic medications for, 236,
    238–240
  self-regulation treatment approach
    to, 183–195
    assessment/evaluation phase,
      184, 187
    complexity of, 183–184, 195
    framework for, 184, 186–187,
      207
    functional impairment
      dimensions and, 185–186
    indications for, 183–184, 195
    organizing therapeutic milieu
      phase, 184, 188–192
    psychotherapy phase, 184,
      192–194
    termination phase, 184,
      194–195
    transition phase, 184, 194
  treatment outcomes of, 195, 212
  treatment strategies for
    complexity of, 183–184, 195,
      197–198
    eclectic, 197–212
    self-regulation, 183–195
Bulimia nervosa (BN)
  antisocial personality disorder
    with, 28, 30–32

avoidant personality disorder
  with, 28, 30–32
  relevancy of, 149–160,
    215–220
  treatment strategies for,
    220–227
borderline personality disorder
  with, 28, 30–32, 34, 49, 71
  relevancy of, 131–145
  treatment strategies for,
    186–195, 197–212
childhood trauma associated with,
  64, 71–72
as comorbidity, 14–15
  assessment difficulties of,
    100–108
  clinical implications of, 34–35
  clinical vignette of, 50
  compulsivity/impulsivity risk
    for, 46–47, 50–51
  diagnostic criteria for, 122–123
  literature review on, 25–26
  personality assessment
    difficulties with, 93–99
  prevalence of, 28, 30–32
  prognosis implications of,
    247–256
  self-injurious behavior and,
    51–52
  treatment outcomes of,
    253–254
dependent personality disorder
  with, 28, 30–32
histrionic personality disorder
  with, 28, 30–32
narcissistic personality disorder
  with, 28, 30–32
obsessive-compulsive personality
  disorder with, 23–24, 28,
    30–32
  relevancy of, 121–128
  treatment strategies for,
    168–176
psychotropic medications for, 241
Burning, skin, eating disorders and,
  50–52
Buspirone (Buspar), 241

C

Caloric restriction, for longevity, 54
  assessment difficulties with, 95,
    105

Calories, as anorexia treatment, 104
Caretakers, abuse associated with,
  66, 70
CAT (cognitive analytical therapy),
  for obsessive-compulsive
    personality disorder, 172
CBT, *see* Cognitive-behavioral
  therapy (CBT)
Chaos, internal, in borderline
  personality disorder, 131
Chaotic eating behavior, assessment
  difficulties with, 103–106
Childhood trauma, 59–72
  assessment challenges of
    Axis II factors, 61
    subject recollection as, 60–61
  Axis II disorders associated with
    assessment difficulties, 61
    intensifying factors of, 67–68
    studies refuting, 68
  eating disorders relationship to,
    70–71
  impaired recall of, psychological
    maneuvers for, 60, 69
  literature search on, 59–60
    limitations of, 60–61, 69
  perpetrators of, confrontation of,
    210
  personality disorders associated
    with
    adult victims studies of, 66–67
    borderline, 65–66, 139, 206
    clinical implications of, 69–72
    eating disorders and, 70–71
    sample populations of, 62–64
  self-injurious behavior associated
    with, 52–53
  type vs. severity of
    as predictive vs. augmentative
      factor, 69–70
    as risk factor, 62, 65, 68
    sequencing model of, 71–72
  witnessing violence as, 65
*Childhood trauma-personality
  dysfunction-eating disorder*
  sequence, 71–72
Children
  diagnostic cautions for, 10–11
  eating disorders assessment in,
    100–102

life experiences of, avoidant
  personality disorder and,
  215, 217–219
sexual abuse of, *see* Sexual abuse
Children in the Community Study,
  11
Chronic restraint, in eating; *see also*
  Restricting anorexia nervosa
  assessment difficulties of,
  103–106
Citalopram (Celexa), 239
Clinical assessment
  of avoidant personality disorder,
  216–220
  of borderline personality disorder
  for eclectic treatment, 198–199
  for self-regulation treatment,
  140–141, 187
  childhood trauma and, 60–70
  of eating disorders, 91–93
  clinical examples of, 91–93
  as comorbidity, 167
  conclusions about, 108–109
  general problems in, 93–99
  special problems in, 100–108
  of obsessive-compulsive
  personality disorder,
  104–105, 108
  of personality disorders, 79–88
  challenges with, 79–80
  clinician bias in, 98–99
  construct problems with,
  93–94
  criteria problems with, 94
  difficulties in, 91–108
  dimensional measures for,
  85–87
  informant problems with,
  98–99
  interviews for, 81, 83–85
  levels for, 17
  measure scale problems with,
  94–95
  sampling/comparison group
  problems with, 95–96
  self-report inventories for,
  80–82
  timing problems with, 96–98
  two-step approach to, 80, 87
Clinician bias, 98–99
Clomipramine (Anafranil), 54
Cloxapine (Clozaril), 241

Cluster A, of personality disorders, 5,
  23, 151
  anorexia nervosa in, 24, 26–29
  binge eating in, 32–35
  bulimia nervosa in, 24, 28, 30–32
  childhood trauma associated with,
  62
Cluster B, of personality disorders, 5,
  24, 151
  childhood trauma associated with,
  62–64, 68
  eating disorders prognosis and,
  151, 248, 250–254
Cluster C, of personality disorders, 5,
  24, 151
  childhood trauma associated with,
  64
  eating disorders prevalence with,
  154–155
  eating disorders prognosis and,
  151, 248, 253
Cognitive analytical therapy (CAT),
  for obsessive-compulsive
  personality disorder, 172
Cognitive-behavioral formulation,
  for avoidant personality
  disorder, 216–218
Cognitive-behavioral therapy (CBT)
  for avoidant personality disorder
  efficacy of, 213–214, 216,
  226–227
  integrative approach to,
  220–221, 226
  stages of, 221–225
  for borderline personality
  disorder, 188
  for eating disorders, 253, 255
  for obsessive-compulsive
  personality disorder, 170,
  176
  for self-injurious behavior, 54
  for social phobia, 214
Cognitive processes
  in avoidant personality disorder,
  153–154, 157
  as negative, 215, 218–220
  treatment strategies for,
  222–226
  in borderline personality disorder,
  140–141
  functional impairment of,
  185–186

restructuring strategies for, 192–193, 203–204

splitting of, 206–208

in obsessive-compulsive personality disorder, as distorted, 171

in target-symptom approach to medications, 235

Cognitive remediation therapy (CRT), for obsessive-compulsive personality disorder, 171–172

Cognitive rigidity, eating disorders and, 54, 123

treatment strategies for, 171–172

"Cohort effect," of personality disorders, 11

Cohort studies, of eating disorders, 101

Collaborative Longitudinal Personality Disorders Study, 62

Common cause model, of borderline personality disorder, 142

Comorbidity(ies)

of Axis I and Axis II, 13–14

eating disorders as, *see* Eating disorders (EDs)

research problems related to, 96, 99

Comparison groups, for personality disorder assessment

with childhood abuse history, 62–64, 67

problems with, 95–96

Competition, in group therapy, 209

Complication/scar model, of borderline personality disorder, 142–143

Compulsivity

definition of, 45

dimensional measures of, 87

in eating disorders, 43–55

assessment difficulties with, 103

bulimia nervosa example, 48, 50

distinctions of, 43–45

prognosis implications of, 248, 255

risk of developing, 15, 34, 46–47

self-injurious behavior with, 26, 34, 48, 50–55

transdiagnostic characteristics of, 47–49

treatment of, 53–54

impulsivity vs., 45

in personality disorders, *see* Obsessive-compulsive personality disorder

Conflict, as influencing factor, 11–12

Conflict management, for borderline personality disorder, 192–193, 205

Confrontation, therapeutic, of perpetrators, 210

Conscientiousness, personality disorders and, 9, 45

dimensional measures of, 86

Constructs, for personality disorders diagnosis based on, 3, 5, 8–11, 16–17, 87

general, 232–233

problems with, 93–94

Contagion phenomenon, in group therapy, 209

Contract/contracting, therapeutic, borderline personality disorder and, 190–191

for high-lethal behavior, 199–200, 210

for low-lethal behavior, 200–201

Cooperativeness, dimensional measures of, 86

Coping, self-injurious behavior associated with, 53

Coping skills, for borderline personality disorder, 204–205

Core beliefs

in avoidant personality disorder as dysfunctional, 218–219

as negative, 215, 217–218, 223

treatment strategies for, 222–226

in borderline personality disorder, restructuring of, 203–204, 207–208

Cosmetic surgery, 176

Court-documented childhood abuse, sample assessments of, 64

Crisis management, 199–200

Criticism, avoidant personality
disorder and, 215, 219
CRT (cognitive remediation therapy),
for obsessive-compulsive
personality disorder,
171–172
Culture
borderline personality disorder
and, 133
role in personality disorders, 4,
11–13, 17, 150
Cutting, skin, eating disorders and,
50–52

D

DAPP-BQ (Dimensional Assessment
of Personality Disorder
Pathology), 85, 87
DBT, *see* Dialectical behavioral
therapy (DBT)
Defectiveness, avoidant personality
disorder and, 217–218
Demoralization, in borderline
personality patients, 202
treatment strategies for, 202–205
Denial
self-injurious behavior associated
with, 53
in self-report inventories, of eating
disorders, 106–107
in trauma recall, 60, 69
Dependent personality disorder
anorexia nervosa in, 26–29
binge eating in, 32–34
bulimia nervosa in, 28, 30–32
childhood trauma associated with,
63, 67
cultural influences on, 12
diagnostic concepts for, 5
Depression, as comorbidity, 3, 10,
13–14
assessment difficulties of, 97–98
childhood trauma associated with,
66
psychotropic medications for, 236
self-injurious behavior associated
with, 52
Detachment, in avoidant personality
disorder, 157

Devaluing, in borderline personality
patients, 202
treatment strategies for, 202–205
Developmental studies, of eating
disorders, 100–102
Developmental trauma, *see*
Childhood trauma
*Diagnostic and Statistical Manual
of Mental Disorders–Third
Edition (DSM-III)*, Axis I vs.
Axis II categories of, 3, 61
*Diagnostic and Statistical Manual of
Mental Disorders–Fourth
Edition (DSM-IV)*
avoidant personality disorder
criteria, 152–153
personality disorders
classification, 4–5, 24, 61,
151
psychotropic medication
evaluation and, 234
personality disorders criteria, 3–4
age appropriateness concerns,
10–11
assumptions as basis for, 5, 93
challenges to, 5–8
models for, 8–10
problems with, 94
*Diagnostic and Statistical Manual
of Mental Disorders–Text
Revision (DSM-IV-TR)*
anorexia nervosa criteria, 122, 140
borderline personality disorder
criteria, 134, 140–141
bulimia nervosa criteria, 122–123,
140
obsessive-compulsive disorder
criteria, 123, 125
obsessive-compulsive personality
disorder criteria, 122–124
psychotropic medication
evaluation and, 234
Diagnostic assessment, of personality
disorders, *see* Clinical
assessment
Diagnostic categories/criteria, for
personality disorders, 3–4
adolescents and, 10–11
assumptions as basis for, 5, 93
dimensional vs. blended models
of, 8–10, 43–44
distinctiveness of, 7–8

eating disorders influence on,
  91–108, 256
maladaptiveness role in, 7, 16
problems with, 93–94
psychotropic medication
  evaluation based on, 234
reliability of, 5–6
validity of, 6
Diagnostic Interview for Borderlines–
  Revised, 136
clinical adaptation of, 136–137
clinical applications of, 199
Diagnostic Interview for DSM
  Personality Disorders–IV
  (DIPD-IV), 84
Dialectical behavioral therapy (DBT)
  for borderline personality
  disorder, 211
for obsessive-compulsive
  personality disorder,
  170–171
Dialogue, establishing, for borderline
  personality disorder, 203
Dimensional Assessment of
  Personality Disorder
  Pathology (DAPP-BQ), 85,
  87
Dimensional model
of eating disorders, 51–52
of personality disorders, 8–9,
  43–44
  classification measures for,
  85–87
of personality traits, five-factors
  of, 9, 86
Disability status, in borderline
  personality treatment, 205,
  210
Dissociation
in borderline personality disorder,
  134, 141
in trauma recall, 60, 69
Dissociative identity disorder,
  childhood trauma
  assessment with, 64
Distortion
cognitive, in obsessive-compulsive
  personality disorder, 171
in eating disorder assessment, 105
self-report inventories and,
  106–107
Diuretic abuse, 51–52

Diversion interventions, in borderline
  personality treatment, 205,
  210
DSM, *see Diagnostic and Statistical
  Manual of Mental Disorders*
  entries
Dysfunctional assumptions, avoidant
  personality disorder and,
  215, 218–219
treatment strategies for, 224–225
Dysphoria, chronic, in borderline
  personality disorder, 131,
  136–137

E

Eating Attitudes Test, 187
Eating disorders (EDs), as
  comorbidity, 13–15, 248; *see
  also* specific disorder
APA treatment guidelines for, 151
assessment difficulties of, 91–108,
  167
  clinical examples of, 91–93
  conclusions about, 108–109
  general personality problems,
  93–99, 256
  special problems in, 100–108
avoidant personality and, 149–160
  assessment of, 216–220
  links of meaning between,
  215–216, 218
  treatment strategies for,
  220–227
Axis II disorders with, 23–24,
  154–157
borderline personality and,
  131–145
  eclectic treatment approach to,
  197–212
  self-regulation treatment
  approach to, 183–195
childhood trauma associated with,
  64, 70–71
complex relational dynamics of,
  149–151
developmental onset of,
  personality pathology effect
  on, 250–251
impulsivity/compulsivity in,
  43–55

clinical vignettes of, 49–50
distinctions of, 43–45
risk of developing, 46–47
self-injurious behavior and, 26,
  34, 48, 50–55, 71
transdiagnostic characteristics
  of, 47–49
natural course of, personality
  pathology effect on, 251,
  255–256
obsessive-compulsive personality
  and, 121–128
treatment strategies for,
  165–178
prevalence of, 14, 23, 26–36,
  150–151
prognostic conclusions about,
  247–248, 255–256
psychotropic medications for,
  237–238
risk factors for, 46–51, 62–64, 71,
  215
symptoms of, personality
  pathology effect on,
  249–250, 255
treatment outcomes of,
  personality pathology
  implications for, 252–254
treatment strategies for
  for avoidant personality
    disorder, 220–227
  for borderline personality
    disorder, 183–195, 197–212
  for obsessive-compulsive
    individuals, 165–178
Eclectic treatment approach, to
  borderline personality
  disorder, 197–212
beginning tasks, 202–205
behavior containment contracts,
  190–191, 199–201, 210
ending tasks, 208–209
entry tasks, 198–202
for groups, 209
indications for, 197–198, 211
middle tasks, 205–208
pitfalls with, 209–211
"Ecological niche," 12–13
Educational resourcing skills, in
  borderline personality
  treatment, 192–193

Ego-dystonic behavior, in
  compulsivity, 45, 54
Ego-syntonic behavior, in self-
  injurious behavior, 44, 54
Emotional abuse, as risk factor,
  62–64, 152
Emotional avoidance, avoidant
  personality disorder and,
  217–219
treatment strategies for, 222–226
Emotional neglect, as risk factor,
  62–64
Emotions, expression vs. inhibition of
  in avoidant personality disorder,
    217–219, 224
  in borderline personality disorder,
    69, 141, 204–205
  eating disorder prognosis and,
    159, 252
  self-injurious behavior associated
    with, 51, 53
Empirical studies, on psychotropic
  medications, 233–235, 239
  of target-symptom approach,
    235–236
Employment
  borderline personality treatment
    and, 205, 210
  personality disorders and, 8–9
Empowerment, borderline
  personality disorder and,
  188–189
Entertainment industry, as
  influencing factor, 11–13
Entry phase, in borderline
  personality treatment
  of eclectic approach, 198–201,
    210
  of self-regulation approach, 184,
    187
Environment, role in personality
  disorders, 139, 232
Escitalopram (Lexapro), 239
Evidence-based medicine, with
  psychotropic medications,
  233–235, 239
Exacerbation/pathoplasty model,
  of borderline personality
  disorder, 142–143
Exercise program, for obsessive-
  compulsive individuals,
  168–169

Experiences, *see* Life experiences
Extraversion, personality disorders
    and, 9, 14
    dimensional measures of, 86

F

Family dynamics/dysfunction
    abuse and, *see* Abuse
    as eating disorder factor, 53, 71,
        126, 251
    as personality disorder factor,
        11–12, 63, 139, 152
    traumatic manifestations of, 63,
        68, 70; *see also* Childhood
        trauma
Family informants, problems with,
    98–99
Fear, *see* Anxiety/anxiousness
Feelings; *see also* Affect/affective
        disorders
    negative, tolerance for, 205
    splitting of, in borderline
        personality disorder, 206,
        208
Fluoxetine (Prozac), 176, 236, 239,
    241
Food, as anorexia treatment, 104
Food and Drug Administration, 232,
    241
Food restrictions
    borderline personality disorder
        and, 144, 202
    for longevity, 54, 71
        assessment difficulties with,
            95, 105, 167
Forensic patients, childhood trauma
    associations of, 66
Foundation Skills, for borderline
    personality treatment, 188,
    193
Frustration, self-injurious behavior
    associated with, 53
Functionality continuum, in
    personality disorders, 17,
    150
    assessment of, 79
    avoidant, 152–153, 157–158

borderline, 138, 140–141,
    185–186, 199
eating disorders and, 140, 249,
    255

G

Gabapentin (Neurontin), 236, 239,
    241
Gender ratios
    in borderline personality disorder
        distribution, 132
    in research, 61
Genetics
    in avoidant personality disorder,
        152
    in borderline personality disorder,
        132, 139
    in obsessive-compulsive
        personality disorder, 126
    predisposition in personality
        disorders, 232
Global Assessment of Functioning,
    17
Group treatment, for borderline
    personality disorder, 209

H

Hair pulling, eating disorders and,
    50–52
Harm avoidance
    dimensional measures of, 86
    eating disorders and, 250, 252
Hippocampus, role in borderline
    personality disorder, 139
Histrionic personality disorder
    anorexia nervosa in, 26–29
    binge eating in, 32–34
    bulimia nervosa in, 28, 30–32
    cultural influences on, 12–13
    diagnostic concepts for, 5
    gender distributions of, 132
Humiliation, avoidant personality
    disorder and, 215, 219
Hypersensitivity, in avoidant
    personality disorder, 157

Hypervigilance
  in avoidant personality disorder, 157
  in borderline personality disorder, 198

I

ICD-10, *see International Classification of Diseases–10th Edition (ICD-10)*
Immobilization, in group therapy, 209
Impulsivity
  in borderline personality disorder, 136–137, 141
  compulsivity vs., 45
  definition of, 44, 46
  dimensional measures of, 87
  in eating disorders, 43–55
    anorexia nervosa example, 48–50
    assessment difficulties of, 95, 99
    childhood trauma and, 71
    distinctions of, 43–45
    prognosis implications of, 248, 250–251, 253–254
    risk of developing, 15, 24, 34, 46–47
    self-injurious behavior with, 26, 34, 48, 50–55
    transdiagnostic characteristics of, 47–49
    treatment of, 53–54, 254
  evolutionary framework for, 44–45
  in personality disorders, 16, 87
  psychotropic medications for, 235–236
  serotonin dysfunction associated with, 235
Inadequacy feelings, in avoidant personality disorder, 152–153, 159
Incarcerated offenders, childhood trauma assessment of, 64
Indecisiveness, personality disorders and, 45
Independence model, of borderline personality disorder, 142

Inflexibility, eating disorders and, 54, 123, 126
Inpatients, childhood trauma assessment of, 62
  adult victims studies, 67
  borderline personality studies, 65
  other personality disorder studies, 66
  outpatient samples combined with, 63, 67
International Classification of Diseases–10th Edition (ICD-10)
  personality disorders classification in, 4–5
  personality disorders criteria of, 4
International Personality Disorder Examination (IPDE), 84–85
Interpersonal psychotherapy (IPT)
  for borderline personality disorder, 188
  for obsessive-compulsive personality disorder, 170
Interpersonal relationships
  in avoidant personality disorder, 157, 159, 225
  in borderline personality disorder, 131, 136–138
    diagnostic applications of, 140–141
    functional impairment of, 185–186
    splitting, 206, 208
    treatment strategies for, 206–209
  cultural influences on, 12–13, 17
  eating disorders and, 53, 71, 250, 252
  personality disorders and, 8–9
Interpersonal restructuring, for borderline personality disorder, 204
Interviews
  for childhood trauma assessment, 61
  for personality disorders assessment, 80, 83
    dimensional examples, 86–87
    problems with, 94–95, 101
    self-report inventories vs., 81
    semistructured examples of, 83–85, 136

Intrapsychic assessment, for
  personality disorder, 17
Intrapsychic splitting, in borderline
  personality disorder, 206,
  208
Introversion, personality disorders
  and, 9
Inventories
  questionnaires as, *see* Interviews
  self-report, *see* Self-report
    inventories
IPDE (International Personality
  Disorder Examination),
  84–85
IPT, *see* Interpersonal psychotherapy
  (IPT)

J

Juvenile delinquents, childhood
  trauma assessment of, 64

L

Laxative abuse, 51–52, 71
Learning disabilities, 60, 69
Life experiences
  avoidant personality disorder and
    early, 215, 217–218
  moderating, 218–219
  openness to, dimensional
    measures of, 86
Life perspectives, developing
  realistic, 205
Lithium, 237, 241
Longitudinal studies, 62
  of eating disorders, 101
  of psychotropic medications,
    234–235

M

Maladaptiveness, in personality
  disorders, 7, 10, 16
  dimensional classification of, 9,
    85–87
  eating disorder challenges with,
    100–108, 249

interviews for, 81, 83–85
measurement scales for, 80–85
Management skills, in borderline
  personality treatment,
  192–193
Mandometer, 169
Manipulation, self-injurious behavior
  associated with, 51, 53
McLean Screening Instrument for
  Borderline Personality
  Disorder, 134, 136
MCMI-III (Millon Clinical
  Multiaxial Inventory–III),
  82, 234
Measurement scales, for personality
  traits/disorders, 9, 79–81
  borderline, 134–136, 187
  dimensional, 85–87
  interviews as, 83–85
  problems with, 94–95
  self-report, 80–83
Medical treatment, for obsessive-
  compulsive individuals,
  168–169
Medications, *see* Pharmacotherapy
  psychotropic, *see* Psychotropic
    medications
Memory recall, of childhood trauma,
  60–61, 69
MET (motivational enhancement
  therapy), 172
Millon Clinical Multiaxial
  Inventory–III (MCMI-III),
  82, 234
Minnesota Multiphasic Personality
  Inventory (MMPI), 82
  in eating disorders study, 103–104
Mirror exposure, supervised, 176
Misrepresentation, in trauma recall,
  60, 69
Mood disorders
  eating disorders and, 15, 141
    assessment difficulties of,
      97–98, 103
    prognosis implications of, 248
  noradrenaline dysfunction
    associated with, 235
  target-symptom approach to,
    235–236
Mood stabilizers, for impulsivity, 54
Morey MMPI Personality Disorder
  Scales, 82

Motivation, borderline personality
disorder and, 188–189
Motivational enhancement therapy
(MET), 172
Muscle dysmorphophobia, 175–176

N

Nail biting, severe, 51–52
Narcissistic personality disorder
anorexia nervosa in, 26–29
binge eating in, 32–34
bulimia nervosa in, 28, 30–32
childhood trauma associated with,
62–63
cultural influences on, 12–13
diagnostic concepts for, 5
Negative automatic thoughts,
avoidant personality
disorder and, 218–220
treatment strategies for, 223–225
Negative core beliefs, avoidant
personality disorder and,
215, 217–218
treatment strategies for, 223–225
Negative feelings, tolerance for, 205
Neglect, during childhood, as risk
factor, 62–64, 139
NEO PI (Neuroticism Extraversion
Openness Personality
Inventory), 9–10
Revised, 85–86
Neurohormonal factors, of
personality disorders, 139,
232
Neurological factors, in borderline
personality disorder, 69,
132, 139
Neurosis, semi-starvation, 103–104
Neuroticism, personality disorders
and, 9
dimensional measures of, 86
Neuroticism Extraversion Openness
Personality Inventory (NEO
PI), 9–10
Revised, 85–86
NICE guidelines, for eating disorder
treatment, 252
Nonclinical studies, of childhood
trauma, 62, 65

Nosological systems, personality
disorders included in, 4–5
Novelty-seeking, dimensional
measures of, 86
Nutritional rehabilitation
borderline personality disorder
and, 202
obsessive-compulsive personality
disorder and, 168–169

O

Obsessive-compulsive disorder
(OCD)
diagnostic criteria for, 123, 125
eating disorders with, 121–122,
126
perfectionism and, 121–123,
126–128
treatment strategies for, 165–166
Obsessive-compulsive personality
disorder (OCPD)
anorexia nervosa in, 23–24,
26–29, 34, 46, 49
assessment difficulties with,
104–105, 108
binge eating in, 32–34
body dysmorphic disorder with,
167, 174–176
bulimia nervosa in, 23–24, 28,
30–32
characteristics of, 165–166
childhood trauma associated with,
62, 71
compulsivity in, 45, 49; *see also*
Compulsivity
cultural influences on, 12
diagnostic concepts for, 5, 9, 87
problems with, 94, 97–98, 105
diagnostic criteria for, 122–124
eating disorders with, 121–128
Axis I vs. Axis II distinctions,
121–122
case report on, 127
definitions for, 122–123
perfectionism and, 121–123,
126–128
prevalence of, 124–126
prognosis of, 248, 251–253

symptomatology of, 165–166
treatment approaches to,
    165–178
treatment outcomes of, 176
treatment setting for, 168
treatment strategies for, 165–178
    assessment difficulties and, 167
    case histories of, 177–178
    cognitive rigidity as target,
        171–172
    eating disorders and, 165–166
    general behavioral techniques,
        169
    medical approach, 168–169
    medications for, 173–176
    perfectionism as target,
        171–172
    physical approach, 168–169
    psychodynamic approaches,
        172–173
    psychoeducational approach,
        168–169
    psychotherapeutic approaches,
        172–173
    specific behavioral techniques,
        170–171
Obstinacy, eating disorders and, 54,
    123
Olanzapine (Zyprexa), 241
Openness to experience, dimensional
    measures of, 86
Organizing phase, in borderline
        personality treatment
    of eclectic approach, 202–205
    of self-regulation approach, 184,
        188–192
Outpatients, childhood trauma
        assessment of, 62
    adult victims studies, 67
    borderline personality studies, 66
    inpatient samples combined with,
        63, 67
    nonconfirming studies review, 68

P

PAI (Personality Assessment
    Inventory), 81–82
Panic attacks, psychotropic
    medications for, 236

Paranoid personality disorder
    childhood trauma associated with,
        62–63, 67
    diagnostic concepts for, 5
Pardon, inability for, eating disorders
        and, 123
Parenting, *see* Family
        dynamics/dysfunction
Paroxetine (Paxil), 241
Path-analytic model, of borderline
        personality disorder, 68
Pathoplasty/exacerbation model,
        of borderline personality
        disorder, 142–143
Pattern recognition skills, in
        borderline personality
        treatment, 192–193
PDI-IV (Personality Disorder
        Interview–IV), 84
PDQ-4 (Personality Disorder
        Questionnaire–4), 82
PDs, *see* Personality disorders (PDs)
Perfectionism
    eating disorders and, 46–47, 104,
        108, 121, 159
    prognosis implications of, 248,
        250–252
    obsessive-compulsive traits and,
        121–123, 167
    relationships among, 13,
        126–128
    treatment strategies for,
        171–172
    personality disorders and, 13–14
Perpetrators, therapeutic
        confrontation of, 210
Persistence
    dimensional measures of, 86
    obsessiveness and, 121
Personality Assessment Inventory
        (PAI), 81–82
Personality Belief Questionnaire,
        217, 223
Personality Diagnostic
        Questionnaire–4, 134, 187,
        233
Personality Disorder Examination,
        136
Personality Disorder Interview–IV
        (PDI-IV), 84
Personality Disorder Questionnaire–4
        (PDQ-4), 82

Personality disorders (PDs)
    abuse as risk factor for, 62–64; *see also* Childhood trauma
    assessment levels for, 17, 80; *see also* Clinical assessment
    blended models of, 9–10
    classification of, 4–5, 24
    clusters of, 5, 24
    comorbidities of, 13–15
    conceptualization of, 3, 16–17
    constructs
        diagnosis based on, 3, 5, 8–11, 16–17, 87
        general, 232–233
        problems with, 93–94
    cultural influences on, 4, 11–13, 17
    definition of, 4, 24
    diagnostic criteria for, 3–4
        challenges to, 5–8
    dimensional models of, 8–9, 43–44
        classification measures for, 85–87
    eating disorders with, *see* Eating disorders (EDs)
    pharmacotherapy for, 231–242; *see also* Psychotropic medications
    prevalence of, 231
    prognostic implications of, 247–256
    temporal stability of, 10–11
Personality styles/traits
    adaptive vs. maladaptive, 7, 16, 80
    adolescent development of, 11
    biosocial model of, 86
    confounding components of, 7–8
    culture as shaping, 11, 17, 150
    eating disorders associated with, 14–15, 140
        assessment difficulties of, 103–106
    instruments to measure, 9
        dimensional, 86
        problems with, 94–95
        timing of, 96–98
    in personality disorder assessment, 17, 80
Pharmacotherapy
    for eating disorders, 104, 240–242, 253

    in obsessive-compulsive individuals, 173–176
    for personality disorders, 231–242
    psychotropic, *see* Psychotropic medications
    for self-injurious behavior, 54
Phenomenological assessment, for personality disorder, 17
Phobias
    body image, 167, 175
        treatment strategies for, 174–176, 226
    social, role of, 214–215
Physical abuse, as risk factor, 62–64, 139
Physical neglect, as risk factor, 62–64
Physical treatment, for obsessive-compulsive individuals, 168–169
Picking, skin, eating disorders and, 50–52
PISIA, in Diagnostic Interview for Borderlines–Revised, 136–137, 199
Placebo effects, with psychotropic medications, 234, 238
Polypharmacy, 237–238
Polysymptomatic disorders, 138, 149–150
Population groups, for personality disorder assessment
    with childhood abuse history, 62–64, 67
    with eating disorders, 101–102
    problems with, 95
Post-traumatic stress disorder, 66, 132, 236
Practice Guideline for the Treatment of Patients With Eating Disorders (APA), 151
Predisposition/vulnerability model, of borderline personality disorder, 142–144
Prevalence rates, of personality disorders
    cross-cultural differences in, 12
    eating disorders and, 14, 23–36
    literature review summary, 24–25
Problem-solving skills, in borderline personality treatment, 192–193, 205

Psychobiological models
    of borderline personality disorder,
        142–143
    of personality pathology, 232–233
Psychodynamic intervention
    for borderline personality
        disorder, 204
    for obsessive-compulsive
        personality disorder,
        172–173
Psychoeducation
    for borderline personality
        disorder, 202–203
    for obsessive-compulsive
        personality disorder,
        168–169
    self-injurious behavior and, 53–54
Psychological maneuvers, for
        impaired recall of trauma,
        60, 69
Psychotherapy
    for borderline personality
        disorder, 184, 192–194
    individual vs. manualized vs.
        institutional, 211
    pitfalls with, 209–211
    contract for, *see* Therapeutic
        contract
    definition of, 192–193
    for eating disorders, 256
    for obsessive-compulsive
        personality disorder,
        172–173
    interpersonal, 170
    supportive, 172–173
    for self-injurious behavior, 54
Psychotic episodes, in borderline
        personality disorder,
        136–138
Psychotropic medications
    for body dysmorphic disorder, 176
    for eating disorders, 104, 240–
        242, 253
    in borderline personality
        patients, 205
    in obsessive-compulsive
        individuals, 173–176
    for obsessive-compulsive
        personality disorder,
        168–169
    efficacy of, 173–176
    general commentary about, 175

    for personality disorders, 232–240
        borderline, 205, 238–240
        evaluation problems with,
            233–235
        mechanism of action, 233
        neurobiology construct for,
            232–233
        prescribing context for,
            237–238
        subtype indications, 234
        target-symptom approach to,
            235–237
    for self-injurious behavior, 54
PsycINFO database, 25, 59
PubMed database, 25
Purging behavior
    in anorexia nervosa
        prevalence of, 28–29
        self-injurious behavior and,
            51–52, 71
    in bulimia nervosa, 52
    personality pathology impact on,
        255

Q

Quantitative models, of personality
        disorders, 43–44
Quasi-psychotic episodes, in
        borderline personality
        disorder, 136–138
Questionnaires, for personality
        disorders assessment
    examples of, 134, 187, 217, 223
    problems with, 94–95
    self-report, 80–82
    semistructured interviews, 81,
        83–85

R

Racial patterns, in borderline
        personality disorder, 133
Realistic view, in borderline
        personality treatment, 205
Recall, memory, of childhood
        trauma, 60
Relapse prevention, for obsessive-
        compulsive personality
        disorder, 176

Relational processes, *see* Interpersonal relationships
Relationship management skills, in borderline personality treatment, 192–193
Relaxation training
  for borderline personality disorder, 205
  for obsessive-compulsive individuals, 168–169
Reliability, of personality disorders categories, 5–6
Repression, of trauma recall, 60, 69
Restricting anorexia nervosa
  assessment difficulties with, 103–106
  borderline personality disorder with, 133
  clinical implications of, 34–35, 71
  impulsivity in, 47, 49, 51
  prevalence of, 26–27
Restructuring, in borderline personality disorder treatment
  cognitive, 192–193, 203–204
  of core beliefs, 203, 207–208
  interpersonal, 204
Revictimization, therapeutic confrontation as, 210
Reward dependence, dimensional measures of, 86
Rigidity, *see* Cognitive rigidity
Risk taking, eating disorders and, 46
Risperidone (Risperdal), 239, 241
Rumination, 165
  treatment strategies for, 174, 226

S

Safety behaviors
  in avoidant personality disorder, 152–153
    automatic negative, 218–220, 223–224
    treatment strategies for, 224–226
  in borderline personality disorder, 191–192
Sample populations, for personality disorder assessment
  with childhood abuse history, 62–64, 67
  with eating disorders, 101–102
  problems with, 95–96
Sampling bias, 95–96
Scar/complication model, of borderline personality disorder, 142–143
Schedule for Nonadaptive and Adaptive Personality Functioning (SNAP), 85–87
Schizoid personality disorder
  childhood trauma associated with, 63
  diagnostic concepts for, 5, 9
  psychotropic medications for, 236
Schizotypal personality disorder
  childhood trauma associated with, 62–63, 67
  diagnostic concepts for, 5
SCID-II (Structured Clinical Interview for DSM-IV Axis II Disorders), 83
  Revised, 126
Scratching, eating disorders and, 50–51
Selection criteria, research, problems with, 95–96
Selective noradrenergic reuptake inhibitors (SNRIs), 174
Selective serotonin reuptake inhibitors (SSRIs)
  for body dysmorphic disorder, 176
  for borderline personality disorder, 239–240
  for bulimia nervosa, 241
  for compulsivity, 54
  for obsessive-compulsive personality disorder, 173–174
  target-symptom approach to, 236
Self-care, in borderline personality treatment, 207
Self-concept
  in avoidant personality disorder, 153–154, 219
    treatment strategies for, 222–226
  in borderline personality disorder, 189–190, 203

Self-confidence, loss of, in avoidant
    personality disorder, 215,
    219
Self-destructive identity, in
    borderline personality
    patients, 202
    treatment strategies for, 202–205
Self-directedness, dimensional
    measures of, 86
Self-efficacy
    in borderline personality disorder,
    189–190
    impulsivity and, 53–54
Self-esteem
    eating disorders and, 141, 215,
    219, 253
    self-injurious behavior and, 54
Self-harm behavior (SHB), *see* Self-
    injurious behavior (SIB)
Self-Harm Inventory, for borderline
    personality disorder,
    134–136
    with eating disorders, 187
Self-injurious behavior (SIB)
    in borderline personality disorder,
    134–136, 138, 141
       contract for containing,
       199–201, 210
       equivalents with eating
       disorders, 144
       treatment strategies for,
       202–205
    eating disorders and, 26, 34, 48,
    50
       childhood trauma and, 71
       impulsivity/compulsivity in,
       44–45, 51
       treatment of, 53–55
    gender distributions of, 132
    most common, 51
Self-management, in borderline
    personality treatment, 188,
    193, 204
Self-mutilation
    with body dysmorphic disorder,
    176
    with eating disorders, 50–52
Self-psychological approach, to
    obsessive-compulsive
    personality disorder, 173
Self-punishment, in eating disorders,
    51–52

Self-regulation, difficulties of, 207
    eating disorders and, 34, 47, 52,
    141
Self-regulation treatment approach,
    for borderline personality
    disorder, 183–195
    assessment/evaluation phase, 184,
    187
    complexity of, 183–184, 195
    framework for, 184, 186–187, 207
    functional impairment dimensions
    and, 185–186
    indications for, 183–184, 195
    organizing therapeutic milieu
    phase, 184, 188–192
    psychotherapy phase, 184,
    192–194
    termination phase, 184, 194–195
    transition phase, 184, 194
Self-report inventories
    for borderline personality disorder
    assessment, 134–136
    for childhood trauma assessment,
    61
    for personality disorders
    assessment
       advantages of, 80–81
       commonly used, 81–82
       denial in, 106–107
       dimensional examples, 85–87
       distortion in, 107–108
       eating disorders and, 101–102
       problems with, 94–95, 101
Self-sabotage, contract for
    containing, 200–201
Self-transcendence, dimensional
    measures of, 86
Semistarvation, assessment
    difficulties related to, 98,
    100, 103–106
"Semi-starvation neurosis," 103–104
Semistructured interviews, for
    personality disorders
    assessment, 81, 83–85
    borderline, 136
    problems with, 94–95, 101
Sensation seeking, eating disorders
    and, 46
Sequencing model, of childhood
    trauma-personality
    dysfunction-eating disorder,
    71–72

Sertraline (Zoloft), 239, 241
Sexual abuse, childhood
    adult victims studies of, 66–67
    assessment challenges of, 60–61
    personality disorders associated
        with, 62–63, 67, 139
    self-injurious behavior associated
        with, 52–53
    timing impact of, 67
Sexual behavior
    cross-cultural differences in, 12
    eating disorders and, 34, 45, 47
SHB (self-harm behavior), *see* Self-
        injurious behavior (SIB)
Shoplifting, compulsive, 47
Shyness, personality disorders and,
        14, 151, 215
SIB, *see* Self-injurious behavior (SIB)
SIFFM (Structured Interview for the
        Five Factor Model), 86
Skills Base, for borderline personality
        treatment, 188, 190,
        192–193
Skin burning, eating disorders and,
        50–52
Skin cutting, eating disorders and,
        50–52
Skin picking, eating disorders and,
        50–52
SNAP (Schedule for Nonadaptive
        and Adaptive Personality
        Functioning), 85–87
SNRIs (selective noradrenergic
        reuptake inhibitors), 174
Social adaptation/adjustment
    in avoidant personality disorder,
        152–153
        automatic negative, 218–220,
        223–224
        treatment strategies for,
        224–226
    in borderline personality disorder,
        136–138
    eating disorders and, 106–107,
        250–251
    personality disorders and, 4, 7–10,
        17
Social anxiety, in avoidant
        personality disorder,
        153–154, 157
    automatic, 218–220

    role of, 214–215
    treatment strategies for, 224–226
Social consequences, of self-injurious
        behavior, 53
Social expectations, cross-cultural
        differences in, 11–13, 17
Social façade, in borderline
        personality disorder, 131,
        138
Social phobia, generalized, role of,
        214–215
Social relationships, *see* Interpersonal
        relationships
Social skills training, 205, 226
Sociology, of personality disorders,
        11–12
Somatic preoccupation
    in body dysmorphic disorder, 167,
        175
        treatment strategies for,
        174–176, 226
    in borderline personality disorder,
        138
Spectrum/subclinical model, of
        borderline personality
        disorder, 142
Splitting, in borderline personality
        disorder, 206, 208
SPM (structural-process model),
        for borderline personality
        disorder, 188–190
SSRIs, *see* Selective serotonin
        reuptake inhibitors (SSRIs)
Starvation, assessment difficulties
        related to, 98, 100, 103–106
State condition/effect, of
        semistarvation, 98, 100,
        103–106, 140
Stress
    childhood trauma associated with,
        66
    gender distributions of, 132
    role in personality disorders, 139,
        232
Structural-process model (SPM),
        for borderline personality
        disorder, 188–190
Structured Clinical Interview for
        DSM-III-R Personality
        Disorders, 136, 234

Structured Clinical Interview for
    DSM-IV Axis II Disorders
    (SCID-II), 83
  Revised, 126
Structured Interview for DSM-IV
    Personality, 83–84, 216
Structured Interview for Personality
    Disorders, 136
Structured Interview for the Five
    Factor Model (SIFFM), 86
Stubbornness, eating disorders and,
    54, 123
Subclinical/spectrum model, of
    borderline personality
    disorder, 142
Subject recollection, of childhood
    trauma, 60
Sublimation, in borderline
    personality treatment,
    204–205
Substance abuse
  borderline personality treatment
    and, 210–211
  eating disorders and, 26, 34, 46,
    51
    assessment difficulties of, 95
    prognosis implications of, 248
  as emotional blocking behavior,
    225
  impulsivity in, 46–47
  mixed, childhood trauma
    associated with, 63, 68
Suicidality
  contract for containing, 199–200,
    210
  eating disorders and, 45, 47, 51–52
    assessment difficulties of, 95
  personality disorders and, 10, 45,
    210
Supervisory neglect, as risk factor,
    62–64
Supportive psychotherapy, for
    obsessive-compulsive
    personality disorder,
    172–173
Suppression, of trauma recall, 60, 69

T

Target-symptom approach, to
    psychotropic medications

essential elements of, 237–238
research limitations of, 234–235
for selection, 235–237
TCI (Temperament and Character
    Inventory), 85–86
Teasing, avoidant personality
    disorder and, 215, 218
Technology, as influencing factor, 11
Temperament, preexisting
  avoidant personality disorder and,
    215
  borderline personality disorder
    and, 69
  childhood trauma manifestations
    and, 69–70
  dimensional measures of, 86–87,
    232
  obsessiveness and, 121
Temperament and Character
    Inventory (TCI), 85–86
Temporal stability, of personality
    disorders, 10–11
Termination phase, in borderline
    personality treatment
  of eclectic approach, 208–209
  of self-regulation approach, 184,
    194–195
Therapeutic confrontation, of
    perpetrators, 210
Therapeutic contract, for borderline
    personality disorder,
    190–191
  for high-lethal behavior, 199–200,
    210
  for low-lethal behavior, 200–201
Therapeutic relationship
  for avoidant personality disorder,
    222, 225
  for borderline personality disorder
    consistency of, 211
    in eclectic treatment, 201–202,
    205, 208–209
    patient role, 190
    in self-regulation treatment,
    188, 191–192
    therapist role, 4, 190, 193
  for eating disorders, 256
Thought-action fusion, 171
Thoughts, *see* Cognitive processes
Thought-shape fusion, 171
Threats, malignant, with childhood
    trauma, 67–68

Topiramate (Topamax), 239, 241
Trait condition/effect
　in eating disorders, 14–15,
　　103–106, 140
　of personality, *see* Personality
　　styles/traits
Transition phase, in borderline
　　personality treatment
　of eclectic approach, 205–208
　of self-regulation approach, 184,
　　194
Trauma
　abusive, *see* Abuse
　developmental, *see* Childhood
　　trauma
Treatment
　anorexia nervosa implications for,
　　252–253
　for avoidant personality disorder,
　　213–227
　binge eating implications for, 254
　for borderline personality disorder
　　eclectic approach to, 197–212
　　self-regulation approach to,
　　　183–195
　　structure for, 188–192
　bulimia nervosa implications for,
　　253–254
　dimensional model basis for, 8–9,
　　43–44
　for eating disorders; *see also*
　　specific personality disorder
　　APA guidelines for, 151
　　indications for, 24, 104, 252,
　　　254–255
　for obsessive-compulsive
　　personality disorder,
　　165–178
Treatment environment
　for borderline personality
　　disorder, 198
　for obsessive-compulsive
　　personality disorder, 168
Treatment outcomes
　of borderline personality disorder,
　　195, 210–212
　of eating disorders, 252–254
　of obsessive-compulsive
　　personality disorder, 176
Triggering events
　for avoidant personality disorder,
　　215–216

for borderline personality
　disorder, 139

U

"Usual self," in eating disorders
　assessment, 103–105

V

Validity, of personality disorders
　categories, 6
Valproate (Depakote), 239, 241
Venlafaxine extended release
　　(Effexor XR), 239–241
Verbal abuse, as risk factor, 62–64
Violence, witnessing, as childhood
　　trauma, 65
Vomiting, self-induced, 52, 144
Vulnerability/predisposition model,
　of borderline personality
　disorder, 142–144

W

War/wartime, as influencing factor,
　11–12
Weight control, in eating disorders,
　52, 54, 71
　assessment difficulties of, 99,
　　107–108, 167
　avoidant personality disorder and,
　　159, 215–216
　borderline personality disorder
　　and, 144
Weight recovery
　antipsychotic agents and, 174–175
　behavioral therapy for, 169–171
　calories for, 104
　personality pathology influence
　　on, 250
　psychotropic medications for,
　　240–241
Worry, 165
　treatment strategies for, 174, 226
"Worry diary," 226

Y

Yale Adolescent Follow-Up Study, 11
Young Schema Questionnaire-Short
    Version, 217, 223

Z

Ziprasidone (Geodon), 239, 241